ON STRIKE AND ON FILM

ON STRIKE AND
ON FILM

MEXICAN AMERICAN FAMILIES
AND BLACKLISTED FILMMAKERS
IN COLD WAR AMERICA

ELLEN R. BAKER

THE UNIVERSITY OF NORTH CAROLINA PRESS

CHAPEL HILL

© 2007 The University of North Carolina Press
All rights reserved
Manufactured in the United States of America
Designed by Kaelin Chappell Broaddus
Set in 10/13 Warnock Pro
by Keystone Typesetting, Inc.

The paper in this book meets the guidelines for permanence
and durability of the Committee on Production Guidelines for
Book Longevity of the Council on Library Resources.

This book was published with the assistance of the Anniversary
Endowment Fund of the University of North Carolina Press.

Library of Congress Cataloging-in-Publication Data
Baker, Ellen R.
On strike and on film : Mexican American families and blacklisted
filmmakers in Cold War America / Ellen R. Baker.
p. cm.   Includes bibliographical references and index.
ISBN-13: 978-0-8078-3083-3 (cloth: alk. paper)
ISBN-13: 978-0-8078-5791-5 (pbk.: alk. paper)
1. Empire Zinc Company Strike, Hanover, N.M., 1950–1951. 2. Strikes and
lockouts—Zinc mining—New Mexico. 3. Mexican American labor union
members—New Mexico. 4. Salt of the earth (Motion picture) I. Title.
HD5325.M721951 .E473   2007
331.892′82345209789692—dc22
2006024952

cloth   11 10 09 08 07   5 4 3 2 1
paper   11 10 09 08 07   5 4 3 2 1

Portions of this work appeared earlier, in somewhat different
form, in Ellen Baker, " 'I Hate to Be Calling Her a Wife Now':
Women and Men in the Salt of the Earth Strike, 1950–1952,"
in *Mining Women: Gender in the Development of a Global
Industry, 1670 to 2000*, ed. Jaclyn J. Gier and Laurie Mercier
(New York: Palgrave Macmillan, 2006), 213–32, and are
reproduced here by permission of the publisher.

CONTENTS

Acknowledgments xi
Abbreviations xiii

Chapter 1. Introduction 1
Chapter 2. Grant County's Mining District 17

PART I. CRISIS
Chapter 3. Class Conflict in the Mines, 1930–1950 45
Chapter 4. Competing Models of Unionism 85

PART II. THE WOMEN'S PICKET
Chapter 5. Political Consciousness and Community Formation 119
Chapter 6. Household Relations 151

PART III. A WORKER-ARTIST ALLIANCE
Chapter 7. The Blacklist 177
Chapter 8. A Progressive Vision of Popular Culture 192
Chapter 9. Anticommunist Assaults 223
Chapter 10. Conclusion 244

Notes 255
Bibliography 317
Index 339

ILLUSTRATIONS

Miners at shift change, ca. 1950	30
Women picketing, summer 1951	120
Women picketers trying to shame strikebreakers	121
Strikebreakers, summer 1951	122
Women and children near the picket line, summer 1951	124
Picketer confronting deputy	132
Picketer photographing deputy	133
Elvira Molano, Fred Barreras, and Sabina Salazar in the Grant County courthouse	138
Women working at Chino during World War II	160
Charles Coleman as Antonio Morales	195
Esperanza confronts her husband Ramón	198
Juan Chacón studying the script of *Salt of the Earth*	209
Virginia and Clinton Jencks on the set of *Salt of the Earth*	210
Angie Sánchez as Consuelo Ruiz	211
Henrietta Williams as Teresa Vidal	212
E. A. and William Rockwell as the sheriff's deputies	213
Meals on the set were provided by the production committee	216
Ramón assaults the foreman	218
Willie Andazola as a striker's son	220
Filming *Salt of the Earth*	221

MAPS AND TABLES

MAPS

1. Grant County, N.M.   18
2. New Mexico   19

TABLES

1. Men Employed in the Mining Industry, Santa Rita and
   Hanover, N.M., 1930   33
2. Employed Women, Santa Rita and Hanover, N.M., 1930   36

ACKNOWLEDGMENTS

A project of this duration incurs many debts, and this book owes much to the generosity and acuity of many people. Linda Gordon, Benjamin Már-quez, Jess Gilbert, Bill Cronon, and Diane Lindstrom gave immeasurable help in revising my Ph.D. dissertation into a book manuscript. Elizabeth Jameson and Paul Buhle wrote timely and incisive critiques that helped me revise an earlier draft. Laurie Mercier, Jaclyn Gier, Pablo Piccato, Greg Mann, Brad Abrams, Adam Kosto, and Sam Roberts carefully critiqued an article that treats many of the themes in this book. And in addition to being interviewed, Clinton Jencks generously read and commented on an earlier version of this manuscript. The labor and peace movements lost a genuine hero when he died in December 2005.

I am grateful to Ricardo Trevizo and Nacho Quiñones for permission to use photographs of Grant County and for help in obtaining them, to Sam Sills for sharing his extensive interviews with Dolores Jiménez and Clinton Jencks, and to Terry Humble for helping me understand Grant County history and politics. Jolane Culhane, Herb Toy, Susan Berry, Terry Humble, Nacho Quiñones, and Juanita Escobedo all helped put me in touch with Grant County residents. Nina Judar, Jena Clouse, Matthew Bernstein, and Dorothea Browder performed exceptionally valuable re-search assistance in New York, New Mexico, and Wisconsin. For their archival help I thank José Villegas of the New Mexico State Records Center and Archives, Velia Miranda of the Grant County court records, David Hays of the Western Historical Collection at the University of Colorado Archives, Stephen Rollins of the Zimmerman Library at the University of New Mexico, and the staffs of the State Historical Society of Wisconsin, the Silver City Museum, the University of Colorado Archives, the New Mexico State Records Center and Archives, the National Archives, and the Center for Southwest Research at the University of New Mexico. A Columbia University Council Grant for Research in the Social Sciences and Humanities, a Mellon Fellowship in the Humanities, a Columbia College Chamberlain Fellowship, and the generosity of Martha Jane Baker made the research and writing financially possible for me. I especially appreciate the hospitality offered by Ellen Mowry, Johan Stolpe, Virginia Chacón, James Couture, Stephanie and Stuart Lipkowitz, Jolane Culhane, Herb Toy, and Annie Baker as I conducted research in Colorado, New Mexico, and Washington, D.C.

Graduate school comrades and faculty colleagues have shepherded this project through its various life stages, from birth as a dissertation topic, through childhood and that awkward adolescent stage of making a dissertation into a book, and on to adulthood as a book manuscript. Throughout it all, Monica Najar blessed me with her wit and unerring critical faculties. Bethel Saler, Tracey Deutsch, Kateri Carmola, and Jennifer Greenfield inspired me with creative approaches to the historical problems in this book. Betsy Blackmar, Barbara Fields, Eric Foner, Matt Jones, Alice Kessler-Harris, Adam Kosto, Barbara Locurto, Greg Mann, Kirsten Olsen, Pablo Piccato, Adrienne Sockwell, and Sonia Wagner have supported me at Columbia University in countless ways, and I appreciate them all. Many thanks are due to Chuck Grench for bringing this book into the University of North Carolina Press and guiding it through the editorial process, and to Katy O'Brien and Mary Caviness for their help.

I love my family and feel fortunate for their support. Annie Baker, Lyman Baker, Talat Rahman, Cynthia Baker, Nameer Baker, Brian Howard, Joan Holt, Bob Holt, Martha Jane Baker, and many aunts, uncles, nieces, and cousins have enriched my life immeasurably. I only wish that my uncle Richard Baker could have lived to see this book, for he was a storyteller and historian extraordinaire. My daughter Rachel arrived just as I thought I was finishing the revisions, and while I cannot honestly say she made it easier to finish, she certainly filled my life with joy. And for this I am forever grateful. To Danny Holt go my greatest thanks—for his keen intellect, for his humor, for putting up with this book for so many years, for editing and proofreading, for making me figure out what I'm trying to say when I really would prefer he do it all himself. All in all he is the best accomplice I could hope for.

Naturally I feel the most gratitude toward those people of Grant County who told me about their lives in the 1940s and 1950s. It is no trivial matter to invite a stranger into one's memories, and I hope they know how much I appreciate what they have given us all.

ABBREVIATIONS

ADTFC	Association of Documentary Technicians and Film Cameramen
AFL	American Federation of Labor
AHA	Alianza Hispano Americana
ANMA	Asociación Nacional Mexicana Americana (National Mexican American Association)
CCC	Civilian Conservation Corps
CIO	Congress of Industrial Organizations
CP	Communist Party, U.S.A.
FBI	Federal Bureau of Investigation
FEPC	Fair Employment Practices Commission
HUAC	House Un-American Activities Committee
IATSE	International Association of Theater and Stage Employees
IPC	Independent Productions Corporation
LAW	League of American Writers
LULAC	League of United Latin American Citizens
Mine-Mill	International Union of Mine, Mill and Smelter Workers
MPAPAI	Motion Picture Alliance for the Preservation of American Ideals
MPPDA	Motion Picture Producers and Distributors of America
NIRA	National Industrial Recovery Act
NLRB	National Labor Relations Board
NMC	Nonferrous Metals Commission

NWLB	National War Labor Board
PD	Phelps-Dodge Corporation
PWA	Public Works Administration
SISS	Senate Internal Security Subcommittee
USSRMC	U.S. Smelting, Refining, and Mining Company
WFM	Western Federation of Miners
WMC	War Manpower Commission
WPA	Works Progress Administration, later Work Projects Administration
WPB	War Production Board

ON STRIKE AND ON FILM

1

Introduction

Early on the morning of October 17, 1950, zinc miners finished the graveyard shift at the Empire Zinc Company in the village of Hanover, New Mexico. They climbed out of the mine shaft and into the sunlight illuminating the mountains in this southwestern corner of the state. Other workers gathered outside the company's property—not to begin the day shift, however, but to begin a strike. Contract negotiations between their union, Local 890 of the International Union of Mine, Mill and Smelter Workers (Mine-Mill), and Empire Zinc had finally broken down around midnight, with the company rejecting union demands for collar-to-collar pay, paid holidays, wages matching the district's standards, and a reduction in the number of job classifications.[1] This last demand was aimed at combating the dual-wage system in which Mexican American workers routinely earned less than Anglo workers, for a large number of classifications made it easier for employers to keep Mexican American miners in low-paying jobs. Striking to press their claims, 140 men picketed two entrances to the Empire Zinc property. Their picket lines completely shut down the mine.[2]

A year later, the picket lines were still in place, still blocking the mine entrances, and Empire Zinc was barely operating. But if the picket lines continued to perform the same function, they had nonetheless been completely transformed: the marching picketers were all women and children, not the men who walked out on that October morning in 1950. This dramatic change had taken place in June 1951. The strike began as a typical conflict between miners and their employer over work conditions and wages, but like many labor conflicts, especially in single-industry towns like Hanover, the strikers depended on a wider community, especially their wives, for support. And when the Empire Zinc Company got a court injunction prohibiting striking miners from picketing, miners' wives took over the picket lines. This role reversal sparked conflict between husbands and wives. Although husbands knew that they could no longer picket, they resented their wives' strike activity, which came at the expense of housework; even worse, women expected their husbands to *do* the housework. Women were frustrated, too, because their husbands refused to help at home and, more fundamentally, because men frequently forbade their wives to picket; some women came to resent that they were expected to have their husbands' permission in the first place. The strike's success in January 1952 rested on women strikers' individual and collective bravery in the face of violence directed against the picketers, and on the ways that women and men negotiated the power relations in the family. Ultimately, union families redefined their community's goals to include equality between men and women.

Yet another year later, in early 1953, women were still marching in circles on a picket line, but they were doing so on a movie set, on a ranch not far from the Empire Zinc mine. Blacklisted Hollywood filmmakers had joined the mining families to make a feature film that would tell the story of the strike, focusing on the conflict between husbands and wives. The Mine-Mill workers and their families played most of the roles and helped craft the screenplay. The product of this extraordinary collaboration, *Salt of the Earth* (1954), represented a spirited—though ultimately limited—resistance to domestic anticommunism, for both groups had ties to the Left and had suffered repression because of those ties. Many of Mine-Mill's national leaders and a few of Local 890's leaders belonged at one point or another to the Communist Party (CP), as did the blacklisted Hollywood artists who helped produce *Salt*. Making the film was their attempt to break through the isolation imposed by anticommunism. Reenacting the strike through an artistic medium was also a way for the mining families to make sense of the changes caused by the strike. But union opponents and Hollywood anticommunists drew upon the political power of anticommunism to try, through violence and intimidation, to prevent the film's completion.

For the miners, the Empire Zinc strike represented the culmination of a decade of union organizing around both workplace equality and civil rights for Mexican Americans. This upswing of Mexican American labor activism coincided with the downward turn in the fortunes of left-wing unions in the United States, and the juxtaposition of these two trends marks an important part of the history both of Mexican Americans and of the American Left. Because Mine-Mill worked for Mexican American labor and civil rights, Mexican American union members were to a great degree inoculated against the raging anticommunism that shaped the political culture and weakened the labor movement elsewhere. From a very different background came the Hollywood filmmakers. Already blacklisted from the movie industry for refusing to disavow communism, these filmmakers conceived of *Salt of the Earth* as an assault against the blacklist and the forces that gave rise to it. Independent movies that told "real stories about real working people" would not only break with conventional Hollywood storytelling but also show other filmmakers how to break out of the constraints of Hollywood studio contracts. The success in producing the film—and the failure in distributing it—show that leftists and working-class activists had some space to mark out an alternative to the emerging Cold War consensus, but not enough to give that alternative the power it would need to reshape the political and cultural terrain.

THE STRIKE

When the miners struck the Empire Zinc Company in Grant County, New Mexico, in October 1950, they believed that Empire Zinc was colluding with other mining companies in an ambitious effort to destroy the union. The strike, then, quickly became not just a test of Mine-Mill Local 890's strength but also a conflict in which the union's recent achievements in advancing Mexican American civil, as well as labor, rights were at stake. In meeting this high-stakes test, strikers drew on a heightened ethnic and class consciousness that they had developed over the 1940s.

Miners picketed uneventfully until June 1951, when Empire Zinc got a court injunction that forced the miners and their union to devise new strategies if they were to maintain the strike. Chief among these strategies was one proposed by miners' wives: women would replace men on the picket lines, thereby obeying the letter of the injunction against picketing miners while defeating its purpose. In an unprecedented move, women took over the picket lines on June 12, 1951. And they held the lines for more than six months, until the Empire Zinc Company agreed to negotiate in January 1952. Miners won wage increases, other benefits, and improved housing conditions, and they considered the strike a victory.

But the strike proved important for more than labor-management relations and the survival of the union: women's picket activity threw gender relations into confusion. On the picket lines women met violence from strikebreakers and law enforcement, while at home they encountered ambivalence—and sometimes outright hostility—from their own husbands. Pushed to the sidelines, many miners resented women's picket activity because it threw into question their own work, their leadership, and thus, to a large degree, their manhood. Leaving the physical defense of the picket to women was bad enough. But actually taking over women's household work, which the women could not perform while picketing, was even more emasculating. Yet that was precisely what their wives demanded. Women used the temporary inversion of the sexual division of labor to assert their independence as political actors and to challenge men's authority in the household. Organizing shifts on the picket line, enduring jail time, holding the line against physical assault—all of these activities convinced many women that they wielded considerable power as a group and that they deserved their husbands' respect as equals. Thus, the victory of the strike consisted also of forcing the union to take serious account of women's place in the class struggle, for it revealed that women existed not at the margins of a struggle waged by men but as fully integral members of the working class.

THE MOVIE PRODUCTION

The Empire Zinc strike reverberated beyond the mining district in which it took place, helping to dismantle the dual-wage system of the American Southwest. But it would probably not have registered as more than a blip on the radar screen of American history had it not also found expression in *Salt of the Earth*. Blacklisted Hollywood filmmakers, enchanted by the story of the women's picket, enlisted the mining families in an alliance to translate strike experiences into a dramatic film that could open cinema to realistic portrayals of working-class life. Mining families brought to the project more than their stories; they also collaborated on drafting the script, played most of the dramatic roles, and organized much of the off-camera production. The film, unique among movies of the period, connected women's domestic labor with men's "productive" labor in a way that presaged later feminist analyses of class and gender. The film's production in Grant County represented an effort of unionists and black-listed artists and technicians to render the blacklist impotent. For that very reason, it drew national attention from anticommunists, who were outraged that the blacklisted were still making films, and violent opposition from those Grant County residents who had opposed the union during the strike. Violence marked the production just as it had marked the strike itself, and the film only barely reached completion. This remarkable victory, however, was diminished since a coalition of anticommunists in the film industry, the American Legion, and even some trade unions prevented the film's distribution.[3] Feeding off the publicity generated by the movie, the federal government targeted Local 890 representative Clinton Jencks and others in Mine-Mill for criminal prosecutions that lingered in the courts for years. *Salt of the Earth* reached audiences only after the blacklist began to disappear in the 1960s. Today, half a century after it was made, *Salt of the Earth* is regularly cited as among the most important American films of the twentieth century.

A SYNOPSIS OF THE MOVIE

Salt of the Earth tells the story of a fictional Mexican American couple, Ramón and Esperanza Quintero, who live and work in Zinctown, a small New Mexican mining town.[4] Ramón works for the Delaware Zinc Company and Esperanza works in the home. We quickly learn that there is tension between them, based on the different ways that they experience working-class life. Ramón enjoys meeting his friends in the beer hall, which Esperanza resents; Esperanza enjoys the radio, which represents to Ramón a degrading dependence on the installment plan by which they are paying for it. Esperanza, pregnant with their third child, heightens the differences between their worlds by comparing Ramón's imminent strike with her imminent motherhood: "You have your strike," she tells him. "I'll have my baby." Yet in contrasting their worlds, Esperanza also establishes the parity of obligations held by husbands and wives.

Their relationship registers the changes wrought by the strike. Ramón enthusiastically supports the strike as an expression of his own manhood and status as a breadwinner. The strike chokes off his paycheck (which distresses Esperanza, who must feed the family every day), but he adopts a longer view, in which life without the union would set them back even further. He recognizes, more readily than Esperanza does, that the union deserves credit for protecting Mexican American workers against Anglo discrimination, and this strike promises to win them equality with Anglo miners. But when women offer to take over the picket lines in order to circumvent "that rotten Taft-Hartley injunction," Ramón opposes their proposal because he does not want to "hide behind women's skirts." Already angry that Esperanza votes against him in the union meeting at which the ladies' auxiliary gets assigned to picket duty, he becomes even more distressed by the changes he soon finds in his home. With Esperanza away, he is suddenly forced to feed the children, wash the dishes, and hang the laundry, and he defends, ever more shrilly, his manly prerogatives in the home. For her part, Esperanza gradually transforms herself from a timid housewife into a vibrant labor activist, and she begins to stand up to her husband.

The conflict between Ramón and Esperanza mirrors the final confrontation between the mining community and the company. Convinced that the company will win out—partly because he overhears company discussions, partly because he cannot accept that women might win the strike—Ramón tells Esperanza that they cannot go on this way. He starts cleaning his rifle, set on joining his equally disgruntled friends on a hunting trip that would take them away from their assignment to the "standby squad." By going hunting, the men would reassert their manhood by engaging in a quintessentially masculine activity and by defying a strike leadership that, they felt, had cast them aside. Esperanza believes that the hunt jeopardizes the strike: she senses that the company is on the verge of "something big," and if the men were to leave, the company might pull it off. But Ramón has lost patience with the strategy of the women's picket, and he seems willing to abandon it even if doing so means losing the strike. Esperanza, though, wants to win. Even more, she wants "to rise . . . and push everything up" as she goes. "And if you can't understand this," she tells Ramón, "you're a fool—because you can't win this strike without me! You can't win anything without me!" Ramón gets angry and grabs her shoulder, prepared to hit her: in this moment we see a history of male authority, enforced by the fist, met by Esperanza's refusal to submit. "That would be the old way," she tells him icily. "Never try it on me again."

Ramón goes hunting with his friends. As Esperanza's neighbor Teresa Vidal comments, "So they had a little taste of what it's like to be a woman . . . and they run away." But Ramón has a change of heart while walking in the woods, and he rallies his friends to return to town. And it is just in time, for the sheriff is at that moment evicting the Quinteros from their company-owned house. As union supporters pour in from all directions, Ramón finally recognizes the power of working-class solidarity, in which both men and women are indispensable. He and Esperanza quietly arrange for women to start bringing the furniture back into the house through another door, confounding the sheriff and his deputies. The community has a dramatic, tense showdown with the sheriff, and the sheriff backs down. The company representatives, watching from a safe distance, agree to settle the strike. Ramón's long view of class solidarity has been refashioned to accommodate a closer view of the household and its critical place in the community.

HISTORICAL SIGNIFICANCE

The strike, the social history of the mining region in which it took place, and the film's production and script have important things to tell us about the Mexican American working class, the Left, and gender in the twentieth century. The left-wing Mine-Mill union offered considerable space for working-class Mexican Americans to challenge ethnic and class inequality, first at work, then in local society and politics, and finally (along with left-wing Hollywood artists) in popular culture. Mine-Mill first appeared in Grant County early in the 1930s, a militant union increasingly close to the Communist Party and, as such, committed to interracial and interethnic organizing. Its efforts were part of widespread and heavily repressed Mexican American labor organizing in the Southwest and Midwest during the Depression, primarily by Communist-influenced labor unions.[5] Mine-Mill stepped up its activity in Grant County in 1941, part of a southwestern organizing drive as the American economy geared up for World War II.[6] Armed with an antiracist policy, Mine-Mill used the wartime labor shortage, the federal government's official commitment to equality in defense-industry jobs, and the union's patriotic no-strike pledge to organize Mexican American workers. If elsewhere, as other historians have shown, left-led unions scaled back their antiracist work in the name of all-out war production, in Grant County the two went hand in hand.[7] Over the course of the 1940s, these workers and organizers collectively began to chip away at, if not eliminate, the dual-wage system in the southwestern mines. After World War II, Mine-Mill members and leaders also expanded the union's mission to include addressing political and social inequality in the mining towns of Grant County.

The story of Local 890, however, was not solely a linear progression from oppression to liberation, or even overlapping and ever-widening spheres of union activity. Local 890's strength was tempered after World War II by the domestic Cold War, when mining managers, eager to reassert their power, confidently wielded the club of anticommunism in labor disputes. Mine-Mill was one of eleven unions expelled from the

Congress of Industrial Organizations (CIO) in 1949 and 1950 for inadequately ridding themselves of communist influence. But in order to understand the local political economy, it is important to reject any easy or apparent symmetry between communism and anticommunism; both were present in Grant County in the late 1940s, but they do not line up evenly in opposing columns. Instead, we find a confusing political terrain in which one version of communism—an especially democratic one—influenced Local 890's structure and actions but could not be openly acknowledged, while anticommunism was used by management as one tool among many in what was essentially an economic contest. Some Local 890 members and leaders belonged to the CP, finding in it a powerful tool for pressing working-class and Mexican American claims. Significantly, the party organized married couples, thus building into its very structure a recognition of women's importance to the class struggle. But despite these complexities, in the discourse of anticommunism, communists were single-minded, uniform, implacable, and devious, insinuating themselves into legitimate institutions and committing unsuspecting members to a program that subverted American democracy. Communist unions were controlled by Soviet agents and served Soviet masters. There was no room in this picture for a left-wing union to be democratic or genuinely to represent the interests of its members. Ironically, the searchlights that regularly swept the nation in the late 1940s and 1950s in order to expose communism failed to throw light on the real meaning of leftist democratic unionism precisely because they forced all progressives to hide any connections to the CP.

Anticommunists were correct, however, in perceiving a threat to the social order: Mexican American miners were threatening to step out of their proper place. In this respect, the miners were part of a wider tradition of Mexican American labor and civil rights activism whose groundwork was laid in the 1930s by left-wing unions and by civil rights organizations like the radical Congreso Nacional del Pueblo de Habla Española (National Congress of Spanish-Speaking People) and the moderate League of United Latin American Citizens (LULAC).[8] World War II catalyzed this activism, as returning Mexican American veterans demanded the civil rights that should have accompanied their military service on behalf of democracy.[9] But by casting that threat to the social order as a monolithic communism that poorly matched union men's union experiences, anticommunists created a disjuncture that convinced unionists that employers had a more sinister agenda. Whether or not they believed or cared that there were communists among them, Local

890's members saw through and were quick and determined to expose management's anticommunism as a cynical pretext to push Mexican American workers back "in their place."[10]

Gender shaped all of these developments, and this book also considers how sexual divisions of labor and attendant ideologies influenced people's experience of class. People are often invested in the work they perform in ways that go beyond the wages they take home. Men develop and reinforce a sense of their manliness through the work they perform, and they frequently act to protect their prerogatives as men even if those actions also threaten what we might consider their "class" interests.[11] Similarly, women frequently defend their prerogatives as caregivers.[12] Sexual divisions of labor, which take place both in the labor market and in families, shape and are reinforced by ideology. In the United States of the nineteenth and twentieth centuries, class formation took place in gendered ways, captured most succinctly in the ideology of the "family wage," whereby men expected to earn a wage adequate to support a family (although the ideology itself masked the degree to which families depended on much more than a breadwinner's wage). Women's productive labor—that which could command a wage and produce a commodity— never followed the blind dictates of capital alone. In deciding whether women would work for wages, families took a variety of concerns into account rather than always seeking the highest income.[13] A family's decision, moreover, was often the outcome of conflict and negotiation among members with different interests. Women's *unpaid* labor was also intimately connected to industrialization, because women's housework materially compensated for men's low wages; moreover, the very invisibility of women's contributions as "work" reinforced the ideology of a male breadwinner being the only worker in the family.[14] Quite apart from industrial capitalism, in fact, women's work in the household has been fundamental to social reproduction, the daily work required to raise children and sustain families. These connections between work and family, between paid and unpaid labor, have been especially important in twentieth-century Chicana history.[15]

Mining towns (and other towns dominated by a single industry) are fascinating places for studying the workings of class, gender, and ethnicity. Mining towns often had skewed sex ratios, especially in the early years, but over time—particularly in the twentieth century—employers found that their workforce would be more stable if men were married. In these contexts, male workers reinforced a masculinity based both on the hard physical labor and courage required of miners and on the breadwinner ethic, affirming their responsibility for earning a wage that could support their families.[16] For their part, women in mining towns found limited job opportunities; they were especially dependent upon marriage at the same time that their unpaid work was especially crucial to the reproduction of the workforce. Because of the power wielded by companies in single-industry towns, labor conflict often affected the community beyond the workplace, and successful strikes often depended on a community unionism that mobilized working-class families and formed cross-class alliances with local businesspeople. Gender ideologies had the potential to forge strong working-class solidarity, but they often fractured that solidarity at key moments.[17] Similarly, ethnic diversity in mining towns could provide a powerful basis from which to challenge mining companies, but those moments of solidarity stood out against a backdrop of ethnic division.[18]

In Mine-Mill Local 890, different models of manhood coexisted and, at times, conflicted with one another.[19] An aggressive masculinity, combined with the breadwinner ethic, proved important in creating class and ethnic solidarity during the years in which workers first built their union in Grant County. Men created fraternal bonds based on shared work experiences in a highly sex-segregated industry, and they used these bonds from which to challenge management's paternalism. But when women's picket duty in the Empire Zinc strike called upon men and women to rethink their household relations, this same model of masculinity suddenly threatened the very class and ethnic solidarity it had helped to build. The union leadership had both encouraged militant masculinity and introduced a more broadly based idea of the working class—one based in the larger community rather than limited to the workplace. In this manner the leadership opened the door to women's participation in union activities, which would, in the context of the Empire Zinc strike, ultimately challenge the power relations predicated upon militant masculinity.

Women's rebellion against male domination lies at the heart of both the Empire Zinc strike and *Salt of the Earth*. It deserves exploration, coming as it did from Mexican Americans (whose culture had a powerful, if complicated, tradition of patriarchal authority) and during a period when the "feminine mystique" permeated Anglo American culture. The women's rebellion grew from their own class consciousness, which both resembled that of their husbands and diverged from it in critical ways. Women's class consciousness had two sources: their own work experiences as Mexican American housewives in working-class mining camps, and their eventual participation, under the aegis of family meetings and the ladies' auxiliary, in union business. Before the Empire Zinc strike, women's activities were clearly auxiliary. But the strike's temporary reversal and general upheaval of gender-based responsibilities threw women into a situation that transformed their political consciousness and permitted them to question male authority in the household. Thus they directed the union's attention to the households that made up the community on which the strike depended. The return to the earlier division of labor after the strike, however, shows that a change in gender consciousness alone did not permanently transform power relations. Without a different sexual division of labor and a stronger feminist movement, the changes proved temporary.

The experiences of these housewives reveal the importance of feminism in Mexican American labor history, even where feminist organizations were absent.[20] I take feminism to mean the recognition that women are subordinate to men, the belief that this subordination is not natural, and the conviction that an end to male domination is both possible and desirable. Mexican American women were introduced to a left-wing feminism associated with the CP, which condemned what it termed "male chauvinism," and this may have given them a language with which to critique male authority.[21] Chicana feminists have rightly challenged scholarship that blindly applies categories and theories developed in Anglo feminism to the situations of women belonging to other groups.[22] The story of this strike shows that feminism as an ideology may have come originally from outside but that working-class Mexican American women understood and used it in the context of their own lives. Encountering their husbands' resistance during the Empire Zinc strike, Mexican American women insisted on profound changes in the relations of husbands to wives. And like other Mexican American activists of the period, these women united community and family concerns in a way that did not affirm the conservative family politics of the 1950s.[23]

It was women's activism and the conflict-ridden but also solidaristic story of husbands and wives that attracted Hollywood filmmakers to Grant County. A shared experience of Cold War repression and similar antiracist class politics brought miners and artists together. These two groups had little else in common: class background, work experiences, and ethnicity divided them.[24] These divisions were exposed, for instance, in the filmmakers' tendency to romanticize "the workers," "the Mexican Americans," "the people." The collaboration on *Salt of the Earth* offers an unusual window on the Left during this period precisely because of these differences. The parties understood that their collaboration would be difficult, and they set up a production committee composed equally of Hollywood people, men from the union, and women from the auxiliary. This formal structure and the centrality of the gender story in *Salt of the Earth* together reflect the power that women had gained in the strike and continued to exercise thereafter. Left-wing artists did not apply rigid formulas to interpreting the mining families' stories, and they permitted the families to exercise final say over the script. Mining families' eager participation and vocal opinions about the way the story should be told show that issues of culture and representation mattered greatly to working-class Mexican Americans—these were not esoteric issues. The history of the film collaboration reveals people laying claim to the ways the world would see them.

NOTE ON TERMINOLOGY

Language is a complicated matter, and my own usage requires some explanation at the outset. The terms people at the time (1930s–1950s) used to describe ethnic, racial, and national identities are confused and confusing: "Mexican," "Mexican American," "Spanish American," "Hispanic," "Spanish-speaking," and "manitos" (a New Mexican word) have been used interchangeably to describe people of Mexican descent. In general, I refer to people of Mexican descent as "Mexican American," adopting usage that union members promoted. This term, however, often conflates Mexican nationals with U.S. citizens; where the distinction is important to the story at hand, I make it. Moreover, vocabulary sometimes reveals a speaker's particular perspectives on class, citizenship, and other issues. In those instances, I try to unpack the term. In keeping with local usage, I use "Anglo" for non-Mexican Americans, regardless of their own national or ethnic background, unless they are clearly identified by other terms.

I should explain how I identify people as "Mexican American" or "Anglo." In general, I have relied on people's surnames as markers of their heritage, although I am fully aware of this technique's limitations, particularly because intermarriage between Mexican Americans and Anglos is not uncommon. But by checking my use of surnames against other evidence, I believe I have arrived at reasonable approximations of the numbers of Mexican Americans and Anglos in the region. A close reading of the manuscript censuses allowed me to track intermarriage and other details, which I was then able to use to make arguments about the pull of Mine-Mill as a Mexican American labor organization. In 1930, the Census Bureau classified Mexicans as a separate race, which in turn caused political protest. The census data are also full of classification oddities, as illustrated by Tom Allison and his family. The census tells us that Tom, a white man, was married to Carmen, a Mexican woman; their children were all classified as "Mexican," as was Tom's mother, Nora, who lived with them.[25]

On a more abstract level, I use the term "ethnicity" in describing the ways that certain identifications mattered, or came to matter, to the people in this story; I use the term "race" when they themselves used the term. Race as a biological category does not exist, and I believe that to use the term uncritically is to grant its use a legitimacy it does not merit and is, itself, a racist practice.[26] Racism and racial thinking are historical phenomena, though, and I do not intend that my use of the term "ethnicity" should erase the politics of racism. Moreover, it is important to keep in mind that many people of Mexican descent have used the term "raza," which does not translate exactly as "race"; instead, it connotes family, history, culture, and politics.[27]

This book is arranged in three parts, after a brief introduction to Grant County's mining district (Chapter 2), and it moves chronologically through several episodes in the strike and film production. Each chapter begins with one such episode then analyzes in detail the themes raised by it. Part I shows what was at stake in the Empire Zinc strike and explains the strikers' organizational and ideological resources in responding to two crises, one generated by the company and the other generated by the union itself in responding to the first crisis. Chapter 3 begins with the court injunction that threatened to paralyze the strike. This injunction serves as a symbol of labor relations early in the Cold War and, more broadly, of the evolving political order that reinstalled anticommunism in management's arsenal. The chapter then explains the Depression-era origins of Local 890 and its development in the changing political landscape of the 1940s. Mine-Mill organized Mexican American men, and some Anglos, by fusing class and ethnic goals in the name of a shared brotherhood and by generating a strong leadership out of the rank and file. Thus, by the time Mine-Mill came under attack for its alleged Communist affiliation in 1948, Mexican American miners were primed to interpret anticommunism as a shabby pretext for returning Grant County to an earlier class and racial order.

   Chapter 4 begins with another scene of crisis, this one occasioned by women trying to solve the injunction problem. In a contentious union meeting, women proposed to take over the picket lines, and their husbands balked. This conflict between men and women arose from a conflict between two forms of unionism, one a brotherhood and the other a family, corresponding to different visions of the union's very composition. In itself, neither type of unionism challenged the family ideal of a male breadwinner and subservient female nurturer; indeed, the two models had developed alongside one another in the late 1940s. But the temporary inversion of gendered responsibility, implicit in the women's proposal, exposed the power relations between husbands and wives that had seemed natural but that now blocked a resolution of the injunction crisis. By setting these two crises—the injunction and the women's proposal—alongside one another, we can see not only their dynamic relation—in responding to one crisis the union created another—but also the complex workings of gender in battles over shared class and ethnic goals. The union's composition and recent history positioned it to respond to the injunction—a threat from the outside—in a creative way that in turn challenged union members' own gendered understandings and expectations of their union's internal composition and goals: Were the men of Local 890 to allow women to assume center stage in this conflict? Because those expectations of women's proper behavior were shared by management, the ability of the men and women of Local 890 to call them into question proved critical to overcoming management's tactical advantage.

   By looking at different aspects of the women's picket, Part II tracks the events that reshaped and consolidated the union community. Both chapters in this part of the book cover the same chronological ground— from the start of the women's picket on June 13, 1951, to the strike's conclusion in January 1952—but do so by examining different themes. Chapter 5 follows women to the picket line and shows their changing political consciousness as they interacted with two political institutions— law enforcement and the courts—and with the international union's leadership in Denver. Out of these interactions, women picketers came to see local political institutions as thoroughly corrupt, which, in turn, helped them to define the boundaries of their community ever more sharply and to perceive its place in the class struggle more clearly. They were joined in the process of marking off these boundaries by other townspeople, who found themselves forced to choose sides. Complicating the story was women's challenge to the international leadership, which fired a popular organizer despite women's loud protests. Chapter 6 follows the picketers back home, where they met with hostility from their own husbands, and explores the power relations in working-class families by examining women's marriage choices and household labor in the context of a job market with few opportunities for women.

Part III examines the creation of a worker-artist alliance and its production of *Salt of the Earth*. Its chapters jump between Hollywood and Grant County, reflecting the difficulties this alliance faced in bridging the gap between two very different groups of people. Chapter 7 introduces the blacklisted filmmakers and describes their experiences of industry and government repression. Chapter 8 centers on the filmmakers' vision of popular culture, one that would bring "real stories of real working people" into commercial theaters, and analyzes the mechanics of the worker-artist alliance that could achieve it. Union families were not just raw material for the screenplay; acting in the film was a way for the women and men of Local 890 to make sense of the conflicts caused by the strike and to make connections to audiences, and the production committee ensured that they influenced the way their story would be told. Chapter 9 traces the connections between national and local anticommunism during the film production. Just as making *Salt of the Earth* gave mining families the chance to make sense of their conflicts during the Empire Zinc strike, so too did local businesspeople's violence toward the film crew recapitulate the violence between strikers and law enforcement —but with an added edge: the presence of blacklisted Hollywood people drew national attention, which in turn fueled local actions against the film crew and union members. The connections between local and national anticommunism were further strengthened by government persecution of Mine-Mill leaders, including Local 890's international representative, Clinton Jencks.

The medium itself—film—transformed the immediate outcome of the strike into an enduring, and constantly renewed, lesson on class struggle, Mexican American history, gender, and the Cold War. As historian Frederick Cooper has shown in his analysis of Ousmanne Sembene's 1960 novel *God's Bits of Wood*, and its portrayal of a 1947 West African railway strike, the artistic representation "both complicates the task of the historian and lends it importance: the written epic may influence testimony, yet the fictional account enhances the sense of participants that their actions shaped history."[28] In the conclusion, I reflect on the significance of the Empire Zinc strike and *Salt of the Earth*, in part by following some of the historical characters into the next decades. Despite, or perhaps in part because of, the repression directed against the film's production and distribution, *Salt of the Earth* has become a part of the film canon. Its ability to bring the story of Zinctown to generation after generation represents a victory for the blacklisted artists and for the mining families in Grant County, albeit a victory far removed from the film's immediate origins. This additional dimension to the history of Mexican American mining families, their union, and their film makes the assessment of what really changed in terms of class or gender relations in Grant County only part of the story.

2

Grant County's Mining District

Grant County lies in the southwestern corner of New Mexico, separated from the Rio Grande by the Black Range to the east and the rugged Gila Wilderness to the north. (See Map 1.) Low rolling hills covered with scrub and grasses are interrupted by sharper inclines and canyons. Winding under the hills and mountains are metals that people want: grains and crystals of gold, silver, copper, lead, and zinc. For two centuries, these metals have been the bedrock of the European American economies here; the social relations that structured their extraction, however, have not been nearly so stable. They changed from systems of large-scale forced labor to individual prospecting by Anglos and Mexicans, then to large-scale wage labor in capital-intensive mines and mills. With this last arrangement came a new racial order, the dual-wage system, in which Mexicans were confined to the poorest-paying jobs. Spreading out from the workplace, this racial order was manifest in housing, school, and social segregation, and it grouped all Mexicans, whether native-born or immigrant, into a single, subordinate class. In this chapter I show the development of Grant County's mining economy alongside its streams of immigrants, ending with the dual-wage system and paternalist labor relations against which miners began to rebel in the 1930s.

Two centuries is hardly anything compared to the millions of years it took to create southwestern New Mexico's metal deposits. On the shore and on the floor of the prehistoric ocean, limestone, shale, and sandstone were gradually pressed into very thick, dense layers. About sixty million years ago, molten rock pushed upward and broke them up. Into the cracks seeped hot water carrying dissolved minerals; as the whole mass

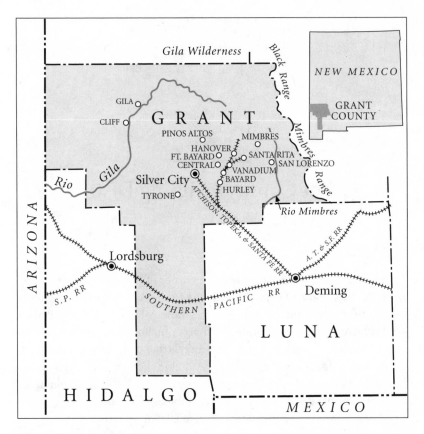

Map 1. Grant County, N.M.

cooled, the water disappeared and the cracks remained full of minerals.[1] But any miner who arrived then, hoping for a big strike, would have decided the ore was hardly worth mining: the ratio of useful mineral to rock was far too small.[2]

These minerals became valuable to people because of erosion by water and air. In the case of copper, this erosion turned pyrite (iron-sulfur deposits) into sulfuric acid. The acid then dissolved chalcopyrite (copper-iron-sulfur) and sent copper solution down through cracks all the way to the water table, where its reactions produced chalcocite (copper sulfide).[3] This was the good stuff: a vast, rock-hard pool of copper sulfide, along with porphyry copper disseminated through quartz. But 35 million years ago, before human beings could get to it, indeed, long before human beings walked the earth, lava and ash buried it. Then water and air eroded the tuff beds and exposed some of the copper in what would come to be

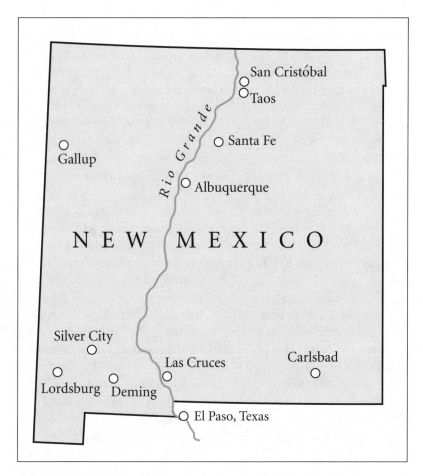

Map 2. New Mexico

known as the Santa Rita mines. North and west of Santa Rita, similar processes distributed gold placer, vanadium ores, lead-carbonate ores, iron, chalcocite-silver ores, and zinc sulfides in the shape of an elliptical ring, about three miles north to south and a mile east to west.[4] It was "the most highly mineralized district" in what would become New Mexico.[5]

MINING IN THE NINETEENTH CENTURY

Native groups, of whom the Apache became the predominant, mined copper for centuries, but their economies rested more on hunting, gathering, and (by the end of the seventeenth century) raiding.[6] Apache territory was roughly encompassed by the Gila Mountains in the north, the Rio Grande in the east, the White Mountains of Arizona in the west, and Chihuahua in the south, and groups of Chiricahua Apache swept a wide circle in their seasonal migrations. Deep in Sonora and Chihuahua they raided Spanish ranchos and villages for cattle, horses, food, and captives. An entire group typically traveled together, with warriors heading off to raid, hunters taking off to hunt, and everyone else making camp. An impressive range of elevation—some 5,000 feet between desert floor and mountain—gave them a range of food; women harvested crops and gathered mescal, piñons, mesquite beans, berries, and other plants.[7]

In 1798, an Apache man showed the Santa Rita mines to a Spanish army officer, José Manuel Carrasco. Carrasco was delighted to "discover" this treasure—one whose worth he recognized because he had grown up near the copper-rich Río Tinto in Spain—but he could not afford to develop the mine himself. He got the help of a Chihuahua banker and merchant, Francisco Elguea.[8] Don Francisco enjoyed leases from the Spanish crown to both land and labor, which is to say that the crown built a penal colony there to supply workers.[9] His adobe fort happily "served the double purpose of controlling the miners and affording protection against Apache incursions."[10] Men descended "chicken" ladders (made either of rope or of a single notched pole of pine) 100 feet into dark holes, and they climbed back out with 200-pound bags of copper—as much as ten tons of ore every day.[11] Beginning in 1804, mule trains hauled copper ingots to Chihuahua for use in coinage. Mexicans continued the trade after independence from Spain in 1821, minus the forced labor and with more and more families settling the district.

Most New Mexican trade headed south to Mexico City, except for some trade confined to the upper Rio Grande. But goods from the Santa Rita area traveled a slightly different route, the "Copper Trail" overland to Janos, Chihuahua, then to Chihuahua City, where it merged with the main trunk of the Camino Real. These different paths have corresponded to different histories of the regions, too. Most historical scholarship has focused on central and northern New Mexico, where Spanish missionaries, soldiers, and settlers first claimed territory for the Spanish crown in the sixteenth century and where Anglo traders began to reshape the Mexican commercial economy in the 1820s. Conflict among Indians, Hispanics, and Anglos marks the history of this region, particularly over land title, labor, and water rights.[12] Grant County, by contrast, was settled much later and much more tenuously, with Apaches defending their territory successfully against Spaniards, Mexicans, and Americans alike until late in the nineteenth century.[13]

If Santa Rita's copper district differed from older New Mexican settlements, it nonetheless shared one feature with them. The mines attracted people of many nationalities whose presence was alternately a boon and an annoyance to the Mexican government far to the south in the period 1820–46. French and American adventurers mined copper in Santa Rita and trapped beaver along the Gila River, among them Kit Carson, who trapped along the Gila when he was not working as a teamster at the mine.[14] Sylvester Pattie and his son James leased the Santa Rita mine in 1825–26, and their party also trapped along the Gila River.[15] Irishman James Kirker arrived in 1824 and "trapped along the Gila every winter . . . , as late as 1835."[16] Robert McKnight and Stephen Courcier ran the mines from 1826 to 1834, and they hired Kirker to guard the mule trains from Santa Rita to the smelters in Chihuahua.[17] Some of these mountain men married Mexican women, just as many trappers did farther north, and their descendants often belonged to Mexican American communities. James Kirker became a Mexican citizen (in order to get trapping permits), married Rita García sometime around 1831, and set up house in Janos, Chihuahua, where he and his wife reared five children.[18]

Unfortunately for all the settlers, and even less fortunately for the Apaches, an American trader named James Johnson arrived in 1837 and arranged "with some Mexicans at Santa Rita to rid New Mexico of the 'Apache menace.'"[19] The Apaches had accommodated some of the intruders, probably because they were more interested in raiding the productive farms and ranches farther south. Many trappers, in fact, were well regarded by the Apaches and considered Apache leaders their friends. But Johnson planned to present the governor of Sonora with the scalps of Apache leaders Juan José Compa and Mangas Coloradas and anyone else he could kill, and for each scalp he expected an ounce of gold. He invited the Apache to a trade meeting, during which he ordered his trappers to open fire.[20] Juan José Compa was killed, as were many Indian women and children who had joined the festivities, but many Apaches escaped and organized a retaliation against not only Johnson and the trappers but the settlers as well. The war, for that was what it quickly became, isolated the mining town and drove all of its settlers south toward Chihuahua. Only a few made it that far; most were killed on the way.[21] Johnson never got his scalps (he barely kept his life), and mining shut down for thirty years.

Mexicans continued to settle along the rivers and to prospect a bit, both before and after the U.S.-Mexican War, which transferred the territory to the United States in 1848, but settlement in the mining district remained sparse until after the Civil War. In the decade following annexation to the United States, mining attracted both families (usually Mexicans) and single men (usually Anglos). Among the miners were two of Jim Kirker's sons, Rafael and Roberto. A few Anglo Americans and Europeans had some capital at their disposal, including a German named Henkel, who founded the town of Hanover in the 1850s and operated a copper mine and smelting works there. One hundred fifty men and thirty women, almost all Mexican, worked for him, the men earning $30 a month and women half that.[22]

But none of Grant County's settlers could feel securely settled. Chiricahua Apaches kept both Anglos and Mexicans on edge, causing miners and farmers alike periodically to pack up and move out. The Apaches were threatened by the glut of people who were destroying their hunting grounds; a gold strike in Pinos Altos in 1860, for example, quickly drew thousands of people. American aggression infuriated the Apaches, most notably when leader Mangas Coloradas was savagely beaten by a group of drunken miners whom he had tried to induce to prospect farther north.[23] Facing more and more settlers who enjoyed more and more military protection, various Apache groups negotiated with the U.S. government for food, livestock, and land in exchange for settling permanently on restricted areas of land, only to find that the U.S. government failed to honor its end of the bargains. A cycle of raids and peace went on for decades, the Apaches making good use of the disruption caused by the Civil War, until the U.S. Army drove them to reservations east of the Rio Grande in the 1880s.[24] They were the last holdouts of the Indian wars that consolidated the continental United States.

Apache strength accounts for another difference between Grant County and other parts of New Mexico: Mexicans and Anglos settled the region at roughly the same time, albeit often in different locales, and both groups were accorded the "pioneer" status befitting anyone who endured Indian threat.[25] This is quite remarkable, for the pioneer myth centered on European Americans moving westward across the continent and, to the extent that the myth acknowledged prior occupants, displacing those occupants under the banner of progress. Mexicans fared poorly in this American origin story. The ideology of manifest destiny gained currency in the 1840s precisely around the time of the U.S.-Mexican War, and Mexicans were routinely dismissed as a degraded race. In fact, this version of racism helped delay New Mexican statehood some seventy years, for Americans elsewhere feared that their polity could not absorb such large numbers of backward citizens.[26]

Under some circumstances, this parallel, if not entirely shared, experience might have kept Mexican Americans and Anglos on some level of social equality, and intermarriage during the period 1850–1900 may have accomplished something of the kind in rural Grant County. Joe T. Morales, a strong Mine-Mill leader and an actor in *Salt of the Earth*, traced his origins to one such family from the Mimbres Valley.[27] In this respect, the Mimbres Valley looks a lot like the San Pedro Valley in southeastern Arizona, where Mexicans, Anglos, and other Europeans together faced the same Apache threats, owned similar amounts of land, and intermarried.[28] This was less true of Silver City, the main town in Grant County, however. Compared to other areas of New Mexico, where "the overwhelming majority of married Anglo men . . . were married to Hispanic women," only a third of such Silver City men were married to Hispanic women in 1870 and fewer than a quarter were in 1880.[29] Moreover, as historian Deena J. González warns us, intermarriage does not necessarily indicate assimilation (in either direction) or cultural unity.[30]

But as the power of Anglo mining companies, cattle ranchers, and other local Anglo notables grew, it eroded what started out and could have remained a situation in which ethnicity did not necessarily mark social status. The transformation from small-scale to capital-intensive mining around the turn of the century decisively changed social relations in Grant County. A local Anglo elite consolidated its power, class divisions were sharpened, and the worst jobs became synonymous with "Mexican" jobs. By 1920, a German like Henkel would have been considered "Anglo," because non-Spanish people were subsumed under that term.[31] The distinction that came to matter most was that between Anglo and Mexican, a distinction manifest most clearly in the dual-wage system that developed in the mining industry.

CAPITAL AND ENGINEERING

Capital-intensive mining became the engine of Grant County's economic growth in the twentieth century. Precious metals like gold and silver continued to be important (and they still attract prospectors to this day), but alone they could not drive Grant County's economy. Silver City and its neighbors would have gone the way of places like Tombstone, Arizona —rapid settlement, lots of money changing hands, rough conditions, and

then depletion of the ore, followed by the disappearance of its citizens—
were it not for the demand for base metals and the development of new
methods for extracting them, methods that required great amounts of
capital and labor. Copper, lead, and zinc had been used for thousands of
years, but with new manufacturing processes that depended on them
came a demand for unheard-of quantities of these metals. Copper's exceptional ductility made it indispensable for electrical wiring. Lead was
needed in storage batteries and telecommunications casings. Zinc was
essential in galvanizing steel and vulcanizing rubber, and it was especially
important in die casting, which enabled mechanized production. The
world production of finished metals increased almost tenfold between
1880 and 1920; in that same period, U.S. production grew at twice that
rate, from 30,200 tons produced in 1880 to 612,000 produced in 1920.[32]
The world smelter production of zinc was 50,000 tons in 1850; by 1910 it
had increased sixteen times to 800,000 tons.[33]

The Empire Zinc Company, formed in 1902, was one of many companies aiming to profit from this demand. Empire Zinc was a wholly
owned subsidiary of the New Jersey Zinc Company, whose own predecessor, the Sussex Zinc and Copper Mining Company, had built the
country's first commercial zinc smelter in 1848.[34] With New Jersey Zinc
behind it, Empire Zinc explored and developed mines in Colorado, New
Mexico, Arizona, Nevada, and Mexico. This required no small investment, because until New Jersey Zinc developed a flotation process that
could readily separate zinc from lead in complex ores, these western
districts were almost worthless.[35] Empire Zinc set up operations in Hanover, a few miles northwest of Santa Rita, and in Magdalena, in neighbor-
ing Socorro County.

By 1920, corporations, many of them large multinationals, had
bought up numerous mining camps and dominated the local economy.
In 1919, only 47 percent of New Mexican metal mines were corporate,
but those corporations produced 98 percent of the value of mine products and employed 96 percent of the state's metal miners.[36] The trend
continued in the 1920s such that half of New Mexico's fourteen copper
enterprises were corporately owned, producing 98 percent of the value of
copper products and employing 95 percent of the state's 2,258 copper
miners. Seven of the eight zinc enterprises were corporately owned.[37]

Individual miners and small firms did not disappear from the landscape, though. Thirty percent of New Mexico's mine operators in 1919
were individuals, and another 23 percent were firms, smaller operations
of one or two miners that often leased claims from other individuals or

from already-existing companies, and that permitted the individualist symbol of an earlier era—the prospector—to persist.[38] But the prospector of the twentieth century was as likely as not to have an advanced degree in mining or metallurgical engineering. Companies turned to engineers, experts who could design and operate new mining technology and who could confirm the worthwhile deposits. Mining claims were risky, and companies needed experts to separate the promising from the disastrous. Mining engineers formed a cohesive bunch, and they came to represent the changing class structure of industrial mining as it developed within the United States and across national borders. As much as they might celebrate the virtues of individualism, they were remarkably similar to one another in background and education. And they depended on corporate largesse at the same time they were striking out on their own paths.

Ira L. Wright was typical of many mining engineers of his generation. He combined a breadth of experience—many kinds of mines, many kinds of ores; mining engineering and metallurgy alike—with an enterprising spirit that made him one of the most successful mine operators in Grant County. Wright was born in 1883 on a farm near Hughesville, Missouri. After graduating from a country school, he went on to the Missouri School of Mines in Rolla.[39] Like any mining school worth its salt, the Missouri School of Mines sent its students to work all over the country during the summer. It was imperative, most engineers and educators believed, to give their students a feel for the work and, importantly, a feel for the workers. Mining engineers could expect to become mine managers in some capacity or another, and the miners who trained them on the job would probably be their employees a few years down the road.[40]

While still a student, Wright did stints in Utah copper mines and Missouri coal, lead, and zinc mines. These were exciting times for ambitious young engineers, who were in great demand around the turn of the century.[41] After he graduated in 1907, Wright went to Bisbee, Arizona, to work for the Calumet and Arizona Copper Company, and a couple of years later he moved to the Silver City area to work for the Savanna Copper Company.[42] These were typical first jobs for a mining engineer, combining surveying, assaying, and reporting on the likely worth of a mine claim. They were also relatively low-paid jobs, for companies mined recent graduates for cheap labor.[43] Wright must have seen the possibilities that additional credentials would open, because he went back to Rolla for a master's degree in mining engineering.

When he returned to Savanna Copper Company, he put this education to good use—his own. Like many engineers, Wright leased claims from the company while working full-time for a regular paycheck. He and his partner, James Bell, had few "resources except unbounded energy and sublime faith," the local newspaper reminisced twenty-five years later. They hired some inexperienced miners to do some of the grunt work, and "one night they actually 'gophered' into a chamber of almost pure gold."[44] The wily Wright did not let on to the others what they had found; instead, he genially suggested that they take the night off to enjoy a local dance. The chamber was safe for him and Bell to exploit as much as they could. Over the next four years, they got somewhere between $50,000 and $100,000 from this Pinos Altos mine, a strike that "electrified southwestern mining circles."[45]

After Pinos Altos, Wright worked as a metallurgical engineer for the Chino Copper Company before opening an engineering and assaying office in Silver City. Around 1920, Wright signed on with the ailing Blackhawk Mining Company, which soon elevated him to general manager. Under his capable management, Blackhawk started to turn a profit on lead and zinc ores that could be processed with the flotation method pioneered by New Jersey Zinc. Wright continued his independent projects while running Blackhawk for the next thirty years. He became one of the local notables, helping found the New Mexico Miners and Prospectors Association in 1939 and reporting regularly on the health of the mining economy.

While mining dominated the economy throughout Grant County, the centerpiece of Grant County's mines was always Santa Rita. Francisco Elguea's heirs, whom the U.S. General Land Office confirmed as Santa Rita's owners, had split the property into smaller claims and sold them to J. Parker Whitney of Boston in 1881. Whitney then subleased the mines to other operators, who took as much high-grade copper as possible and left the low-grade ore as waste.[46] By the turn of the century, the remaining ore was low-grade, and only expensive new technology could extract valuable copper from useless gangue. Moreover, low-grade ore promised a profit only if mined on a scale that the lone prospector could not achieve. Processing the ore required new mills for crushing rock, new chemicals for separating minerals, new reverberatory furnaces for smelting. The depletion of high-grade copper, at a time when people were eager to cash in on the copper market, set the stage for technological and social change in Grant County.

The catalyst for this change was a mining engineer named John Sully. Sully was born in Dedham, Massachusetts, in 1863, and earned a B.S. in mining engineering from the Massachusetts Institute of Technology in 1888. He spent fifteen years working in Montana, California, and Alabama mines before landing in Grant County in 1903. There, he inspected Santa Rita's prospects on behalf of General Electric.[47] General Electric soon lost interest in the project, but Sully did not, and after an interlude of a few years in Mexico, he returned to Santa Rita in 1908 as a consulting engineer for the Santa Rita Mining Company. Ten months of surveying convinced Sully of Santa Rita's worth. It had, he declared, something on the order of 3,217,060 tons of developed copper ore, plus more than 5 million more tons of what he called "expectant" ore. But the copper content was only about 2.73 percent (2.39 for the expectant ore), so only new methods of mining and milling could make it pay off.[48] Instead of digging tunnels and stopes underground, Sully thought that digging a wider and wider hole, and hauling the ore from the pit in railroad cars, would make it both possible and profitable to exploit the deposits.

In this he followed the lead of another mining engineer, Daniel Cowan Jackling. Jackling made a name and a fortune for himself by starting the massive open-pit mining operation in Bingham Canyon, Utah, and he would come to influence Santa Rita's development, too.[49] Like Ira Wright, Jackling was a Missouri farm boy who made his way to the School of Mines. As a teenager he was making $14 a week as a farm hand when he realized there was little future in it: the agricultural ladder that supposedly led the hardworking farm laborer up into farm ownership ended abruptly on the wage-earner rung. He worked for railroads to pay his way through school and graduated in 1892 with a degree in metallurgy. After teaching for a year at his alma mater, Jackling headed west, arriving in Cripple Creek, Colorado, with three dollars to his name.[50] The gold mining camp of Cripple Creek was in its heyday, a microcosm of the emerging industrial order where miners jockeyed for prospects and investors alike.[51] Jackling hooked up with other young men on the make, and through them he made contacts with wealthy investors in Colorado Springs and Denver.

Later in the decade Jackling was cashing in on one such contact. He supervised a cyanide plant at Mercur, Utah, and in 1898 the company president asked him to test ores from Bingham Canyon. Bingham Canyon was rich in copper, but it was "porphyry copper": the metal was diffused through quartz, so recovering any of it meant mining all of the surrounding rock. This was a problem. Jackling's solution was to use steam shovels to tear big chunks of rock from the earth and then to mill it with new methods that made a richer concentrate of copper. He had gotten this idea from seeing similar shovels at work in the Mesabi iron range in Minnesota. Building the equipment he proposed would require massive capital investment, and, just as in Sully's case six years later, the company declined to make that investment. But Jackling was a pro at getting financial backers—fortunate, since he had no money of his own— so he formed the Utah Copper Company in June 1903 to undertake the Bingham Canyon project himself. A few years later, when he was ready to start mining the open pit, the Guggenheim family invested in his company. Jackling quickly began building a 3,000-ton concentrator in Copperton, the first mill to process the same kind of porphyry copper that Santa Rita held.[52]

By 1909, Jackling's mine and mill were so successful that his approval alone secured investment in Sully's proposal to create the new Chino Mining Company as a subsidiary of Jackling's Utah Copper. The Chino Mining Company operated the Santa Rita mines and, in 1911, a new mill at Hurley, a railroad depot eight miles south of Santa Rita.[53] Thus did Chino join a vast empire of copper mines, coal mines, and food production. Part of what made companies able to sit out a long stretch of losses in a new mining venture was its vertical integration, or the degree to which the same company controlled many aspects of production. In the case of mining, a company like the American Smelting and Refining Company (Asarco) owned mines, mills, smelters, refineries, and transportation—in short, all the stages of production.[54] Jackling's company, too, controlled many levels of production. All of Santa Rita's and Hurley's store provisions were shipped in, some $340,000 worth in 1937. Companies in which Jackling invested, such as the Gallup American Coal Company and the Great American Sugar Beet Company, provided the coal to run its steam shovels, trains, and mill, and the foodstuffs to feed workers in Santa Rita and all the other mining camps.[55] And there were many mining camps, all pulled into a set of corporate relationships that shifted, shrank, or grew according to the demands of the metal market and the ambitions of the mine operators. Utah Copper was bought by Nevada Consolidated in 1922, which was itself bought by Kennecott Copper Corporation in 1933. But Jackling kept control over most of the western operations for many years and sent his mining engineers from one property to the next, spreading technological skill and helping consolidate these men, and their families, into a cosmopolitan class.

AN INDUSTRIAL WORKFORCE

Capital was one thing, and corporations like Empire Zinc and Chino had it. But they also needed a large workforce. No machine could be trusted to blast holes, drive trains, lay new track, or repair the machines themselves. Thousands of men, Anglo and Mexican alike, took jobs in Grant County's mines between 1910 and 1950.[56] Industrial mining and milling were complex processes that required many people to fill a wide variety of jobs. Many mine workers were craftsmen plying trades common to any industrial enterprise: blacksmiths, boilermakers, electricians, carpenters, plumbers, machinists, and railroad brakemen and engineers. The miners themselves were a varied group; "miner" is both a generic term for any employee of a mine, itself denoting operations both above and under the ground, and a specific term for the individual who gets the ore.[57] Subsuming the varied occupations in one term provides a useful shorthand for discussing the employees of the entire industry and their identity as workers in masculine jobs. But it also obscures the wide range of work required in Grant County's mines and mills, a range that both reflected the industry's complexity and reinforced the discrimination attending ethnic distinctions.

Grant County's miners shared similar work processes and rhythms. An underground miner's day began early in the morning or mid-afternoon, depending on his shift.[58] First he changed into work clothes, if the company provided a changing room; this was an amenity won by unionized miners in the 1920s, but no unions took root in Grant County until the 1930s. Next the miner went to the main shaft and descended in a cage with twenty or so other workers.[59] The main shaft traveled downward hundreds or even thousands of feet, either vertically or at an incline. A massive hoisting mechanism, hung from a headframe above the mine opening, allowed the cages and skips to be moved up and down the shaft at speeds reaching eight hundred feet per minute for men, and even more for other materials.[60] The hoistman, as the Mine-Mill union observed, held "at all times men's lives in his hands [and handled] some of the company's most expensive property."[61]

A station surrounded the shaft on each working level, and at each station the cager directed the comings and goings of men and materials. Crosscuts, or horizontal passageways, led from the shaft to the vein of ore and created a dense hive of rooms and working areas. Raises and chutes connected levels to one another, generally fifty to a hundred feet apart. Timbermen built the chutes, made the ground a safe working surface, and repaired timber supports. Trackmen and pipemen installed the critical transportation system of tracks, pipes, and trams.

Metal mining, also called hard-rock mining, depended on controlled explosions to drive tunnels from the shaft to the ore face and wrest ore

Miners at shift change, ca. 1950. Photo courtesy of Ricardo Trevizo.

from its deposits. Miners excavated the ore in a series of stopes, or step-shaped hollowed-out blocks. This method increased the number of rock surfaces, which in turn made the blasting process more precise and efficient.[62] First a miner drilled a series of holes, entering the rock face at different angles. Into these holes he loaded the proper type and amount of explosive (or powder), and then he attached wires to the cartridge's blasting cap. Moving some distance away, and warning his helpers and nearby workers, the miner ignited the cartridge, blasted the rock, and waited for the dust and debris to settle.

Muckers helped load explosives, supplied the miner with steel drills, and then shoveled the ore into chutes or cars that brought it back to the station. In many instances, muckers did exactly the same work as miners, but they were never paid the same wage. By the mid-1940s, mucking machines and air-driven hoists had begun to relieve some of the back-breaking physical labor, but the machines themselves were dangerous and hard to manage.[63] Crushermen, as their name implied, crushed over-sized boulders into pieces that would fit in the cars. Trammers moved the cars along tracks or, as at the Peru Mining Company in Hanover, dumped and refastened ore buckets that moved along aerial trams. Grizzlymen, also called underground pocketmen, unloaded ore cars and helped the cager load the skips heading back to the surface, often drilling and blast-ing those rocks that were too large for the skips to lift. At the surface, toplanders helped men in and out of the cages and dumped ore and waste into railroad cars; their job resembled that of cagers. Railroads took the ore to a mill for processing.

Chino's open pit was a different sort of operation entirely.[64] The open pit expanded downward and inward in concentric circles, eating away the land under Santa Rita. The town was gradually confined to a peninsula that jutted into the pit, and the company had to move all its buildings, and the cemetery, to accommodate the ever-expanding pit; by 1960, the original site of Santa Rita had disappeared altogether. Open-pit miners were not subject to the dangers of underground mining, but their work was hazardous nonetheless. On each working level, or bench, miners drilled holes fourteen inches in diameter and sixty feet deep, typically ten or twenty feet from the edge of the bench, and blasted between twenty and fifty holes at once. Twenty-five tons of explosive, for instance, would dislodge a quarter million tons of rock.[65] Shovel operators loaded rock tons at a time into railroad cars. Because the working surface changed so frequently, trackmen were always needed to lay new track along the newly blasted levels. In the 1920s, Chino replaced the steam shovels with electric shovels; during World War II it further electrified the operations and replaced the trains with gigantic trucks that hauled fifty or more tons, their drivers sitting sixteen feet above the ground.[66]

In Grant County, companies both mined and processed ores. Ore processing entails separating the desirable minerals from each other and from useless rock in a series of stages. The first stages take place in a mill, later stages in smelters and refineries. There were four mills in the Cen-tral mining district: Chino treated all its copper in Hurley; Empire Zinc and Asarco each treated lead and zinc in Hanover; and later the U.S. Smelting, Refining, and Mining Company treated lead in Bayard. Other companies sent their ores to local mills for initial processing or sent them straight to El Paso, Amarillo, and points east for milling or smelting. Chino built its own smelter in Hurley in 1938.

Millmen ran huge crushing and grinding machines that broke the rock into smaller and smaller pieces, often down to powder. Gravity separated metals from other rock. To the metal powder, men in the flotation department added chemicals that made the ore float to the top, from which others skimmed it—now more or less a mud—into separate tanks. After another round or so of concentration, mill workers shoveled the ore into bins for weighing and then onto railroad cars for shipping.[67] Smeltermen added heat to the process. After mixing mill concentrates with silica and limestone, they melted it all down in a reverberatory furnace. The upper level was slag, or waste, that they hauled to waste dumps; the bottom layer was a copper matte that they further reduced in furnaces. Copper bars or molds were then shipped east for use or for further refining.

The men who came to Grant County's mines in the twentieth century soon learned who belonged where. In the American Southwest, ethnicity came to determine the allotment of jobs and, as we will see below, the location of homes. As Table 1 shows for Santa Rita and Hanover mines, Mexican Americans outnumbered Anglos but were disproportionately clustered in the "laborer" category, which included very few Anglos. Mexican American men typically started as general laborers and, until the 1940s, seldom advanced far. In 1934, Chino general laborer Julián Horcasitas, for example, was earning $3.65 a day; track laborer Francisco Costales, who had started working at Chino in 1923, earned $2.60 a day.[68] There was no chance for Mexicans to advance above a very low ceiling. Many Mexican jobs—like laying track for the train cars that hauled ore out of the open pit, or repairing train cars in the railroad yard—had no lines of promotion leading away from them; José M. Martínez, for instance, started working as a track laborer in 1918, and he retired from that position in 1953—thirty-five years in Chino's lowest-paying job. The only way a Mexican American could hope for a promotion was to get transferred to another department altogether.[69] So few Anglos worked as "laborers," in fact, that the job title was probably a euphemism for "Mexican."[70]

Craft and some railroad jobs pulled the highest wages and went almost exclusively to Anglo men. The railroad industry was extremely segregated all over the country, and Grant County barely diverged from the national pattern. As a matter of policy, the "Big Four" railway brotherhoods, which represented engineers, conductors, brakemen, and firemen, excluded Mexican Americans and other people deemed nonwhite; in nonunion areas like Grant County before the 1940s, however, the firemen (who fed the furnace in the engine room) were occasionally

Table 1. Men Employed in the Mining Industry, Santa Rita and
Hanover, N.M., 1930

Occupational group	Santa Rita		Hanover	
	Mexican	Anglo	Mexican	Anglo
Laborers	420	5	113	8
Helpers	11	23	1	4
Miners	11	6	26	18
Skilled railroad workers and other craftsmen	20	157	0	18
Other mine employees (drillers, hoistmen, pumpmen, cranemen, etc.)	12	90	12	24
Office employees	5	8	0	4
Security	2	4	0	0
Engineers, scientists, and doctors	0	13	0	11
Foremen, managers, and owner-operators	3	28	0	15
Prospectors	0	1	0	3
Contractors	0	0	0	1
Total	484	335	152	106

Source: 1930 manuscript census, New Mexico, Grant County, Precincts 11, 13, and 16
(Hanover, Vanadium, Bayard Station, and Santa Rita).

Mexican.[71] V. H. Crittenden started work at Chino as a steam shovel
fireman when he was teenager. He was probably helping support his
widowed mother, who ran a boardinghouse in Santa Rita. By 1934, when
he was just over thirty years old, he was a crane and shovel operator
earning $5.25 a day.[72] Locomotive fireman and engineer Joseph W. Bax-
ter, who started working at Chino in 1920, earned $5.15 a day in 1934.[73]
There were some important differences between the mines in Santa Rita
and Hanover, however, with respect to other craft jobs: twenty Mexican
men held such jobs in Santa Rita (11 percent of the total skilled railroad and other craft workers), while none did in Hanover. By contrast,
while the same number of Mexican men in both Santa Rita and Hanover
worked as "other mine employees"—such as drillers, hoistmen, pump-
men, and cranemen—this number (twelve) represented very different
proportions of that workforce (12 percent of Santa Rita's versus 33 percent of Hanover's).

Managers were almost always Anglo, some homegrown and some
brought in from other Jackling operations. Horace Moses, for example,
grew up in Grant County and worked at Chino from the beginning. He

had graduated from the State Teachers College in Silver City, but even without formal training as a mining engineer he was appointed general foreman in 1912. He held that position until the 1920s, when Nevada Consolidated, which bought Chino in 1923, appointed him general manager of its coal mines in Gallup, New Mexico. He returned to Santa Rita in 1938 to superintend the whole Chino outfit.[74] By 1930, only three Mexican American men had made it into the ranks of Chino foremen; the other twenty-two foremen were Anglo. Those Mexicans who did enter management did so after a much longer stint in wage work than was required of their Anglo counterparts. Felipe Huerta, for instance, began working for Chino in 1912, the same year as Horace Moses. He was a general laborer for thirty years before his 1941 promotion to the powder department, which tended the open pit's explosives; in 1950, he was finally promoted to powder foreman.[75] The situation was not much different in Hanover, where no Mexicans worked in any supervisory or clerical position in 1930.

If ethnic segregation generally defined Grant County's mining industry, sex segregation was even more extreme, to the point that it barely warranted notice. The sexual division of labor, present everywhere, is especially pronounced in mining districts, where women have rarely found work in the mines. Women's exclusion from North American mining has a long history. Individual nineteenth-century women found their way into prospecting and placer mining, occasionally accompanying their husbands or partners; anecdotal evidence points to some women managing mines even earlier.[76] In some instances, mining—or at least the aboveground processing of ore—was evidently considered suitable work for women. Indian women mined, transported, and smelted lead in the upper Mississippi River valley until the 1830s, when their communities were pushed out of the region, and California Indian women integrated mining into their seasonal work during the gold rush. Mexican women played some role in Henkel's Hanover mine, and other Mexican women could be found sorting ore in Guanajuato silver mines as late as 1907.[77] A few women worked in Appalachian coal mines in the mid-twentieth century, despite male miners' resistance.[78]

But if women occasionally worked aboveground in various aspects of mining, they seldom worked underground. Cornish miners believed that it was bad luck for women to go into the mines, and they brought this idea to North America.[79] Just such a distinction may account for the differing attitudes expressed in 1904 by the Western Federation of Miners (WFM), Mine-Mill's predecessor. A paean to the "idol of Groom

Creek Miners Union," one Mrs. H. H. Keays, celebrated her accomplishments as miner and as member in her own right of Local 154. Keays accompanied her husband in his prospecting, "endowed with a sublime fortitude that [would] challenge the fearless intrepidity of the most courageous men," yet she "lost none of the feminine graces that [made] her a queen in her home."[80] Contrast this with the hellish vision of Belgian women and girls of the same era working underground, sometimes as deep as 4,000 feet: "female slaves of toil spend[ing] 12 hours of imprisonment in the bowels of the earth to earn the pittance that prolongs a life of miserable poverty."[81]

Seemingly insignificant distinctions can carry weighty ideological baggage. Both Keays and the Belgian women worked in the mining industry, but their place and conditions of work, ages, and presumed relations with men differed in critical respects. Keays and her situation met the requirements for a progressive vision of American history, particularly as played out in the American West. She exemplified "woman," who, "by the very force of her character, has swept hoary conventionalities into the grave."[82] Keays's work with her husband did not threaten gender divisions because she performed it within certain accepted conventions (which did not, evidently, get swept away): she was married to her coworker, not working alone or with strange men; she worked above ground in prospecting and placer mining, not in the mine shafts; and her work did not compromise her femininity, since she retained her "feminine graces." The individual prospector assumed an important place in the myth of the ruggedly individualist West, and the WFM was willing to laud the occasional exceptional woman as well. But not those women, especially young women, working underground. The situation of Belgian female miners was no golden opportunity but rather a sad misfortune in the eyes of an American labor movement concerned over horrific industrial conditions and, just as important, over the proper place for women in European and American industrialism. Belgian women miners belonged to an inhumane system that denied working men a family wage—a system that American labor leaders feared in their own country as well: while "the American citizen, whose bosom swells with patriotism, may censure the dynasty of King Leopold, . . . in the 'Land of the free and the home of the brave' the mills and factories of the cotton kings present a spectacle that makes Belgium look like 'A garden of the gods.' "[83]

Miners had little to fear that industrialism would directly threaten the lives of their wives and daughters, for few women worked in industrial settings in Grant County's mining district. Few women worked for

Table 2. Employed Women, Santa Rita and Hanover, N.M., 1930

Sector	Santa Rita			Hanover	
	Mexican	Anglo	Black	Mexican	Anglo
Service[a]	58	12	1[b]	12	3
Sales (in store or house-to-house)	4	8	0	0	0
Clerical[c]	0	5	0	3	5
Agriculture[d]	0	0	0	0	2
Labor[e]	0	3	0	3	0
Landlady (apartments)	1	0	0	1	0
Professional[f]	3[g]	22	0	0	13
Total, by town and ethnicity	66	50	1	19	23
Total, by town		117		42	

Source: 1930 manuscript census, New Mexico, Grant County, Precincts 11, 13, and 16 (Hanover, Vanadium, Bayard Station, and Santa Rita).
[a] Service includes servant, maid, waitress, dishwasher, cook, washwoman, housekeeper, boardinghouse keeper, dental assistant, and beauty specialist.
[b] Wife of a gardener; the couple worked for John Sully.
[c] Clerical includes clerk, stenographer, telephone operator, bookkeeper, office manager, railroad agent, postmistress, and census enumerator.
[d] Agriculture includes ranch helper and farmer.
[e] Labor includes seamstress, laundry laborer, and railroad brakeman.
[f] Professional includes teacher, school principal, school superintendent, nurse, and religious practitioner.
[g] Includes two teachers, both of whom taught Spanish in a private school.

wages at all, although this varied considerably by town. In Hanover, for instance, 42 out of approximately 105 adult women (40 percent) were employed for pay in 1930—a fairly high number. In Santa Rita, by contrast, only 117 out of approximately 1,100 adult women (11 percent) were so employed.[84] As Table 2 shows, those women who worked for wages in Santa Rita and Hanover in 1930 were primarily in the service sector, if they were Mexican American, and in the professional sector, if they were Anglo.

The differences between Hanover and Santa Rita might be related to another difference: the number of female-headed households.[85] Santa Rita, with ten times the population of Hanover, had slightly fewer female-headed households than that town, sixteen in Santa Rita, compared to eighteen in Hanover. In both towns, most female heads of households were widows—itself evidence of how little shielded women actually were from the ravages of industrial mining—but the ethnic compositions were almost mirror opposites of each other. Fourteen (88 percent) of Santa Rita's female heads were Anglo, compared to only three (17 percent) of Hanover's female heads. Fewer female-headed households in Santa Rita might account for a lower labor force participation rate; it leaves open, of course, why there was such a big gap between otherwise similar towns. It is possible that in this stricter company town, it was harder for women to keep their houses or leases if the male mine employee left or died. I return to the issue of women's employment in Chapter 6.

THE SOCIAL GEOGRAPHY OF MINING TOWNS

In order to attract the kind of miners the companies wanted—men who would come to remote areas, who would not disappear at the rumor of better mines elsewhere—many companies in the 1910s and 1920s built towns to house workers and their families; if miners lived with their families, perhaps they would find it harder to leave. Companies' control over housing often meant control over many aspects of a mining family's life, although this power was not always bluntly exercised.[86] Grant County's mining towns fell along a spectrum, from towns owned outright by Chino (Santa Rita and Hurley), to towns where more than one company operated mines and owned housing (Hanover and Vanadium), to relatively independent towns (Bayard and Central). These towns kept their basic characters through the mid-1950s, when Kennecott dramatically changed the landscape by selling off the towns of Santa Rita and Hurley.

Daniel Jackling's vision of a vast system of interlocking parts had a local component in the paternalism he and Sully used to organize Chino's production and housing. The company would care for its employees as a father would care for his children. Once Sully started open-pit mining, he found that he needed "to take care of a great number of employees ... at Santa Rita and Hurley."[87] His solution was to build towns. Santa Rita already existed, but the company razed all the buildings to start from scratch. Hurley—site of the company's mill and, beginning in 1939, its smelter—was merely a railroad depot until Sully laid a grid of streets. In both places, the company "built a large number of comfortable houses," mostly for the Anglos.[88] It leased land instead to Mexicans, who built their own houses in Santa Rita's Mexican Town and in North Hurley. Chino also owned the schools and paid the teachers, owned the mercantile store, owned the hospital and hired its doctors, and hired the deputy sheriff and the mortician. Chino owned everything.

Empire Zinc did not build the town of Hanover, which had instead been built on Henkel's $47,000 investment in the 1850s, and the company was not the sole operation, for Peru Mining Company and Blackhawk

Mining Company came to employ many people there from the 1920s onward.[89] In these respects, Hanover was what historians Yvette Huginnie and Elizabeth Jameson have called "semi-independent" towns.[90] But Empire Zinc nevertheless made its mark: its officials served on the school board, it owned many of the houses, and by 1920 its wage workers (almost all Mexican or Mexican American) had replaced the hundred or so Anglo miners and ranchers, none of whom worked for wages, who had lived there in 1910.[91]

Services in these mining towns were marked by racial distinctions, which corresponded closely to class distinctions. Santa Rita and Hurley were both segregated from the very beginning. The "comfortable houses" that Sully built were indeed comfortable: they were "lighted by electricity and furnished with water and connected with sewer systems," amenities that were even more impressive for a remote area in 1910.[92] But only Anglos could rent those houses. Mexicans typically lived in the houses they could afford to build on the lots they could afford to rent. Bill Wood's family, for example, lived in the three-room house that his father built out of one-by-twelve boards and one-by-four slats, filled in with construction cardboard.[93] Similarly, Arturo Flores grew up in a house his family built out of wood boards, two-by-fours, and cardboard.[94] Empire Zinc striker and Auxiliary 209 president Mariana Ramírez bitterly remembered growing up in Hurley, where her father worked for $2.40 a day: "On the north side of the tracks the Negro and Mexican-American people lived in shacks. The Anglos had company-built dormitories and no Mexicans were allowed on the South (Anglo) side after nine o'clock. No Mexican-American family was allowed to entertain at his house, unless permitted by the Justice of Peace. . . . You could even hear the Anglo kids say that on the North side of the tracks live the bad and mean people. They picked this up from the grownups."[95] Similarly, Hanover's Mexican residents typically paid less rent than Anglos did. The rent differential, however, did not reflect the company's special concern for Mexicans so much as the inferior quality of the property available on the Mexican wage.[96]

Occupational segregation in Grant County's mining towns was extremely rigid, and geographical segregation was almost as much so. On this foundation grew a social segregation that all residents, Anglo and Mexican American alike, perceived from childhood onward. It was apparent in schools, churches, civic organizations, and recreation, and it was reinforced by the local political structures that favored Anglo over Mexican American in almost all arenas.[97] Santa Rita, Hurley, and Silver

City schools were segregated through the third grade, while Bayard, Hanover, and Central schools were too small to provide separate facilities for Anglos and Mexican Americans. St. Mary's Academy, a Catholic school in Silver City, served both Mexican American and Anglo youth. Aurora Chávez and Alice Sandoval both recalled that the Santa Rita schools and Hurley High School had separate bathrooms and drinking fountains for Mexican and Anglo students.[98] Whether integrated or not, students quickly learned central facts about the relative value of Anglo and Mexican culture: the teachers and principals were all Anglo, with very few exceptions, and students were discouraged from if not outright punished for speaking Spanish on school property.[99] And while Spanish-named students were the majority of eighth grade graduates, they were the minority of high school graduates. Mexican students, for whatever reason, were less likely to graduate from high school than were their Anglo counterparts.[100] Many Mexican American boys, of course, expected to work in the mines, and they stayed in school only until they were old enough to work. "According to legend," Chino labor relations manager Bernard Himes recalled, "a company official, driving by a school playground that was segregated for those of Mexican descent, remarked, companionably, 'There's my next generation of track laborers.' "[101]

Social and civic organizations were similarly segregated. Fraternal organizations, which represent the kind of social and economic ties people make with one another, rarely crossed ethnic lines, although they frequently included both small businesspeople and skilled workers: Elks, Eagles, Masons (and their ladies' auxiliaries, too) admitted only Anglos to their brotherhood; the Alianza Hispano Americana and the Catholic Youth Organization served social and insurance needs of the Mexican Americans.[102] These same patterns were established among youth; Girl Scout and Boy Scout troops generally had either Anglo or Spanish-named members, with only a few—like the Girl Scout troop at St. Mary's—including both.[103] Religious communities paralleled the civic organizations. Few Mexican Americans belonged to Protestant denominations, although Baptists and Methodists occasionally held services in Spanish for their congregants. Both Anglos (or, more accurately, Irish) and Mexican Americans belonged to the Catholic Church; Central and Silver City's parishes seem to have consisted of both groups, but the smaller parishes, like Hanover's Holy Family Church, were mostly Mexican Americans.

Recreation was often segregated. Movie theaters seated Mexican Americans apart from Anglos, although some Mexican American moviegoers refused to obey this informal rule, and dances were usually advertised as "Anglo-American" or "Spanish American," with an occasional "Everyone Welcome" notice appearing after World War II.[104] The swimming pool in Hurley was reserved for Anglos until Sunday, when Mexican Americans were allowed to swim—just before the pool was cleaned for the week. Sports, however, proved to be one arena in which Mexican Americans and Anglos participated together; company baseball teams were integrated and very popular among both groups of people.

Grant County's political structure favored Anglo over Mexican American in almost every realm. Poll captains and election judges, who did not necessarily wield concrete power but were well integrated into the local political machinery, were almost all Anglo in Grant County through the 1940s. The few exceptions—in one Silver City precinct, in North Hurley, in Fierro, and in some towns on the Mimbres River—only proved the rule that Mexican Americans rarely laid claim to the workings of electoral politics. In 1951, when precincts in Hurley and Silver City were integrated, Mexican Americans disappeared from election boards altogether.[105] Mexican Americans were important to county politics because they voted, but they rarely held elected office in the political, law enforcement, or judicial arenas.[106] From county commissioners to mayors to justices of the peace, almost all elected officials were Anglo in the 1940s. Exceptions were the constables of Hanover and Fierro throughout the 1940s, and one member of Bayard's town council in 1950.[107] Moreover, almost all of the Anglo local officials came from local commerce. Finally, Anglos always outnumbered Mexican Americans on the juries of New Mexico's Sixth District Court during the 1940s; out of the typical pool of thirty-six jurors, no more than eight ever had Spanish names.[108]

The sharp lines between Anglo and Mexican were occasionally blurred, however, by intermarriage. William Villines, for example, was the son of a French German father and a Cherokee mother. Villines married a woman named Margarita, herself the daughter of a Mexican man and an Apache woman. While Margarita bore and raised twenty-one children, William worked as a hoistman.[109] Jim Blair was a Texan who drifted into Grant County late in the nineteenth century, working first as a saloon piano player, then as Grant County's sheriff, and finally as Santa Rita's deputy sheriff. He and his family, as well as his brother John, who lived next door, lived in a Mexican American neighborhood (named Blair Hill), probably because they had both married Mexican women. Whatever the conflicts between Anglo and Mexican in Santa Rita, Jim Blair was a force for conciliation. Many Mexican Americans remember him as an especially fair lawman; the fact that he stands out only emphasizes that intolerance was the norm. Mexican American and Anglo women alike called on him during domestic disputes.[110] William Fletcher was born in 1881 in New Mexico. Early in the twentieth century he married a Mexican-born woman named Abigail. By 1920, the Fletchers, with five children, were living in Hanover, where William was a foreman in a zinc mine. They owned their own home free of mortgage. But when their son Frank entered the labor market in the 1940s, he found that the Mexican part of his parentage outweighed the Anglo part. He was given a job as a shop laborer.[111]

Paternalism was a system that partly rested on managers' personal acquaintance with workers. At first the managers knew each man by name, but in later years all hiring and firing was done at a lower level. Daniel Jackling was proud of his own working-class origins, and he used that to make connections of some sort to the workers.[112] Pride in his humble origins did not make him humble, though. He cut a grand figure, sweeping into town a few times a year in his personal Pullman car, the *Cyprus*, which also brought his wife, his valet, his male secretary, and several other servants.[113] Hurley and Santa Rita would crackle with excitement at Jackling's arrival. After meeting with the local management, Jackling and his family would typically stay at Hub Estes's ranch near Whitewater, where Jackling and prominent local men—the district judge, other mine owners, Chino's higher management—would go big game hunting.[114] John Sully was a bit more modest in comportment, and many workers and residents found him quite approachable and easygoing.[115]

Grant County's paternalist mine managers frowned on collective action by workers and successfully resisted unions until the 1940s. Unionism, in the eyes of managers like John Sully and Daniel Jackling, was only ingratitude for all the good things the company did and gave. There is little evidence that unions made much of an impact in the copper or zinc camps during the 1910s and 1920s, although that did not keep management from worrying about them. Steam shovelers struck unsuccessfully in 1912 and lost their jobs to men the company had brought from elsewhere. The strikers left town, although it is unclear whether they left voluntarily or by force.[116] But mining companies were not above using force. In July 1917, at the height of a strike against the Phelps-Dodge Company in Bisbee, Arizona, the sheriff and his "citizen's alliance" rounded up a hundred strikers—many of them members of the Industrial Workers of the World (IWW), or Wobblies—boarded them on trains, and sent them east across the New Mexico border, depositing them in the desert near Columbus.[117] This dramatic event reverberated in Grant

County's mining district, where Sheriff Herbert McGrath was eager to take a stand against radicals, too. There were no Wobblies to speak of in Grant County, though, and apparently too few labor agitators to be rounded up under the pretense of protecting the citizens against Wobblies. Farther north, however, the Gallup (New Mexico) American Coal Company, a subsidiary of Utah Copper Corporation, staged its own deportation of thirty-four radicals for having in their possession "inflammatory literature" or belonging to the IWW. This action received less local support, however, because the United Mine Workers, which represented coal miners, mounted a powerful protest that also served to dissociate itself from the IWW.[118] Elsewhere in Jackling's mining empire, labor strife met with severe repression.[119]

What mine managers wanted did not change in the 1930s, but their ability to impose it did. With the help of a revitalized Mine, Mill and Smelter Workers Union and federal legislation sanctioning union organization, Grant County miners would begin to challenge the paternalist dual-wage system during the Great Depression, enjoy new successes during World War II, and face renewed opposition after the war. The Empire Zinc strike of 1950 culminated almost twenty years of this struggle across changing political terrains.

PART I

CRISIS

3

Class Conflict in the Mines,

1930—1950

THE INJUNCTION

A hundred people gathered outside the Empire Zinc Company's mine and mill in Hanover, New Mexico, on a June morning in 1951. Some were employees, others worked in other local zinc and copper mines. Still others were miners' wives and children. The workers belonged to Local 890 of the International Union of Mine, Mill and Smelter Workers (Mine-Mill) and had been on strike against Empire Zinc for eight months. Having failed to break the strike through attrition and an anemic back-to-work movement, the company was ready to reopen the mine by force.

Force came in the form of Sheriff Leslie Goforth and his twenty deputies. Thin and bespectacled, Goforth looked a bit like a retired schoolteacher or an elderly Harry Truman. He belonged to one of the "pioneer families" of Grant County. After serving in World War I, he surveyed mining claims and ranched; like other men of his class, he moved easily in and out of local law enforcement, ranching, and mining. Ironically, he probably owed his 1950 victory over Democratic incumbent Bartley McDonald to Local 890, whose members had come out in force against McDonald because of an ugly police brutality case in 1949.[1] McDonald lost by only three votes and demanded a recount. Answering his rival's claim that "special interests" lay behind Goforth's election, Goforth took pains to clarify his relationship to Local 890. The union had helped, he explained, but he was in no way beholden to it.[2]

Sheriff Goforth got the chance to demonstrate his impartiality when he commissioned his deputies. Empire Zinc announced on June 7 that it would reopen its mine and mill, and Goforth spent the next several days lining up his men, over union objections that they served the company. Goforth stood his ground. "I'm choosing my own men," he insisted. "I will not allow [them] to take any sides in this dispute. . . . If a man trying to go to work hits a picket, he will be thrown in jail. So will a picket if he hits a man trying to go to work."[3] Still, the sheriff's impartiality took a peculiar form. He declined to deputize any union men, and he conceded that Empire Zinc had requested and paid for the deputies.[4] Among the deputies was Lester Williams, the elected constable for the nearby town of Central.[5] Known as "Tex," though born in Alabama, he favored cowboy hats and western-style shirts. He was tall and somewhat stocky, with a slight double chin. Robert Capshaw, another deputy, had moved to Grant County as a youngster in the mid-1930s from Oklahoma's lead-zinc mining district.[6] Capshaw and Marvin Mosely, a former Silver City policeman and now a resident of Central, would become the most notorious of the deputies. Not all deputies were Anglo, though: Silver Citians Jack Madrid, Manuel Montes, and Mike Terrazas joined the force, too.[7]

Strikebreakers and strikers faced one another on June 11. They "sparr[ed] around" for a few hours, but no one crossed the picket line except company officials. One strikebreaker watched the scene at the north entrance of the mine from a front yard in Hanover. "Go to work?" he asked. "Sure, I'll go if some other guys do. But go thru [sic] that line all by myself? Hell, no. Not me."[8] Around ten in the morning, the sheriff received instructions from District Attorney Thomas P. Foy to clear the roads. Goforth first arrested Clinton Jencks, the union's international representative, then ten more men. As each left the line, another came forward to take the picket sign: Max Doñez, David García, Wallace García, Tomás Gómez, Ray Marrufo, Claudio Padilla, Julián Perea, Daniel Salas, Sal Vásquez, Mariano Zamora. Elvira Molano, married to an Empire Zinc striker, shouted at the deputies until they arrested her, too. Hauled before Justice of the Peace Andrew Haugland, they all pleaded not guilty and were released on bail. They returned to the picket line and union hall the next day.

Only twelve people were arrested: hardly a big event in the scheme of labor conflict in the twentieth century. Still, the union members understood this to be a turning point in their strike, and they awaited the company's next move. Again Sheriff Goforth delivered it, the very next day, but this time in the form of a temporary restraining order. Judge A. W. Marshall had granted Empire Zinc's request for an injunction prohibiting all members, officers, and agents of Local 890 and of Mine-Mill from blocking the public road to the Empire Zinc property.

On the surface, the picketers' dilemma seemed simple: picket and go to jail, or not picket and stay out of jail; either way, the strike would be lost. But their dilemma was not simple. It must be understood in the context of the complicated class relations of the early Cold War, when management once again wielded pre–New Deal tools such as court injunctions against mass pickets, while left-wing unions like Mine-Mill enjoyed few government protections. How the union men would choose their next step, or mitigate the effects of that choice, or slip around the dilemma altogether, would depend on the kind of union they had built over the course of the 1930s and 1940s. In the eyes of its members, Local 890 was a militant, democratic union that had done more than any other institution to improve local working and living conditions, especially for Mexican Americans, and it had done so by affirming rank-and-file power. The union's political bent, structure, shifting legal and economic advantages and disadvantages, and accomplishments positioned the Empire Zinc strikers to see the stakes in their strike as especially high, to look to their own ranks for creative strategies, and to implement those strategies with remarkable unity.

This chapter moves chronologically through three periods—the Great Depression, World War II, and the early Cold War, each defined by a distinct set of issues. It concludes with the events of the Empire Zinc strike leading up to the injunction crisis. During the Great Depression, miners collectively challenged the social order for the first time. Constant company intimidation made workers at the Chino mine and mill organize secretly; survival was their main objective, and even that proved almost impossible when the company shut down from 1934 to 1937. Still, two developments in this period set the stage for later organizing. First, the Chino local was organized by both Anglos and Mexican Americans, working together, a remarkable accomplishment made possible by radical changes in the international union's policy. This made the union's cross-ethnic organizing in Grant County during World War II much easier than in other southwestern mining districts, even to the point of Mine-Mill's winning the loyalty of skilled Anglo workers, who would later stick with Mine-Mill even after their jobs fell under other unions' jurisdictions. Second, while the economic crisis suspended most of Mine-Mill's activities in Grant County, it also brought federal relief projects, which installed the federal government in the local political landscape. When Chino refused to rehire any known union men upon reopening in

1937, Mine-Mill forced the company to do so by bringing federal leverage to bear on local labor relations.

Federal machinery remained one of Mine-Mill's tools during World War II, the subject of this chapter's second section. What had been a fight for the union's very existence in the 1930s became a fight against ethnic discrimination during the war, as well as a jurisdictional battle with unions affiliated with the American Federation of Labor (AFL). Mine-Mill used the government's wartime policy against racial discrimination and its protection of union security, and took advantage of the labor shortage, to carve a place for itself in the mining economy, to erode the dual-wage system, and to earn workers' loyalty. Mine-Mill also used the rhetoric of patriotism in its fight against ethnic discrimination, arguing that discriminatory practices against Mexican Americans stunted the war effort. At the same time, it continued to attract Anglo workers, who appreciated the concrete benefits of membership and who were not, apparently, put off by the union's assaults on the dual-wage system.

The postwar years leading up to the Empire Zinc strike were marked by acute class conflict in Grant County, and in the third section of the chapter I analyze the dimensions of that conflict. The local union's structure, leadership, and history of political activism shaped its response to a new management offensive and alienation from the mainstream labor movement during the period 1946–50. Mining management reasserted itself in the context of national anticommunism, using federal anticommunist legislation and a tighter labor market to try to weaken the union. Meanwhile, Mine-Mill locals in other parts of the country were being ripped apart over the issue of communism (some of them even seceding from Mine-Mill and joining the rival United Steelworkers in the years 1947–50), and the international union was expelled by the Congress of Industrial Organizations (CIO) in 1950 for failing to fire Communists from its leadership. Those Mine-Mill leaders who were Communists, like Maurice Travis, had resigned from the party in order to sign affidavits required by federal legislation, yet this did not protect them from federal prosecution in the 1950s, a topic I revisit in Chapter 9.

But Mine-Mill persisted into the 1960s, and it held on especially strong in the Southwest. A disjuncture between national and local conditions helps explain Mine-Mill's endurance. While the arena for labor activism—especially for leftist unions—was shrinking throughout the country, Local 890 was in the process of expanding. It was strengthening its leadership from the ranks and expanding its struggle against discrimination from the workplace to Grant County society more broadly. Communism played a role in Local 890's internal politics, but seldom the controversial one seen elsewhere, probably because the version that influenced Local 890's structure and mission was an especially democratic one. A few union men became unhappy with what they saw as communist domination of the local, but most believed that the union remained *their* union, whether or not communists also belonged to it. Thus union men met management's attacks with even greater militancy, challenging management each day at the workplace and rebuffing their employers' crude attempts to red-bait them and their international union.

THE GREAT DEPRESSION AND
THE GREAT LABOR REVOLTS

During the Great Depression, Grant County miners launched their first successful union drive. After Congress passed President Roosevelt's National Industrial Recovery Act (NIRA) in 1933, workers all across America joined labor unions in unprecedented numbers; many people believed that President Roosevelt *wanted* them to join unions. One provision of the act, Section 7(a), protected collective bargaining and encouraged companies to accept employee representation.[9] NIRA came at a moment of transition in Chino's management. John Sully died in 1933 and was replaced by Rone B. Tempest, a "reserved, quiet man" who had been assistant general manager for ten years.[10] Tempest came from Utah, having worked in Jackling's Utah operations, and he was no more a fan of unionism than Sully had been. Still, he saw the need for some kind of employee representation to stave off more threatening forms of unionism, so in July 1933 he set up an Employee Representation Plan to channel worker complaints. It did not work out quite right.

The first employee representative in Tempest's program was a Texan named Joseph I. Kemp, who had moved to Santa Rita with his wife and four children in the 1920s. He earned a good wage as a compressorman, enough to pay a stiff $25 monthly rent on their house.[11] But good wages presumably did not compensate for poor work conditions or the indignities suffered under paternalist management, because Kemp soon turned Tempest's plan on its head. In the spring of 1934, he wrote to the Mine-Mill international secretary for membership cards and began organizing his coworkers into a union quite distasteful to management. On March 24, 1934, Local 63 received its charter from the international union.[12] The same thing had happened at Kennecott's coal company in Gallup, New

Mexico. Horace Moses, the general manager at Gamerco, Kennecott's subsidiary, invited his employees to form a union in July 1933, just as Tempest had done in Santa Rita, but the meeting in which miners were to elect their officers resulted in something quite different: "Two men from a nearby mine . . . convincingly argued against a company union and suggested that a district union would provide additional advantages of independent strength and unity."[13] The assembled miners adjourned the meeting and later joined the National Miners Union, a Communist alternative to the United Mine Workers.[14] And across the Southwest, both before and after the passage of NIRA, Mexican workers increasingly allied themselves with CP-led unions in manufacturing, warehousing, and agricultural work. The reason was simple: Communists stood up for them in the face of considerable violence.[15]

Railroad workers, craft workers, common laborers, Mexican American workers, Anglo workers: all kinds of miners joined the Mine-Mill union at Chino, with Anglos typically organizing other Anglos and Mexicans other Mexicans. Within six months, Santa Rita's Local 63 had over 300 members and Hurley's Local 69 had 59. The first officers of Local 63 were six Anglos and three Mexican Americans; the first two officers of Local 69 were both Mexican American.[16] Attracting both Anglos and Mexican Americans was a remarkable achievement, one that did not always take place in other southwestern mining camps. When it came to persuading Anglos to join the Grant County union, organizers were probably helped by the fact that several Anglos, many of whom became the biggest union supporters, were married to Mexican women—even locomotive engineers, whose occupation was one of the most rigidly segregated and whose unions excluded nonwhites as a matter of policy.[17] Indeed, a decade earlier, the composition of a Mine-Mill union in Grant County would have been all Anglo, or "American." The possibilities for cross-ethnic organizing were created in some measure by the family ties that cut across ethnicity in Grant County, by changes in the national union's class and racial politics in the forty years since its inception, and by the fact that Mine-Mill had organized before AFL unions or the Railway Brotherhoods got a foothold in Grant County.

Mine-Mill began in 1893 as the Western Federation of Miners (WFM), a union of "hard rock"—metal, as opposed to coal—miners. The WFM distinguished itself by its rhetoric of class warfare in the evolving mining industry, one that witnessed many dramatic clashes between labor and capital. Labor was the source of all wealth, the WFM proclaimed, and mine owners had better give workers their due. The "bread and

butter unionism" championed by the AFL, in which workers would satisfy themselves with wage gains and other benefits, rang hollow for WFM
members eager to bring capitalism down. The WFM promoted industrial
unionism over craft unionism and helped to launch the Industrial Workers of the World (IWW) in 1905.[18] Yet the WFM, and later Mine-Mill,
fostered a militant class consciousness that was sharply racialized: the
union organized white workers on the explicit basis of excluding Mexican
workers, even going so far as to destroy bridges to derail trains carrying
Mexican workers. In a bitter 1902 strike in Cananea, Mexico, for example, the WFM tried to organize white workers and deliberately ignored all
Mexicans—this in the Mexicans' own country.[19]

In 1916, the WFM changed its name and its philosophy, largely
because of dissension over socialism and the IWW and because of government repression during World War I. Renamed the International
Union of Mine, Mill and Smelter Workers and belonging to the AFL, the
union confirmed its expansion, already under way, into associated industries and into other regions of the country. It claimed to represent all of
the United States, Canada, and Mexico, but it never extended far into
Mexico, which had its own increasingly powerful miners' union that,
quite understandably, distrusted the United States and its unions. No
longer stating Mine-Mill's agenda in revolutionary terms, the union's new
preamble modestly advocated greater safety measures.

But Mine-Mill's expansion proved short-lived, for in the 1920s the
union lost members and shrank geographically.[20] Now confined to the
core of unions from which the WFM had sprung—chiefly in Montana,
Idaho, and Utah—Mine-Mill leaders annually lamented the postwar decline of the labor movement at their conventions, a decline they attributed to the Red Scare and to cheap Mexican labor. Delegates to the
union's 1928 convention, for example, supported the Box-Harris Immigration Quota Bill to restrict Mexican immigration. "It is almost impossible," the union declared, "for the American citizen to secure employment in the southwestern States, particularly in the mining industry due
to this influx of Mexican immigrants, and [it] is an utter impossibility for
American citizens to live on the basis being established by these Mexican
immigrants[, which] places in jeopardy the American standard of living."[21] In 1929, Mine-Mill had only 3,000 members.

The New Deal changed the political landscape. Like many other
unions, Mine-Mill made great use of NIRA's Section 7(a) and, after the
passage of the 1935 Wagner Act, of the National Labor Relations Board
(NLRB). The union organized new locals throughout the West and in the

Alabama iron district. The Connecticut brass industry came under the Mine-Mill umbrella beginning in the late 1930s, and locals arose in urban settings such as Chicago, San Francisco, and Newark as the union tried to consolidate jurisdiction vertically from mining through processing and manufacturing. By 1940, 153 contracts covered approximately 70,000 workers.[22]

Starting in 1934, leaders associated with the CP increasingly influenced Mine-Mill, and this opened the way for the union drives among both Anglos and Mexicans in Grant County.[23] Within the AFL, Mine-Mill helped form the Committee on Industrial Organization and, when the AFL expelled those unions in 1935, helped form the rival Congress of Industrial Organizations (CIO). Mine-Mill readopted the class-conscious preamble to its constitution, but now the class-conscious rhetoric was matched by a formal commitment to racial and ethnic equality, manifest in its opposition to the poll tax and support for antilynching legislation. Mine-Mill leaders abandoned their anti-Mexican stance in 1934, fretting more over foreign competition—"slave labor" in South America and Africa—than over Mexican Americans in the Southwest.[24]

The same year that Mine-Mill abandoned its anti-Mexican policy, it was invited into Grant County by Chino worker Joseph Kemp. The union sent out membership cards, a charter, and an organizer, Verne Curtis of Bisbee, Arizona. Curtis's father had belonged to the WFM, and Curtis himself started working in the metal mines before he was seventeen; they were both charter members of Bisbee Miners' Union 30. Though Curtis was a seasoned organizer, Chino was a powerful adversary that could draw on the experience of managers in Kennecott's other mining camps. Workers in Gallup had struck Kennecott's subsidiary, Gamerco, in 1933, and Gamerco's general manager, Horace Moses, severely repressed this strike and later, when another battle broke out in 1935, arranged for some of the activists to be deported to Mexico.[25] (Moses would return to Grant County to manage Chino in the 1940s.) Foremen and superintendents at Chino pressured workers to steer clear of Mine-Mill. "Why are you such a strong union man?" assistant mine superintendent Roy Grissom demanded of Felipe Huerta, a Santa Rita laborer, who responded that he wanted better work conditions. Grissom warned him, "It is better for you to think it over or not vote for the union because this camp has been working and operating for twenty-five years and you have been protected. If the Union is successful the camp will stop for a year and you will lose your work, possibly you will not get it again. It is better for you to take your Union with the Company, put the Superintendent in as presi-

dent and leave those outsiders out."[26] Claude Dannelly, a foreman at
Hurley, told Marcelo Avalos that a vote for the union was "not agreeable
to the Company."[27] Harry "Hap" Thorne, open-pit superintendent, conceded that unions were generally a good thing—but not in the Chino
camp.[28] Apparently, the organization of Mexicans especially galled the
company. Antonio Cruz got under Thorne's skin by "constantly exciting
and constantly agitating the Mexicans."[29] Grissom warned José Portos
that workers ought "to be careful and vote the proper way, especially the
Mexicans."[30]

Company intimidation forced Curtis, Kemp, Huerta, Avalos, and
other pro-union workers to meet in secret, often "at midnight after shift
work," as Benigno Montez recalled. "There was always company officers
watching to see what was going on, so we had to have the meetings in
different places."[31] An abandoned cabin by Whitewater Creek was one
such meeting place.[32] This intimidation angered many union men, who
allegedly started to threaten company officials.[33] "When the union [gets]
control in Santa Rita," shovel operator Victor Crittenden was said to have
declared, "all non-union men [would be] going down the canyon, and
Captain Thorne would be leading them."[34] Dutch Stewart allegedly told
the pastor of Hurley's Community Church, "They will meet our demands
or we will wreck their trains, blow up their shops, burn their houses, and
get Tempest and Thorne."[35] Tempest worried that his children would be
kidnapped, and "it was said . . . that [he] took to carrying a pistol in the
glove compartment of his car."[36] But Mine-Mill's efforts paid off in September, when the majority of Chino workers in Santa Rita voted to join
Local 63. Hurley workers opted instead for their own local, Local 69,
which then lost the representation election.

Santa Rita workers voted in September for Local 63 to represent
them, but they had little chance to enjoy their victory: only a couple of
weeks later, the company shut down completely. The union men were
furious, and they complained to the NLRB that the company's closing
was an antiunion tactic that constituted an unfair labor practice.[37] But the
reality was that Chino had been hobbling along for three years, barely
operating more than fifteen days a month and shutting down for a few
weeks from time to time. The company had not turned a profit in over a
year, and the economy gave no signs of improving. Chino had ground to a
halt. Thus, the NLRB's ruling against the union was reasonable.

Chino's shutdown devastated Grant County. Already, people were
suffering from the Depression. With mines operating only part time,
workers had barely enough income to pay their bills. Once Chino shut

down completely, many families (chief among them union supporters) were evicted, and the county could no longer count on the company's taxes. Chino worsened the situation by insisting on a lower tax valuation, which threatened to reduce Grant County's classification for purposes of receiving state funds for education, health care, and other services.[38] Empire Zinc also closed its mine and flotation mill in Hanover from 1931 to 1937.[39]

At the very moment when people needed more support, the county was able to provide less. Public relief in New Mexico, or any kind of public welfare, had long been measly at best. For gathering and administering public relief for the destitute, Grant County relied on a voluntary organization, the Grant County Welfare Association, which was staffed by local mining managers, other prominent male citizens, and their wives, all of whom, the union alleged, discriminated against union families.[40] The relief rolls were growing at the same time that funds were evaporating; the number of families on relief almost doubled between January and July 1934, from 242 to 452—this before Chino even shut down—and the Welfare Association's monthly expenditures "jump[ed] from approximately $1,200 in January to $7,200 in November."[41] Families were evicted, and the hospital was boarded up. Most families moved away or returned to the small farms from which they had come. Several literally uprooted their houses and moved them to the newly incorporated town of Bayard, midway between Santa Rita and Silver City.

It was in this context that many New Deal social programs came to Grant County. In addition to direct relief, which never fully met the need, the New Deal offered work programs for youth and adults. NIRA created the Public Works Administration (PWA) and the Civilian Conservation Corps (CCC), and the Emergency Relief Appropriation Act of 1935 created the Works Progress Administration (WPA, later called the Work Projects Administration). Money and enrollment were channeled through the states, which in New Mexico meant through quasi-public agencies like the Grant County Welfare Association. In New Mexico, the CCC drew 32,385 young men into its eight camps.[42] Both Anglo and Hispanic youths found their way into the CCC.[43] Women were much more poorly served; a dozen or so girls joined a National Youth Administration training program in domestic science, and a few dozen women were employed on WPA sewing projects. But most of the jobs were in construction—highways, public buildings, dams—and they went to men.[44] Interestingly, even though they were no longer employed by Chino, some of the men working on the highway through the Black

Range kept up the union spirit. Writing to Governor Clyde K. Tingley in 1935, Joseph Kemp protested their mistreatment and signed his letter "Local 63."[45] Similarly, Ysmael Moreno, formerly a mill worker at Hurley and still the secretary-treasurer of Local 69, alerted Tingley to the desperate need for jobs and relief in Grant County.[46] Grant County workers turned to other sources of income and, perhaps more important, came to see the government as bearing some responsibility for their welfare. This shift in attitude, reinforced by the greater presence of federal agencies, would prove critical in labor relations.

Late in December 1936, Chino announced that it would reopen its operations in Santa Rita and Hurley. "Let us start up again clean," W. S. Boyd, Kennecott's executive vice president, told Chino superintendent Rone Tempest.[47] "Clean," of course, meant union-free, and union men soon found themselves on Tempest's blacklist. James L. McCraney, a crane operator, approached his former foreman, Harvey Forsythe, for a job in the spring of 1937. McCraney had started out as a steam shovel operator in 1923 and had been promoted twice, but his union record overshadowed his accomplishments on the job. "We are not putting back any of the old men, the union men," Forsythe told him, adding that it would be useless to appeal to general foreman Harry Thorne.[48] Angus Gruwell, another steam shovel operator, had no better luck. Fifteen years before, when Chino reopened after a yearlong shutdown, the company had tracked Gruwell down in Arizona to invite him back to work.[49] This time, Gruwell had stayed in the area during the shutdown (perhaps because he and his wife now owned their own house), but in 1937 he was refused work. Chino had done even more to bring Ysmael Moreno back to Hurley from Los Angeles in 1922: by special delivery it sent him an invitation and railroad tickets back to New Mexico. But Moreno "cut his neck when he joined the union," his foreman explained, and the company would not take him back in 1937.[50] Some miners did not even bother to apply, having heard from relatives and friends that the company would not rehire union men.[51] In Forsythe's words, they lacked "character." The blacklist extended beyond the mines, too, underscoring Chino's control over its town: even the "radical-leaning barber" was refused permission to reopen his shop. He "set up shop in Bayard and for 50c" one could get a haircut and "perorations on the evils of capitalistic enterprise."[52]

One hundred and sixteen men filed a complaint with the NLRB, alleging discrimination on the basis of union membership, and the NLRB ruled in their favor.[53] But Chino kept this case in the courts for years, until finally, in 1942, the U.S. Supreme Court upheld the NLRB ruling against

Nevada Consolidated, Chino's parent company.[54] In the meantime, Locals 63 and 69 pushed hard for contract negotiations. Tempest stood just as firmly against them, remaining "outwardly unflappable, [but] the union issue raised the specter of radicals, threats against managers and families, [and] riots," and ultimately the stress became too great for him.[55] On May 7, 1938, a state district court ordered Tempest to turn over the company's books. That night he shot himself in his garage. Tempest's unexpected suicide took the wind out of the union's sails more than his recalcitrance had, and the union campaign stalled for a number of months. Only with defense mobilization for World War II did Mine-Mill begin again to organize with vigor.

WORLD WAR II AND MINE-MILL'S APPEAL
TO MEXICAN AMERICANS

When Mine-Mill renewed its organizing efforts in the early 1940s, it centered its new campaign on fighting discrimination against Mexican Americans.[56] Mine-Mill used its competition with the AFL to stress its commitment to Mexican American rights, and the strategy worked: Mine-Mill won recognition and negotiated contracts at all the major mines in Grant County. Moreover, Mine-Mill was well positioned on the political landscape of defense mobilization to take advantage of three things: the labor shortage, which gave the union greater leverage with companies; new federal policy, which forbade discrimination in defense industries; and the political culture of patriotism, which set the parameters of legitimate social activism.

Mine-Mill began a regional organizing campaign throughout the Southwest in 1940, starting with the Asarco smelter in El Paso, Texas. The national union soon extended the campaign to camps in Arizona and New Mexico, creating the Southwest Industrial Council and assigning a dozen organizers to the region in 1941 and 1942.[57] By visiting all of the districts, the organizers developed a sense of the regional political economy. Organizers who worked in the Silver City area included Verne Curtis and George Knott, both of whom had worked in the metals industry for many years; Glenn Gillespie and James Robinson, long involved in Mine-Mill; and Harry Hafner, a veteran of the Spanish Civil War. Curtis knew the region especially well because he had already helped organize Local 63 in Santa Rita. Like many Grant County union men, Curtis had been rewarded for Bisbee union activity in the 1930s by getting himself blacklisted. A reputedly good motor swamper at the Calumet and Arizona Mining Company, Curtis was refused reinstatement after a 1935 strike. "In 300 years we will give you fellows a job again," the company's employment manager told him.[58] Organizer Arturo Mata, who first came to Grant County in 1942, also had firsthand experience with labor repression. He had lived as a child in Morenci, Arizona, where his father had participated in strikes during World War I. In retaliation, local authorities deported the entire family to Mexico. Arturo Mata returned to the United States in the 1920s and joined unionizing and civil rights efforts.[59]

Organization and collective bargaining paid off first at Asarco, which operated the Ground Hog mine in Vanadium and a mill in Hanover. In April 1941, Asarco workers elected officers for Local 530 (with Mexicans and Anglos elected in even numbers), and four months later they won the election for union recognition by 165 votes to the AFL's 34.[60] When contract negotiations broke down at the end of October, the miners held a strike vote as a show of strength. It worked. Early in November they signed a contract, the first ever negotiated in the mining district, and one that raised wages between fifty and fifty-five cents a day; the larger increase went to the lowest-paid workers. Miners now took home $5.75 a day (a 10 percent increase), and "all other workers" got $4.69 (a 13 percent increase). The union asked for but did not get a closed shop and a union checkoff, but the company agreed to a week's vacation for all employees who worked a year or more.[61] The following spring, the NLRB certified Mine-Mill as the representative for Asarco mill workers, and Local 530 negotiated a similar contract for them.[62]

The Chino locals were revived in February and March 1941. Opening a meeting in May 1941, Local 63 vice president Julián Horcasitas announced, "The union is here to stay come hell or high water."[63] After Asarco workers negotiated their contract, Mine-Mill organizers built their district campaign around Chino. The plan was to win at Chino and then "to attack each of these small plants . . . and crack them in logical order."[64] Membership grew rapidly in 1941: 122 people joined Hurley's Mine-Mill Local 69 in March 1941, and they elected an all–Mexican American slate of officers the following month. Membership increased steadily to 208 in July and then jumped to 316 the next month. In Santa Rita, Local 63 followed a similar path; seven out of its eight officers elected in April were Mexican American.[65]

The Chino campaign heated up in the spring of 1942, when competition became fierce with the Chino Metal Trades Council, which comprised eleven AFL craft unions. The Supreme Court's ruling against Nevada Consolidated boosted morale among Mine-Mill supporters, as did a series of rousing meetings in April and May 1942. Mine-Mill ultimately won representation for all production workers but lost craft workers to the AFL.[66] The Chino Metal Trades Council signed the first contract ever with Nevada Consolidated early in June 1942, and Mine-Mill signed its first contract in July.

Peru, Blackhawk, and Empire Zinc all followed suit over the summer of 1942. Mine-Mill soundly defeated the AFL in the Peru election: 105 workers at Peru's Pewabic and Copper Flats shafts voted for Mine-Mill, and only 2 voted for the AFL.[67] At Empire Zinc, the AFL had "been ruled off [the ballot] because it could not produce any proof of membership."[68] Here 110 workers voted for Mine-Mill and 67 voted for no union.[69] Thus only at Nevada Consolidated did the AFL end up representing the craft workers; in all the others, Mine-Mill became the exclusive representative of all workers, Anglo crafts included. Consequently, the Mine-Mill locals at Santa Rita and Hurley, consisting entirely of production workers, were more heavily Mexican American than were Locals 530 (Asarco) and 604 (Peru, Blackhawk, and Empire Zinc), which included craft workers.

With few exceptions—such as Arturo Mata—the organizers who came to Grant County in 1941 and 1942 were Anglos. But the union's constituents were largely Mexican American, and Anglo organizers had to craft their appeals in ways specific to this group because Mexican Americans did not inhabit the same world of work that their Anglo "brothers" did. This was not hard to do, in large part because Mine-Mill's competition provided a perfect foil. The Chino Metal Trades Council and the railway brotherhoods were also trying to organize at Chino.[70] Their poor track records in organizing Mexicans, or even accepting them, drove almost all Mexicans into the Mine-Mill camp. For example, the Operating Engineers, an AFL union, found that its discrimination against Mexican Americans caused it to lose jurisdiction at Chino. "If a man's name was Hernandez," observed later Chino labor relations director Bernard Himes, "he could not apply for membership in the Operating Engineers. No Lopez or Candelaria could aspire to operate a bulldozer or power shovel. This bargaining unit, the largest, most crucial of all units, quickly passed to Mine-Mill, opening at last hundreds of job opportunities to Mexican-Americans and transferring great bargaining power to Mine-Mill Locals 63 and 69."[71] Earlier in the century, Mine-Mill had used the desire for racial exclusion to organize Anglo workers; now the union used the injustice of racial exclusion to organize Mexican Americans.

Both the CIO and its opponents promised higher wages and better working conditions, but there were signs that Mine-Mill had especially close ties to the Mexican American community. For example, when Reymundo de la Torre, a young Mexican American boy, won the regional spelling bee in May 1941, the Mine-Mill locals all chipped in to send him to the national competition in Washington, D.C.; none of the AFL unions contributed.[72] Similarly, Mine-Mill conducted its business in Mexican American neighborhoods and local establishments like Lucero's Tavern in Hanover and El Rancho in North Hurley. Mine-Mill's big rally before the Chino election in 1942 took place on the "Spanish side of Hurley," and at least one large meeting was held in an Alianza Hispano Americana (AHA) hall.[73] Meetings for the AFL's Metal Trades Council met instead on company property, which suggests that craft workers felt at ease there.[74]

Not every meeting followed this pattern, of course; Local 63 sometimes met in Santa Rita's International Pool Hall (itself an astonishing fact, in contrast to the clandestine organizing of the 1930s), and the AFL's Metal Trades Council held a family meeting at El Rancho.[75] And at least one AFL organizer tried to improve the federation's bad reputation. Addressing the Metal Trades Council on October 9, 1941, Ernie De Baca of Albuquerque announced that his own appointment to the New Mexico State Federation of Labor was "a new symbol of unity among all the laboring men of New Mexico"; moreover, the state convention elected a Spanish American president and appointed an equal number of Anglo and Spanish American regional directors. To De Baca, these moves signaled a "whole-hearted cooperation between American citizens, whether of Spanish extraction or otherwise."[76] Still, none of the Chino Metal Trades Council officers in its early years had Spanish names; by 1948, six of eighteen did—a significant improvement but one that resulted more from Mine-Mill's aggressive promotion of Mexicans into the skilled jobs that fell under AFL jurisdiction than from AFL efforts at promoting Mexican American leadership.[77]

De Baca's defense notwithstanding, Mine-Mill organizers constantly denounced the AFL for excluding Mexicans as the two sides geared up for the National Defense Mediation Board elections to be held May 26, 1942. These elections would show the relative weight and appeals of the industrial unionism of Mine-Mill and the craft unionism of the AFL. Mine-Mill organizer George Knott invited AFL representatives to a debate on May 24. "In this meeting," he announced, "the question of the Spanish worker will be discussed, the discriminatory attitude of the AF of L to these workers will be brot [sic] out into the limelight, the unfair effort . . . to coerce workers into the ranks of the AF of L by threatening them with high initiation fees if they don't join now, by telling the Spanish worker on the job that even if they do vote their vote won't count, all of these organizational malpractices will be exposed."[78] Three hundred workers belonging to the AFL and Mine-Mill came to the debate, but the AFL debaters never appeared.[79] Arturo Mata also led a "well-attended" meeting of Peru workers in Hanover, which "three AFL stooges crashed . . . [speaking] their usual line of americanism."[80] The Mexican American workers were probably gratified to see "Mata [take] them apart so bad that they weren't even able to answer and left the meeting in disgrace."[81]

What exactly did members of Mine-Mill gain from their new affiliation? More than anything else, they got contract language that destroyed formal discrimination against Mexican Americans and contract provisions that gave workers a way to protest unfair working conditions. Even the *Silver City Daily Press*, which would later oppose many of the union's activities, applauded Mine-Mill's first contract with Chino in July 1942: "It is felt that the signing of this contract will have far-reaching effects in the southwest as it is the first time that racial discrimination has been voluntarily abolished in this area, thru [sic] the collective bargaining . . . , which was very fair thruout [sic] the entire proceedings and is to be congratulated on fair labor practices."[82] Seniority—not race, creed, color, or national origin—would now determine layoffs, rehiring, and promotions. This meant that anyone in Mine-Mill would have a chance at the craft jobs that had previously been reserved for Anglos. Daily wages would remain at "the prevailing rate," which ranged from $4.60 for unskilled workers to $7.50 for skilled. Employees who worked a year or more could look forward to paid vacation, and all workers under the agreement could bring grievances before a five-man committee.[83] Later that month, Mine-Mill organizer George Knott reported that "about fifty of our Spanish Americans" had gotten promotions and increases in pay at Chino. Moreover, miners immediately flooded the company with grievances, evidence that they took seriously their opportunities for redress.[84]

In at least one instance, the union stood up for Mexican American workers against the wishes of skilled Anglo workers. The converter cranes had always been run by Anglos in the Hurley smelter. When the union forced smelter superintendent E. A. Slover to promote a Mexican American to this position, Anglo workers threatened to walk out. Verne Curtis told Slover that Mine-Mill Local 69 would not recognize the Anglos' picket line and would instead readily fill all the jobs with qualified people.[85]

Mine-Mill's accomplishments in Grant County's mining district are all the more impressive when one considers how many Anglo workers joined a union that explicitly attacked Anglo privilege, even when there was an alternative like the AFL or the railway brotherhoods. At all the camps except Chino, Mine-Mill won jurisdiction over craft and industrial laborers, and Anglo workers both joined the union and entered its leadership. From August to December 1942, monthly initiates into Local 604 (representing Peru and New Mexico Consolidated workers) were always predominantly Mexican, but Anglos made up increasing percentages, from 23 percent in August to 46 percent in December.[86] This percentage dropped significantly by the late 1940s, however. In January 1948, only three of the forty-six initiates were Anglos.[87] Asarco Local 530's Anglo initiations ranged from a low of 31 percent of the total in April 1941 to a high of 45 percent in December; for the next two years, Anglos comprised between 40 and 44 percent of the total initiates.[88]

Even at Chino, where the AFL Metal Trades Council and the railway brotherhoods defeated Mine-Mill's bid to represent craft workers, some craft and railroad workers stuck with Mine-Mill. These were typically men who had joined the union in the 1930s, had been blacklisted for that action, and saw in Mine-Mill a union that would stand up for them.[89] The 1942 Supreme Court decision against Nevada Consolidated came at a crucial moment in the Chino organizing drive. By forcing the company to rehire blacklisted union men and to give them seniority retroactive to 1937, the Supreme Court's ruling infused the Mine-Mill campaign with energy and probably convinced Anglos, whether themselves affected by the decision or not, that Mine-Mill was a militant, principled union that would fight for them. Anglo workers who joined Mine-Mill may also have done so because they preferred industrial unions over craft unions on principle. Quite apart from the exclusive interests of Mexican American workers, Local 63 and 69 went to great lengths to protect their union security clause that would protect Anglo and Mexican alike: they demanded that Chino fire 160 workers who did not pay dues guaranteed to the union by the contract's maintenance-of-membership clause.[90]

The cross-ethnic organizing in Grant County's mines was quite different from that in other districts like Clifton-Morenci, Arizona, where Anglos and Mexicans were openly hostile to one another. One Anglo worker in Clifton-Morenci penned an astonishingly nasty song about CIO organizers and Mexican workers. Carlos Castañeda, an investigator for President Roosevelt's Fair Employment Practices Committee (FEPC), excluded this song from his committee's public reports because it was too vulgar.[91] Many things caused this tension, but one may have been that in

Clifton-Morenci, the AFL organized first. It laid claim to Anglo worker loyalty from the beginning, while in Grant County the Mine-Mill union was the only game in town during the 1930s.

Mine-Mill's appeal to Mexican Americans was not new in the 1940s. But it grew much bolder then, its boldness generated by the strategic advantages that Mine-Mill enjoyed under war conditions: a labor shortage, legal and political leverage, and patriotic credentials. With these advantages Mine-Mill began to erode the dual-wage system. By the end of the decade, Mexican Americans still held the vast majority of "laborer" positions—in fact they held an even greater percentage in 1949 than in 1944—which suggests that whatever changes in job segregation took place, Anglos did not take many "laborer" jobs.[92] Still, Mexican Americans slightly increased their presence in craft jobs, although they made no inroads into skilled railroad jobs. Even more important was Mine-Mill's attack on the large number of job classifications, which permitted employers to assign Mexican Americans to lower-paid jobs that were essentially the same as differently named jobs held by Anglos. By 1952, contracts guaranteed that Kennecott's wages were more equitably distributed among a smaller range of occupations.

World War II effectively ended the Depression for Grant County and sent thousands of people back to work. The mining industry kicked back into gear in 1941, before the United States even entered the war, and mining payrolls were up by October.[93] More people were working, and, just as important, they were working for higher wages. In 1941 alone, before any unions signed contracts with it, Chino granted a fifty-cent increase in wages for everyone. This pushed the daily wage for an unskilled worker from $3.85 to $4.35, and for a skilled worker from $6.75 to $7.25.[94] So many workers flooded the mines that the Work Projects Administration, the New Deal work relief program, could not fill all of its Silver City jobs in the summer of 1942.[95] But even with these new workers, and higher wages to retain them, mine operators faced competition from the military and from better-paying employers. In November 1942, Horace Moses, general manager of Chino, reported that "approximately 275 men have left this organization to join armed forces and a substantial number of skilled workmen have left to accept positions with contractors who are engaged in other defense industries."[96]

By 1944, Chino's copper production had declined because of the labor shortage.[97] Despite its labor needs, the mining industry did not import Mexican workers, as the agricultural and railroad industries did during the war; there was no Bracero Program for the mines. Chino hired

Mexican American women to work in the open pit, mostly as track laborers, and brought some 250 Navajo workers and their families to Santa Rita.[98] Perhaps Horace Moses's Gallup contacts played a role in bringing Navajo families to Santa Rita (he was a "founder . . . of the annual Gallup Inte[r]-Tribal Indian Festival" while living there); certainly Navajos employed off the reservation during World War II found hostility greatest in those towns closest to their reservation and, consequently, preferred to work farther away.[99] Chino built a separate "Indian village" for them, "just west of the great waste dumps on the road to the precipitation plant."[100] This was the worst housing, consisting of tar-paper shacks located close to a creek bottom "rusty with copper precipitates."[101] The entire village shared one water tap. The Navajos did not join the Mine-Mill union in great numbers but rather engaged in their own collective actions: the entire extended family would confront Chino's management, one spokesman articulating the complaint and the rest backing him up with their sheer numbers.[102]

The nationwide mining labor shortage led the War Manpower Commission (WMC) in September 1942 to declare the entire western region, consisting of twelve states, including New Mexico, a "critical labor area." No one employed in mining, milling, or smelting any of twenty-one minerals could quit without a "certificate of separation" issued by the United States Employment Service.[103] In 1943, the WMC lengthened the minimum work week to forty-eight hours and then to fifty-six, and it began releasing soldiers from the army to work in the mines.[104]

The WMC decree was quite a repressive exercise of executive power. Many labor historians, in fact, see in World War II's enhancement of executive power the seeds of later union bureaucratization, not to mention the immediate repression of labor's rights.[105] But Mine-Mill often turned this executive power to the union's advantage in Grant County. The WMC, charged with granting or denying wage increases during the war, sometimes reduced wage discrepancies among mine companies in the Grant County mining district and between companies in this district and those elsewhere. The latter was especially important in undermining a justification for the dual-wage system—that a lower standard of living for Mexicans in the Southwest warranted lower wages in that part of the country.

Mine-Mill used several federal agencies in this manner. One of its resources was the FEPC. President Roosevelt created this committee by Executive Order 8802, which forbade discrimination in defense industries. Its mandate was to hold public hearings in regions or industries in

which there was some evidence of systematic discrimination. The FEPC
was always weak; it never had the funding it needed, and Congress shut it
down before the war ended.[106] But it was nevertheless important in the
class relations of the Southwest, not least because Mine-Mill called on it
to investigate conditions there. Those conditions impressed FEPC investigators enough to plan public hearings in El Paso. These plans were
scuttled because companies persuaded the government that "public reve-
lations [of discrimination] would damage the nation's posture in Latin
America."[107] The very threat of hearings, however, helped Mine-Mill organize in the Southwest, and the union redirected its research on wages
and job segregation toward cases brought to the National War Labor
Board (NWLB), which replaced the NLRB during the war. The union
brought seventeen complaints to the FEPC at Chino in 1944 as part of the
committee's regional investigation; nine complaints were dismissed the
following year because the complainant was unavailable, four were dismissed on the merits, two were held for further investigation, and two
were satisfactorily resolved (that is, the worker now held the job from
which he had been barred).[108] The FEPC concluded that the entire southwestern mining industry followed "the general policy and practice [of
restricting] Spanish-speaking Latin-American citizens of Mexican extraction to . . . [c]ommon or unskilled labor positions in all departments
[and] [s]emi-skilled jobs in departments manned totally or almost totally
by Mexicans."[109]

The various defense industries were brought under the supervision
of the War Production Board (WPB). The WPB's copper program did not
explicitly prohibit discrimination, but Mine-Mill's Southwest Industrial
Council interpreted the program—which promoted "improved working
conditions and ventilation, better servicing of miners and better utiliza-
tion of miners' skills"—as an opening to fight discrimination against
Mexican Americans.[110] Mine-Mill insisted that the Nonferrous Metals
Commission (NMC), which regulated metal mining for the War Production Board, investigate wage discrimination in the Southwest. In 1943,
just two months after gaining recognition and before signing its first
contract with Asarco, Mine-Mill Local 530 brought the case of timekeeper Arnulfo Holguín before the NMC.[111] Holguín had first been hired
as a surface laborer and truck driver in 1939, earning $3.43 per six-hour
day, and two years later he accepted the job of timekeeper for $110 a
month. His predecessor, however, an Anglo, had earned $135 a month
when first hired. Ultimately the NMC ruled that Stanley Campbell, Holguín's predecessor, had more prior office experience before beginning as

timekeeper, and that this difference adequately accounted for the salary difference. But it is interesting to note that this was not exactly the company's defense: Asarco alleged that Holguín was "inexperienced and untrained" and thus had required much "supervision and assistance." Campbell himself, however, testified to the contrary: not only had Holguín "caught on" at once, but the job also included more responsibilities than when Campbell held it; moreover, Holguín had graduated from New Mexico State Teachers College and had taken courses in bookkeeping and business psychology.[112]

The Holguín case was limited to comparing two individuals, but in another case brought by Mine-Mill in Arizona, broad patterns of discrimination became the object of investigation. In 1944, three Arizona companies were forced to submit payroll records to the NMC, which revealed "a consistent pattern of discriminatory rates for 'other employees'" (i.e., non-Anglos).[113] These records devastated the companies' defense, which had been that wage differences and job segregation arose from "cultural tradition, skill variations, and jurisdiction conflicts between craft and industrial unions."[114] The NMC told the three companies to end this pattern, and eventually this principle spread throughout the Southwest.[115]

Like most CIO unions, Mine-Mill was eager to influence production decisions for the war effort. The WPB encouraged labor-management production committees for war industries and even sent two representatives from the Labor Production Division to help start one at Nevada Consolidated. But this committee mostly exhorted workers to work harder. With the help of the WPB and the U.S. Army, it sponsored a parade in August 1943 "to build in the men on the home front a fighting spirit to match our boys in the front lines"; guns, tanks, soldiers, and airplanes paraded through the county's mining camps.[116] The committee also put its energies into enforcing the WMC's decree prohibiting workers from changing jobs.[117] Organized labor was being channeled, willingly or not, into enforcing restrictions on labor mobility rather than helping to shape management decisions. If the experiences of other unions, and of the CIO on a national level, are any indication, it is likely that management stood squarely in the way of any intrusion into management decisions. Companies were happy for unions to police their members and to encourage greater productivity, but they did not want to be told how to run their operations.[118]

World War II eased economic distress considerably, and everyone rejoiced in the flush of high-paying jobs. But the war accomplished this economic miracle while also taking sons (and a few daughters) to the front lines, and the early Pacific campaigns drove home the cost of the war. Grant County's first reported casualty, Eddie Driscoll, died in the first week of the war with Japan.[119] But much more devastating was the fate of the 200th Coast Artillery Battalion, Anti-Aircraft, to which many Grant County youth belonged. Stationed in the Philippines, this National Guard unit was heavily bombed by the Japanese in December 1941. It retreated to Bataan early in 1942 and finally surrendered in April. The defeated battalion was forced on the infamous Bataan Death March, during which thousands of soldiers died or were killed; those who survived did so as prisoners of war for three years in horrific conditions. The day after the 200th had surrendered, dozens of men went straight to the Silver City enlistment office, most hailing from the mining camps at Hurley and Santa Rita.[120] Grant County people were acutely aware of the real cost of the war effort. Dozens of families, Anglo and Mexican American alike, did not know for months, sometimes years, what had happened to their relatives in the 200th Battalion.

It was in this context that Mine-Mill resumed organizing in 1941. Mine-Mill used both its badge of patriotism—a rally for all-out production and a pledge not to strike for the duration of the war—and an explicit commitment to racial and ethnic equality in order to attract workers and to justify its place in the local political economy. Mine-Mill had opposed U.S. entry into the war during the Hitler-Stalin pact of 1939–41, but once Germany invaded the Soviet Union in the summer of 1941, and especially after Japan bombed Pearl Harbor, the union backed the war effort in full force. Just days after Pearl Harbor, and even before the CIO signed a no-strike pledge in Washington, Mine-Mill locals in Grant County promised not to interrupt war production. Organizer James Robinson announced on December 11 that the three locals would "give 100% support to national defense as loyal Americans in this time of peril."[121] Robinson also spoke at the AFL-sponsored Victory Parade, held in Silver City on December 20, 1941, and reiterated his call for around-the-clock production, defense bonds, and efforts to detect sabotage.[122]

By standing firmly behind the CIO's no-strike pledge, Mine-Mill was able to undertake an ambitious organizing drive in Grant County without risking condemnation for threatening war production. The no-strike pledge may have weakened workers' shop-floor strength; certainly this is the conclusion drawn by labor historians studying unions elsewhere in the United States. But in Grant County, upholding the no-strike pledge did not entail simply accepting company policies. Instead, the pledge increased the union's political capital, and this political capital lent legit-imacy to Mine-Mill organizers' arguments that agitation against ethnic discrimination actually supported the war effort.[123]

Companies in the Central mining district worked with the local de-fense bond committees to sign up workers for payroll deduction to buy bonds, a key component of the war effort, and Mine-Mill joined the defense bond drive, too.[124] Those Chino workers who signed up for pay-roll deduction in February 1942, for instance, were identified as "CIO workers," shorthand for "Mine-Mill workers."[125] That spring, organizers Verne Curtis and Glenn Gillespie challenged all companies in the area to donate a day's profit each week to the war effort, just as miners were offering to give a day's wages each week to defense bonds. Mine-Mill's defense bond committee, under Curtis's leadership, even drew the praise of the *El Paso Times*, which organizers described as a "reactionary pa-per."[126] By 1943, 81 percent of the workers in the Central district's mines were donating a portion of each paycheck; these 2,453 workers, in fact, accounted for more than a third of Grant County's war bond sales.[127] The union locals held contests to reward workers who put their wages into defense bonds, and in 1944 the Santa Rita local unanimously voted again to give a day's pay to the Grant County War Chest.[128]

Mine-Mill pointed to the Southwest's military contributions in order to fight antiunion legislation. In 1943, the New Mexico legislature con-sidered an "anti-racketeering" bill to ensure war production, and labor unions across the state protested to Governor John J. Dempsey. Mine-Mill's Southwest Industrial Union Council reminded Dempsey, who op-posed the bill, that "in the battle of Bataan . . . New Mexico lost many of her native sons. Many of your friends and mine were killed or are lan-guishing in Jap prison camps. . . . [We find] that very many of them were working men and members of labor unions. They went willingly to fight for the American Way of Life. . . . Will they return only to find that we on the home front have lost *our* battle to perpetuate this same American Way of Life?"[129]

ANTICOMMUNIST BACKLASH

Patriotism worked well for Mine-Mill when the union's politics were aligned with the larger political culture. Working for all-out production during World War II gave Mine-Mill locals patriotic credibility that was vital in a region like Grant County, which suffered so many losses of life.

But patriotism was no longer available as a tool for labor after the war, because it was redefined exclusively as anticommunism. And it was a tool bluntly wielded against unions like Mine-Mill. In one respect, however, Mine-Mill managed to lay claim to patriotism by highlighting the number of veterans in the union, which I discuss in Chapter 4.

A New Management Offensive

It was not immediately obvious that when the war ended labor would be thrown on the defensive. Toward the end of the war, Mine-Mill was optimistic that, in contrast to the post–World War I period, organized labor could not only hold onto its gains but also strengthen the nation's social welfare through laws maintaining wartime price controls and subsidizing new housing. Even the American Mining Congress made its peace, of a sort, with collective bargaining.[130] The labor movement was strong and getting stronger; almost fifteen million workers belonged to unions at the war's end, and five million of them went out on strike in the year following Japan's surrender in August 1945—the biggest strike wave in United States history.[131] The desperate unemployment that followed World War I had never been far from the thoughts of labor and industry leaders as they anticipated reconversion to a peacetime economy after World War II, and in 1945, as the nation began to demobilize, labor seemed strong enough to make President Truman listen to noncorporate voices, too.

Soon, however, a combination of antilabor legislation and battles over communism within the CIO—and within Mine-Mill itself—began to sour the prospects for left-wing unions. Management pointed to the strike waves as evidence not merely of workers' power but also of unions' irresponsible use of that power. Many opponents of the Wagner Act of 1935 (and of the Fair Labor Standards Act of 1938) believed that it unfairly favored workers and labor unions. They were particularly alarmed by the prospect of supervisors and other salaried employees seeking collective bargaining rights, which threatened to deprive "management of its fundamental right to control its operations."[132] The period after the war appeared to be a good time to curb some of labor's power, to restore balance, as they put it, to the relative strengths of labor and capital.

Congress responded with the Labor-Management Relations Act of 1947, better known as the Taft-Hartley Act. Taft-Hartley affirmed workers' right not to join a union, made it easier to get a court injunction against strikers—a return to the years before the 1932 Norris-LaGuardia

Act limited such injunctions—and forbade many union tactics as "unfair labor practices."[133] One of its most dangerous provisions, from the perspective of left-wing unions like Mine-Mill, was a requirement that all union officials sign affidavits denying membership in the CP. Those unions that did not file noncommunist affidavits lost access to the NLRB.[134] Outraged at this abridgement of free association, leaders of the CIO refused to sign the affidavits for over a year.

Taft-Hartley presented an opening for the mining companies to shoulder Mine-Mill aside. In the summer of 1948, Kennecott, Asarco, and the U.S. Smelting, Refining, and Mining Company (USSRMC) all announced that they would negotiate new contracts in Grant County only if Mine-Mill signed the noncommunist affidavits.[135] On May 1, Kennecott denied a request by Local 890 for contract amendments, hinting that Mine-Mill did not legitimately represent Chino workers and suggesting that union members become "good Americans."[136] The term "good American," of course, was shorthand for both "noncommunist" and "native-born." For all of its odious provisions, the Taft-Hartley Act did not actually prohibit negotiations if unions failed to file the affidavits; it stipulated only that unions could not appeal to the NLRB. But companies used the union's inability to protest to the government as an opening to weaken the local union in Grant County. Kennecott fostered a rival organizing campaign of the International Association of Machinists because it knew Mine-Mill could not appeal to the NLRB in this jurisdictional dispute. As Clinton Jencks told Senator Dennis Chávez in 1949, when Congress was considering new legislation, the affidavit "was the big club every mining company in New Mexico picked up. This was their smokescreen, their bar against decent wages and working conditions."[137]

But the union transformed the company's obstacle into a tool for the union to reassert local workplace power. National, industrywide bargaining, which the union sought throughout the 1940s and which was blocked by the companies' anticommunist maneuvers, had proven both a strength and a weakness. National bargaining helped secure better wages and, especially important to Grant County, an equalization of wages: it guaranteed fewer regional differences in wages, and companies could not as easily insist on "local custom" to justify a discriminatory dual-wage system. But there were drawbacks to national bargaining, which frequently produced contracts that forbade strikes and paid little attention to local conditions. Difficult as it was, the new situation created by the mining companies and their use of Taft-Hartley nevertheless gave Local 890 the chance to remedy some of the problems created by national bargaining.

When companies refused to negotiate in 1948, union members first worried that they could not defend themselves without a contract. But they quickly found room to maneuver without the contract, using walk-outs, sit-downs, and strikes. If the company did not want to negotiate a contract, then workers, in international representative Clinton Jencks's words, would "negotiate conditions every day on the job."[138] At Kennecott, for instance, the union rallied on the front steps of the superintendent's office on June 11 and voted right there to authorize a strike. Whole departments went together to the manager's office to demand redress on a range of grievances, both new problems and those that had accumulated over the years. The result was chaos with just enough whiff of worker power to make the companies eager to sign new contracts, even without the Taft-Hartley affidavits. Kennecott's general manager promised to observe the old contract if the union would only stop its members from coming in every day with grievances.[139]

The new anticommunism also created conflicts within organized labor itself, sparked by management offensives and political imperatives that made unions finally sign the noncommunist affidavits, as well as by political conflicts that had long existed within unions. The 1948 presidential election sharpened these conflicts: anticommunist and liberal labor leaders threw their weight behind President Truman and thereby committed themselves to Truman's anticommunist foreign policy, while leftists and other progressives supported third-party candidate Henry Wallace, who criticized Truman's escalation of the Cold War. On the new political terrain, support for Wallace came to be treated as the telltale sign of a union's subordination to the CP.[140] In 1948, the CIO leadership finally agreed to sign the noncommunist affidavits. This decision came out of battles in the labor movement—within CIO unions and between them—over communism and the power of left-wing leaders.

In Mine-Mill, the issue of communism came to a head at the 1949 convention. The representatives of some locals, mostly in Connecticut, had long wanted to sign the noncommunist affidavits. Some sensed that Mine-Mill could not continue to resist the raids by hostile unions and that only the help of the NLRB could protect its locals; others felt that communism was a genuine problem in the union and that the affidavits would weed out CP union leaders.[141] There had always been a left wing and a right wing of the union, long before the CP even existed, and the right wing became stronger after World War II. Many right-wing delegates came from the East Coast brass industry and from the die-casting industry, neither of which had been organized for long by Mine-Mill, and the fight over affidavits led some locals to secede from Mine-Mill. The international union that weathered these storms was firmly in the leftist camp—but one that agreed, finally, to sign the affidavits. Maurice Travis, Mine-Mill's financial secretary, formally and publicly left the CP. It was a case of too little too late, however, and the CIO expelled Mine-Mill, along with ten other left-wing unions, in 1949 and 1950.

The Mine-Mill locals in Grant County stayed at some distance from these battles. Certainly their members held a range of political opinions. But with the exception of Local 530 (discussed below), the Grant County locals were not shaken up by the question of communism and generally supported the left-wing national leaders. After the union was expelled from the CIO, Local 890 told Mine-Mill president John Clark: "We will back you, and our brother officers of Mine-Mill 100% against the phony trials brought up by [CIO president] Phil Murray."[142] Most importantly, those trade unionists close to the CP developed their own brand of progressive unionism, which I discuss in the next sections.

Amalgamation and Shifts in Leadership

Internal conflict did appear when the Grant County Mine-Mill unions changed their structure in 1947. The five local unions amalgamated into one district union, Local 890, with individual units representing workers at the different mines. Some leaders and members criticized this centralization and the changes in leadership that accompanied it, but only later did they couch their criticisms in terms of anticommunism.

The case of Rafael Lardizábal illustrates the conflict over amalgamation. Lardizábal had strong union credentials; his father had been a blacksmith and union supporter at Chino until it shut down in 1934, and Rafael was the very first to sign the membership book of Asarco Local 530 in 1941.[143] Over the next decade he stayed active in the local, but in 1952 he was reprimanded for missing too many stewards' council meetings. Lardizábal told shop steward council president Bud DeBraal that he did not want to attend meetings with "outsiders" like Clinton Jencks.[144] "Outsiders" was a code word, it seems, for communist leadership. A few months later, Lardizábal came forward to support the "organizing efforts" —or raids on Mine-Mill—of the United Steelworkers. He had been ambivalent at best over the amalgamation, he explained in 1952. He had feared that it would give "too much power to one man—and it has happened. Every bit of publicity, or any thing that the membership does is directed by the international representative."[145] Mine-Mill's expulsion from the CIO in 1950 had also troubled him, and he became convinced that the union's international leaders "were guilty of following the Communist line." The local leadership (primarily Clinton Jencks) was just as guilty; Lardizábal described pictures of convicted CP leaders on the walls of Local 890's union hall and declared, "Jencks must have been aware that the international officers sent money to the convicted communists' children for Christmas, when we were pleading for help to make a Christmas for the children of the Empire Zinc strikers."[146] Apparently Lardizábal changed his mind about the Steelworkers after he heard a talk by Asbury Howard, an African American Mine-Mill leader from Alabama, about Steelworkers' raiding there. But news of his return to the fold came only from Local 890's Ernesto Velásquez, not from Lardizábal himself.[147]

Lardizábal's story was part of a larger story of power shifts in Asarco Local 530. From its beginning, this union's membership and leadership was composed of roughly 60 percent Mexicans and 40 percent Anglos; after the war, though, Mexicans made up approximately 80 to 85 percent of the membership at the Vanadium Ground Hog mine and 60 to 80 percent of the membership at the Hanover mill.[148] In 1946, some Anglo officers were defeated in a fight between left and right, paralleling the conflict in Mine-Mill on the national level.[149] Among the displaced leaders was Leslie T. White, the financial secretary, who four years later explained that he, Charles Smith, and others "quit the union or became inactive when it became apparent that Communist influences had taken control."[150] They also left their jobs in the mine industry: White became an accountant and Smith opened a garage in Bayard.[151] It is unclear, though, whether they left the union because they left mining, or left mining because they left the union. Only in the heat of the Empire Zinc strike, when these three former union men became some of Local 890's most active opponents, did they frame their 1946–47 departures as a response to communist infiltration. For their part, union loyalists insisted that White and Smith were ousted because of graft.

The Mine-Mill unions had indeed become centralized in 1947, and Jencks had pushed for this change when he arrived in Grant County as an international representative. In fact, amalgamation was needed for the five locals even to afford a full-time representative.[152] But the simple fact of centralization under Jencks's guidance does not capture the nature of the changes that took place in Grant County from 1947 to 1950. Rafael Lardizábal saw centralization taking place around a single person, with union leaders and members serving only as mouthpieces for international representative Clinton Jencks, and that person an outsider who, by definition, could never have the rank and file's interests at heart and therefore could never truly represent them. But Local 890's executive board consisted of representatives from each plant, and the board's meetings featured their animated participation, as well as Jencks's steady presence: they were hardly mouthpieces for any individual.[153] Moreover, these union leaders were often veterans, men who came from Grant County but whose absence had made them relative outsiders after they returned from the war. The distinction between insider and outsider was murky, and it did not correspond to a clean distinction between authentic and false representation.

Years later, some union activists believed that amalgamation helped to consolidate Mexican American leadership in Grant County, a development that they believed was long overdue.[154] This is an important observation but one that perhaps says less about the number of Mexican Americans in leadership positions, which did not change radically, than about the *kind* of Mexican American (and Anglo) leadership that developed. Numerically, most locals were dominated by Mexican Americans from the outset, and increasingly so after the war.[155] In Local 530, one of the more evenly represented, plenty of Anglos remained after White, Smith, and others left. Floyd Bostick, for instance, first joined Local 530 in October 1943 and then rejoined it when he was rehired at Asarco in July 1947, soon becoming an officer.[156] Bostick had been "a dirt farmer in Oklahoma" before he brought his family to New Mexico because of his wife Flossie's health.[157] Never having lived among or worked with Mexican Americans, and coming with the stream of migrants from the South and Southeast, Bostick shared a background with many Anglos who kept Mexican Americans at arm's length. Yet, unlike those who later volunteered as deputies for Sheriff Goforth, he clearly found in Mine-Mill a community for himself and his family. Whatever else a stronger Mexican American leadership meant, it did not mean driving away sympathetic Anglos like Bostick.

The centralization that so worried Rafael Lardizábal, in fact, went hand in hand with deeper and broader training of leadership, and with wider and wider spheres of union activism.[158] Earlier in the decade, the Mine-Mill organizers had been responsible for vast areas in the Southwest, and they made only loose connections with the rank and file. Organizers typically stayed in a motel, worked on some grievances and negotiations, gave a speech at a union meeting, and then moved on to the next town.[159] These men worked hard on behalf of Mexican American miners, but they rarely worked to develop Mexican American leadership. Local union officers gathered grievances and, guided by membership meetings, articulated what kind of contracts the rank and file wanted. But they ultimately relied on the international representatives to direct the actual negotiations and to pressure the companies on grievances. In one case of a Mexican American's promotion to the job of bulldozer operator, for instance, Santa Rita Local 63's grievance committee reported to the regular meeting, "It seems that we didn't get very far with [Santa Rita superintendent] Mr. Goodrich. So we are going to take this grievance up to [Chino superintendent] Mr. Moses, and if we can't fix anything with Mr. Moses, we will see our Organizer so that they will take this case higher up."[160]

And even though international representative Verne Curtis actually did live in Silver City for some of the period from 1941 to 1947, it is telling that everyone I spoke with believed that Clinton and Virginia Jencks, who moved to Grant County in 1946, were the first organizers to live among them. That the Jenckses "lived among them" is indicative of the kind of relationship the Jenckses had with union members and of the work they did in building local leadership. While the Jenckses were also Anglos from outside, there seems to have been something different about their involvement in the Grant County unions. Virginia Chacón recalled that it did not matter that the Jenckses were Anglo, "because they didn't act like they were even *americanos*. They acted like one of us. That's the kind of feeling they always gave, and you can ask a lot of people here in Grant County about it. And his name wasn't even Clint. They used to call him Palomino."[161]

Clinton and Virginia Jencks came to Grant County from Denver late in 1946. They brought with them their two children and years of activism in labor and social-justice causes. Clint was born and raised in Colorado Springs, Colorado, where his father was a mail carrier and his mother was active in the Methodist Church. He discovered social concerns through his Christian upbringing and attributes his activism to a belief in the brotherhood of all mankind. Still, religious activism went only so far for him, particularly when he encountered hypocrisy. As a high school student, for instance, Jencks delivered food baskets to striking coal miners only to discover that the eviction notices on workers' houses were signed by a bank vice president—none other than Jencks's own Sunday school superintendent.[162]

Jencks attended the University of Colorado, the tuition for which he paid by holding several jobs, and earned a bachelor's degree in economics in 1939. In Boulder, he found political action taking place in student groups like the Student League for Industrial Democracy (SLID) and the Young Communist League.[163] Gradually he came to see that the people doing the most to improve social conditions were Communists, and their commitment—particularly to antiracist work—deeply impressed him. "Long before the civil rights movement," he remembers of his years in Colorado, "we sat in on local restaurants to break racial barriers." After college he did clerical work for a John Deere distributor in St. Louis, where he started to learn about tenant farming issues through his work in the Interfaith Youth Council.

Virginia Derr grew up in St. Louis. As a teenager in the Depression she worked at a sweatshop and picketed it along with other young women workers.[164] She joined the St. Louis Youth Council, which focused on issues like industrial pollution and tenant farmers' rights. It was here that she met Clinton, and with him she observed the Southern Tenant Farmers' Union's dramatic highway sit-down strike outside Sikeston, Missouri, in 1939.[165] Clinton joined the Army Air Force, and he and Virginia got married at an air base in 1942. Virginia moved to California while he served abroad. After the war, the Jenckses moved to Denver, where Clinton got a job working for the Globe Refinery, an Asarco plant organized by Mine-Mill, and he quickly made union work his second job. Virginia was evidently no stranger to the union headquarters, and when Clinton got the chance to move to New Mexico as an international representative, there was no doubt in their minds that the two of them would do the work together. Thus the locals in Grant County suddenly got two organizers for the price of one. When Verne Curtis was transferred to Globe, Arizona, in 1947, the Jenckses took over as full-time union representatives.[166]

Clinton Jencks has commented that he was working to put himself out of a job by developing leadership from the rank and file.[167] He went about this in concrete ways that suggest his understanding of the psychological and personal dimensions of the men with whom he worked. While early organizers were careful to focus on grievances specific to Mexican Americans, Jencks went a few steps further. More than anything else, he tried to develop leaders from the bottom up and to impress upon them that ultimate authority lay with the workers they represented. Jencks organized several leadership training schools, making sure that they were conducted in both Spanish and English. (This meant that someone else helped run the sessions, because Jencks was not fluent in Spanish at the time.)[168] Any "CIO Man" could attend these training sessions, although they were aimed particularly at stewards and elected officials.[169]

A person attending the stewards' training would encounter basic Marxist economic theory, expressed in the preamble to Mine-Mill's constitution:

> We hold that there is a class struggle in society, and that this struggle is caused by economic conditions.
>
> We affirm the economic condition of the producer to be that he is exploited of the wealth which he produces, being allowed to retain [a portion] barely sufficient for his elementary necessities.
>
> We hold that the class struggle will continue until the producer is recognized as the sole master of his product.
>
> We assert that the working class, and it alone, can and must achieve its own emancipation.
>
> We hold that an industrial union and the concerted political action of all wage workers is the only method of attaining this end.
>
> An injury to one is an injury to all.[170]

Mine-Mill's Education Department in Denver also provided a chatty introduction to Adam Smith's labor theory of value, illustrated with references to contemporary corporations and working conditions, and a film strip (translated into Spanish) called "Why Work for Nothing."[171] Supplementing the written and visual materials were discussions of current politics, geared at explaining, as one flyer put it, "how *your* political action can save *your* union, *your* freedom."[172]

Stewards did not just sit quietly while Jencks lectured to them about economic abstractions. They combined workers' theater from the Depression with a Mexican tradition of oral performance. Stewards themselves chose a grievance and acted out its resolution in front of everyone. This technique loosened people up and let them make fun of management and each other. They did not rely on a script but rather drew on their own experiences at work, using humor to critique social relations. In the course of play-acting grievances, they began to see some of the larger issues in labor relations. And, importantly, the classes were not boring.[173]

Beyond learning economic theory, stewards worked directly on the nuts and bolts of organizing coworkers. As Arturo Flores recalls, Jencks showed them how to "talk to the guy next to us . . . and then have that guy talk to other guys," thus building a strong network person by person.[174]

They learned how to design their own leaflets and to operate mimeo-graph machines. They learned that stewards should always carry a "5¢ notebook and a pencil tied to it with a string" in order to be ready to take down a grievance on the spot.[175]

After learning some basics of trade unionism, leaders put them into practice. Chairmanship of Local 890's executive board rotated among the representatives from the different units, a policy aimed at the dual goals of training many people and of preventing any one person from assuming too much control.[176] At one meeting in which executive board mem-bers discussed the union's finances, Alberto Muñoz, Brígido Provencio, Charles Morrell, and Art Flores all weighed in with complex analyses of the union's finances, while Jencks played a comparatively low-key role, which suggests that he did not jealously guard such critical information but shared it with the other leaders.[177] As further evidence that Jencks was not running a one-man show, the union's weekly radio spots, deliv-ered in both English and Spanish over radio station KSIL, frequently showed signs of having been written first in Spanish, which Jencks could not have done.

Union work often had social, cultural, and educational dimensions. In 1948, Jencks wrote to the Taller de Gráfica Popular (People's Graphic Arts Workshop) in Mexico City for a portfolio of pictures of the Mexican Revolution. "We are very anxious to obtain these pictures," he explained, because "as much as 95% of our membership is Mexican-American and feel the closest ties with the people of Mexico."[178] He leased films from the state university and from the international office; the union's pur-chase of a film projector suggests that the executive board believed that films were a necessary part of union business—not a luxury.[179] Cipriano Montoya, Local 890 president in 1951, continued this tradition when he asked the international office for information on "progressive" films pro-duced by the United Nations.[180] And by holding meetings in Spanish, as well as English, and by making documents available in both languages, union leaders affirmed Mexican American culture—sometimes against company opposition. In 1949, for example, the Asarco bargaining com-mittee was told that the contract would be printed in both languages. But Asarco superintendent T. H. Snedden and attorney J. F. Woodbury later balked at publishing it in Spanish. According to the union minutes, Sned-den and Woodbury insisted that "this country was American speaking and would not tolerate it, but Brother Jencks says that he hasn't read anything in the 'Constitution of the United States' that says anything of it being strictly American speaking."[181]

Jencks encouraged union leaders to develop confidence and concrete skills. But strength of leadership was never meant to overshadow where the real strength lay: in union members themselves. Rather than seeing themselves as the experts who could solve all the problems, stewards and elected officials were instructed to "try to get *all* the workers in [their] department *using* their rights, using their steward, learning to be union members in action."[182] To this end, stewards refused to take up griev-ances by telephone. Only when a worker was ready to talk face-to-face with a foreman was he, in Jencks's estimation, likely to follow through on the grievance. If a worker was not willing to do this, "he wasn't ready to win."[183] Many Mexican American workers were used to Anglo inter-cessors and, indeed, had little reason to believe that their efforts alone would get them very far in an Anglo-dominated setting. Jencks believes that the policy of pursuing grievances in person helped show workers— rather than merely telling them—that they themselves made the differ-ence. Stewards' training brought this message home: a good steward "tries to get all workers to bring up grievances, take part in union ac-tivities, and support all parts of the union's program." He "tries to help the workers to stand on their own feet, independent of the boss, in the shop and out of the shop."[184]

The example of Arturo Flores shows how Mexican American union leaders of this period made use of both their own experiences of discrimi-nation and the opportunities that Mine-Mill offered for effectively repre-senting workers and improving their lives in material ways. Flores thrived in the new environment of the late 1940s. Coming of age in the Great Depression, he learned stonemasonry in the CCC. But he could make little use of his trade when he applied to the Chino mines in 1940: the company hired him only as an unskilled laborer. "They didn't ask for a résumé," Flores remembers. "They just asked for my first name and my last name, and my last name determined where I was going to work. No matter what." Confined to a job shoveling the ash dumped by a coal-powered locomotive, the young Flores soon discovered and joined the then-clandestine Mine-Mill organizing effort.[185]

From 1942 to 1946, Flores served in the navy as a metalsmith for aircraft and, later, as an instructor. The war sharpened Flores's perception of discrimination. He encountered segregation in the navy, but only for African Americans, not Mexican Americans; Flores bunked and worked with Anglos. His problems were not with "the navy types" but rather with Anglo civilians. Flores described an incident that took place when he was traveling home and stopped in Dallas to change trains:

There was a soldier there, an Anglo soldier, real nice guy, nice fellow. He said, "Let's go uptown, have a bite to eat. The food here is terrible at the station." "Okay," I say, so we start walking towards town and we started crossing a street, along with a bunch of other people, and a cop jumped on *me*. And he said, "Didn't you see the light? I'm gonna put you in the can if you keep on jaywalking." Here I was walking with all these people! And they said, "We were all walking!" And he said, "You shut up. I'm not asking you. I'm asking him." Well he intimidated them, of course. . . . I was in uniform, and the soldier said, "Gee, you know, I can't understand." "Well," I said, "some people in some of these parts here don't like blacks, and they figure Mexicans are probably the same."[186]

Then, after being rebuffed in a bar—"We don't serve Mexicans here"— the two soldiers gave up and went back to the railroad station. When he left the service, Flores "made up [his] mind that [he] was gonna be an instrument of change, here in Grant County."[187]

Flores returned to Chino, this time as a truck driver in the open pit, a position he held for decades. When he complained in meetings about the treatment Mexican Americans got in the mines, his coworkers elected him steward. His first case concerned a Mexican American who should have been promoted. "The contract clearly specified that our people had the right to bid for jobs that were open," Flores recalled. When an oiler job opened, Ramón Hurtado applied and expected the promotion because he was next in line; the job, however, went to someone else. Flores quickly filed a grievance. "I was told right away, 'We don't put greasers with oilers.' That's what the foreman told me. I said, 'But the contract here says different.' He says, 'Well I don't care what your contract says.' "[188] Flores and Hurtado successfully appealed the decision, and Hurtado became an oiler. When management had insisted to Flores that "your people" could not operate the shovels, Flores declared that the union did not care if Mexican Americans were able or not—it wanted to give them the opportunity to try it out. And, according to Flores, after trying it out, Hurtado became an outstanding shovel operator in the open pit, "the best they ever had."[189]

Mexican American workers used Mine-Mill effectively to challenge discrimination at work, and they soon directed their energies toward reforming Mine-Mill's international leadership. Throughout the Southwest, these union men pressured the international executive board to live up to its commitment to ethnic equality by bringing more Mexican Americans into the leadership. They found a good deal of support from board member Chester Smothermon, who represented the Southwest (District 2) and who became convinced that Mine-Mill's efforts in Superior, Arizona, required the skills of a Mexican American union representative. Smothermon solicited Local 890's Cipriano Montoya for the job.[190] The international also hired Arturo Flores to help repel a raid by the Steelworkers in El Paso.[191] At the 1951 convention, Mexican American delegates caucused and concluded that the national executive board "would not function right without a Mexican American on the Board." They blamed the international for not providing adequate leadership.[192] Secretary-treasurer Maurice Travis recognized the paradox of Mine-Mill's appeal to African Americans and Mexican Americans. Because those workers were "so responsive to organization and to leadership which fights in their behalf[,]" he wrote to Smothermon in 1951, "they become among the most militant trade unionists, and we therefore, as a form of escapism, rely upon them to carry the organizational load . . . , rather than facing the much [more] difficult organizational task of [getting] white and Anglo workers to accept some of that responsibility."[193]

Meanings of Communism in Local 890

There are plenty of signs that Local 890's leadership shared many of the principles articulated by the CP; the entire executive board in summer 1949, for instance, subscribed to the *People's Daily World*, a CP newspaper published in San Francisco. Communist explanations of the political economy meshed with many Mexican Americans' own perceptions of discrimination. They could see, moreover, that the union pushed companies hard and that union members became stronger the more they stayed active in challenging management prerogative. As Anita Torrez put it, "If this is what they're gonna call communist, fine: Let's all be communists then! Because we're fighting for our *rights*."[194] Virginia Chacón said that for her and her husband, Juan, communism was part of strong trade unionism, "part of getting us to learn and walk further and see things the way they were happening. As far as we were concerned, Juan and I . . . didn't think anything of the Communist Party. We just joined because we wanted to be in it, it had good principles, and it still does."[195] Lorenzo Torrez found in the party an encouragement to read widely and think deeply about class issues. He began to get interested in communism because the press called the most active and militant people communist: "I began to get curious and I used to invite them to a bar, for example, after a meeting. And I would ask them, 'Well, why is it that they're calling you a communist?' And they would relate their experience in the union, how they were all stewards or something like that, and how they handled grievances, how they had built the union, how they had eliminated discrimination. Well, for me, that was the way it's supposed to be. . . . But they never admitted that they were [communists]."[196]

The CP in Grant County was very small, but it organized effectively at the workplace—attracting people like Lorenzo Torrez—and among married couples. It was "an advantage to have the couple instead of the husband [without] the wife," Anita Torrez observed. "It makes it very hard on the couple if *he's* in the party and the wife isn't. It's a strain on the family."[197] Club meetings were essentially discussion groups; members read Marxist theory and related it to their experiences as workers and as targets of government harassment. Communists in Grant County focused on local politics and union activism. In the course of the Empire Zinc strike, according to Lorenzo Torrez, they "learned which side the politician is on, which side the newspaper is on, which side the government is on, so politics became very central to [them]: how to change it, how to gain representation, all of those things."[198]

Membership in the party, though, took a back seat to trade unionism, if the two were ever to conflict. And they did conflict once Mine-Mill decided to sign the noncommunist affidavits in 1949. For Clinton Jencks, the choice was not difficult: he resigned from the party, and he signed the affidavit on October 15, 1949.[199] The irony, of course, was that one's political principles did not begin and end with actual membership in the party. Anticommunists realized this, and they angrily denounced union leaders like Mine-Mill's Maurice Travis for paying only lip service to Taft-Hartley.

Democratic centralism was supposed to define CP structure; in Mine-Mill, it is apparent that the "democratic" part of centralism was much stronger than in the party's version. A commitment to democracy lay behind Local 890's efforts to train leaders up through the ranks and its policy of leaving all important decisions to the membership. But Local 890's was still a centralism in that it developed a strategy for particular situations and contained dissent within the bounds of the union, and the secrecy surrounding CP membership certainly complicates any discussion of democracy.[200] In a crisis, according to Lorenzo Torrez, the party committee would meet in advance to discuss strategy, and then its members would present the options to the membership at the regular meeting.

The members voted and voiced their opinions, but they did so within parameters set by leaders. The same stewards' training that emphasized workers' independence also emphasized the steward's loyalty to the union in terms that were established to diminish internal criticism in the name of the workers' interests: "[The steward] always defends the union's policies, even if he didn't vote for them. He always defends the democratic wishes of the union members. . . . He never says anything anywhere that can be used to weaken or disrupt his union. . . . He is constantly alert to any and all attempts to weaken or destroy the union."[201]

Most union members generally brushed off the charges of communist domination and criticized the motives behind the charges. Empire Zinc strikers, for example, were offended by the company's claim that "leaders" ran everything, a not-so-subtle charge that the union was run by communists. "The leaders don't dictate to me what I want," Jesús Ríos told Empire Zinc. "I tell them and back them on what is best for me and all the workers." Or as Luis Horcasitas explained, "We tell the leaders what we want, not like the Company says, that our leaders tell us. We back our leaders on our just demands."[202] Rarely did union defenders deny outright that the leaders might be communists; they focused instead on the reasons their opponents would level charges of communist domination.

THE EMPIRE ZINC STRIKE

Mine-Mill was a beleaguered union in 1950, cast outside the pale of the mainstream labor movement that it had helped build; struggling in a hostile political environment, the Mine-Mill locals that held on scrambled for creative solutions to difficult problems. In Grant County, though, mining managers found that anticommunism was not as strong a weapon as they had hoped, because the miners there not only found ways to defend themselves against it but even mounted a counteroffensive. Just as anticommunism in the labor movement was taking off, the Grant County unions were building on their recent successes. Many miners believed that the Empire Zinc strike would be the place where companies would try out new tactics, having failed to break the union during either a bitter strike at Asarco earlier in 1950 or a successful representation campaign waged by the nominally independent Grant County Miners Association at USSRMC.

The Empire Zinc strikers had direct experience with democratic unionism, both before and during the strike, and it was this experience that enabled them to persist and respond to company offensives. When the strike began on October 17, 1950, committees quickly assumed responsibility for strike relief, negotiations with the company, publicity, legal and police relations (which were friendly in the first eight months, until Sheriff Goforth swore in his deputies), recreation, and fund-raising. The negotiating committee and the chairs of the other five committees determined strike policy, which union members reviewed weekly and subjected to referenda.[203]

The company responded with an attrition policy, hoping to outlast the strikers, whose strike benefits barely met their needs. By wintertime, the attrition policy began to show results, and families felt the pinch of limited rations spread over too many people. "The men on the picket," Local 890 president Cipriano Montoya reported to Maurice Travis, "are holding the strike solid but require assistance in the basic needs of food and fuel." Montoya requested another $1,000 in strike relief—but also sent Travis "two small checks for the National Heart and Cancer Research funds."[204] The union paid strikers' electric, gas, fuel, and utility bills and "an occasional car or furniture payment, so that [their] striking brothers [wouldn't] have their property taken away."[205] Food for each family cost about forty dollars a month. The union bought beans, rice, chilies, flour, corn tortillas, cheese, oil, potatoes, milk, cereal, sugar, and soap in bulk at Southwestern Foods, a local grocery store, and gave it away at the union hall.[206] Families found no meat, eggs, or butter in their weekly food baskets, although one man (employed at one of the other mines) brought "a big thing of bologna" every payday to the picket line.[207]

Some men wanted release from picket duty to look for other work, and others, who had found new jobs, resented turning over a quarter of their wages to the strike fund.[208] Anita Torrez remembered "meeting after meeting, discussing and discussing" the question of looking for outside work. "We were lucky," she said, "we had only one child. But there were others that had big families, and [they felt] 'we can't go on like this, I need to go out and look for a job.'" Her husband, Lorenzo, an Empire Zinc striker, recalled that "the discussions went along well. . . . It was agreed that those that had bigger families should try to get work and those that had less, the union would help us maintain. Finally it came to a certain weekly allowance. I think we went through the whole strike with something like $12.50 a week."[209] These weekly discussions changed policy. By February, strikers who took other jobs reduced their contribution from 25 to 15 percent of their wages. Even that seems to have been hard to collect, for the international office in Denver found the payment "haphazard and poorly organized."[210] Strikers who held jobs elsewhere either resented paying strike dues or were out of communication with the union.

In March 1951, the Empire Zinc Company started a back-to-work campaign, flooding workers' mailboxes with letters from Superintendent S. S. Huyett. Workers had suffered too long, and for what? The union leadership was keeping the strike going despite workers' desire to return to work. The company's effort backfired. Instead of rallying to the company gates, Empire Zinc workers and their families offered their own interpretation of the strike's unfortunate duration. Mrs. Antonio Rivera conceded, "Yes, Mr. Huyett, our families have suffered. No doubt about that. But for my part I don't want my husband to work without the conditions the other companies have within the district." Jesús Bustamante told the company, "QUIT spending our money on letters. Spend it on collar-to-collar and paid holidays and other benefits that prevail in the district." Antonio Macías resented that the company did not even pay the correct postage: "I have had to pay an extra 2 cents to get their letter from the post office. Next time I am going to return the letter." And Lorenzo Torrez suspected that the company was "not sorry for the $1,800 [he] lost but for the profits [they] lost."[211] The back-to-work movement failed, even with the help of Jesús Avalos, former Local 890 steward, and Charles Graves, Empire Zinc's "top labor relations expert," who was flown in especially to deal with the strike. And the effort to reopen the mine by force failed. The injunction served by Sheriff Goforth was the company's next step. Fortunately for Local 890, its members were primed to entertain unorthodox proposals of their own. They would encounter one in the union meeting that they convened to deal with the injunction crisis.

4

Competing Models of Unionism

THE UNION MEETING

The court injunction delivered by Sheriff Goforth electrified the union community, and the union scheduled a community meeting for that very evening, June 12, 1951. Everyone associated with Mine-Mill was invited —Empire Zinc strikers, workers in other camps, wives, children, sisters, parents. Word of the injunction and the meeting to discuss it spread from home to home and from shift to shift. After their suppers, families walked or shared rides to the union hall in Bayard. On the outside, the union hall was a utilitarian box that looked like a military barracks, which, in fact, it had once been. But if the outside lacked character, the inside was a different story. Walls were decorated with posters and announcements ("Oppose the Smith Act! Down with Taft-Hartley!") and Mexican wood-cut illustrations; below the decorations hung sign-up sheets for picket duty and other committee work. At the front of the room, the American flag was displayed near Local 890's Mine-Mill charter. The union had not always had a meeting place of its own. Locals and then units of the amalgamated union met wherever they could rent or borrow a space— usually a local tavern or the pool hall in Santa Rita, spaces that men were comfortable in, but not women. Then the local bought a government surplus building and had it moved north from Deming's air force base to Bayard to serve the broader community of Local 890.

Around 7 P.M., the hall was starting to fill up and buzz with greetings and gossip. Women served coffee from the back of the hall. Folding chairs scraped and clattered as people made their way into rows of seats.

Kids were shushed by their parents, and parents were quieted by the sharp rap of President Montoya's gavel. He told the audience that they were there to decide what to do about the injunction. Montoya read the court order aloud, first in English and then in Spanish, and opened the floor for discussion. For awhile, the men argued over their pitiful options. A general strike? Too provocative, too risky, even though the union was strong in almost all of the local mines and mills. Ignore the injunction? Fines would multiply and men would be jailed in such numbers that the union would be destroyed. Give in? Absolutely not.[1]

After quite some time of this back-and-forth discussion, one woman raised her hand and was given the floor. She rose and asked, "Why not have women take over the pickets? The injunction spoke only of 'striking miners.'" Women were not miners, she reminded the audience, "so they could picket and the sheriff would have no authority to stop them."[2] Surely no union man would object to such an ingenious way to circumvent the injunction without violating it.

But union men could object, and object they did. "What are you gonna do with the children?" they asked. "I'm sure not gonna take care of them!"[3] Some men were afraid their wives would be physically hurt on the picket, while others, Virginia Chacón later recounted, thought that "shenanigans" would take place on the line—their wives would run off with other men.[4] Her own husband, Juan, unequivocally opposed the women's picket.[5] But most of the women were fired up by the chance to take over the picket, eager to defend the union. The "stronger" women, in Anita Torrez's words, declared that they would find something to do with the kids: If the men did not "want to share in working the problems out then we were gonna do our own problem-solving."[6]

As much as the proposal seemed spontaneous, a bolt out of the blue, it was actually planned in advance by three women. Earlier that afternoon, Virginia Jencks, Virginia Chacón, and Aurora Chávez met to figure out how women might help the picketers. Just as a core of 890 leadership would often meet ahead of time to set a meeting's agenda, these women in the ladies' auxiliary had caucused ahead of time.

The union meeting was contentious and heated and lasted far into the night. Except for international representatives Clinton Jencks and Bob Hollowwa, men generally opposed a women's picket.[7] Women belonged at home. They had clothes to wash and kids to tend, and no one could take their place. The picket line was unpredictable; who knew how women might behave on it? How would it look for men to hide behind their women? And if women were hurt, men could only blame themselves for having exposed their wives and daughters to the violence, for they knew how rough the picket line could be.[8] Women, by contrast, generally supported the proposal. They were excited at the prospect of something new, impatient with men's closed-mindedness, and eager to get down to business. "We had a hard time convincing the men," Braulia Velásquez commented later. "But we finally did by a vote."[9] Around 2:30 in the morning, with women voting alongside men—a provision granted to all auxiliaries by the international—Local 890 decided to send women to the pickets.[10] The women immediately gathered to start planning their shifts. The first would begin at dawn.

The meeting on June 12 was so contentious and the arguments so hard-fought because the stakes were so high. The union faced a powerful enemy, one made even more powerful by its apparent control over local law enforcement. Women and men alike agreed that the union needed to be defended.[11] Not only had Local 890 secured better wages, especially for Mexican Americans, but it had also pushed beyond the mines, mills, and smelters to challenge discrimination against Mexican Americans in local schools, stores, and government. Men and women, Anglos and Mexicans alike, supported the union's mission.

But there was more at stake than defending the union against outside enemies: the very nature of the local union was in question, and battling it out in the union hall that night were two models of unionism. One was based on a brotherhood of men—and exclusively men—who had protected one another against the dangers of mining, their exploitation by management, and the calamities of unemployment, and who had asserted Mexican American dignity against an unjust political and social system. These experiences had, moreover, reinforced men's claims to household authority as the breadwinners in their families. The other union model was based on a larger family of union supporters who, during strikes, made short-term sacrifices for long-term economic security, and who helped consolidate the union's power beyond the workplace. The two models of unionism had coexisted peacefully until the injunction crisis forced the differences between them into the open. Under the new terms of labor conflict, either model could work only at the expense of the other.

Local 890 was used to crises that forced its members to rethink their tactics, and in this respect the injunction crisis was similar to episodes like the 1948 contract negotiations or the 1949 unemployment crisis: it opened up a space for a group of union supporters—in this case women—

to scramble for creative solutions to a difficult problem. But the women's proposal also differed from those situations. While union men certainly understood that Empire Zinc held the tactical advantage, they were nonetheless uneasy at making such a radical departure from the familiar tactics that had worked before. They did not want to commit to a course of action that would disrupt the normal workings of the family and thereby undermine their authority within the family. The prospect of such a disruption of the family order, which had served as the foundation for the union that men had built over the preceding few years, was deeply unsettling. For how could emasculated men ever defeat a powerful mining company? Moreover, women's behavior in the union meeting threw open the question of who would decide the union's course of action. As union men approached their dilemma based on the militant, democratic union that they had built during the 1940s, they were shocked to discover that the decision was not theirs alone to make.

For women, too, the proposal to take over the pickets was a startlingly new idea, although once the proposal was made, women saw that it followed logically from their recent auxiliary work. Its novelty gave the proposal a lot of power, for it was not what their adversaries expected of them—any more than their husbands did. The injunction crisis carved out a space for women to make a bold new move; it was the occasion for amplifying the union's repertoire of tactics. This process was as exhilarating for women as it was disturbing to men. The proposal could only have been made by people who had come to sense their own power, which these women had done by gradually getting more involved in the union over the previous three years. The story of the women's picket, then, a story taking place both on the line and in people's homes, shows women and men debating their understandings of the union community and, in the process, remaking it.

THE UNION BROTHERHOOD

Mining was indisputably men's work. Everywhere that work went on, whether in the open-pit mine, an underground mine, a mill, or a smelter, men were doing it. As many historians have shown, mining has always had a masculine character, but masculinity has taken different forms in different settings and has changed over time. "Masculinity was clearly linked to class ideology," historian Steven Penfold has argued, "but there was no automatic relationship between manhood and class. Indeed, gender definitions and their implications were highly contextual."[12] Over the course of the twentieth century, for example, Appalachian miners fostered two kinds of masculine identity corresponding to different periods of workers' mobilization. Unionized miners of the 1930s defined true manhood as a worker's vigorous challenge to management prerogative (and to management's paternalism). But in a period of union retrenchment, these miners articulated and acted upon a different definition of manhood: one marked by hard work and the breadwinner ethic.[13] In Chile, American capitalists tried to regulate workers' sexuality and other behavior in order to create a more stable workforce. Miners resisted this effort with masculine practices like drinking, gambling, and refusing to settle down in marriage, yet they also drew upon their responsibility as breadwinners and upon the honor they attained through hard work in order to demand a family wage and fair treatment.[14]

Similar complexities mark the history of masculinity in Grant County's mine industry. As miners built their union in the 1940s, they drew on, deliberately or not, models of the family to shape their relationships with one another. Already familiar with the horizontal and vertical relationships inherent in families, union men drew upon three sets of relationships—those of brothers, husbands, and fathers—in structuring the union. The union became a brotherhood made up of equals bound to one another by mutual needs, particularly the need for safety, and reinforced by the exclusion of women. Their fraternal equality (the *kind* of brotherhood they felt) was itself partly based on another set of family relationships: these men were equals not only because they had the same experiences at work but also because they each headed their own household, or aspired to do so. Male breadwinners exercised authority over the women and children in their families, quite apart from the fictive family in the union hall. Yet men achieved the status of breadwinner, from which their authority in the home derived, in the workplace. The democratic structure of the union was rooted in this brand of social equality. Still another dimension of their fraternity was its grounding in shared ethnicity and, at the same time, its capacity to transcend ethnic barriers and to attract Anglo workers to a brotherhood that affirmed the social equality of Mexican Americans and Anglos.

The miners' union was much more than a fraternal club, of course. Its central purpose was to deal collectively with a powerful adversary: industrial management. Here, too, family relations and masculinity came into play, but with a twist. Management insisted that a family relationship structured the workplace. As Kennecott labor relations expert James K.

Richardson instructed the New Mexico Miners and Prospectors Association, "Labor negotiations should be, in my opinion, family affairs. Don't wash your dirty linens in public!"[15] As in any industry, it was common for managers to speak of the company as one big family, working together but headed by a father; this approach corresponded to a notion that any differences between labor and management were "merely a misunderstanding by each party of the aims of the other. Each has a basic willingness to promote a free enterprise system."[16] In exerting paternalist control, management reassured workers that it knew best what workers' interests were (because they were the same as the company's) and how best to protect them. Managers were parents and workers were children. In the Southwest, this paternalism took on another dimension: Anglos were parents and Mexicans were children.

The union men, both Anglo and Mexican American, would have none of this. By no means did they consider themselves children. Manhood, after all, encompasses both masculinity and adulthood, and to accept the status of child meant to forego the status of man. Rather than behaving like the children in the company "family," union men insisted on acting like adults. But what did it mean to act like an adult? Men taking responsibility for their union brothers and private families—the markers of manhood within the union—meant nothing to an employer who was trying to infantilize them. The situation required a different kind of masculinity: a combative, militant, aggressive masculinity. The relationship between worker and management was adversarial and not familial, and in rejecting the family model at the workplace, union men were laying claim to their own manhood. In parallel fashion, they rejected any natural Anglo authority over Mexican Americans.

Brothers

This masculine character cemented the bonds of brotherhood, which were reinforced by the union's language of brotherhood, a lexicon shared by all male unions, and its practice of holding its meetings in male spaces like bars or pool halls, which connected the work organization to masculine forms of leisure. Bars were an exclusively male preserve; few women entered them, and never alone. Thus men's effort to build on and strengthen class and ethnic ties took place literally in the same space that fortified their sense of brotherhood.

Masculinity characterized mining; danger defined mining's essence. Each time that trackman Felipe Bencomo hammered spikes into new track on a bench of the open-pit mine, that cager Cruz Torrez took men down hundreds or thousands of feet into an underground mine's shaft, that powderman Luis Alvarado took dynamite out of its magazine or miner Pat Moreno loaded that dynamite into a hole, they put their lives and those of their coworkers in danger. To survive this danger, miners had to trust and protect one another. Their mutual dependence fostered fraternal bonds, as miners imported a form of family duty into the workplace. Reviewing several incidents in which men faced that danger can help clarify the relationship between men's work processes and the obligations they felt toward one another, obligations that they strove to meet through their union.

Dynamite was one of the miner's primary tools. Without careful handling, precise timing, and clear communication among workers, it was deadly. Communication turned out to be faulty in Peru Mining Company's Kearney shaft on March 29, 1947.[17] It was a Saturday night, and Delfino García and his partner, Joe Dimas, were drilling holes into the rock face on the 500-foot level. At the end of their shift, close to 11 P.M., they loaded the holes with dynamite and attached wires to each cartridge's blasting cap before making their way the 300 to 400 feet from their stope to the shaft, where a cage was waiting to take them to the surface. J. D. Hughey was ready to detonate the charges they had just set. Hughey was a conscientious miner, already having made sure that the men on the next level down were clear in case debris fell down the chutes from the blast level, because, as he put it, "you have to watch out for yourself and your buddy." To make sure the men on the blasting level were safe, he called out, "Is everyone clear?" One miner yelled back that Red and his crew were the only ones who might still be there. Another miner said that Red had already left, so Hughey threw the switch and the dynamite exploded, choking the area with dust and debris. But there were two men nicknamed Red, and only one had left the drift near the explosion. Oscar "Red" Jones was still on the 500 level with Jesse Worthington and Harry Porter. Men at the shaft station saw Red Jones stagger out of the blasted drift, ribs broken; they found the other two men deeper in the drift. They "tried to get [Worthington] to go out but he wanted to see about Porter first." Porter, though, was dead from a skull fracture and lacerated brain. He was thirty-six years old, and this was his first shift at Peru. He left it in a bucket.

Miners at every camp were concerned with one another's safety, but certain work arrangements made accidents more likely. The contract system, for instance, created risks because the lines of authority, responsibility, and communication were not always coextensive. Phelps-Dodge owned the Burro Chief mine at Tyrone and leased the fluorspar workings to H. E. McCray, a Silver City mining engineer. McCray, in turn, contracted with John Zelitti (himself a miner) to bring a crew to work each day. McCray and his foreman, Julio Tafoya, told Zelitti which stopes the miners should work each day. Tafoya was supposed to check conditions before each shift started, but he did not always then have time to tell the miners whether the rock needed barring down or timbering.[18] This arrangement offered at best a loose net for safety, one through which miner LeRoy Jones fell to his death on May 9, 1947. The night before, Tafoya had noticed that part of a hanging wall—a twenty-five-foot slab of rock that looked deceptively stable—had fallen down in one of the stopes, but in the morning he "had to do some other work" and did not tell Zelitti. "I just forgot, I guess, but [the workers] are supposed to [check] it."[19] Jones and his partner, Jack Hales, were raking ore into a chute on the 265-foot level after a blast. After a while Hales went to cool off, and then he heard the "hanging wall" pull away from the "real" wall. He never saw it; "the wind from the concussion . . . knocked my light out." Jones called to him, "Jack, pull me out," but Hales could not reach him.[20]

When paid by the amount and grade of ore they mined, miners were apt to take shortcuts in safety. But pressure to take shortcuts also came directly from the manager, not just wage-hungry miners. Zelitti described three good mining practices and admitted that the Burro Chief followed only one of them—timbering—and then only "where it was bad enough." Tafoya observed that McCray was sometimes a day late in getting timber to the site, once even failing to bring it at all. McCray told workers not to blast the hanging walls, because they were only waste ore, and a few weeks before the accident McCray yelled at Jones for blasting such a wall and ruining a car of high-grade ore.

Miners took their responsibility for one another very seriously, and concern for mine safety often engendered other forms of support. Often unions were first organized so that workers could give one another money when disaster struck; in this way they were like other kinds of fraternal organizations, which typically gave death benefits to workers' families. Many such organizations existed in Grant County, and many funerals were arranged (if not always funded) by them. For the most part, fraternal-minded Mexican Americans did not belong to the same organizations as Anglos, choosing instead the Alianza Hispano Americana. The AHA was formed in Tucson in 1904, and within ten years the first Grant

County lodge was organized in Silver City; by the 1940s, there were dozens of AHA lodges in the mining camps.[21]

Concern for mine safety also laid the basis for collective action. As one anonymous miner told the *Silver City Daily Press* shortly after the 1947 Peru explosion that killed Harry Porter, "It looks like the miners will have to join forces to make themselves stronger in order to live." He demanded that the district court investigate the Peru mine, where two men had recently been killed and eight others injured.[22] Safety was also the focus of Mine-Mill's own activism from 1916 to 1934, the period when the union abandoned its call for class struggle.

Husbands and Fathers

Men's shared status as the breadwinner in their families was also key to the union's brotherhood. The breadwinner ethic held that men should provide the income for their families while women tended the home; in its working-class version, employers were expected to pay wages sufficient to support a family—the family wage. The breadwinner ethic prevailed in most parts of the United States, but it was especially strong in places like mining towns, which were built around industries with exclusively male workforces. Men and women alike frequently endorsed this division of labor, many women believing it their right to have a husband who provided for his family. During the Great Depression, for example, American men and women expressed outrage at women taking precious jobs away from men who needed to feed their families, even though many women were the sole providers for their families.[23] Certainly not all miners headed households; a man's work life usually started before his marriage, if he married at all. But the breadwinner was the standard for mining.

The breadwinner ideal underpinned much union activity, most obviously in the union's demands for wage increases to match the rising cost of living. But we can see it in other aspects as well. Aware of its responsibilities to workers' families, for example, the union tried to bring housing into company negotiations. Meeting with Empire Zinc's management on August 29, 1949, Local 890's bargaining team asked the company to promise not to raise rents on its Hanover houses. Mr. Francis, the company's representative, cut off this discussion: "You talk as though the company must meet the cost of living. There is no guarantee to meet any cost of living. . . . Purchasing power theory is not true. [Rent increases] don't belong in negotiations. The company is willing to discuss the things which belong here."[24]

Men were understood to be the principal breadwinners even when they were out of work. After World War II, lead-zinc miners suffered two particularly harsh spells of unemployment when the market bottomed out. Because unemployment was not precisely a "workplace" issue—the problem obviously being one of *not* having a workplace—it was not taken for granted that a labor union would step in to address it. That Mine-Mill did shows that its members extended their responsibilities to one another beyond the workplace. Moreover, dealing with unemployment required union resources beyond the usual contracts and grievance machinery. Unemployed miners quickly organized themselves through Mine-Mill, gathering information on unemployed miners' dependents and veteran status, both of which indicated male responsibility and status, and lobbying the governor and state legislature for extended unemployment benefits.

All of these actions reflected union men's concern over being able to support their families and their sense that they could rely on their union brothers. Ernest Rodríguez, a member of Local 890's Unemployed Committee, for instance, felt that it was important to organize the miners for reasons beyond the cash benefits they hoped to see. An organized community of miners would prevent "disorganized migration, which is an evil because it causes misery to children. It interrupts their education [and] makes it impossible to receive medical attention when needed."[25] At meetings for unemployed men, Local 890 took down the names and ages of each unemployed man's dependents.[26] The union used this information not only in allotting food relief but also to demonstrate how deserving of support these men were. Similarly, the union kept close tabs on the numbers of military veterans among the unemployed. Of fifty-four men on one list, eighteen identified themselves as veterans, though some people did not answer either way.[27]

Grant County did not immediately suffer from the postwar recession that everyone had feared. Employment dropped in 1946, but then it leveled out and even increased over the next two years; this was quite different from the years right after World War I, when Chino and Phelps-Dodge both shut down during a terrible recession.[28] Unemployment, while troubling for any family, proved to be a transient problem in the years right after World War II. But by early February 1949, state employment officer Ray Strickland began to notice a shift in the pattern of layoffs, a shift that could not be explained by normal seasonal changes. Men were being laid off from jobs they had held for years.[29] That spring, Peru Mining Company and the U.S. Smelting, Refining, and Mining Company (USSRMC) started laying off workers and curtailing production.

In early June, people still hoped that this was only a short aberration. The state employment service told Grant County's anxious chamber of commerce that employment looked even better in 1949 than it had a year before. But just ten days later, miners found reason to disagree: Peru and Kennecott both stopped production at their zinc shafts, one in Hanover and the other in Santa Rita, and laid off 170 workers.[30] A week later, sixty Empire Zinc workers faced layoffs as the company announced a reduced work week to begin July 1. But the biggest layoff bomb fell at USSRMC. That company announced on June 27 that it would completely shut down in Grant County the following day, throwing some 400 to 500 workers out of work with no warning. Crowds of them filled the local employment office.[31] All told, about a thousand Grant County miners lost their jobs by the end of the month, driving the county's unemployment rate to 15 percent, three times the rate for New Mexico as a whole.[32] And it got worse from there. Despite promises that it would stay open, Asarco stopped all ore production in mid-July, laying off another 150 men.[33] Strickland reported in August that 25 percent of Grant County's workers were unemployed.[34] The effects soon spread to "every important industry in the area between September and November."[35] Weekly unemployment benefits of $20 lasted only twenty weeks, and the state legislature was not in session to extend or increase them.

Faced with a dismal present and a worse future, unemployed miners began to organize immediately after USSRMC closed. They centered their activities in the union and soon expanded into the community at large, using a combination of publicity and pressure on particular political and government figures. They insisted that they were not asking for a "handout": their past military service and present responsibilities as breadwinners entitled them to work.[36] The day after USSRMC closed, Tony Queveda, Charles Morrell, Fidel Aragón, and Ernest Rodríguez formed a union committee and visited the local employment office. They demanded a special session of the state legislature to consider the unemployment crisis, a new public works program, and an end to the red tape that kept unemployed miners lined up around the block outside the employment office.[37] Ray Strickland could do nothing to meet the first two demands, which required the governor's, if not the president's, inter-

vention. That the miners went to him first thus appears somewhat misguided, a desperate scramble for help without finding out the proper
channels. But their action is reminiscent of similar activism in the early
1930s, when unemployed councils and workers' alliances pressed local
authorities to come through with relief, thereby exposing the ineffective-
ness of the system as a whole.[38] Perhaps because he felt the gravity of the
two demands he could not meet, Strickland immediately responded to
the third: he brought in more employment officials to process claims
more quickly. The unemployment office placed 300 unemployed miners
in agricultural jobs, sent 38 to a Utah mine, and assigned another 210 to
fight forest fires.[39]

The unemployed miners next organized a delegation to Governor
Thomas J. Mabry. Six miners, all veterans, left Bayard on July 5, stopping
to speak to interested crowds in Hot Springs and Socorro before arriving
in Santa Fe the following morning.[40] Governor Mabry barely gave them
the time of day. As Ernest Rodríguez, a member of the delegation, noted,
"He gave us a quick answer." Clinton Jencks elaborated: " 'Good morning,
good night, good-bye—that's all I care to discuss.' "[41] Mabry would not
call a special session of the legislature at the miners' request, but he said
he might respond to similar pressure if it came from legislators. Over the
next two months, Local 890's unemployed committee showered state
representatives with descriptions of the miners' plight and appeals for a
special session.[42] But Mabry still declined to call a special session, choosing instead to appoint a commission to study the problem. "The cure," he
said, "should stem from Washington."[43]

Mine-Mill's unemployment activism relied in part on public spectacle. In mid-August, forty-two unemployed miners, veterans, and wives
of unemployed miners traveled the state by caravan, each car "decorated
with 5 full sized posters demanding jobs, no discrimination, and equal
pay."[44] By the time they reached Santa Fe, however, Mabry had left town
on vacation. The delegates met instead with Lieutenant Governor Joseph
Montoya, requesting public works jobs and an extension of unemployment benefits beyond twenty weeks.[45] Some unemployed workers got
jobs building state roads, but the legislature did not extend their unemployment benefits. Local 890 then lobbied for surplus food to be delivered
to unemployed miners' families and for the state welfare department to
provide more funds to indigent families, and the union's membership
authorized a transfer of strike funds to an unemployment fund. Only with
the gradual reopening of the mines in 1950, however, did mining families
regain some financial security.

Rejecting the Status of Sons

Masculinity often carries with it one form or another of individualism, an assertion of self against other. The same workplace danger that required mutual help also required individual courage, and women's absence from mines and mills ensured that this courage would be associated with men. Mine-Mill asserted workers' individual and collective adulthood against management's treatment of them as children. In the eyes of mining managers, Mexican workers were docile, prone to laziness, and indifferent to work conditions that "Americans" would not tolerate, and they needed the firm paternalistic governance that a mining company provided. This position, with its strands of class, culture, race, and gender ideologies, contributed to and justified the dual-wage system.

There were, of course, plenty of examples of Mexican and Mexican American workers who forcefully pressed their claims upon a bewildered management, both in Mexico and in the Southwest. Chino general manager Horace Moses probably had clear memories of Mexican American coal miners rising up in Gallup, where during the 1920s and 1930s he oversaw the Gallup American Coal Company and its violent repression of labor organizing. But these counterexamples only underscored, for management, the need for discipline. Managers variously saw Mexican Americans as docile or unruly and interpreted both as evidence of Mexican Americans' cultural immaturity and inferiority. But from the standpoint of Mexican American miners, when they challenged management by joining Mine-Mill and demanding better wages and work conditions, they were also challenging both the cultural definition of Mexicans as ethnically or racially inferior and the paternalistic labor relations in the mines and mills. They vindicated both their manhood and their Mexican ethnicity by rejecting the deference that companies expected from them.

Two features of Mine-Mill fostered this kind of masculinity. First, by the late 1940s, many of its members were war veterans, and returning veterans were little disposed to tolerate the old racial order. They wanted to be treated with respect; they wanted their dignity and manhood honored. Veterans often took the lead in pursuing grievances, ensuring that management promoted workers according to clear lines of seniority, and organizing their fellow workers. The union leadership clearly valued this infusion of veterans. Union records regularly noted whether someone was a veteran, and the leadership stressed its members' veteran status in its appeals to local opinion or state government. And although plenty of women served in the armed forces, the status of veteran was very clearly a masculine one: these were men who had risked their lives fighting for the country.[46] In this manner, affronts to these men's dignity and manhood— as, for example, might be found in a paternalist mining company—were cast as affronts to the nation's own honor.[47]

Second, Mine-Mill itself became more adversarial toward the companies after World War II, a change that reflected changes in Communist Party (CP) policy. As we saw in Chapter 3, once the United States entered World War II, Mine-Mill observed the no-strike pledge to the letter; the party and the union alike pressed for all-out war production. For many labor leaders in the United States at the time (and for historians since then), this policy fundamentally compromised workers' power. But in the Southwest, Mine-Mill organizers used the no-strike pledge to claim legitimacy. With this political capital, they insisted that discrimination against Mexican Americans jeopardized war production. During the war, then, Mine-Mill abandoned one aspect of militancy—strikes— while reinforcing another aspect—uncompromising assaults on the dual-wage system.

After the war, the CP rejected what was labeled "Browderism." Earl Browder, longtime leader of the U.S. party, had imagined that the United States and the Soviet Union could and likely would coexist peacefully (he based this on Roosevelt's and Stalin's behavior at the 1943 Teheran conference); as a corollary, Browder predicted a softening of class struggle in the United States and less need for communists to have a political party. Toward the end of World War II, though, pressure from abroad persuaded American Communists to abandon this "revisionist" position and prepare for a full-scale assault by capitalists, which would culminate in a war of capitalism against socialism.[48] Along similar lines, Mine-Mill in the Southwest reclaimed strikes and shop-floor conflict as definitive characteristics of militancy. Leo Ortiz, an international organizer who occasionally visited Grant County, urged Kennecott locals to prepare "for the [coming] negotiation . . . , which is going to be a tough one to settle, because the odds are against the working man since the war ended. So we must really get down to business and work harder than ever so that we can keep all of the things that we gained during the war by the aid of the War Labor Board."[49] "If we have the guts to stand firm," the chairman of the national Kennecott Council told his union brothers, "we'll get at least the national pattern. If we're gutless we throw away those millions [of Kennecott's profits] and lose our self respect, and the Companies will laugh up their collective sleeve."[50]

American industrialists did in fact go on the offensive after overwhelming waves of strikes in 1945 and 1946. Moreover, companies like Asarco and USSRMC used the unemployment crises of 1949 and 1950 to try to win wage concessions from its workers. Mine-Mill's insistence that it was both militant and democratic was part of its strategy to deal with the turning political and economic tide: it was militant because it rejected what it considered the class collaboration of other CIO unions, and it was democratic because its members voted on all questions before it. It was a "fighting union" that was not afraid to stand up to the bosses.

Local 890 went on the counteroffensive. As we saw in Chapter 3, workers without contracts started striking at the slightest provocation. Some union grievances hinted at workers' attempts to defend their dignity, and the rhetoric of masculinity regularly appeared in the union's descriptions of encounters with management. Utimio Udero, for instance, protested a foreman's "unjust" complaint against him and reported with satisfaction that the foreman "got pretty bad marks for himself" as a result.[51] Clinton Jencks exhorted union men to "sit up tight against the company and show our powers. . . . The unions are to be prepared to stop [it] in [its] tracks."[52] Later that month, Jencks asked Chino general manager Horace Moses, "What's it going to be, strike or settlement?" Moses first balked, but then, seeing that the Kennecott workers would go out on strike, he changed his mind. As Local 63's secretary recorded, "So far we have reached the point that we have made the company say uncle although the fight is not over yet. We got to maintain our readings because we got fighting to do. Keep pressure up."[53] This union officer connected forceful action with the political education that Mine-Mill provided, both tactics helping to establish new class relations in the mines: forcing a company to "say uncle," after all, is hardly the action of a dutiful son. A final area of Mine-Mill activism took place at the inquests held to investigate mine fatalities. Beginning in 1947, Jencks started attending these inquests. At first he was not permitted to ask questions, but soon he became a regular figure at the inquests and joined in questioning the witnesses and managers.

Certainly the union enjoyed no monopoly on asserting masculinity. Albert Mracek, editor of the *New Mexico Miner and Prospector* in Silver City, burst with gendered rhetoric when he exhorted mining men to join the New Mexico Miners and Prospectors Association in April 1944:

> If you want to be out in front where the danger is, and where the men get separated from the boys; if you want to be dug into the fox holes of industry when we've liquidated the last of the Huns

and the little yellow b-b-brothers; if you want to be in there
cursing and pounding the table in the interests of fair play and
common sense when the post-war plans are being drawn in final
form; if you want to tackle reconstruction with the cold steel of
confidence in your outfit; if you want to play your part in fighting
off government of the bureaucrats, by the bureaucrats and for
the bureaucrats; and if you want to look 'em in the eye as they
come back from the hell of Europe and the South Pacific, and
not flinch.[54]

ACTION BEYOND THE WORKPLACE

Companies extended their power far beyond the district's mines, mills,
and smelters, and Mine-Mill soon felt powerful enough to challenge the
wider political economy. Some companies owned their camps outright;
others influenced schools, churches, and town governments indirectly.
Segregation, which defined most aspects of local society, was not neutral;
it was pernicious, and union men assaulted it with the same urgency that
characterized their work-related dealings with companies. Mine-Mill Local 890 became more than a labor union in the late 1940s. It became a
political and civil rights organization, too, attacking those institutions
that favored rich over poor, Anglo over Mexican American.[55]

Politics

Not all of this was new, of course; Mine-Mill had formed a political action
committee as early as 1942, when it endorsed Democratic candidates and
registered voters.[56] Political work moved to center stage in the fall of 1944
when the CIO's Political Action Committee mobilized unions across the
country to register voters. Seferino Anchondo and Verne Curtis, international representatives for Mine-Mill in Grant County, opened an office
on Bullard Street in Silver City to promote Roosevelt's candidacy and the
sale of war bonds.[57]

But there was a difference between this activism and that which took
place later in the decade. In 1948 the union launched its own candidates
under the banner of the New Party (later called the Independent Progressive Party). This move signaled that union men were abandoning a
second-class status, that they were laying claim to the political tools long
denied them; it also indicated the union's distance from the mainstream

CIO and closeness to the CP.[58] Early in January 1948, Local 890's executive board started talking about a third party. Local 890 voted unanimously to endorse Henry Wallace for president at its February 26 meeting and linked the two main parties to monopoly capitalism, which it held responsible for deepening racial discrimination. "Workers in this section of our nation," the union declared, "particularly feel the pressure of the corporations and their straw bosses. Mexican-American workers see monopoly capital used to keep discrimination alive. Any division of race means lack of unity in contract demands. Men divided, even by the myth of race superiority, cannot fight effectively for better wages and working conditions."[59]

Nominated for U.S. senator was Brígido Provencio, a forty-two-year-old Kennecott employee at Hurley. Provencio grew up in Grant County and farmed before heading to the mines. Before the amalgamation, Provencio was an officer in Local 69; afterward, he represented the Hurley workers on Local 890's executive board. Also running were Clinton Jencks for U.S. representative, Juan Chacón for state senator, Magdaleno Luján for Grant County sheriff, and Henry Jaramillo for state representative.[60] About thirty people traveled to El Paso for a Wallace rally in October, with Local 890 covering some of the transportation costs.[61]

Local 890 did not completely abandon the Democrats: Albert Muñoz, who presided over Local 890's Santa Rita unit and represented Santa Rita workers on 890's executive board, filed that year for the Democratic nomination for state senator.[62] Muñoz had lived in Santa Rita all his life, except for a brief stint at Eastern New Mexico Junior College in Portales, and he studied law by correspondence with LaSalle University in Chicago. Like many Mine-Mill activists, Muñoz served in the armed forces during World War II, first as a machine gunner and then as a laboratory technician with the medical corps.[63] He lost the Democratic primary in June but garnered a respectable 1,344 votes to C. C. Royall Sr.'s 2,471.[64]

The Wallace campaign failed in Grant County as it did all over the country. Grant County voters backed Harry Truman over Thomas Dewey by 3,530 votes to 1,997; Wallace claimed 107 votes. Local New Party candidates, though not winning office, fared slightly better. Provencio got 129 votes, Jencks got 149, and Chacón got 126; Magdaleno Luján, though, got only 75 votes.[65] Some voters had faith in the abilities and commitment of Jencks, Chacón, and Provencio, but they did not follow those union leaders into Wallace's camp.[66]

Muñoz's bid and the Wallace campaign failed, but they revealed a sense of entitlement: Mexican Americans believed themselves worthy of holding elected office. Backing Juan Chacón, Brígido Provencio, and others signaled that some people in the union believed that Mexican American workers had something to offer.[67] They built on the groundwork laid by a few Mexican Americans who gained prominence in state and county party machinery. Among them was Joe V. Morales, a cousin of Joe T. Morales, who worked at Santa Rita and who portrayed Sal Ruiz in *Salt of the Earth*. Joe V. Morales owned the Silver Tavern, a bar in Silver City. He spoke regularly at political rallies in Grant County and was "in demand as a spellbinder over the state, his speeches in Spanish especially arousing partisan enthusiasm among the native people."[68]

If Mexican American candidates were relatively new, the "Spanish vote" was already understood to be important, at least in some elections. Many campaigns went by in which no candidates specifically appealed to Mexican Americans, but two Silver City mayoral elections, in 1947 and 1951, suggest that a Mexican American voting bloc mattered to candidates and, possibly, to Anglo voters.[69] By the 1950s, Mine-Mill held the balance of power in many local elections. Even if politicians disliked the "red" union, Local 890 activist Lorenzo Torrez recalled, they liked its members' votes.[70] Candidates often sought union endorsement, which suggests that the union either reflected or shaped the voting practices of its members.

Local 890 supporters were decisive in at least one 1950 election. In the fall of 1950, shortly after the Empire Zinc strike began, Local 890 mobilized its members and their wives to drive Sheriff Bartley McDonald, a local rancher and Democrat associated with an explosive case of police brutality in the town of Fierro in May 1949, from office. They backed Republican Leslie Goforth instead, and Goforth edged McDonald out by a slim margin. As became obvious during the Empire Zinc strike, however, Goforth hardly proved a steady friend to the union.

Asociación Nacional Mexicana Americana

The Fierro case, as the 1949 police brutality incident came to be known, sparked the formation of a local chapter of a new national civil rights organization, the Asociación Nacional Mexicana Americana, or ANMA.[71] ANMA's mission was to promote Mexican American dignity by defending Mexican Americans' political and cultural rights.[72] Wherever Mexican Americans suffered police brutality, be it in Fierro, New Mexico, or Los Angeles, California, ANMA came out in protest. Early in the 1950s, it boycotted *The Judy Canova Show* because of the stereotyped cartoon character "Pedro," whose simpering voice was provided by Mel Blanc, and persuaded the show's sponsor to withdraw support.[73] ANMA worked with the left-wing Committee for the Protection of the Foreign-Born to defend Mexican Americans, particularly working-class leaders, against deportation.[74] The organization publicized the difficulties facing miners in New Mexico and beet workers in Colorado. And when the Empire Zinc strike began, it organized a campaign to support the strikers, identifying the strike as one of the most important in protecting Mexican American rights.

ANMA's defense of young Mexican American men in the Fierro case was an example of union members' assertions of dignified manhood not only in the workplace but also increasingly in society at large. The case grew out of a confrontation between two deputy sheriffs, Lem Watson and Albert Parra, and some young miners at the Fierro Nite Club on the night of Saturday, April 30, 1949. Rubén Arzola, one of the miners, left the dance hall with a friend around midnight, and Watson arrested him outside the club for drunk and disorderly conduct; Arzola's friend protested, and Watson arrested him as well.[75] First Watson told the two friends to get in the back seat of his police car, but then he told them to move to the front seat. At this point, the accounts by union people and the deputy sheriff sharply diverged.

In the union version, Watson began to beat Arzola when the latter tried to move to the front seat. A crowd soon gathered outside the dance hall. "The dancers verbally protested against Watson's physical abuse of Arzola," stated an ANMA-produced fact sheet. "Thereupon Watson— who is notorious throughout Grant County for his anti-Mexican feelings —pulled out his pistol. He first shot Rubén Arzola in the leg, and then giving way to his inner feelings, shot his guns into the crowd. Under this rain of bullets two others were wounded; Lopi Márquez in the leg and Valdemar Herrera in the arm. . . . It was only after Watson had fired his guns, that the people in self-defense and anger began to throw rocks at his car and finally overturned it."[76] ANMA criticized Watson alone, making no mention of Parra, a Mexican American.

The deputy sheriffs saw things differently. Relating their account, the *Silver City Daily Press* emphasized the risk that both officers took during the incident: "The mob—an estimated fifty persons—attacked the two officers and turned the prisoners loose. . . . Arzola was shot while assertedly [sic] fleeing [and] Lupe Rodríguez 'apparently was hit by a stray bullet.' Watson and Parra told [Sheriff Bartley] McDonald that they had to draw guns in self defense after the mob swept over them, hit Watson with a rock, and overturned their automobile."[77] Arzola went to the county jail, and Márquez, according to ANMA, went to the hospital.

But the episode did not end there, for the next day the sheriffs rounded up several more men at the Zarape Nite Club in Bayard. Two union representatives, Jencks and Local 890 president Angel Bustos, went to the police station to see who had been arrested. They could not get a full list, so Jencks returned Monday morning. McDonald told Jencks that "only a minister, a lawyer or a doctor could see the prisoners." "He told me," McDonald continued, "he was counsel for the prisoners and I told him he wasn't a lawyer and, as far as I was concerned, could quit meddling with the case."[78] Jencks left, and the sheriff's department continued to arrest men in the mining district; ten men in all spent time in jail. Jencks returned on Thursday with attorney C. C. Royall Jr., in order to check the disposition of those cases that had not yet reached the docket of Justice of the Peace Andrew Haugland. Local 890 was worried that the detainees were not having charges brought against them and were not being permitted to see their families.[79] This encounter ended with a "one-punch fight." McDonald told Jencks that they "were arraigning the prisoners as fast as possible." Then, McDonald continued, "[Jencks] called me a liar. I got mad and let him have one. I'm sorry it happened but I don't like to be called a liar."[80] Jencks did not admit having called McDonald a liar. "I [was] not trying to stick up for anyone who is guilty," he explained. "[I wanted] to see that those who are arrested get an even break. McDonald got mad and hit me."[81]

The shootings, arrests, and assault led Mine-Mill leaders to call a meeting for the following evening, May 6. Three hundred people reportedly showed up to hear testimony "of police brutality [from] those who had been picked up or interrogated." They created the Grant County chapter of the Asociación Nacional Mexicana Americana, electing officers and issuing four demands:

1. Guarantee the constitutional rights of anyone arrested.

2. Removal of Deputy-Sheriff Lem Watson from the police force.

3. An end to "trigger-happy cops" and the abuse of justice.

4. The hiring of lawyers for the defense of those arrested and the wounded.[82]

A month later, ANMA financial secretary Arturo Flores reported that petitions to remove Watson had over 300 signatures, 200 people had joined ANMA, and the Fierro defendants now had a defense committee and lawyers to represent them.[83]

ANMA continued its defense of young Mexican American men in Grant County, even when the organization was otherwise defunct. By 1953, the national office listed no members in New Mexico or Texas, and ANMA letterhead was widely in use as scrap paper, if Local 890's archives are any gauge.[84] Yet there is some evidence that Grant County's ANMA revived its activities when a particular situation called upon its expertise. Early in 1953, for instance, union notes made during the filming of *Salt of the Earth* refer to getting ANMA's help for two Mexican American youth. Pete Peña, a sixteen-year-old from Hurley, was hard of hearing and had difficulty in school. His teacher wanted to put him in reform school, and ANMA tried to get a doctor's statement documenting Peña's medical condition. ANMA also secured legal services for Louis Márquez, age seventeen, who was in jail awaiting trial for stealing a crank shaft.[85]

ANMA was the most concrete example in Grant County of class-based organizing to redress racial discrimination in all areas of society. While it was intended to be a cross-class organization of Mexican Americans and sympathetic Anglos, all of its leaders were affiliated with Mine-Mill. Its mesa directiva (board of directors) in 1949 and 1950 included Alberto Muñoz, president; José Carrillo, vice president; Arturo Flores, financial secretary; and members Cipriano Montoya, Clinton Jencks, Henry Jaramillo, and Albert Vigil. Women were conspicuously absent from leadership positions in Grant County's chapter of ANMA, a fact all the more remarkable given ANMA's use of family iconography and its efforts to organize families, not just individuals, in California.[86]

ANMA entered politics both locally and in the state at large. It registered voters in Grant County, and with help from Local 890's Political Action Fund, it paid workers for the wages they lost if they spent election day driving voters to the polls. It even sent its own members to El Paso to register Mexican Americans there, which was a bold challenge to the political order because Texas was well known for its disfranchisement of African Americans and Mexican Americans. Lorenzo Torrez, who led ANMA's state chapter in 1951, recalled the campaign to elect a Mexican American mayor in El Paso: "The problem in Texas was that in order . . . to register to vote, you had to have property. So we went, and we recruited people to register, and we argued successfully—I don't remember if we had lawyers—that a *ring* was property. A *watch* was property. And in that way we forced the county to accept the registration of hundreds of voters. You had to transport them to the courthouse, so we went from Bayard. And the mayor got elected when it came to vote."[87] Torrez remembered that ANMA helped bring legal suits against restrictive housing covenants.[88] The state chapter of ANMA, over which Arturo Flores presided in 1949, also tracked the situation of *braceros* in El Paso and lobbied state officials about Grant County's unemployment.[89] And in league with the union's ladies' auxiliary, ANMA publicized school segregation in Silver City. It hoped to use the information it gathered—on the quality of schools, facilities, books, and teachers—to present a case before New Mexico's Fair Employment Commission.[90]

ANMA accomplished a great deal, both nationally and in Grant County, but it existed only a short while. There are hints that membership was flagging in the early 1950s, which one activist, writing to Mine-Mill's Maurice Travis from California, attributed to top-down leadership. But the real demise came at the hand of the U.S. attorney general, who promulgated a list of "subversive organizations" that, by definition, were required to register with the Department of Justice as foreign agents. Many leftist organizations landed on this list, and the measure harmed the designated organizations whether they registered properly or not. For ANMA in 1953, already weakened by threats of deportation of several leaders, the general atmosphere of McCarthyism, and its own structural problems, the attorney general's list was the last straw: ANMA disbanded in December 1953.

Influencing Local 890's and ANMA's activism was the CP's theoretical position on Mexican Americans. Recognizing that oppression of Mexican Americans was similar to that of African Americans, Communists relied on considerations of "the Negro Question" in interpreting Mexican American conditions. But Communists also recognized that Mexican Americans occupied a social, economic, and historical position different from that of African Americans; for this reason, there came to be a greater—albeit inconsistent—emphasis on culture and nationality as Communists connected "Anglo chauvinism" and American imperialism to the denigration of Mexican culture. Anglo chauvinism combined national and racial prejudices.[91] While Anglo chauvinism possessed different historical roots from white chauvinism, the consequences were similar: appalling living conditions, poor health, few job opportunities beyond manual labor, and residential segregation.[92] San Antonio labor activist Emma Tenayuca and her husband, Texas Communist leader Homer D. Brooks, wrote one of the most penetrating analyses of the conditions facing Mexican Americans and Mexican nationals in the Southwest. They advocated a program that took language and culture into account, as well as the material conditions of segregation, economic exploitation, and political repression.[93] All of these considerations found expression in the activism of Local 890 and of ANMA in New Mexico.

THE UNION FAMILY

Local 890 broadened its mission in the late 1940s to include civil rights activism, and the union's leadership saw that this larger mission required a wider and deeper base of support. Moreover, many union men understood how much workplace struggles—especially strikes—depended on family and community support. Wives who misunderstood why their husbands went on strike were likely to pressure their husbands to go back to work. Consequently, at the same time that Local 890's leadership promoted a masculine militancy, it was also advancing a different vision of the union community—the union family.[94]

The impetus for women's and community organization lay with the Jenckses, both of whom had backgrounds in community organizing and were familiar with labor history, in which women's participation had proven critical. "Without women," Clinton Jencks later observed, "the union was organizing with one hand tied behind its back."[95] Moreover, the Jenckses belonged to a political culture that was beginning to refine a class-conscious feminism. The CP had drawn many women into its activities, especially in neighborhoods ravaged by the Depression. But the party had been rather theoretically vacant on "the Woman Question," as the problem of sexism was called. To Communists, feminism was, by definition, bourgeois, for it masked the real class struggle and advanced bourgeois women at the expense of working-class women. Feminists argued for an equal rights amendment in the 1930s and 1940s, while Communists, trade unionists, and progressives opposed it for fear of dismantling the protective labor legislation that, they believed, benefited women workers.[96] At some odds with this model were "labor feminists," as historian Dorothy Sue Cobble has called them, who also opposed the equal rights amendment and used labor organizing of working-class women to advance a broader agenda of social justice.[97]

Still, the late 1930s and 1940s had witnessed some Communist considerations of the Woman Question that transcended the simplistic maxim that women's status could approach equality with men's only after a socialist revolution. Mary Inman's 1939 book, *In Woman's Defense*, began with Friedrich Engels's *Origin of the Family, Private Property and the State*: men began to subjugate women when men began to accumulate private property.[98] To this Inman added the insight that housework was a form of productive social labor worthy of Communist organizing and agitation.[99] This was not a new insight—Socialist women earlier in the century had similarly critiqued housework—but it would prove central to the gender politics depicted in *Salt of the Earth*.[100] The party hierarchy, however, disavowed Inman's analysis.[101] Still, even though the CP barely acknowledged women's issues, it was an institution in which men could be criticized for being "backward on the Woman Question."[102] This room to criticize men for sexism made the CP unique among male-dominated political institutions.

And more than in official publications, the Woman Question received attention in informal discussions and in organizations beyond the party's direct control. There we find hints that women were raising substantive issues that men, and male leaders, were likely to dismiss as trivial. Betty Millard, a Communist journalist who wrote on Latin America (and visited Grant County on one of her speaking tours), authored the pamphlet *Woman against Myth* (1948), drawing attention to women's history and to the psychological, economic, and legal dimensions of "delimiting . . . women to the role of wife and mother."[103] Her pamphlet is notable for its celebration of nineteenth-century feminists without dismissing them for their class background; in it Millard lamented the vast historical ignorance of women's struggles. In this respect, *Woman against Myth* resembles the work taken up by the Congress of American Women (CAW), a women's organization that attracted women from a range of political beliefs. The CAW pushed a leftist agenda that did not trivialize women's issues and emphasized the importance of women's history; prominent women's historians Gerda Lerner and Eleanor Flexner belonged to this organization.[104] It should come as no surprise, then, that Millard belonged to the CAW.[105]

Inspired by new views like these, as well as by her own background in political organizing, Virginia Jencks walked house to house in Grant County's mining towns, knocking on doors and striking up conversations with miners' wives. She encouraged them to come to union meetings, where families would eat, play games, perhaps watch a movie, or talk about political issues. Virginia Chacón, who soon joined Jencks, found that "some women were interested, but it sounded like they were scared" of their husbands.[106] Indeed, it took some doing to get men to invite their wives to union meetings. Clinton Jencks worked first on the executive committee, repeatedly urging union officers to bring their wives to meetings, and these men then tried to persuade others in their work units.[107]

The power of voting probably helped some women get more involved in union activities. At Local 890's meeting to discuss the injunction, women were voting alongside men—or, more accurately in this case, against them. Their numbers ensured that the resolution would get taken seriously; had men alone voted, there is little chance that the women's picket would have taken shape. The right for auxiliary members to vote was a provision of the international union, confirmed at its 1936 convention. There Ida Smith and T. L. Williams of Montana's newly formed auxiliaries reminded their union brothers that the auxiliaries paid fees to the international and to deny women the vote was to practice taxation without representation. Their resolution carried, and the women also helped defeat a counterresolution that would explicitly deny women voting privileges.[108] Women in other CIO auxiliaries were "astounded beyond words" that Mine-Mill women were "given a voice and a vote on the convention floor."[109] The Mine-Mill union thus granted a formal right that Local 890 would extend into the local union's business.

The parameters of Local 890's woman suffrage are unclear, however, and we should not exaggerate Mine-Mill's commitment to women's equality. The international auxiliary had no money to work with— just the international's postage, for which they were duly thankful—and found few men actually willing to help local auxiliaries get started.[110] Auxiliaries always got the leftovers. In 1941, one auxiliary complained that "the membership books provided by the international offices for the auxiliaries are of such a poor quality that they fall to pieces after a year's use, and . . . so outdated that they state on the front cover that we are affiliated with the A.F. of L.—which we resent."[111] And, most importantly, men seem to have been uneasy about women's participation in their conventions. There was a lot of nervous jocularity about women wearing the pants, or men trying to keep women tied to the bedpost, comments that diverted serious discussion into frivolous channels that eventually dried up. In 1940, for instance, men constantly resorted to jokes when they introduced or responded to women speakers. But Ora Valentine of Park City, Utah, put her foot down. "I don't know why it is that every time the ladies get up it is taken for something funny. That is all right. You are laughing at us. You fellows earn your money and bring it home—and I hope you give it to your wives to spend—but unless your wives are organized, they do not care whether the money goes for a union-made article or a scab article."[112] To protest that behavior, as Valentine did, was to run the risk of even more ridicule; that she was not further ridiculed testifies to the willingness of at least some men to accord her some respect.

Conflict over communism was refracted through Mine-Mill's gender politics, too. In 1947, the president of the international auxiliary, Mary Orlich of Butte, Montana, began agitating against the international's left-wing leadership. Montana Mine-Mill activists denounced her "for meddling in union men's affairs." Fights over communism were ugly everywhere, but because of the particular relation of the auxiliary to the international union, the conflict took on a gendered dimension: the international executive board was in a position to dissolve the auxiliary, essentially deeming it unfit to govern itself.[113] President Maurice Travis told all local auxiliaries to pay dues only to the international Mine-Mill office, not to the international auxiliary leadership, and declared that the funds would be held in escrow until the auxiliary problems were resolved.[114] The executive board soon tried to revive the auxiliary, but the bitterness of these events debilitated the Montana auxiliaries.[115]

Grant County union women formed Ladies' Auxiliary 209 in 1948, after the uprising in the international auxiliary was quelled, and anticommunism does not seem to have figured at all in its internal politics. Instead we find that auxiliary activity was a source of women's class consciousness, which ultimately gave them the confidence to propose that women take over the pickets and the strength to defend the proposal. It is not immediately apparent that ladies' auxiliaries would foster class consciousness, given that they did not take up workplace concerns, much less confront management directly. They were, instead, often the engine of endless rounds of potluck suppers and bingo games, as one recording secretary indicated by adding "bingo $\div$ bingo = bingo" to meeting minutes in 1949.[116] But their distance from the workplace, both in terms of activity and relation to management, should not blind us to their possible role in class formation.

In the United States and Canada, most union auxiliaries were formed in the midst of crisis, usually a strike during which women shouldered the burden of providing food, clothes, cash, and morale to strikers' families. Demonstrations, pickets, parades, medical assistance, visits to the homes of strikers and strikebreakers, and lecture tours rounded out auxiliary strike activities. Auxiliaries also typically promoted the union label (particularly among AFL auxiliaries), pushed for public relief, worked for prolabor figures in local politics and civic organizations, and generally spread the union gospel as far as possible. That there were endless rounds of potlucks is not too far from the truth, since most auxiliaries faced the decidedly unglamorous task of raising money through bake sales, lotteries, and socials.

What did such activities mean for women? One way to understand them is to place them along axes that stretch from the "domestic" to the "social" and then to the "political," or from the "traditional" to the "nontraditional." Traditional activities projected women's domesticity onto the union community; they included organizing socials and dances, cooking, offering medical care to wounded strikers, and buying only union-made products and services. They were often associated with domestic life and, importantly, with what historian Patricia Yeghissian calls the "nagging wife syndrome"—the hostility of wives toward their husbands' union, and especially toward strikes. Nontraditional, political activities, by contrast, could broaden women's perspective and make women into staunch unionists; these activities included demonstrating, speaking in public, picketing, and joining political campaigns. Many historians have found women following a trajectory from the social to the political, often through the course of a strike. Women in the 1937 Flint sit-down strike auxiliary, for example, started out staffing the kitchens and moved on to perform in the Living Newspaper, a Works Progress Administration theater project. Journalist Mary Heaton Vorse observed that women started out helping their husbands but ended up discovering themselves and developing a social awareness.[117] Arizona women in the 1983 Phelps-Dodge strike contrasted their work in the 1980s with that of earlier auxiliaries: they believed it was now more "political."[118] Thus in this configuration, women developed class consciousness by moving beyond the domestic. Of course, as the example of the international Mine-Mill auxiliary shows, a movement into the "political"—in this instance, into the conflict over communism—could embroil an auxiliary in conflicts with the male-led union.

In explaining women's class consciousness, many historians have been perhaps too quick to speak in terms of a public/private dichotomy, even to the point of assuming the concrete existence of separate spheres.[119] Often, though, the boundaries were permeable. Women in Kansas mining towns of the 1920s, for instance, would shame their husbands publicly by refusing to bring lunch (a domestic task) to the mine.[120] Auxiliaries occupied a contradictory position: they were based on women's secondary, "helpmeet" role, but once women acted at all they were thrust into the public sphere, which in turn altered domestic relations.[121]

A second way to understand women's developing class consciousness is to root it in the domestic realm itself, either because women's household conditions fostered a class perspective on the world or because the domestic realm extended beyond the immediate household and into the community. Women food rioters in Barcelona around the turn of the century, for example, acted collectively and defiantly because high prices prevented them from meeting their families' needs; their riots were not based on a feminist consciousness that questioned the sexual division of labor but rather on a "female consciousness" that strenuously upheld it.[122] In the 1970s, one Kentucky coal miner's wife declared, "Ain't no man gonna take *my* husband's job and git away with it!"[123] Like the Barcelona food rioters, this woman, acting through the union auxiliary, struggled to stave off a direct and personal threat to her own well-being, dignity, and survival. Women in Lawrence, Massachusetts, early in the twentieth century moved in and out of the paid workforce, but they always kept close family and community ties to the local textile mills. Their domestic world extended beyond their individual houses and into the streets of their neighborhoods. And out of the networks that women formed with their neighbors, out of the "material reality of everyday life," came their unprecedented support for the textile strikes in 1912 and after.[124]

Related to this interpretation is a third, in which women develop class consciousness out of their own experiences as working-class household laborers. Coal miners' wives in Ludlow, Colorado, supported their husbands' 1913 strike because they had direct experience of the company's abuse of power. They lived in a company town, in which the Colorado Fuel and Iron Company owned or otherwise controlled the houses, the stores, the schools, and the churches, and it was hard work to raise children, clean houses, and budget food in such a setting.[125] Similarly, a defense of their own interests pushed Canadian women to join auxiliaries of the International Association of Machinists early in the twentieth century.[126]

Tracing the progression from domestic to political action does help explain the activities of the ladies' auxiliary in Grant County, though theirs were without the conflicts over communism experienced by the Montana local auxiliaries. Auxiliary 209, like the union as a whole, did not single-mindedly wage class struggle. It frequently confined itself instead to the stuff of ladies' auxiliary legend: potlucks and bingo, or social activities that seemed an extension of women's domestic life. The mathematical discovery that "bingo ÷ bingo = bingo" points both to the tedium inherent in much auxiliary work and to one anonymous woman's impatience with it. Enchilada suppers, dances, bingo, and socials were all part of women's work to raise money for the union. Women brought food to picket lines, registered voters, lobbied against school segregation, and lobbied the state government regarding unemployment, thus matching the "political" side of the auxiliary coin too.

But equally important is to consider what women's participation—and, more broadly, gender—meant for the *union's* activism, for the range of issues that the union believed it should address. From this angle, we can see two important markers regarding gender in the union. The first is the degree to which women joined a union movement in an industry that almost exclusively employed men. Women's participation in Local 890's activities—whatever the source or goals of those activities—can thus be understood as one gauge of the union's critique of existing power relations and its breadth of political vision. For if women were involved, then the union perceived the need for action beyond the mines, mills, and smelters, into which hardly any women entered. The second marker regarding gender is the degree to which power relations between men and women concerned the union. Some of the most stirring moments in *Salt of the Earth*—and, importantly, some of the most comic—are when people throw precisely those power relations into question. But the union as a whole did not concern itself with relations between men and women before the Empire Zinc strike.

When the Empire Zinc strike began in 1950, women and men were keenly aware of the threat to their union. True, the Korean War made employment more secure, but mining companies still enjoyed anticommunist weapons that a hot war against communism would only make more powerful. Within the first month of the Empire Zinc strike, the ladies' auxiliary unobtrusively began to support the strikers. Wives and sisters of Local 890 members served on all of the strike committees save the negotiating committee. With the auxiliary's help, the local sponsored a Christmas benefit and then a "Jamaica" party, or carnival, complete with the coronation of township queen, in February.

For the first eight months, then, women's work looked very much like the "traditional" or "domestic" activities of many auxiliaries. But the seemingly trivial nature of these activities should not obscure the serious groundwork being laid for sustained, and difficult, organizing. The auxiliary integrated existing leadership, like Virginia Jencks, Virginia Chacón, and Clorinda Alderette, with newly active women like Braulia Velásquez, the wife of the negotiating committee's chairman. Velásquez admitted

that she "had never been an active woman in Union affairs up to the time
the strike occurred." "I had always been blind as to what my husband was
doing in his Union affairs," she said. "I first got a vague idea of what the
Union meant when the Empire Zinc Company started discriminating
against my husband in 1948."[127] Yet despite women's own reasons for
supporting the strike, and their participation in all facets of the strike
except the picketing, union documents continued to identify women
as secondary players at best. Publicity and internal union documents
consistently referred to "strikers" and "striking brothers" rather than to
"strikers' families." Men were still considered the workers on whom the
strike centered. This would change during the summertime.

Using this first measure—the mere presence of women's organization—we can see that some women were very committed to the union,
and that, importantly, their commitment took an institutional, rather
than haphazard or casual, form. But there is the second level on which to
analyze women's participation in Auxiliary 209. When Local 890 expanded its membership to include women, it did not thereby expand its
mission to include addressing issues defined as "women's" issues. In other
words, inviting women to join union activities did not necessarily mean
placing women's issues within the union's purview. Before the Empire
Zinc strike, the class and community goals toward which the union and
its auxiliary directed their energies did not question relations between
men and women.

And there were certainly hints that all was not well on the domestic
front. Cipriano Montoya, an 890 leader, was known to abuse his wife,
Feliciana (Chana), but the union leadership—and the party leadership,
for both Montoyas were in the party—did not broach the subject with
him.[128] Even if Cipriano Montoya's abusive behavior interfered with his
wife's much-valued contributions to the union movement, people simply
did not discuss such personal affairs.

There is room in comments like Clinton Jencks's—"without women
the union was organizing with one hand tied behind its back"—to imagine how untying that hand might also unleash a power struggle. For men,
the family model was uncomplicated. While union men astutely refused
to accept the company as a "family," seeing it instead as an antagonist
trying to mask its class interests with family rhetoric, they were in no
position to consider the relations between men and women as anything
other than naturally harmonious.

On many occasions in women's history, feminist questions about
the relative power of men and women, questions about women's proper

"place," come up only after women have begun to participate in social movements that ostensibly had nothing to do with gender issues. Only in responding to male hostility did female antislavery activists, for instance, begin to develop principled arguments about women's equality in the mid-nineteenth century. The Empire Zinc strike of 1950–52 would transform women's participation from a defense of community into a challenge over domestic relations and, simultaneously, transform the very community that women had set out to defend. The rift between men and women was partially closed by the definitive vote at 2:30 in the morning. The family vision held sway; the unity that women and men achieved was imposed by one side winning out over the other. But events on the picket line and back at home would prove men correct in one sense: the natural order was threatened.

PART II

THE WOMEN'S PICKET

5

Political Consciousness and
Community Formation

The road was about fifteen feet wide, unpaved, uneven. It was an easy walk in work boots but a little trickier in ladies' shoes, especially in predawn darkness. Older women held the arms of their neighbors, sisters, or daughters as they walked to a hut within sight of the massive headframe above Empire Zinc's mine. From down the road came cars, one or two at a time, slowing and then edging off the road to park; more women and kids got out and joined the group at picket headquarters. The picket captain took charge and formed them into a circle in the middle of the road. As the sun came up the women's picket was well under way.

Dolores Jiménez was one of the women who had come from a distance, carpooling with neighbors for the twelve-mile drive north from Hurley. Her husband, Frank, worked at Kennecott, but she had heard about the Empire Zinc strike and its need for women's help, and she had been encouraged to join by her friend Clorinda Alderette. Dolores was young, just twenty-one, but already had two sons under the age of five. It would have been harder to go to the picket that morning had not another woman, a grandmother herself and "not even from working people," offered to watch the children.[1] Other women had children they could still carry, but some picketers, like Anita Torrez, who brought her infant daughter, soon found it very tiring to hold a child while walking all day. The best situation was to have children who no longer needed constant attention, like Daría Chávez's two teenaged sons. It was her family situation as much as her skill and enthusiasm that made Chávez one of the

Women picketing, with men and women on the hillside nearby, summer 1951.
Photo courtesy of Luis Ignacio Quiñones.

picket captains; her sister, Elena Tafoya, found it next to impossible to go to the picket with her many children under age ten.[2]

Beyond the circle of women and children, against a hill by the road, stood a group of men. These were fellow strikers waiting to see if the new strategy would work; they were also husbands and brothers and fathers, waiting to see how their women would behave. The picketers walked "in circles and circles and circles," Dolores Jiménez later recalled, "talking, laughing, singing."[3] They sang "our 'Solidarity Forever,' our union songs" as they walked—or danced, when some men brought guitars to the picket.[4] Some crocheted or knitted. It was, Henrietta Williams thought, the most beautiful thing she had ever seen.[5]

But before the festive mood set in fully, more cars arrived, this time carrying Sheriff Goforth, his twenty-four deputies, and the handful of men who wanted to cross the picket line to work at Empire Zinc. Climbing out of his car, Goforth saw women where there should have been men. Some were no doubt familiar to him; Elvira Molano had been arrested two days before, and Virginia Jencks was already well known. But most were strangers, all were women, and Goforth did not quite know what to do. He may have been among the county officials who "opined that the women were not technically union members and there-

Women picketers trying to shame strikebreakers.
Photo courtesy of Luis Ignacio Quiñones.

fore would not be affected by [Judge] Marshall's order."[6] In any case, he chose to watch carefully rather than act hastily, and the *Silver City Daily Press* reported that "quiet was the rule" on the picket that day.[7]

The strikebreakers were probably also surprised by the women's picket. To Anglos like Grant Blaine or Denzil Hartless, the women were unfamiliar, distinguishable one from the other only by age.[8] Hartless lived in Hanover, but he lived with his family in the Anglo section and probably

Strikebreakers trying to go onto the Empire Zinc property, summer 1951.
Photo courtesy of Luis Ignacio Quiñones.

had little reason to visit the other side of town. Only seventeen years old, he had left school after eighth grade and was working with his brother Carl digging ditches when Empire Zinc announced that it would reopen in June 1951.[9] The two brothers simply saw this as a way to earn some money, not as the start of a career in mining; in Carl's case, he was waiting for induction into the army.[10]

Unlike their Anglo counterparts, Mexican American strikebreakers like Francisco Franco and Jesús Avalos came from the same community as the picketers. Franco had lived in Hanover and the nearby village of Fierro since at least 1939, and Avalos had even been a steward in Local 890—that is, until the union suspended him for helping the company organize its back-to-work movement in April 1951.[11] These two men became special objects of the women's derision as the strike went on, and they responded with insults, abuse, and, at one point, a shotgun.

Things heated up the second day of the picket, when strikebreakers tried, and mostly failed, to sneak onto the company property. Women may have had "problems catching the sneaking scabs, crawling through the pine trees," but few strikebreakers, if any, slipped through their grasp.[12] That night, June 14, women swept into the union hall, eager to tell stories of the picket. "No scabs were crossing our lines," Aurora Chávez announced. Elvira Molano and Daría Chávez exhorted the assembled women—"We don't need men"—to join the picket the next morning. The hundreds who answered their call found the pickets an exciting place to be.

The women's picket, from June 13 until the end of the strike the following January, generated tremendous solidarity. Violent conflict with strikebreakers showed women a collective strength that did not depend on men. On June 15, for example, the strikebreakers were ready to act forcefully against the picketers. Jesús Avalos tried to drive through the line, but the women and children threw rocks and pushed his car back. Grant Blaine and Denzil Hartless tried to move through on foot, but the picketers "grabbed them and tore their shirts."[13] Most of the time, certainly, life on the picket was routine: day after day of walking in circles, making lunches in the picket hut, writing letters to the newspaper, apportioning strike rations. But these activities built the framework for catalyzing, interpreting, and responding to events that were quite out of the ordinary; they required women to organize, and the strength of their organization became apparent in the moments of intense conflict that punctuated the long stretches of routine picketing. Furthermore, by calling into question the injunction's scope, the women created a backdrop of legal uncertainty against which the confrontation between the picketers and the strikebreakers played out while the enforcers of the law could only stand back and wait for the courts to clarify the bounds of their authority. By the time the legal authorities caught up with them—extending the injunction, issuing warrants, making arrests, and hauling them off to jail—the women had gained the collective strength to resist new legal measures. They had filled a legal vacuum with their own solidarity.

The reactions of local police and the courts to picket violence further convinced women picketers that those authorities were aligned with the mining companies and therefore corrupt. This distilled the contest down to one between an illegitimate power structure and a righteous union community. Picketers' confrontations with deputies and judges were confrontations with the institutions of political power, and they generated more than solidarity: they carried lessons about power itself. The women's picket stripped away the mask of power. Women were not just asserting that different people should occupy the positions of power in

Women and children near the picket line, summer 1951. Rudy Chapin, age fourteen, is seated at far left; Daría Chávez, picket captain, is standing at far right. Photo courtesy of Luis Ignacio Quiñones.

Grant County. They were reinvigorating the very concept of legitimacy, basing it in what they considered true justice.[14]

As the Empire Zinc picketers were marking the lines between themselves and their opponents, they found support among many local merchants and businesspeople, but other people increasingly found themselves alienated from the strikers who, opponents believed, were disrupting the community by following the instructions of outsiders. Opponents of the strike were outraged at women's behavior. They laid claim to the legitimacy of citizenship and denied it to the strikers, a denial that drew upon both anticommunism (communists were "un-American") and racism. Alignments gradually hardened over the summer, and by autumn they were explicit, emerging generally, but not always, along ethnic and class lines and finding expression in debates over communism.

JOCKEYING FOR POSITION

By June 15, Sheriff Goforth had gotten over his surprise at seeing the women on the line. That day, District Attorney Tom Foy issued warrants to arrest six women and ordered Goforth to break up the road blocks so that cars with replacement workers could reach the Empire Zinc mine. The following morning, Goforth tried to clear the road. Three women threw rocks at one car, and a deputy pushed Virginia Chacón out of the way of strikebreaker Francisco Franco's car. "So the rest of the women went around me and pushed the car—it was not very far," Chacón recounted. "[They pushed it] back and the other ladies were running up . . . to put [some rocks] on the sides of the road so the car would not go by. And these scabs were pretty much mad at us, were very angry and began calling us names, and were just dirty to us."[15] The women "surrounded the deputies and pushed the car back down the road to an intersection."[16]

Around 10 A.M., the sheriff and his deputies raised the stakes. "[They] took red-covered tear gas grenades, held them in their hands and looked toward the picket line, which consisted then of women and children. Men . . . sat or moved about on the hillside above the road."[17] Into this tense scene a deputy "let go one of the gas grenades. It skewered and rolled among the pickets, spewing the white gas and dispersing the screaming women." But the wind was in the pickets' favor, and they soon reorganized their line.[18] On a hill, "about a hundred women and children . . . cursed and jeered the sheriff. . . . For a moment officers feared violence."[19]

The officers had, of course, committed some of the violence, but Goforth moved in to arrest as many women as he could haul away, in a manner that would later be quite faithfully depicted in *Salt of the Earth*.[20] Once arrested, the women did not resist the deputies. "But until the moment of arrest, sheriff's deputies said, they resisted bitterly."[21] Three carloads of women and children, with Goforth scrambling to round up a school bus for more arrests, made their way to the Grant County jail, which adjoined the courthouse in Silver City. Goforth's arrests, though, did not disperse the picket line; some 300 women remained on the line in Hanover. Lucy Montoya was "proud to be the one who started the second picket line . . . after the D[istrict] A[ttorney]'s gunmen broke [the] first one."[22] "We can keep arresting them," Undersheriff Lewis Brown remarked, "but they keep moving in. We could clear the road, but someone would be hurt in the process."[23]

Fifty-three women were ultimately arrested, and they took their children to jail with them. Braulia Velásquez carried her newborn infant; most of the kids were between the ages of six and ten. Virginia Chacón had never seen the inside of a jail before and was very nervous at first. But when the sheriff told them they could leave if they agreed not to return to the picket, she recounted, "we all responded at the same time we would not go home, we would go back to the picket lines and help our strikers, help our union members."[24] The women refused to leave individually on bail or to make any deals with the district attorney.[25] After that, the women "had a very good time" playing cards, singing, and making "all kinds of noise."[26]

The jail cells were filthy and the food unappealing. "All we had for lunch," Virginia Jencks complained, "was cold beans and a few loaves of bread we couldn't eat."[27] Union attorney David Serna sent food and soft drinks, which jailer Jim Hiler refused to deliver because "orange peelings stop[ped] up prison plumbing and jail rules forb[ade] glass bottles." (Hiler finally ladled soda from a bucket.)[28] Children posed special problems; one had a nosebleed, and Braulia Velásquez's infant cried for its formula.[29] The women made such a racket in the county jail—"the worst mess" that Hiler had ever seen—that Goforth released them that night. "It looks like an endless job," he admitted.[30] And it was. The women returned to the picket that night and the following morning, setting up a picket tent with a stove, cots, and food: a home away from home.[31]

Women's festive and resolute solidarity blossomed in these new circumstances, but it had grown out of their recent history of organizing themselves as miners' wives. The sheriff's offer to release them provided they not return to the picket, for instance, sparked an immediate response—rejection—because the women already knew and trusted each other, and their ultimate victory over the sheriff deepened their faith in one another and in their collective endeavor. The national press failed to perceive the level of organization that permitted women to launch a jail protest. The New York Times, for instance, described the women's resistance to police on the line as "screeches and fingernail attacks," conveying a picture of wild animals.[32] The Communist Party (CP) press also tended to play up the spontaneous and spectacular elements of the jail scene, although it did mention in a light-hearted way that the "wives and children of the miners organized themselves even in jail."[33] The sympathetic CP press reacted to the unusual situation with outrage at the brutality, but it also reported with humor the incongruity of women taking on the local authorities.

Women's organization enabled them to respond to the threats from outside, the most important of which was direct, physical violence, and they often responded violently themselves. Throughout the summer of 1951, violence continued to characterize the relations between the picketers and the sheriff, his deputies, and strikebreakers. These episodes solidified the community spirit that animated the pickets. As Anita Torrez reflected many years later, "At the moment when the ladies took over, there was a lot of fear. [But] being among these women every day, . . . more ladies were eager to participate, [and] we gained confidence. [There was] a moment when you let go of your own fear."[34] In fact, she commented, "once the violence started, everybody wanted to be there. Everyone."[35] The cumulative effect of this violence was not to inure people to it, to make them dismiss it as constituting the normal course of events, but rather to see in its very unexpectedness and intensity the embodiment of the true nature of local power. It sharpened tensions and raised union complaints against local officials to a higher pitch, even as it ennobled the women whose valor was on public display.

To legal authorities like Silver City justice of the peace Andrew Haugland and Sixth District judge A. W. Marshall, these women were far from noble. The scene on the picket line was chaotic, disruptive, and fundamentally at odds with the law and order the judges were bent on enforcing. And to bring that scene into the courthouse, as a hundred picketers and their supporters did on June 18, was truly shocking. That morning, forty-five of the jailed women were scheduled for arraignment, and they "jammed the courthouse corridors" waiting for Haugland to open court. "It's like a picnic," said one woman. "We're having fun—and we're going to stay on the picket line, too."[36] District Attorney Tom Foy had decided not to charge anyone younger than sixteen, and one younger girl complained, "But I fought the sheriffs. I fought 'em good. I hit one real hard and I spit in another's eye."[37] Recording the deputies' complaints and finding all of the arraignees delayed the hearings by almost two hours, and Haugland, a sober Methodist, must have been grinding his teeth by the time the women entered his courtroom in groups of five.[38] All pleaded not guilty. Haugland released them on their own cognizance and ordered them bound for district court. Their case then moved into the jurisdiction of Judge Marshall, who "took elaborate precautions to prevent any outbursts of sentiment during the hearing" on June 21: no photographs, no radio broadcast, no overflow crowd on the floor where the courtroom was located, no standing-room visitors, no entering or leaving during recesses. And no children.[39]

On June 29, in a separate legal case, Judge Marshall decided that the temporary restraining order against the mine workers also covered women and children as agents of the union, and on July 9 he made that injunction permanent.[40] But the new ruling did not cause the same dilemma as the temporary injunction had done on June 12. The women's picket had taken the sheriff and company by surprise; this surprise resulted in a power vacuum that women filled through their numbers, particularly during and after being jailed, and through their solidarity. The point at which Marshall ruled that the injunction covered women and children came after women had shown the futility of mass arrests: women had changed the terms of the conflict. For their part, law enforcement officials took from this the lesson that women were acting outside the law, and when those officials reasserted power, it was more closely and obviously connected to the company's agenda. This convinced women of the corruption of legal authority and the righteousness of their own cause.

PICKETERS, STRIKEBREAKERS, AND SHERIFF'S DEPUTIES

Failing to stop the women's picket, the permanent injunction instead prompted a new round of picket-line clashes. Whenever violence broke out on the lines, women mobilized car caravans to bring more people to the lines, and children walked out of school to join their parents.[41] Some 300 women showed up on July 11, the day the permanent injunction took effect, to defy the order and confront the strikebreakers, who were escorted by several deputies. Strikebreaker Grant Blaine, who had apparently made it into the Empire Zinc mine and done a day's work, "was inching his way out [in his car] when one woman threw a rock and broke his windshield."[42] Deputy Robert (Bobby) Capshaw tried to arrest her but found himself "ganged up by several others," according to Sheriff Goforth. One of them, Mrs. Antonio Rivera, even managed to seize Capshaw's blackjack. Then "the whole bunch ganged up on about seven deputies and the battle wound up as a standoff."[43]

This was not what Bobby Capshaw had signed on for. He was twenty-two years old when Sheriff Goforth assembled his deputy force in June. He was not a miner himself, but he had lived in several Grant County towns while growing up and knew the district well. His family had moved to Santa Rita in the mid-1930s when his father, Jessie, could no longer find work in Oklahoma's lead-mining district. Jessie Capshaw was killed in a mine explosion in 1939, leaving his wife, Ann, with six children (fortunately, the two eldest were adults) and fifty dollars a month from Chino.[44] Ann took a correspondence nursing course and got a job at Fort Bayard Hospital, and she also got the help of her brother-in-law and of Tom Foy to build a house in Whiskey Creek. Ann remarried, and early in the war the family moved to San Diego, where Bobby's brother Ross was stationed in the navy and his stepfather worked in the shipyards. Bobby and his brother Dorman soon returned to Grant County alone. By the time the Empire Zinc strike began, their mother and sister had also come back to Grant County, and it is possible that Ann's work for Tom Foy's 1948 campaign for district attorney brought Bobby to Foy's and Goforth's attention.[45]

Picketers especially disliked Deputy Marvin Mosely. On July 12, he drove his green Buick into the picket line and struck fourteen-year-old Rachel Juárez, Aurora Chávez's younger sister. Mosely claimed that Juárez "deliberately threw herself on the left fender of my car. I stopped to get her off and she cussed me."[46] Mosely had particularly bad relations with Elvira Molano, the picketer who had landed herself in jail even before the women had taken over. Molano refused to go to jail on July 20 without her children. Silver City justice of the peace Andrew Haugland, who had ordered Molano committed in lieu of $500 bond, told Mosely, "The children stay out. You take as many men as you think you need and put her in jail."[47] Mosely successfully got her to the door of the jail when his luck ran out and Molano fought back. Later she claimed that a peace officer, presumably Mosely, had spanked one of her children, and in retaliation she "'spanked him in the face and then . . . gave him this.' She swung her foot in a high kick and indicated she was aiming for the groin."[48]

Even away from the picket line, strikers faced violence. Tomás Carrillo, a child at the time of the Empire Zinc strike, was awakened one night by a knock at the door. "My stepmother asked, 'Who is it?' No answer. '¿Quién es?' No answer. My bedroom was right there, and I saw a man, a silhouette, in the light of the moon. I knew if I moved the guy would think I was my dad and he'd shoot me. My dad had a rifle, and he said, 'Who is it? If you don't tell me I'll blow your head off,' and boom— the man took off."[49] In another incident, strikers Henry and Anselma Polanco were driving to the Hanover picket on August 21 when a car driven by Francisco Franco hit and overturned their vehicle. They claimed that Franco hit them deliberately; Franco denied it, telling Assistant District Attorney Vincent Vesely that "he didn't know of the accident until he looked behind him and saw Polanco's car rolling along the highway."[50] Mine-Mill union men saw the incident and drove the couple to the Silver City hospital, where both were treated for severe bruises; Henry Polanco suffered serious cuts and a broken ankle as well. Franco and his passenger, Marvin Mosely, continued on to the picket and, according to the union, taunted the women there with obscenities.[51]

Obscenities were directed at other pickets as well. Pete Loya and Denzil Hartless, both working inside the Empire Zinc plant, were charged with separate counts of "indecent exposure in the presence of minors" on August 18, 1951. Loya and Hartless were alleged to have exposed themselves to a group of children on the picket line on August 8, and Loya was also charged with having done so on July 22 near his home, "in front of a group of minor girls." Both pleaded not guilty and were held in bond of $1,000 each; a few weeks later, charges against Hartless were dropped but Loya was ordered held for district court.[52]

Of course, picketers committed violence as well. Five men attacked Luis Hinojosa, a strikebreaker, and there is some question of whether they also attacked his pregnant wife when the couple was leaving the Empire Zinc area. Women threw red pepper on the strikebreakers and poked them with straight pins. Children threw rocks at strikebreakers, and they sabotaged strikebreakers' cars by burying boards with nails in the dirt roads and by stuffing gas tanks with tailings from the mine.[53]

An even more serious conflict flared on August 23. Five cars of strikebreakers approached the picket line, which was blocking the road with about forty women and children. "The cars neared the line and stopped," according to the *Silver City Daily Press*. "Then, bumper to bumper, they moved into the picket line as the pickets struggled to hold the cars back."[54] One car and a pickup truck made it through the line, and in the meantime four pickets were seriously injured. Consuelo Martínez, who was with her five children, had her leg broken when a car ran over it, and another car ran down Bersabé Yguado, who had been sitting on a bench some ten feet from the side of the road.[55] Martínez reportedly lay on the ground for forty-five minutes. A call to the Kennecott hospital at Santa Rita, which residents not associated with the company had often used for emergencies, met with flat refusal to send an ambulance: "If this call is for the pickets," the hospital spokesperson allegedly declared, "we have no ambulance. The pickets will have to take care of themselves."[56]

For the first time, guns were used for more than show. One strikebreaker "jumped out of the car with a gun in his hand and began shooting" at the women.[57] He wounded thirty-four-year-old Augustín Martínez, a war veteran who had been discharged from the army just nine days earlier.[58] And, according to a Mine-Mill Civil Rights Committee report from late September, for the first time a woman joined the attack: A "gunman woman by the name of Mrs. Clanton," the report claimed, exchanged blows with a woman picketer after first "trying to stomp" on

Rachel Juárez, who was injured again after having been hit by a car a month earlier.[59]

The events of August 23 came just days before Mine-Mill was scheduled to begin a nationwide strike in the copper industry. Local 890's Kennecott and Asarco units had voted early in the month to join that strike, set for August 27, but the violence on the Empire Zinc picket prompted 1,400 members of Local 890 to walk out several days early. The union issued a call for reinforcements over radio station KSIL, and, according to the managers of three companies, men walked off the job by noon.[60] By that point, Local 890 had held two emergency meetings to set up strike committees. In Grant County, AFL and CIO unions observed the pickets, but elsewhere in the nation those unions crossed the picket lines in order to deliberately weaken Mine-Mill. The relative respect shown Mine-Mill in Grant County suggests that CIO and AFL workers were disgusted at the violence directed against the Empire Zinc picket.[61]

All of these events on the picket line convinced picketers that the police were in the company's pockets. "It took . . . the sheriff department almost twenty-four hours," Anita Torrez complained, "to approach the scene of the accident where my husband was deliberately run over by a car."[62] Not only did Sheriff Goforth pay the deputies with Empire Zinc money, but the very deputies keeping "order" on the picket line were also sometimes strikebreakers. Daría Chávez was disgusted to see Mosely and Capshaw sneaking to work at Empire Zinc early on the morning of August 10. "It certainly seems funny to us women on the line," she said, "to see these so-called peace officers, who are supposed to be neutral, now working as scabs. And these are the men the court told us we should respect. . . . They have gone from one dirty job to another. What could be lower than a scab?"[63] After a court hearing in which Marvin Mosely was acquitted of assault charges, Elvira Molano commented, "I had never in my life been involved in courts or the law until the Empire Zinc strike. I thought the law of Grant County was to protect us, not throw us in jail like animals and beat us with blackjacks."[64]

The picketers did not meekly accept this version of law and order. Around noon on July 21, a hundred men visited Sheriff Goforth in the county courthouse. One man told him, "We want Mosely fired before someone gets hurt"; another reminded him that "we are the ones who put you in office"; and a third explained that Mosely lacked even the qualifications to vote in Grant County, having moved there too recently. "If you keep this man on," another told him, "there may be trouble." Goforth

Picketer confronting deputy, possibly Marvin Mosely, who is armed with ammunition and a camera. Deputy Robert Capshaw is standing at far left. Photo courtesy of Luis Ignacio Quiñones.

promised he would meet with them at 2 P.M. From the back of the crowd came one last shout: "If you don't get him out of there, we will do it!"[65] Sheriff Goforth started out of his office, expecting to get lunch, only to find a group of women blocking his way. Elvira Molano pointed at Mosely and declared, "We don't want him."[66] Then began an even noisier confrontation. The women would not wait until 2 P.M. "Now! Now! Now!" they shouted. Molano called for silence—"*Silencia, muchachas*"—and one woman tried to explain: "Sheriff Goforth, you're okay but that man (ges-

A picketer (far left) turning the tables on the photo-taking deputy while women pose for another camera. Photo courtesy of Luis Ignacio Quiñones.

turing to Mosely) isn't."[67] Sheriff Goforth did not fire any of his deputies, but he did suspend Mosely and Capshaw for a few days late in August.

PICKETERS AND JUDGES

Alongside the picket-line battles that summer, arrest warrants and court proceedings drained Local 890's bank account at the same time as they shored up people's resolve. In almost every instance, the local justice of the peace, whether in Bayard or Silver City, and the district judge ruled against the union and its members. Justice of the Peace Andrew Haugland routinely dismissed charges that picketers brought against the deputies, and sometimes he went a step further by criticizing or punishing the complainants instead. On August 8, for example, not only did he dismiss the women picketers' assault charges against Marvin Mosely and Robert Capshaw, but he also commended the deputies. The complainants had not "come to the court with clean hands," he explained, "and any injuries [they] may have sustained they brot [*sic*] on themselves."[68] Haugland dismissed assault charges brought against Mosely by Rachel Juárez's parents, explaining that the charges were based on hearsay, and, according to the union, he then cited her parents for "contributing to the delinquency of a minor by permitting her to go to the picketlines."[69]

The justice of the peace is a holdover from the English common law, hearing charges of minor crimes and either ruling on them right away or sending the alleged miscreants to district court. Into his office (often his home), the sheriff or deputy brought a string of people arrested for drunkenness, fighting, petty larceny, juvenile delinquency, burglary, or just plain disturbing the peace.[70] Sometimes the justice of the peace appeared on coroner's juries, too. The office required no formal training. Mexican Americans seldom served as justices of the peace, but they were elected constable in several Grant County towns. The men—and it was almost always men—typically came from the ranks of small business or the professions, and in Grant County they were elected every two years.[71]

It should come as little surprise that many Grant County justices came from the mining industry, whether as managers or as people with their hands in one or two mining ventures alongside their main occupation. But it is somewhat surprising to find that wage workers held court as justices of the peace. Bob Brewington of Hanover, for example, served as justice from at least 1947 to 1951 while still working for Empire Zinc.[72] But Brewington did not exercise jurisdiction over the cases that came out of the Empire Zinc strike.[73] Perhaps more palatable to the political leaders of Grant County was Bayard justice of the peace Robert O. Day. Day had been a wage-earner at Chino and a member of Local 890 from 1941 to 1947. He left the mining industry that year and opened a service station. Day was interested in local politics and law enforcement, and in 1950 he was elected justice of the peace in Bayard. Just like Haugland, Day typically ruled against the picketers, dismissing, for example, Elvira Molano's assault charge brought against Marvin Mosely.[74]

Also at work in Grant County was the state's district court, which heard felony cases and was empowered to issue injunctions, as A. W. Marshall did in June and July, and to cite individuals for contempt of court, as he did in July and August. Marshall traveled the circuit of New Mexico's Sixth District, hearing cases twice a year in Silver City, then moving on to Deming, Socorro, and other county seats. Marshall claimed descent from U.S. Supreme Court justice John Marshall and from pioneering parents in the railroad town of Deming, southwest of Silver City. He had little patience with rabble to begin with, and hearing crowds in the courthouse hall only reinforced his sense that he stood between order and disorder.

Marshall counted among his friends Horace Moses, Chino's superintendent, Hub Estes, a big rancher, and other men of the local elite. He was probably inclined to support the Empire Zinc Company against picketers because Empire Zinc represented order and property against disorder. This is not to say that the judge was blatantly biased; to the contrary, he would have prided himself on the rational deliberation with which he decided the cases before him. But he moved in the circles of people whose sense of public order was closely bound up with the protection of property. There did not need to be any backroom deals precisely because Grant County's legal authorities shared with mining managers the worldview in which strikes, by their very nature, ran contrary to how things should be. All of Grant County's lawyers had ties of one sort or another to mining concerns, whether they were retained as regular counsel for Chino (as was the firm of Woodbury and Shantz) or belonged to the same social, civic, and religious organizations.[75]

That said, there does seem to have been something of a backroom deal in the meeting that leaders of the Grant County Bar Association held with Judge Marshall shortly before noon on July 23 to "plan an appeal to the governor for aid in preserving peace."[76] That same day, Marshall ruled that Mine-Mill, Local 890, and six local union leaders—all men—were in contempt of court for, as Empire Zinc claimed, violating the June 12 injunction. He fined the international and local unions each $4,000 and sentenced the six members of the bargaining committee to ninety days in the county jail. He said he would suspend the jail sentences and remit half of the fines if the union and its officials obeyed the injunction, and he accepted $8,000 bond from the union and $500 bond each for the individuals.[77] By this time, Local 890 had gotten the help of prominent attorney Nathan Witt, who had once served on the National Labor Relations Board and who, during the McCarthy period, defended left-wing unions like Mine-Mill; he was regularly red-baited himself. At the contempt hearing of July 21, Marshall denied Local 890's motion to dismiss the company's claim, and the union officials and attorneys walked out of the hearing. Witt told Marshall, "Our clients are convinced that law and order have broken down as far as protecting their lives on the picket line is concerned. Women and children have been thrown into jail on the least excuse and have been held in unreasonable bond. It has come to a point where their confidence in law and order here is broken."[78]

Just as in their relations to Sheriff Goforth and his deputies, the picketers became bolder in confronting the county's political and legal authorities, while those authorities tried harder and harder to control the situation. After the contempt hearing, Local 890 broadcast a call over radio station KSIL for a massive demonstration. Three hundred cars drove into Silver City late that night, horns blaring all the way, and rallied outside the courthouse. A thousand people "gathered on the courthouse lawn to hear the six sentenced members of the bargaining committee and their wives pledge to carry on the fight against Empire Zinc."[79] They carried signs saying "No Marshall Law" and "Fooey on Foy."

Some of Grant County's legal authorities were deeply alarmed by the rowdy caravan into Silver City and the union's inflammatory accusations of corruption. The day after the courthouse rally, Marshall issued another contempt ruling, this time for Mine-Mill, Local 890, Jencks, international treasurer Maurice Travis, and Cipriano Montoya. The ruling concerned two occasions on which the union had criticized the local judiciary. On June 15, Mona Lucero broadcast a union message over radio station KSIL: "They have bought and paid for a restraining order to break our strike. They have failed."[80] And five days later, before a public meeting in the Fierro nightclub, Travis predicted that Empire Zinc would get its permanent injunction: "They've got enough people bought off to get it, I think. I think that Brother Witt is the best lawyer in the country. But I also think that if we had three of Brother Witt with us in this thing the company would still get its injunction. The company has enough money to do this. We don't have that much money."[81] These comments infuriated the president of the Grant County Bar Association, C. C. Royall Sr., who persuaded Marshall to issue the contempt citation. "We lawyers do not intend to stand by and let the courts be insulted and be flaunted," he said. "We intend to come to the defense of the courts because if we don't our system of justice will be endangered."[82] To Marshall's complaint that the Empire Zinc strike was getting out of hand, strike committee chairperson Ernesto Velásquez replied, "The only thing getting out of hand is the eagerness of company bootlickers in politics and at the bar to smash the only organization that has been able to raise the living standards of the working people, especially the Mexican American workers, of Grant County."[83] Local 890 charged the Grant County Bar Association with "unwanted interference" in the strike and wrote to Governor Edwin Mechem to counter the bar association's alleged misrepresentation of the situation in Grant County.[84] Mechem offered to mediate, and Local 890 accepted—but Empire Zinc refused the offer.

Criticism of the union's radio message extended only to male union officials; the union's opponents dismissed Mona Lucero's participation as simply something manipulated by the men. This was a key to the union's success: women's participation was highly visible and disruptive at the same time it was not fully comprehensible to the local authorities or to Empire Zinc. As Daría Chávez put it, "The reason the Empire Zinc co. hasn't noticed the wives of the strikers is because the company need[s] glasses."[85]

Local law officials began to employ a new tactic to control the strikers in August: the "peace bond." If someone (typically a deputy, strikebreaker, or relative of a strikebreaker) declared that a person threatened him or her, a justice of the peace could require the alleged intimidator to post a peace bond. If then, on the word of the complainant, the defendant did anything questionable—arguing with a deputy, for example, or taunting a strikebreaker—the defendant forfeited the peace bond and was jailed. Henrietta Williams, her sister Mary Pérez, Elvira Molano, Sabina Salazar, Fred Barreras, and Antonio Rivera all stayed in jail for a week late in August rather than pay peace bonds, which they understood as a blatant attempt to tie up the union in excessive court costs. "We are the peaceful ones," they declared from the Grant County jail. "What have we done? The ones breaking the peace around here are those gunmen who have charged us, who come to the lines after working as scabs, and always try to start trouble."[86] A "Citizens' Committee" petitioned Justice Haugland to release them without the peace bonds, but he refused. By going to a higher authority—district judge Charles Fowler in Socorro, New Mexico—the six gained release on a writ of habeas corpus. Fowler criticized the peace bonds as "so drastic a restraint of the freedom of individuals that a judge must be scrupulous in seeing that any complaint fulfills exactly all of the requirements of law."[87] Scrupulous the local judiciary was not, and the union strenuously objected to the tenor and outcomes of the court proceedings. It circulated a petition to New Mexico's attorney general for a grand jury proceeding to address "the atrocities of the District Attorney and the Sheriff of Grant County."[88] For their part, the newly released strikers were strengthened by the experience. Henrietta Williams was "happy to be together with the sisters in the picket line. She [felt] glad and not ashamed of being in jail," while Sabina Salazar thought that after "staying eight days in jail, she could stay in longer if necessary." The union supporters voted to extend their August 22 meeting by fifteen minutes, and the four recently jailed women "came up front to sing 'We Shall Not Be Moved' in Spanish[,] accompanied on the piano by Brother Juan Antonio."[89]

Authorities at some distance from Grant County proved somewhat more even-handed in the course of the strike. U.S. senator James Murray of the Senate Committee on Labor and Public Welfare was "greatly shocked by newspaper accounts of the jailing of pickets, including women and children." He asked that Senator Hubert Humphrey, of the Senate Subcommittee on Labor and Labor Management Relations, consider investigating the Empire Zinc dispute.[90] Governor Mechem, a Republican

Elvira Molano, Fred Barreras, and Sabina Salazar, three of the six picketers jailed on "peace bonds," in the Grant County courthouse. Deputy Louis Rhea (generously nicknamed "Horseface Rhea") is at left. Photo courtesy of Luis Ignacio Quiñones.

elected the previous November, was suspicious of communist involvement in the strike, but his actions suggest that he was at least equally suspicious of Empire Zinc's sincerity in resolving the crisis. He spoke over the radio on July 28, offering to mediate, and while he dispatched the state police on occasion, he never declared martial law, as some Grant County Anglos had asked—and as plenty of earlier governors had done in labor disputes, including Mechem's own father.[91] State police chief Joe Roach, in fact, actually helped restore order in Grant County. He publicly criticized Goforth and Foy for "magnifying minor complaints and . . . criticizing our system. If the condition again gets out of hand," he continued, "it can in all probability be directly chargeable to the sheriff and the district attorney and this department would rather have no hand in it."[92] It took a judge from Socorro, some 200 miles away, to draw the brakes on the peace bonds. And the National Labor Relations Board indicted the New Jersey Zinc Company for "refusal to bargain" on August 14. This measure did not, of course, force the company to take any action;

unlike the injunctions against unions, a Taft-Hartley injunction or ruling against a company carried no enforcement provisions.

THE PICKET SEEN FROM OUTSIDE

The strike reverberated beyond the picket lines in Hanover, forcing people only indirectly connected to the picketers to choose sides. Many believed the union cause was just, the company intransigent, and law enforcement compromised. Late in June 1951, for example, all of Central's business managers, owners, and operators save one petitioned Empire Zinc to negotiate with the strikers and to fire strikebreakers and armed deputies.[93] They accepted the union rationale for the strike and saw their own interests tied to the strength of the union. Gertrude Gibney, a Central hotel proprietress, explained that "the feeling of the business people in the town of Central is that if Empire Zinc cannot do as much for its employees as the other companies in the district do for theirs, they might as well sell out, and let another mining company that knows how to treat its employees try to do a better job." Grant County would "go backward, instead of forward," if the company denied the union its demands.[94] The company may have prevailed in local courts, local businesspeople intimated, but it was also on trial in the community: "Failing to grant these established district-wide conditions to your employees, your management and company will stand further convicted in the eyes of the people of ours and other communities in this district, as fully responsible for prolonging the strike and for all future violence or bloodshed connected with [the strike]."[95]

Some businesspeople matched their nominal support with concrete aid. Fred Sullivan, owner of El Zarape nightclub, regularly opened his floor to union meetings and benefits; José Martínez donated food from his two businesses, Mi Ranchito and the Central Commercial Company.[96] In September, Gertrude Gibney again came forward for the union, this time testifying before Justice of the Peace Haugland on behalf of Rudy Chapin and his mother. Rudy was a teenager, a regular picketer and, apparently, handy enough with rocks to infuriate Sheriff Goforth's deputies. He found himself in danger of being sent to the boys' industrial school (reformatory) at Springer, New Mexico, and Haugland was also considering punishing his mother for contributing to his delinquency. Chapin's mother was a widow, Gibney explained to Haugland, and she was doing the best she could with her son. It was a hardship for her to report weekly to the juvenile officers because she was sick and on relief and had to travel twenty miles round-trip.[97] Gibney probably understood how hard it could be to run a household; she herself had married at age fourteen and by the time she was in her mid-twenties was running a household consisting of two children, her husband Ruben, her father-in-law, and her husband's cousin.[98] In any case, Haugland was unmoved. He was being "extremely lenient," he replied, and (according to the union's press release) he "wanted to make it tough for the Chapins."[99]

Catholic priests generally supported the strikers, especially Father Francis Smerke of Hanover's Holy Family Church. On October 14, 1951, for example, he held a special high mass "to pray for the successful conclusion of the . . . strike."[100] Father Smerke had come to this parish in 1948, a time when Mine-Mill was starting to push its agenda beyond the workplace, and his parishioners were almost entirely working-class Mexican Americans. Other Grant County towns, like Santa Rita, Silver City, and Central, had Catholic congregations that crossed class and ethnic boundaries; in Central, for example, Tom Foy's family attended the same services at Santa Clara Church that many workers' families did. We cannot make too much of a distinction between Holy Family and the other Catholic parishes, however, because Father John Linnane, who served Silver City's San Vicente Church, also helped the strikers and, the following year, the filmmakers. In fact, the Catholic churches in the region, in addition to St. Mary's Academy, were probably the only churches integrated to that degree; all other churches seem to have had either Anglo, African American, or Spanish-speaking congregants of similar class backgrounds.

If Empire Zinc strikers and their supporters believed that the Empire Zinc Company was responsible for escalating the conflict, other townspeople laid the blame at the feet of the strikers. Illustrative of the complicated fissures the strike opened in Grant County is the case of C. B. Ogás, a Mexican American insurance agent in Bayard. Ogás felt that the strike got out of hand, with both sides to blame. For years he had sold policies to the poorer people of Grant County and witnessed firsthand the difficult and dispiriting conditions in which many lived.[101] Long a friend of Tom Foy, Ogás had managed the campaign that got Foy elected as district attorney in 1948. By 1951 he was managing the Copper Real Estate Company, which Foy owned.

Ogás sympathized with the Empire Zinc strikers, but on terms different from those prescribed by the union leadership. He adopted what he considered to be an even-handed attitude toward the strike, and he deplored the effect of outsiders on the community. To his way of thinking, the company should not have tried to import scabs, nor should the union have brought in "outside agitators" like Clinton Jencks. The escalating violence that galvanized community support struck Ogás as evidence that the situation had gotten out of control. "One woman," he recalled, "even put her newborn child in front of a truck. It got that bad."[102] The strikers seemed to be provoking violence almost as much as suffering from it, or possibly even using it for their own propaganda purposes. The horror of the brutality could make any such efforts appear at best cavalier, at worst immoral.

Ogás's perspective shows how the strike spread beyond the confines of the Empire Zinc mine and into the lives of people only indirectly connected to the union or to the individual strikers. As an agent of Tom Foy's business, Ogás felt he could not sign the Copper Real Estate Company's name to a petition supporting the strike circulated by Local 890 among Bayard businesses. He saw his refusal as simple business practice: the name was not his to sign. (At the same time, however, he did sign a petition that claimed "neutrality" regarding the strike and repudiated the union's attempt to solicit help from businesspeople through a petition.) The union saw this as a fundamental betrayal of the community. For the petition was not simply the union's means of soliciting support: it was a means of marking out the union's supporters from its detractors along a clear axis. There could be no middle way, and Ogás's attempt to forge one cost him dearly. He was seen not just as a union opponent but as a traitor to his fellow Mexican Americans. His own family relations were ruptured as his cousin denounced him for not supporting the strike. The union published the list of those businesses that did not sign its petition and then boycotted them. In Ogás's case, the boycott effectively drove him out of business by 1955 and out of town shortly thereafter; only in the 1990s did he and his wife return to Silver City from their thirty-year exile in Santa Fe.

This was a divided community, and in some respects Ogás was correct in attributing blame for the widening division to both sides. This does not mean that we can satisfy ourselves with a facile "there are two sides to every story" explanation. Instead, it is worth examining the mechanisms by which Local 890 members both built and inhibited "community." The strike laid bare some of the class and ethnic divisions that had long existed. The company's intransigence consistently ratcheted up the stakes, and the strikers—witnessing the apparent collusion of local officials with Empire Zinc—identified their strength in a simple unity to match that of the powerful. Local 890 reached out to Mexican Americans throughout the district and, significantly, attracted many non-Mexican Americans to its cause. In staffing the pickets, squaring off against the judicial system, and trying to get the word out to the public, the union made people into genuine "brothers and sisters." But in some ways the strength of their bond lay in the sharply etched divisions between this group and the rest of the community. The perceived clarity of the political situation—the company against the "community"—actually obscured circumstances that might have made an individual refrain from supporting the strike in the ways staked out by the union. People like C. B. Ogás fell through the cracks of the community that 890 built.

Some initially sympathetic businesses, like Ogás's real estate firm, also had financial reasons for ceasing to support the strike. Silver City's only radio station, KSIL, had broadcast Local 890's weekly "Reporte a la Gente" ("Report to the People") since May 1949, prefaced by an editorial disclaimer. After the violent episode of August 23 and the subsequent districtwide strike, under pressure from the station's advertisers, station manager James Duncan asked that the union submit the "Reporte" ahead of time for censorship. But even this did not satisfy the station's advertisers, who forced KSIL owner Carl Dunbar to cancel the show early in September. The radio program, he explained, was "contrary to the public interest."[103]

Southwestern Foods had supported Local 890 during previous strikes. Almost all of the strike relief receipts for the Asarco and Empire Zinc strikes came from this Bayard grocery store, and on occasion it wiped the account books clean as a donation to the union. Its generosity notwithstanding, the store's management also benefited from Local 890's coffers; according to Virginia Jencks, the union had spent "over $17,000" at Southwestern Foods over the previous four years. By September, though, the store began to curtail credit to striking families. A picket of women, children, and men demonstrated against this new policy that month. During the demonstration, perhaps angry that the strike seemed to be spreading beyond Hanover—or perhaps just angry—a crowd of "businessmen and cowboys" gathered around the picketers and pushed them onto the street, where cars were positioned to run them down. The crowd called the picketers "dirty Communists" and told them to "get the hell out of there." Southwestern's butcher, David Gray, came out of the store and joined in the fight. He tried to grab a sign from the hands of a little boy, and Virginia Jencks told him "to pick on someone his own size."

After that he attacked her—and her daughter—by pulling her hair and slapping her.[104] Jencks was also assaulted by local residents L. H. and Vivian Patton. She told Justice of the Peace Andrew Haugland that L. H. Patton "smashed me in the eye with his fist [and] was insolent."[105] Only when the picketers dragged a policeman from across the street, where he had been watching the fight, did the brawl end.[106] Gray and the Pattons each pleaded not guilty of assault, and Gray charged Jencks with "unlawfully touching [him] in a rude and insolent manner."[107] Gray admitted that he "had grasped Mrs. Jencks and her 14-year-old daughter, Linda, by the hair in the fracas." But he claimed he did so only after Virginia Jencks attacked him.[108] On September 27, Jencks was found guilty while her attackers were acquitted of assault charges.[109]

Families of strikebreakers were particularly angry at the women's picket because they bore the brunt of union hostility. Mary Hartless, the mother of Denzil and Carl, was furious at the Empire Zinc strikers for mistreating both the strikebreaking workers and the community more broadly, and she was convinced that the Jenckses were the cause of all the trouble. "For ten months it's been a fight, scratch and growl," she declared. "The people of Local 890 have insulted and spit at the people of the community. It's a shame we have to put up with this. The people acted decent until Clinton Jencks and his wife came here, started their rotten talk, and stirring the people up."[110] She and her husband, Odell, had come to Grant County in the 1930s, each having grown up on farms in Oklahoma, Texas, and eastern New Mexico, but unable to make a living on the farm in the Depression. Memories of the Depression made them glad for employment in Grant County, even though Odell's work made the family move frequently from town to town.[111] For this reason Mary especially resented the Empire Zinc strikers, who aimed to keep her sons and husband from bringing home a paycheck. The strikers' refusal to work did not seem to her a sacrifice for a principle; instead, it was proof of the strikers' laziness. "Just as long as there are anyone giving Local 890 handouts they are not going to work. Why should they? As long as their families are taken care of it's much better they don't have to work."[112] The Hartlesses may not have known what a typical company house for Mexicans looked like (their own company house had three bedrooms, electricity, running water, and a regular bathroom), so the workers' complaints may have seemed precisely that: complaining.[113]

As frustrated as Mary Hartless was, the strike was probably more difficult for her daughter Betty Jo, a seventh-grader at Hanover School. She had been a quiet student, and during the strike she tried to keep to herself. But the polarization engendered by the strike extended even to the schools, and fights, even among girls, broke out in the schoolyard. Strikers sometimes blocked the road leading to the Hartlesses' house, too. Conflict with picketers became so intense that the family moved to Bayard, where Betty Jo finished out the school year.[114]

Families only indirectly connected to the strike felt the pressure to choose sides, too. Juanita Escobedo's parents, for example, covered the back of their pickup with a tarp to protect the children from rocks as they drove near the picket line to visit a brother, Pete Quintana, who lived in Fierro and continued working at Empire Zinc. "Of course, we knew why they were striking," she recalls. "But there was no room" to explain to angry picketers why the family was going through the picket line.[115] Cecilia Pino was a child whose grandfather crossed the picket lines, and she recalled considerable abuse by strikers—enough that fifty years later she was still distressed by it.[116]

Anger at the picketers helped spark the August 23 incident, in which picketers were injured. Thirty strike opponents met with Goforth on August 22. "We are tired of having to face rock throwing and having pepper thrown in our faces as we go to and from our homes," they explained.[117] Catalyzing the next day's violence was "an alleged assault upon a car driven by Roy Sanders, bookkeeper at the company's office for a number of years."[118] Many of those who went to Goforth stressed that they were simply Hanover residents, although a closer look reveals that many were strikebreakers, or relatives of strikebreakers. And some of the strike opponents certainly behaved the same way as the strikebreakers. Oleta and Homer McNutt, for example, threatened Vicente Becerra with a gun.[119]

Violence on the part of union opponents was seldom punished. Sheriff Goforth required a $250 peace bond from both Oleta and Homer McNutt (but required a $500 bond from Becerra), and the district attorney charged Jesús Avalos with discharging a weapon in a settlement, but law enforcement generally left the strike opponents alone. Sheriff Goforth was a little uneasy, though, when a vigilante group was formed in September. In response, Goforth organized a posse consisting of five men, all ranchers and former law enforcement officers, but made a point to exclude "hotheads and . . . misfits."[120] Goforth chaired a meeting on September 24, 1951, organized by the "law and order" group who had approached him in August. About 150 people attended, among them Local 890 official Joe T. Morales. Goforth agreed to give him the floor, and Morales stated that he too disliked having the women and children on the picket line. He also declared that the communist issue was irrelevant. The audience applauded him when he finished.[121]

Some Grant County residents saw in the opposition to the Empire Zinc strike the chance to settle old scores, some of which dated from the 1947 amalgamation of Locals 530, 69, 63, and 604 into Local 890. Robert Day, formerly an Asarco worker and secretary-treasurer of Local 530, was elected a justice of the peace in Bayard in 1950.[122] Charles J. Smith had served as Local 530's first president. Both men lost their union offices to Mexican Americans at the time of amalgamation into Local 890, and Smith went on to run his own garage and gas station. Day, Smith, and Earl Lett, a druggist who came to Grant County in 1949 from Deming, were cornerstones of a "law and order committee" that solicited Governor Mechem to impose martial law on Grant County after the August 23 incidents. Earl Lett singled out Clinton Jencks, assaulting him on a Bayard street on October 1. He then dropped by Justice of the Peace Day's house for punishment—a fine of one dollar.[123]

Charles Smith insisted that he was not antiunion: he was proud of his work organizing workers into Local 530, and he was only angry that the wrong leaders had gotten control of the union. "What," he asked, "can American citizens do to protect themselves from a group of irresponsible leaders who are following the communistic line and using good American citizens, and an American institution, 'Unionism[,]' as a front, to get by with what has been going on here lately?"[124] To show his support for the right kind of unionism, Smith and his committee invited the United Steelworkers to raid Local 890 in September and October; the Steelworkers organized an opposing union, aimed at all of Local 890's jurisdiction, under the name Grant County Organization for the Defeat of Communism.[125]

In this the Steelworkers were using the same tactic they had been using since the late 1940s: sending in organizers to persuade workers— sometimes through direct violence and intimidation, often through race-baiting, and always through red-baiting—to abandon Mine-Mill. Arturo Flores, for example, had recently taken a job as international representative in order to fight just such raids in Arizona and El Paso. Raiding, or trying to lure union members from one union into another and ultimately to win jurisdiction over a set of workers, was nothing new in the 1940s; Communist unions, in fact, had routinely raided AFL unions during the CP's "dual-union" period of the 1920s and early 1930s until the Popular Front strategy directed them to work within existing unions. After World War II, raiding became a weapon used against left-wing unions by rivals motivated by anticommunism, opportunism, or a combination of the two. These raids were extremely disruptive, whether the existing union was displaced or survived. In its 1945 raid on the Food, Tobacco, Agricultural and Allied Workers in California, for example, the Teamsters violently attacked FTA workers and organizers and ultimately defeated what had been a progressive force for Chicana labor rights.[126] Steelworker raids on Mine-Mill locals often divided communities and families regardless of the jurisdictional outcome. And in Anaconda, Montana, gender played an important role in crafting both Steelworker and Mine-Mill propaganda during these campaigns; Mine-Mill's stifling of the women's auxiliary in the 1940s compromised the community unionism that was needed to resist Steelworker raids in the 1950s.[127]

Still, throughout the 1950s, the Steelworkers' political attacks failed either to dislodge Mine-Mill locals in the Southwest, where Mexican American loyalty was important to Mine-Mill's survival, or to eradicate it elsewhere in the United States. Like most southwestern Mine-Mill members, Local 890's members—Anglo and Mexican alike—were not swayed by the Steelworkers' appeal.[128] They "spoke bitterly about some of the businessmen who . . . asked CIO Steel to the district [and] recalled the weak local they had until Mine-Mill organized the area."[129] Asarco worker Cornelius "Bud" DeBraal explained, "We never knew where our dues went, or what good we got from them. The money just disappeared when those birds, who used to be our officers, got it. And today they are the same businessmen telling us we should have another union."[130] The Grant County Organization for the Defeat of Communism elevated the anticommunist tenor of the strike's opposition (which had been remarkably muted until the summer of 1951), but it did not thereby weaken either Local 890 or the Empire Zinc strike.

Both instances of physical assault away from the Hanover picket lines were directed against the Jenckses. There are several possible explanations for their being targeted. The Jenckses did come from "outside"— Colorado—and the press and local antagonists consistently labeled them "outside agitators." Related to this was the fact that they were Anglos who forthrightly threw in their lot with the district's Mexican Americans. In the eyes of union opponents, local Mexican Americans' agitation for civil rights was bad enough—and in fact likely to have arisen only when outsiders stirred them up—but Anglos struggling alongside Mexican Americans was unthinkable. Virginia Chacón believes that Anglos were furious that the Jenckses would ally themselves with Mexican Americans.[131] The

Jenckses exposed the social system's inequities that, for the privileged, had remained "natural" and therefore comfortably unexamined. It was this publicity—and not the material or social inequalities between Anglos and Mexican Americans—that, in the minds of union opponents, created a race problem where none had previously existed. As the *Silver City Daily Press* commented in July 1951, the "worst feature of the situation now is the continued effort to stir up animosity between anglos and the people who—judging by letters to the Daily Press—prefer to call themselves Mexican-Americans. . . . The two races are here and doing pretty well in this prosperous mineral district. They get along alright, too, except when politicians and walking delegates get 'em stirred up."[132]

Conflict with strikebreakers and their families caused some Empire Zinc strikers to sharpen their understandings of ethnicity. Teenager Lupe Elizado, for instance, wrote an impassioned letter that raised the danger of Mexican Americans being treated as badly as African Americans were. "We are not going to give ourselves to slavery and be treated as colored people," she announced. "The treatment that is given to colored people is nothing to be proud of. They are human beings just like we are. Their color makes no difference as long as they're decent people."[133] Elizado challenged Mrs. Tex Williams, wife of one of the deputies, for calling the kids on the picket line "brats" in a letter to the *Silver City Daily Press*.[134] Elizado took a stand on the proper names for Mexican Americans: "You know why we're living here, Mrs. Williams? Because we have a right to do so, even more than you Anglo-Americans because this land once belonged to Mexico. We're not Spanish or Spanish-Americans as you call us. We are Mexican-Americans, our parents came from Mexico, not from Spain."[135] Not only did Elizado lay claim to her Mexican ancestry, but she also rejected the label "Spanish-American" as an Anglo term. In fact, it was common for Anglos and Mexican Americans alike to refer to the "acceptable" Mexican Americans as Spanish. By calling this usage an Anglo practice, Elizado was implicitly condemning those Mexican Americans who also used the term for rejecting their Mexicanness.[136]

As women picketers refined their understanding of the local political economy, they transferred this newfound confidence to their dealings with the international union. Relations between Local 890 and the international took a turn for the worse in September 1951. Shortly before the Mine-Mill convention in Nogales, Arizona, the executive board hastily dismissed international representative Bob Hollowwa. Hollowwa's dismissal resulted from the conflicts between Local 890 and area businesses,

specifically the Law and Order Committee. Hollowwa was a rather con-
frontational leader, and the international leadership believed that he
pushed otherwise neutral people into the opposite camp.[137] Hollowwa's
correspondence with Cipriano Montoya the following winter and spring
hinted that the real issue was that "top brass" like Orville Larson and
Maurice Travis objected to his militancy.[138] Precipitating his dismissal
was publicity generated by the Steelworkers in their attempt to discredit
Mine-Mill. Hollowwa, they revealed, had served four years in San Quen-
tin on a 1934 kidnapping conviction and, along with his wife, reputedly
attended CP meetings.[139]

If Hollowwa was unpopular with moderates and a magnet for anticommunist agitation, he was very popular with the women picketers. He
had pushed for women to take over the picket line; he had accompanied
them when they tried to get the *Silver City Daily Press* to publish union
messages about the strike violence; and he showed tremendous confidence in the women's abilities. At a September 19 meeting, he was quick
to point out that the women were crucial to the strike but he was not.[140]

Local 890 was confused and indignant over Hollowwa's dismissal in
the middle of the strike. At the September 19 meeting, men and women
commented that Hollowwa's past problems should have been dealt with
long ago, and not in the middle of the strike. Braulia Velásquez denounced the "propaganda" as "part of the move to disrupt the union." Her
statements stirred the people to extend the meeting by fifteen minutes,
during which time the local voted to send another telegram to the international. Vicente Becerra suggested that the local "chip in to pay for
Brother Hollowwa if necessary," and Joe Ramírez praised Hollowwa for
his hard work on the strike. Thirty-one women sent a very strong message to Mine-Mill president John Clark on September 26, demanding
that the international meet with the local to explain the dismissal and,
ultimately, reinstate him. "Should this not be granted," the telegram concluded, "we shall take action ourselves."[141]

Clearly these were not deferential union members. The women and
men who gathered in the union hall that September night proved quite
adept at pushing to the political heart of the matter, even when such
effort meant challenging their national leaders. Local 890 members suspected that behind the dismissal lay personal differences that should
not influence the union's strike strategy. In the same way that a left-
wing union like Mine-Mill might question the motives or timing of government or corporate actions, so too did the local members penetrate

beyond the surface of claims of the national leadership to question that leadership's motives and timing.[142]

Experience on the picket line, in the courtroom, and in jail showed women their collective strength in the face of hostile local authority, often without any help from men. It strengthened their solidarity and contributed to new understandings of the local political economy, shaping their ideas, as historian Dana Frank has put it, of "who they believed was in power; what they thought should be done to alleviate their stress, and, most importantly, how they believed they as women could affect the economic system in which they were enmeshed."[143] Lola Martínez, for example, complained that "justice was not for the working people" in Grant County. Her comment came after Assistant District Attorney Vincent Vesely backed strikebreaker Jesús Avalos in a dispute over armed scabs trying to cross the picket line. Avalos, Vesely declared, did not mean to shoot at women picketing the mine. On the picket line, women witnessed the supposedly neutral sheriff actively transporting strikebreakers across the line; if the women interfered with a scab-bearing car, as did Henrietta Williams, Mary Pérez, Eva Becerra, and Elvira Molano, they were arrested and held on a peace bond.

The strike persisted into a second year. Aid from other unions throughout the country kept food baskets reaching strikers' homes, and the legal snares that the union dealt with each day only drove home the lessons in political economy that its members had learned during the summer. After another series of violent incidents in early December, the company finally agreed to negotiate early in January 1952. The settlement hammered out between the parties provided wage increases totaling 39½ cents, vacation benefits, collar-to-collar pay, and a new rate classification. Striking Empire Zinc workers ratified the contract unanimously at the amalgamated union meeting of January 24. Thus, the fifteen-month Empire Zinc strike ended with substantial, though not overwhelming, contract gains and, as Clinton Jencks stressed, "substantial recognition" won by the women of the district. It was, strike chairman Ernesto Velásquez said, "the entire membership [that] made it possible for us to bring the fight to the end."[144]

The women strikers had their own understanding of where the thanks lay. Back in September, spirits had been flagging. People were tired. The women met on September 11, 1951, to discuss the "picket line problems," and they "decided to form competing teams for picket line duty, with awards or similar recognition going to top teams." Schoolchildren would be allowed to volunteer on Saturdays "to relieve those with household duties."[145] The women picketers thus relied on the strength of their organization to pull themselves together to address the problem and think up a solution. But they sought spiritual help in other quarters as well. A group of about twenty-five women (possibly the same as those who in October asked Father Smerke for a high mass) pledged to make a pilgrimage to the Church of San Lorenzo, some fifteen miles away in the Mimbres Valley, if God willed that the strike should succeed. When the strikers won in January, the women fulfilled their pledge. From Bayard to San Lorenzo they walked, their physical effort expressing their gratitude.[146]

Actually, the strike did not end there. The legal cases that Empire Zinc refused to drop against 890 officials and members constituted more than "aftermath": they formed a central part of the story and also one of the many links to the Hollywood filmmakers who would approach Mine-Mill and Local 890 to produce a feature film about the strike. District judge A. W. Marshall fined the union and twenty members a total of $37,750 on March 10; the union posted a $76,000 bond to keep the twenty out of jail while they appealed the verdict.[147] On March 18, twelve Mine-Mill defendants appeared in district court. The union paid $600 in fines and charges without contest because it still faced around seventy-five additional cases. "We had to clear away the 'underbrush,' " a union spokesperson explained, "to be able to concentrate on more serious charges."[148] In September, serious charges resulted in ninety-day jail sentences for Ernesto Velásquez, Cipriano Montoya, Clinton Jencks, Fred Barreras, Vicente Becerra, and Pablo Montoya. Their attorney, former governor A. T. Hanett, could not persuade Judge Marshall that "it was unfair that the union had been hauled before the court when the National Labor Relations Board had ruled against New Jersey Zinc."[149] As a special punishment, the jailer isolated Jencks from the others. Union members did enjoy one victory that fall: Although Tom Foy held onto his office, voters defeated Sheriff Goforth in his reelection bid. And the following spring, Sheriff's deputies Marvin Mosely and G. W. Clanton tried to parlay their Empire Zinc service into elected office. They were both defeated soundly in the Hanover constable race by Cecilio Torres, a union man.[150]

6

Household Relations

Agustín Chávez was not happy. As a striker at Empire Zinc, he worried about taking care of his family on limited strike benefits. He and his wife, Aurora, had three children, the eldest only nine years old, and Aurora was pregnant with their fourth. But now he had something bigger to worry about: his wife on the picket line. He confronted her after the union meeting on June 12, 1951, despite—or perhaps because of—her having been one of the women to propose the women's picket. He "didn't like it at all. He knew how it was gonna be and he didn't like it," Aurora recalled. Agustín Chávez feared the violence that his wife would face, and he also feared—correctly—that he would have to take care of the children.[1]

Aurora Chávez, though, stood her ground against her husband, because over the past nine months she had become very personally invested in the strike. At first she had taken "very little interest in the whole affair," but as she worked with the ladies' auxiliary she came to "understand that this is not simply a fight for higher wages." "That is but a minor part of our demands to help improve our standard of living," she explained. "What we are mainly concerned with is the health and safety of our husbands and brothers while on the job."[2] Health and safety, not just wages, would improve the standard of living, and at age twenty-seven she knew well what the standard of living for mining families was—and what it should rightly be. Her parents both arrived in Grant County from Mexico as children during the Mexican Revolution.[3] Her paternal grandfather, a miner, died shortly after bringing his family from Guanajuato.

Her grandmother opened a boardinghouse, and her father gave up school and started working for Chino at the age of thirteen. By the time of Aurora's birth in 1924, he worked in Chino's powder department, blasting the sides of the open pit copper mine with explosives so that railroad cars could haul the ore away for processing. He and his young family lived in Santa Rita.

The oldest of ten children, Aurora had begun helping her mother around the age of six or seven. Her mother worked at a bakery during the Depression: with children all under the age of ten, the family relied on her outside employment to make ends meet rather than sending one of the children into the labor market. Even with substantial household responsibilities, Aurora managed to continue school until she was eighteen years old. That was when she married Agustín, a twenty-year-old Empire Zinc miner whom she had met at a dance. After their marriage, the Chávezes set up house in Hanover, renting from Empire Zinc a three-room house that had few modern conveniences. There was a water tap outside but no bathroom indoors. Aurora used a woodstove for cooking and a coal one for heating, and she had to chop the wood and carry the coal to keep both stoves stoked. She did this while bearing and raising three children within nine years.

Aurora ultimately prevailed against her husband regarding the women's picket, but not because her husband agreed to look after the children. Instead, Aurora's father sent her teenaged sister Rachel to help out while Aurora walked on the women's picket line. Thus the Chávezes resolved their conflict by preserving Agustín's prerogatives in one area—not performing child care—but challenging them in another: Aurora would face the violence on the picket lines, and Agustín would stand to one side. He still was not happy about it, but it was the agreement they reached. Importantly, the couple resolved their conflict by turning to the wider family, one in which male authority also carried great weight. Aurora's father, Domitilio Juárez, had the authority to send one of his daughters to Hanover and to persuade Agustín that this was a reasonable solution. Domitilio regretted his decision a month later, when sheriff's deputy Marvin Mosely struck his daughter Rachel Juárez with a car.[4]

The picket brought women from all corners of the mining district into one lively place. But the picket's effects extended outward, too, into each woman's home. With women walking the pickets for hours on end—often stretched even longer by women's reluctance to leave at the end of their shift—men found that their houses were not nearly as well kept nor their children as well tended as they expected. Men confronted their wives for abandoning these responsibilities, which posed an implicit challenge to men's authority in the home. As Local 890 officer Angel Bustos later remarked, "We had a lot of trouble with some of our members that the women should not take any positions or defend any picket lines in any labor movement."[5] Children picked up on these conflicts and compared notes on them, trying to understand the changes they were witnessing but not allowed to discuss with their parents. "You should have heard the fights last night," one youngster would tell another. "Yeah," the other would reply. "My dad's sleeping in the living room."[6] The story of the women's picket, then, became a story of women's rebellion, not just against the Empire Zinc Company but also against their own husbands. Women did not begin their strike activities with gender relations in mind; they aimed only to defend the union community. But the resistance women encountered from their husbands made them realize that there was perhaps more at stake than first met the eye. It made them argue explicitly for *women's* rights to work for the union movement on their own terms and, if necessary, to reorganize their households.

Women and men argued at home, and some women even carried this discussion right back into the union hall. Just two days after the momentous vote, Chana Montoya insisted upon "more help from men on the jobs off the line. More help on the job we cannot do at home while we are doing this job."[7] Montoya spoke with some authority. She was married to Local 890 president Cipriano Montoya, so her words probably carried weight in a union meeting. But her candor is all the more remarkable given the sad fact that her husband regularly abused her. Many people knew this; no one discussed it. She was probably speaking from her own experience at home, and for her even to hint at domestic conflict is astonishing. Clearly she felt that the union community was an authority to which she could appeal and the union hall a safe place in which to voice women's needs. Perhaps her call was made easier by Cipriano's absence from that particular meeting.

Cipriano Montoya was, however, present at—indeed he presided over—another important union meeting, where he hinted at women's proper duties. In October 1951, Local 890 celebrated the first anniversary of the Empire Zinc strike. While strike chairman Ernesto Velásquez praised the women as "veterans," a term fully laden with masculine honor, Cipriano Montoya congratulated first the entire membership and then the women, for "knowing that they have work to do at home."[8] At this meeting, meant to reflect upon the difficulties they had faced and the victories they had won, Montoya chose to remind women of their household duties and to limit his praise to their meeting those obligations. Chana did not speak at this meeting.

Conflict strained the relationships between husbands and wives, and everyone understood that it jeopardized the unity needed against a mining company. But women and men disagreed on the source of the conflict. Women understood their picket duty as a temporary assumption of male duties, similar to the "deputy husband" role that historian Laurel Thatcher Ulrich has described for colonial American women: under unusual circumstances—most notably widowhood or the temporary absence of a husband—women took on men's responsibilities without posing a serious threat to the normal order of things.[9] Many men, on the contrary, believed that women did not belong on the picket lines for two simple reasons. First, exposing their wives to violence made the men look weak, which challenged husbands' sense of manhood. Second, this threat to their manhood was made even more serious when women expected men to assume women's duties at home. Men did not see this as an equal exchange. While women might assume the role of deputy husband, it was quite another thing for men to take on women's work. In other words, men and women generally agreed on a division of labor and of responsibilities, but that division did not entail a *symmetry* of responsibilities. The sexual division of labor was by definition asymmetrical, and male authority depended in part on this asymmetry. Any disruption of male authority at home risked undermining the strength and stability of the household, the foundation of the union "family's" strength.

A household has a dual nature. It may be considered a single unit, its members sharing the goal of bringing together cash and noncash resources in order to feed, clothe, and house themselves as well as to produce and raise children. But the household is also a composite of individuals—men and women, adults and children—exercising different kinds of power and having distinct material interests.[10] Its unity is a fiction, not in the sense of being false or untrue, but in the sense of being created by the people within the household and by society more broadly. The fiction needs to be maintained, and in systems of male dominance its maintenance demands that male authority be able to override female authority at critical moments, whether by cultural prerogative or by physical force. While a family might pursue a shared goal—sending some children into the workforce, for instance, so that the mother might remain at home—the compromises made over which goals to pursue and how to pursue them are products of unequal power relations between men and women in the household.[11] The apparent unity of the family results from men's and, to some degree, parents' ability to impose that unity upon the family's actions. Thus, to understand how families worked together to make the women's picket succeed, and how the picket, in turn, affected families, we must uncover the power relations that lay beneath the appearance of unity behind a common goal.

Divisions of labor are not only gendered; as we have seen, a central organizing principle of Grant County's economy was an ethnic division of labor. These two divisions of labor share certain features. In both situations, people ascribe different values to different types of work—some work is considered dirty and debasing, other work ennobling—and assign that work to people based on ethnicity or sex. This ascription is a social process, not a natural one, but it is made to seem natural and unchangeable. Ultimately it serves to mark and reinforce power differences between groups or individuals. Still, there are some important differences between ethnic and sexual divisions of labor, and these differences bear on the varied ways that working-class people built solidarity in Grant County's mining district. The key difference lies in the family: the sexual division of labor resides in the family (as well as in the larger labor market); the ethnic division of labor does not. Both divisions entail a certain symbiosis, but of very different sorts. The sexual division of labor in the household is maintained by the emotional and practical ties that bind a family together. There are no such emotional ties binding Mexican American workers to Anglo workers. The definition of "Mexican" work, of course, depended on a counterdefinition of "Anglo" work. But the ethnic division of labor, unlike the sexual division, does not entail interdependence so much as complementarity. And whereas the sexual division of labor allows families to pursue shared goals, the goals advanced by the ethnic division of labor are not workers' goals but rather those of their employers. As much as Anglo managers and workers might speak of the ethnic division of labor as natural, efficient, and contributing to the benefit of all, the people on the bottom—the Mexicans—are more likely to see those divisions as artificial, unjust, and harmful. By contrast, family members on both sides of the sexual division of labor constantly experience the ties that bind them to one another, and it is hard to alter some of those ties without sundering them altogether. This does not mean that the sexual division of labor *is* natural, or necessarily desirable, but that family members of both sexes receive some benefits from it.

In this chapter I analyze these household relations, considering both the ways that people made their families and the ideology that supported particular arrangements, in order to see what women were rebelling against and how they experienced and understood the conflicts that shook up their families. The breadwinner ideal, discussed in Chapter 4, was manifest in women's desire to marry, in the economic structure that limited women's options outside of marriage, in women's daily household work and management, and in husbands' attitudes—accompanied by the power to enforce their beliefs.

CHOOSING MARRIAGE

Most women in Grant County got married, usually quite willingly. Dolores Villines, for example, had grown up very shy, very reserved, and forbidden to date boys. Frank Jiménez was her first and only boyfriend, and she was struck, as she called it, "love blind." "I just loved that man very much. For me he was everything." She married him when she was only seventeen years old, and she had both of her sons by the time she was nineteen.[12] For girls tired of their parents' restrictions, marriage promised excitement and the release from childhood. Elena and Daría Escobar grew up under close supervision by their mother, who raised them and their eight siblings alone by taking in boarders. Neither girl was allowed to date boys, or even to walk through the neighborhood unescorted; Daría used the time when her mother was at church to run quickly from one neighbor's house to the next, desperate for some social contact.[13] Marriage provided an escape from this cloistered upbringing. To some women I spoke with, marriage was something they had wanted very much—at least at the time they decided to get married; perhaps there was some wistfulness at the eagerness with which they had gotten married, or some regret at the mistakes of the young. But in all cases, they implied that marriage was something definitive, perhaps inevitable.

If marriage played a part in most women's graduation to adulthood, it was also a choice heavily influenced by the job market and cultural expectations. There were material reasons why staying single was a difficult path to follow: it was hard for a woman to support herself or her family without a male wage-earner. "A woman could work in the stores," Josie Flores remembered. "Or in the restaurants," added her husband Arturo. "Just hardly anything else."[14] As is discussed below, job opportunities for women, regardless of their ethnicity, expanded and contracted within the economic sectors of clerical, sales, service, and, to a lesser extent, professional work. Ethnicity further determined women's opportunities. Anglo women were more likely to work as professionals and clerical workers than were Mexican American women.[15]

Marriage often ruled out a paying job, though this was not the case with two of the Empire Zinc strikers and *Salt of the Earth* actors: both Henrietta Williams and Clorinda Alderette worked outside the home while married. But many women I spoke with laughed off the suggestion that they could have done both. When asked what happened to the jobs they had held as young women, Dora Madero and Alice Sandoval both gave the same explanation, "I got married." Sandoval said that her husband did not want her to work—"I guess I wanted to get married more than I wanted to work"—and Madero hinted as much.[16] Virginia Chacón worked for five years as a nurse's aide for a doctor she respected, but she turned down his offer to transfer to Phoenix and go to school at his expense. Recounting the story fifty years later, Chacón first laughed when she explained her decision: "Oh, I got married!" She paused, then confessed regretting her choice "in a sense, because [Dr. Meyers and his wife] were such good people to work with. They were so good to me."[17]

DIVISIONS OF LABOR

When women boldly suggested that they take over the Empire Zinc picket line in June 1951, they were acting on the basis of class and ethnic consciousness that reflected both their own work histories and their recent union activism. When men agreed to "let" women assume picket duty, their actions, too, were based on class and ethnic consciousness. But as discussed in Chapter 4, the arguments unleashed during that contentious union meeting suggest that there was more to this class and ethnic consciousness than meets the eye. Since it provided the basis for different stances, its meanings seem to have varied for men and women. Experiences in jobs and families provided the basis for both men's and women's consciousness, but the work they performed, the responsibilities they met, and the authority they held in the family were very different.

Women's virtual absence from mining—the region's dominant industry—was a critical feature of the economic structure that limited their opportunities and made marriage a necessity for many, if not most, women. Put simply, women enjoyed few opportunities for paid work. Western mining camps of the nineteenth century sprang up wherever ore was discovered, not according to a well-planned model of urban expansion, and although some operations eventually became industrial processing centers themselves, they were typically located far from urban industrial centers that might have offered a range of jobs to women. The Silver City area presented a greater range of occupations than some mining regions because Silver City was the county seat and also home to the state teachers' college. But it was by no means a "city" with a diverse industrial base, and most mining families lived in the smaller towns ten to fifteen miles from Silver City. Some women commuted to Silver City, but limited transportation kept many women isolated in their homes and small towns.[18]

Only a minority of women in Grant County belonged to the paid labor force, although the number and percentage grew from 1940 to 1950.[19] In 1940, 1,126 (17 percent) women aged fourteen and older considered themselves part of the labor force; this number rose to 1,585 (22 percent) in 1950. Most employed women worked in sales, clerical, and service jobs, their numbers more than doubling between 1940 and 1950 from 169 women (15 percent of the female labor force) to 453 (28 percent of the female labor force).[20] Only 41 women worked as factory operatives in 1940, and, while that number almost doubled to 74 in 1950, it still represented only 1 percent of adult women and just under 5 percent of the adult female labor force.[21] Over the same period, the professional ranks remained relatively stable. The number of professional women increased from 236 to 307, but the proportion of women professionals in the adult female labor force actually dropped from 21 percent in 1940 to 19 percent in 1950. Teaching, nursing, and administrative work were the most common professions for women.

Of course, these jobs were not distributed equally: ethnicity determined women's jobs as much as it did men's. Anecdotal evidence—job notices and descriptions of individuals in the local newspapers—as well as the 1930 census data suggest this job segregation.[22] Professions were almost exclusively Anglo through the 1950s, as were most clerical positions, but both Anglos and Mexicans held sales jobs.

Exceptional circumstances brought a few dozen Grant County women into local mines and mills during World War II. Chino hired several dozen women to fill the male labor shortage, although all 63 underground workers in 1944 were still men. That year, 29 women joined the track gangs that laid, repaired, and moved the railroad tracks on which cars hauled ore from the Chino open pit mine in Santa Rita.[23] Guadalupe Fletcher, divorced and responsible for her daughter's care, quit domestic service to work on the track gang.[24] Younger women worked there, too, among them Dora Madero, a Silver City teenager. Walking to school one morning, she and a friend happened upon some girls boarding a Santa Rita–bound bus in Silver City. "Let's get on the bus," Madero told her friend, "and see what happens." "[We] rode all the way to Santa Rita, and believe it or not . . . were hired right way," Madero explained. "They didn't even ask your age, or nothing. Not even if you had social security or anything like that. They just hired you. So they gave us a little money, and they had a company store and we went up there and we got our safety shoes, and a lunch box, and a safety hat." They stayed until the bus left for Silver City at 4 P.M. Madero normally came home from school at 3:30, however, and her suspicious mother met her at the door. She looked at her daughter's new safety shoes. "Where were you all this time?" she wanted to know. "I've been worrying about you." Madero was supposed to graduate from high school but insisted on working at Santa Rita instead; she would finish school after the war, she told her mother. Only because the family needed money—Madero's father had run off ("like most men do," Madero commented) and Dora's mother was raising her daughters alone—did her mother finally come to accept her daughter's job and overlook her daughter's willfulness.[25]

Madero enjoyed the work, the camaraderie, and the money (even though she had to turn it over to her mother). Her foreman was less thrilled to have a group of young women working under him. "You women," he complained. "First snowfall we get, you're going home. You're not staying here and you're going to mess up everything. We're not going to have nothing to work with, nobody." But all of them stayed on the track gang. And apparently her foreman liked her enough to let her drive other girls to their work sites in a little car and then to let her work as "water girl," bringing water to all the workers in her car.[26]

A handful of women also worked as laborers in other Santa Rita departments. One woman worked as an electrical laborer, another in the machine shop, four in the carpentry department, and two as drill laborers in the powder department.[27] None of these occupations was considered skilled labor, which suggests that the wartime labor shortage drew women selectively into the workforce. Any consideration of the work appropriate to women apparently did not turn on the question of physical danger: most women's jobs were demanding and difficult. Chino hired women in large blocks separately from the men hired in the same departments; moreover, women were singled out and identified on the seniority lists as "F" for "female." This suggests that Chino's management opened the doors to women's employment in a conscious and regulated way. The two powder drill laborers, for instance, occupied a new, sep-

Women working at Chino during World War II. Photo courtesy of the Silver City Museum.

arate classification; there were no male powder drill laborers. Peru Mining Company and its subsidiary, the New Mexico Consolidated Mining Company, also employed women during the war, as did the American Smelting and Refining Company (Asarco), but not in the numbers that Chino did.[28] Clorinda Kirker, a Mexican American woman, worked underground at the Blackhawk mine when she was nineteen years old; she was in charge of the pumps at the 500-foot level, and she joined Local 604 in December 1942. "Probably she is the first girl in this part of the country to take over such duties," the *Silver City Daily Press* commented, "but it is said that she performs her task with exceptional ability and carefulness and that there aren't many men who could do much better."[29] In the context of wartime emergency, the occasional female worker could be accommodated. Later, Kirker married Frank Alderette, and in 1952 she played the role of Luz Morales in *Salt of the Earth*.

After the war, women left the mining industry. A few stayed on at Chino through 1945 and part of 1946, but by 1947, three of Kennecott's four female employees were maids. The exception, Guadalupe Fletcher, continued to work for Chino and was eventually promoted to truck driver in the 1950s, retiring in 1983.[30] Whether other women left voluntarily or were fired is unclear. But the employment history of Rita S.

Jiménez suggests that she, in any case, did not wish to leave the mining industry altogether. After leaving Chino in 1945, Jiménez worked in Asarco's Hanover office at least until April 1947, continuing as a union member once Mine-Mill gained certification to represent Asarco's office staff. The 1950 census reveals 14 Grant County women engaged in primary metals manufacturing (mills and smelters), compared to 892 men. Only 22 women worked in the mining industry as a whole, compared to 1,313 men.[31] While the wartime employment of women in mining was temporary, it nonetheless may have allowed some women to imagine alternatives to low-paid or unpaid work.

WORKING IN THE HOME

In Grant County, almost all adult women kept house, whether or not they also performed paid work.[32] Indeed, throughout New Mexico in 1950, according to one marketing survey, New Mexican housewives "outnumber[ed] the women in all other roles combined, by a ratio of more than three to two."[33] By contrast, very few men kept house, even if they did not belong to the labor force.[34] Male unemployment, then, did not free up men to do housework: the basic asymmetry in the sexual division of labor overrode the seemingly similar experience of not holding a paid job.

Women's relative absence from the formal paid labor force did not divorce them from the local economy. The family wage economy was intimately, and thoroughly, tied to the formal economy of wages and production industries. Within the household economy, a clear division of labor prevailed. Men in mining families provided most of the family's income from wage labor, and women, whether also working for wages or not, assumed almost complete responsibility for household work. Men and women alike were invested in marriage and stable families and in upholding the distinctions between men's and women's work.[35] Moreover, women's household working conditions resulted from their own, albeit indirect, relationship to corporate power, which was manifest in the housing available to workers and the credit arrangements in company stores.

Women's unpaid work sustained the paid labor force. Feminist scholars of the 1970s and 1980s have interpreted household work as "reproductive labor," which complemented the productive labor to which most Marxist analysts had long given their exclusive attention. Feeding and clothing their families, housewives maintained the living standards that enabled men, and sometimes children, to work for wages. The unpaid nature of housework, far from representing a holdover from precapitalist social relations, was instead an inherent feature of the industrial capitalism that developed in Europe and the United States. Capitalists' ability to pay low wages effectively rested on the unpaid—and often unacknowledged—labor of women.[36]

Surveying the living and working conditions of women in coalmining families in 1925, the Women's Bureau of the U.S. Department of Labor drew similar conclusions about the importance of women's housework to the entire industry:

> The mine worker's wife occupies a position of peculiar industrial and economic importance whether she falls in the class of gainfully employed or not. . . . The bunk house and the mine boarding and lodging house long ago proved themselves inadequate to attract a requisite number of workers or to maintain a stable labor supply. Only the presence of his family can keep the mine worker in the mining region, and because of the isolation of so many mining operations the mine worker's wife assumes an unusual importance to the industry. The mine worker can not at will substitute the restaurant for family table as can the wage earners in other important industries. He is more continuously dependent upon his home for the essentials of health and working efficiency.[37]

In a practical sense, women's housework consisted of a series of tasks that promoted their families' well being: cleaning, cooking, laundering, buying food, and taking care of children. Alice Sandoval recalled her mother "always cooking, baking, praying, or nursing."[38] Uneven technological advances in municipal services and household appliances made working-class housework dramatically different from that performed in middle-class homes. Women could delegate some chores to children, but only the middle classes, both Anglo and Mexican American, could afford the labor-saving appliances that might lessen for housewives the defining burden and drudgery of housework, or the domestic servants who would relieve the burden altogether. Housework also had a managerial dimension. Housewives managed the family's money, figuring out each day how to stretch a small income to cover many financial needs. Budgeting that portion of men's wages that made it home did not mean, however, that women fully controlled the family's money. Not only did working-class men bring home small incomes, but they also took out what they wanted before handing over the pay packet to their wives. Thus, household chores and family budgeting both acquired political and economic dimensions that underscored local class and gender power relations. Finally, women's work in the home had an emotional aspect: women were caregivers, and the definition of their role in the family as that of nurturer shaped the ways in which they performed and thought and felt about their work.

Tracing the day's work of a housewife allows us to analyze the implications of new technology and municipal services for women's work. A woman's work day began while her husband was still asleep. Cooking breakfast for her family entailed much more work than simply pouring a bowl of cereal. Into the 1930s, many Mexican American women still made their own tortillas at home, which required pounding corn or wheat masa by hand, rolling out the dough, and cooking the tortillas over a wood stove. Some women prepared tortillas to sell to neighbors, as did Bill Wood's mother.[39] By the late 1940s, Eligio's Tortilla Factory, run by Eligio Ynostroza and perhaps also his wife, provided tortillas to nearby restaurants and housewives in the Bayard vicinity. It is likely that women still made their own tortillas, but only for special occasions, like Christmas.[40] But even without having to make tortillas by hand, as some women continued to do into the 1950s, preparing the day's first meal required a number of steps from which most middle-class women were free by the 1920s.

First and foremost, few miners' houses had indoor plumbing, and Mexican American families were generally worse off than Anglo families in this regard. By the end of the nineteenth century, most urban areas had running water, if only from a tap in a tenement courtyard. But rural Americans carried water from an outdoor pump or well long into the twentieth century.[41] The difficulty of getting and using water affected almost every aspect of housework, whether cleaning, laundering, or feeding one's family. In the mid-1940s, Virginia Chacón, for example, enjoyed no indoor plumbing in her North Hurley house. Her husband, Juan, "had to make a cistern and he'd carry water from Hurley." She explained, "We bought a jalopy truck, and a friend of his built him a tank, and he'd fill that tank with water every evening when he got out of work. . . . And then we bought a little electric pump and he installed the water inside."[42] This kind of small electric or gasoline-motored pump became common in rural areas in the early part of the century.[43] The Chacóns improved their water facilities only gradually: prior to installing the electric pump, Virginia Chacón had to bring the water inside for every chore, and even with the pump, she had to heat the water on the stove and then dispose of waste water outside. As historian Ruth Schwartz Cowan reminds us, tap water is only a "small [part] of what we now consider the total water system. The full system contains pipes to conduct water into more than one room . . . , devices for heating some of the water and distributing it, as well as specialized containers . . . which make it fairly easy to use water for different purposes and to dispose of it."[44] Most or all of this system was lacking for many Grant County mining families.[45]

Insurance agent C. B. Ogás, visiting Grant County homes in the late 1940s, found that frequently "one [outdoor] water faucet took care of three or four homes with no indoor facilities" and that outdoor privies were the norm.[46] Most of Hanover's Mexican American residents lacked even a tap on the side of the house. Elena and Raymundo Tafoya shared a well with other town residents, and Matías Rivera, growing up in Fierro and Hanover in the late 1940s, had indoor plumbing in neither childhood home. His mother put him to work hauling the water. He was fortunate when his family moved, because Hanover's well was closer to home than Fierro's well had been.[47] This deplorable situation did not change quickly for miners and their families. At the time of the Empire Zinc strike, fewer than half of Grant County's dwelling units had "running hot water, private toilet and bath, and [were] not dilapidated."[48]

Stoves generally burned wood, which required chopping, hauling, and igniting before a woman could cook the family's meal, calling to mind the indignant tirade of Luz Morales in *Salt of the Earth*: "Listen, we ought to be in the wood choppers' union. Chop wood for breakfast. Chop wood to wash his clothes. Chop wood, heat the iron. Chop wood, scrub the floor. Chop wood, cook his dinner."[49] Wood-burning stoves created more grime than did gas or electric stoves, and grime meant more work for a housewife. These stoves could prove dangerous, too. Adelaida Martínez Sánchez of Turnerville was badly burned when her stove exploded; a week later she died in the Santa Rita hospital.[50] Local authorities traced many Grant County fires to faulty kitchen and heating systems. An oil-burning stove, for instance, seemed like an advance over a wood-burning stove to the Hubble family in Bayard, but an overflow of oil caused a small fire in their apartment.[51]

Cooking was a constant activity for a woman, who had to accommodate the varying schedules of her husband, family, and (frequently) boarders. A husband who worked on the graveyard shift, for instance, needed meals at unusual times of the day. The combination of fatigue, difficult work schedules, and dangerous living conditions combined in a tragic fire that killed one miner's wife and her children in 1950. Anita Domínguez, a twenty-eight-year-old housewife, had gotten up on August 22 to prepare breakfast for her husband, Manuel, who was at work on the graveyard shift at Asarco's Groundhog mine. Evidently she fell asleep again, and the wood stove burned down the wood-frame house early that morning. She and two of her children, ages ten and one, died before neighbors could get them out.[52]

Constant meal preparation also meant constant food gathering. The daily shopping might involve walking between one or more grocery stores to find the lowest prices; women knew which stores had the best deals for which items. Many stores delivered groceries to miners' houses, and often mothers sent their children to the stores with lists if, as was likely, the family had no telephone. A woman often needed to shop every day because few families had refrigerators to store perishables. Refrigeration required electricity, which was more common than indoor plumbing, but often houses "were wired just for lights"; Matías Rivera and Aurora Chávez used kerosene lamps into the 1940s because their houses had only a single overhead light.[53] Refrigerator prices reached affordable levels for many middle-class families in the 1920s and then dropped considerably in the 1930s.[54] Anita Torrez recalled that after a year or so of marriage, she and her husband were able to purchase a refrigerator—one of the few appliances they had in their two-room house in Hanover.[55] Growing up on a ranch near Hanover, though, Albert Vigil watched his mother use a cold spring as a refrigerator in the 1920s and 1930s. She eventually moved into Bayard, in fact, because of the conveniences there, leaving her husband to run the ranch without her.[56]

If refrigerators made it into some homes, washing machines did not. Fifty-two percent of American homes had power washing machines in 1941, according to the Bureau of Labor Statistics, but only the middle classes did so in Grant County.[57] Laundering clothes and linens without a washing machine was difficult. Matías Rivera and his siblings hauled the water and heated it on the wood stove so that their mother could wash the clothes on a washboard, as did Bill Wood for his mother.[58] Then came another round of hauling and heating for rinsing the clothes. It is little wonder that laundering has been one of the most eagerly abandoned household tasks for American women, and for women in mining towns, as in industrial cities, washing took on an even more odious dimension because mining was such filthy work. Men brought their sweaty, dirty clothes home (although changing rooms allowed some men to leave their work clothes at the mine), and women had to make those clothes presentable again. There were a few self-service laundries in Bayard: Mr. and Mrs. L. H. Gray ran Ruby's Help-U-Self Laundry and D. F. Christopher ran Porter's Help-U-Self Laundry. Clearly some residents made use of their services, but most working-class women did the work themselves.[59]

With clothing washed and hung outside to dry, women would then prepare to iron. Here, too, women, and sometimes children, worked without the benefit of the electrical appliances that became common elsewhere in the United States during the 1920s through the 1950s. A woman heated an iron on the stovetop, removing or replacing it frequently to regulate the heat. Performed in winter, this chore could heat up the kitchen pleasurably; performed in summer, it was stifling.[60] The first appliance that Bill Wood's mother got was an electric iron, which eased her son's work hauling wood.[61]

Not all of Grant County lacked amenities like indoor plumbing or electricity. The Phelps-Dodge company housing in Tyrone, which closed when the mine closed in 1921, offered utilities to many of its residents, even some Mexican American families; Chino's company housing outside of Santa Rita provided them to the Anglo workers.[62] Silver City boasted substantial municipal services very early in its history. By 1887, it had telephone service, electric lights, and a public water system.[63] The local newspapers regularly advertised gleaming electrical appliances like stoves and washing machines. But these examples, far from diminishing the deprivations suffered by the majority of miners' families, instead underscored a critical aspect of local conditions: the maldistribution of technology and services.

While Silver City provided considerable amenities for some of its residents in the late 1880s, photos of the Mexican neighborhood of Chihuahua Hill from the period reveal dilapidated buildings, graphically demonstrating that municipal services were unevenly spread.[64] As late as 1944, Chihuahua Hill residents petitioned for a sewer line; they got a gas line in 1946 when a gas main was extended to a new housing division just beyond Chihuahua Hill.[65] Brewer Hill, southeast of downtown and the home of Mexican Americans and Silver City's few African Americans, lacked adequate water connections. Its streets were so bad that firefighters had trouble reaching and then extinguishing a fire there in July 1948.[66] In Santa Rita, recalled former resident George De Luna, the "Anglo side [of town] was paved by the company, while on the Mexican side, every time it rained the [dirt] roads would be washed out."[67]

And when Juan Chacón brought water home every evening, it was precisely because, unlike the Anglo houses in Hurley, Mexican American homes in North Hurley lacked indoor plumbing.[68] The situation was the same in Hanover. The Empire Zinc Company, which owned much of the housing there, provided indoor plumbing for its Anglo workers but not for the Mexican Americans.[69] As Anita Torrez commented during the Empire Zinc strike, "Empire thinks us second-class workers," undeserving of the plumbing that Anglos enjoyed.[70]

The prevalent myth that housewives did not "work" hardly reflected the reality of working-class women's lives. Mining men in particular were not likely to think of their wives as working, when "work," for them, connoted dangerous, physical work in the mines—not unpaid housework, divorced as it was from the very concept of the breadwinner. In *Salt of the Earth*, Luz Morales insists that women "ought to be in the wood choppers' union" because women did hard work. And she resented the added insult of her husband's attitude: "And you know what he'll say when he gets home. [Mimics husband Antonio] What you been doing all day? Reading the funny papers?"[71]

MONEY

One way to understand the family wage economy is to consider both money and its absence. The flow of money and the effort to substitute housewives' goods and services for commercial ones illuminate the relations between husbands and wives, and between the family and society. A miner's wife typically managed the household's budget, but this managerial duty took place within considerable constraints that operated on two levels, one from outside and the other from within the household. First, while mining paid better than many jobs, the work was frequently interrupted by layoffs during the downswings of the mining economy and strikes during contract negotiations (once the union was recognized). During wartime, a miner's wife dealt with shortages of fats, sugar, and other necessities, and if she lived in a company town she had to pay inflated company-store prices. And a husband's injury or death on the job was a constant possibility, regardless of war or strikes. Second, the household's income passed first through the filter of her husband's personal spending patterns. Wives in Grant County employed a number of strategies to keep their families afloat within these constraints, and constraints and strategies alike placed housewives firmly within, not beyond, the local economy.

The primary constraints within which a woman managed the household budget were the amount of wages and what she could do with them. Metal miners typically earned decent wages compared to local workers who performed other forms of labor, and over the course of the 1940s and 1950s miners' wages doubled from between six and eight dollars a day to twelve or more dollars a day. Mexican American housewives, though, could count on their husbands to be at the lower end of the wage scale because of occupational segregation that resulted in a "Mexican wage" far below what Anglo workers earned. Serious unemployment crises in 1949–50 and 1952–53, as well as strikes, quickly dried up any family savings and made it hard for a housewife to make ends meet. Only a steady income could accomplish that, and the ebbs and flows of metal production—and the periodic strikes—made income unsteady. Moreover, a housewife was constrained by the cost of goods and services—costs that rose ever higher during the war (even with price controls) and then again once the U.S. Office of Price Administration lifted the controls in 1947. Prices remained stable through the early 1950s, but, again, this stability must be seen against the backdrop of unemployment surges.

Also shaping the decisions a housewife could make were her husband's spending patterns. Men often turned over their pay to their wives, but not before taking a cut themselves. By cashing the check in a local bar, for instance, a man had the opportunity—if not the obligation, if he owed a tab—to leave some of the wages behind. Anecdotal evidence that men frequently cashed their paychecks in bars finds corroboration in the actual canceled checks from union bank accounts.[72] One evening in October 1943, a distraught Tony Sena told police that he had been robbed on the highway. The investigation revealed, however, that Sena had lost the forty-three dollars gambling and "feared to go home without the money."[73]

First among women's strategies for coping with limited incomes was to live on credit. Every grocery store in the Central mining district extended credit at some point to its customers, and every person I interviewed recalled having kept a running bill at the grocery store. During strikes, some stores, like Southwestern Food and Sales of Bayard, extended credit and occasionally erased the union's strike accounts altogether. Small businesses generally saw their own well-being tied up in workers' wages. For example, while the Empire Zinc strike stretched the bonds of this limited cross-class solidarity, it is noteworthy that most of the bonds posted to keep strikers out of jail were provided by sympathetic local businesses.[74] Checks paid to union members—reimbursements, or rewards for signing up new members during organizing drives—were frequently cashed at grocery stores and other retail establishments.[75] Stores might have functioned as banks simply because they were convenient; with only two banks in the district—the American National Bank of Silver City and the Grant County State Bank in Bayard—someone who needed to cash a check on the weekend or in one of the smaller towns would have been out of luck if stores did not cash customers' checks. It is reasonable to infer that sometimes the check casher left some of the cash in the till to pay off debts.

Besides living on credit from month to month, most working-class wives kept expenses down by replacing purchased goods and services with goods they produced themselves; at other times, they simply did without. They supplemented the family's income by working for wages, taking in boarders, or marketing goods produced at home. None of women's paid work eliminated housework. Indeed, for those women who took in boarders, the work was an extension of their existing housework and increased that workload. Elena Tafoya's mother ran a boardinghouse, first in Santa Rita and then in Bayard in the late 1930s, feeding meals to miners each day. Matías Rivera's mother was providing the same service to miners in the late 1940s, as well as running a bar that another son owned. Boarding and lodging characterized life in mining camps, in the United States as elsewhere, but much less so by the 1950s.[76]

Many women had to work outside the home in order to make ends meet, and they performed this work on top of whatever housework they could not delegate to children. Paid workers were always the minority of Grant County women. But the difficulties facing families with uneven or inadequate income—or, especially, those without a male breadwinner—made some female employment a part of many a family's strategy to survive.

POWER STRUGGLES

Cooperation and conflict shaped working-class marriages in Grant County. Men and women frequently agreed on the obligations of husbands and wives; men should provide wages, and women should make a home. The terms of the family wage economy were not necessarily at issue. But individuals could not always meet their obligations within that economy, and couples could not always agree on exactly what constituted meeting them. The relative power of husbands and wives both reflected and determined these negotiations.

Despite the interdependence that defined the family wage economy, not all couples stayed together. During and after World War II some men left their families, either to find better work elsewhere or to escape altogether. Several—almost all Mexican American—found themselves hauled before District Court Judge A. W. Marshall for abandoning their families. Sentences ranged from six months to a year in jail, sometimes with hard labor, but the judge typically suspended the sentence if the husband agreed to support his family.[77] Dislocations of wartime accounted for a rash of divorces in 1946 and 1947. The *Silver City Daily Press* commented on "the usual grist of divorces filed" in November 1946 and on the "flourishing divorce business" of the year as a whole: 179 of Grant County's 304 civil cases were divorces.[78] Perhaps because of the cost and the Catholic proscription against divorce, proportionally fewer Mexican American than Anglo couples divorced; the ratio was approximately one to five.[79] In addition, some Mexican Americans lived in common-law marriages, which would have made divorce unnecessary for those couples who wanted to part ways.

Domestic violence disrupted many households. Dolores Jiménez, for example, was brutalized by her husband, Frank, during both of her pregnancies, before she was even twenty years old. "I shouldn't say this," she said later. "That was the greatest thing, to have my two boys. But that's one of the things I didn't care [for in] being married. Because I was abused, every which way. Pregnant and everything. I don't think it's right. But I wouldn't change my two sons for anything, and I'll go through fire for them, but that's one of the things I didn't like. If I had to have kids again and go through that, there's no way. There's no way I would let it happen. Being dragged, being hit."[80]

Rarely did this kind of violence make it onto the public radar screen, much less into the courts. But in Grant County there were enough published notices of husbands charged with assaulting their wives to dispel any idea that this was a completely hidden crime.[81] Both Anglo and Mexican American husbands tried to keep control over their households by beating their wives. Certainly these were not private conflicts, in the sense of no one else knowing of them; neighbors were very likely to hear violent conflicts. But they remained private in that rarely did anyone intervene to stop them. The case of the Montoyas is illustrative. Cipriano was a physically imposing man, used to exercising power at home, as well as in the union hall. Feliciana ("Chana") had married him when she was quite young, and she had few resources with which to resist his violence. Other union officials, including men close to the Communist Party and familiar with its critique of male chauvinism, knew about this abuse, but no one confronted Cipriano or tried to help Chana.

Rarely did these conflicts end in divorce. Dolores Jiménez tried to deal with Frank's violence by running out of the house. She did not want to leave him because he was a good provider—even though she also knew that he had been unfaithful to her.[82] One exception is the McNutts, a couple who often tangled with the Empire Zinc picketers (see Chapter 5). Homer McNutt was charged with assaulting his wife on several occasions in 1946. She had evidently had enough by 1948, when she successfully sued for divorce, yet just four months later Homer again pleaded not guilty of assaulting his wife.[83] Sometimes these conflicts resulted in shootings, if weapons were handy, and even if a woman got out of the marriage, there was no guarantee that she had escaped the power of an angry ex-husband. Certainly most families did not experience this kind of violence, but the examples serve to underscore how men possessed a prerogative to keep their families in line by force.

AN UNEASY RESOLUTION

Women's awareness of the interdependent nature of the family, and their knowledge of the critical contributions they made with the work that defined each day of their lives, proved essential to their ability to imagine, contemplate, and eventually insist upon playing an active and ultimately transformative role in the Empire Zinc strike. They arrived at that awareness over time, as they became more involved in the union. The film's matter-of-fact depiction of Esperanza's and Ramón's work shows a recognition, generated by the Empire Zinc strike, of women's and men's respective contributions to the family's survival, of women's unpaid housework as *work* on a par with that performed by the "breadwinner."

The women's picket challenged husbands to shoulder some of their wives' responsibilities, and some men did change, at least temporarily. "It sure was a shock to us women," one picketer remarked, "to find out that our husbands were such good cooks and housekeepers and the shock to the men that their women could hold the picket lines as well as they have."[84] Clinton Jencks, Bob Hollowwa, and Cipriano Montoya explained the process to the international's executive board in August 1951. Interestingly, they focused on the problem of men helping women at the picket location, although housework had also been under discussion; they were trying to cast the strike in the most positive light possible, and perhaps introducing another level of complexity ran counter to their aims. "In the past few weeks considerable improvement has been made in organizational problems which have come up from time to time," they reported. "Such problems as the participation of strikers in helping the women with work in and around the picket line—such as hauling water, chopping wood, furnishing transportation to women pickets, carrying out the numerous odd jobs required at the picket line. Solving these problems have been accomplished by and thru 'frank' discussion of all the people involved."[85] Symbolizing these changes was the preparation for a dinner to celebrate the first anniversary of the strike. Local 890 president Cipriano Montoya asked which woman would head the food committee. Mariana Ramírez, captain of the women's picket, asked if the dinner was meant to honor the women; reassured that it was, she suggested that Montoya ask "what *brother* would volunteer to head the food committee, because, personally, she expected to *sit* all through the celebration and be honored." Ramírez got what she requested. "The evening of the dinner the men were at the tables serving the food and cutting the hams and sweeping the floors."[86]

But even with men assuming some of women's duties, women often relied on other women to pick up the slack. "All those women we didn't see," Dolores Jiménez recalled, "they were taking care of our kids. The men were maybe taking care of the kids, some took us to the picket, some were busy, some were in the bar drinking. And some were angry, [wondering] how long is this gonna go on."[87]

Ernesto Velásquez provides a good example of the complexities bound up in men's experiences of the women's picket. An employee of Empire Zinc since 1948, he quickly assumed leadership within the Empire Zinc unit of Local 890. Velásquez chaired the strike negotiating committee and emerged as one of the women's most consistent supporters. Unlike Cipriano Montoya, who generally referred to the strikers as "brothers," Velásquez acknowledged women as full-fledged union members. (He was by no means alone in this; several men did so.) He frequently and publicly encouraged women to participate, and the steady participation of his wife, Braulia, speaks to his willingness, on some level, to put his money where his mouth was. On the occasion of the strike anniversary, for instance, he described to the union brothers and sisters how he felt "as a newborn, . . . good as to how solid everything has been over the past year. One year of suffering of our strikers. . . . The women . . . knew nothing about strikes but [now] they are veterans. The women were tear-gassed, jailed, these women have suffered."[88] In stressing women's suffering, Velásquez did not dwell on men's failure to protect their wives. Instead, he cast it as women's strength in the face of company assaults. Such a picture drew on an unassailable cultural value, that of women's patient strength. Moreover, he acknowledged that he *himself* had been transformed: he was the newborn, birthed by these women.

At the September 1951 Mine-Mill convention, Velásquez again expressed appreciation for the women picketers. But here, in this national setting, a convention primarily of men, he also expressed ambivalence. Joking about the role reversals effected by the women's picket, Velásquez revealed some of his discomfort and, perhaps, his way of easing it: "We will see what my wife says—and I hate to be calling her a wife now—she's the boss of the family. It so happened the 13th of June she took over the household. We have a little baby and she said you go home and wash the dishes and change the diapers. That puts me in an embarrassing situation. I have washed the dishes and I have swept the house, but one thing I cannot get myself to do and that is change a diaper. Let's see what Sister Velásquez has to say."[89] Sister Velásquez had nothing to say about "taking over the household"; instead, she described the picket and her time in jail. There are any number of reasons why she might have remained silent on the topic that her husband had so clearly and so publicly raised. Perhaps she believed that nothing of substance had changed, or that the subject was too touchy to be aired in this public setting. Perhaps she felt that Ernesto had used humor to trivialize the extent and meaning of changes in gender relations and had thereby won over the largely male audience to his own perspective. For what could be more ridiculous than a female "boss of the family"? And how could a man boss the family if he had to change diapers? What, indeed, could changing diapers represent, if not the debasement that necessarily accompanies wifehood?

Enough men accepted the changes, at least for the duration of the strike, for the strike to succeed. In January 1952, the Empire Zinc Company finally returned to the negotiating table and agreed to a contract that granted many of the union's demands. Some weeks later, the company quietly agreed to add indoor plumbing to all of its company houses —a demand raised as early as 1949, but one that the male negotiating committee had quickly abandoned when it was challenged.

Throughout the summer and fall of 1951, then, women undertook two sorts of defensive actions. The first was to defend their community against the company and the scabs, police, and local court functionaries that the company marshaled. The second was to defend their actions against the resentment and active opposition of their own husbands, who believed that domestic relations should remain constant lest the community be fractured. Convinced that their motivations and actions were just, women picketers bristled at the opposition they encountered from husbands and insisted that the real threat to stability and unity lay with men's "backward" ideas.

Once the strike ended, however, the pull of the old ways proved very powerful. Men and women alike desired things to get back to normal, even if they were not sure exactly what that would look like. They all had a stake in making the family unit work. The Empire Zinc strike may have made many couples rearrange the assignments of authority and responsibility, but the strike's conclusion did not consolidate those changes for all of them. Strike families' experiences making *Salt of the Earth* show both how household power relations were still uncertain and how women were making use of their strike experience to continue to shape those relations.

PART III

———

A WORKER-ARTIST ALLIANCE

7

The Blacklist

It was late in the summer of 1951, and the Jencks family was driving out of Silver City for a short vacation. They were exhausted by the Empire Zinc strike, which was becoming more tense as the deadline for a national copper strike drew nearer, and they knew the strikers could run things perfectly well without them: committees had long been in place to print leaflets, write radio programs, write bulletins, and try to talk to the company.[1] The Jenckses drove up the Rio Grande Valley to San Cristóbal, a small town near Taos pressed into the Sangre de Cristo range and watered by creeks running from 12,000-foot mountains into the Rio Grande a mile to the west. Their destination was a ranch owned by their friends Jenny and Craig Vincent.

This was not an ordinary ranch. Its mission was not raising livestock so much as fostering community among progressives looking for a refuge from the battles of the Cold War. On any given Saturday night, guests and neighbors of the San Cristóbal ranch gathered for song, dance, and socializing. One week might offer a square dance, the next a revue staged by kids at the summer camp run by the Vincents. They performed songs popularized by left-wing folksingers of the 1930s and 1940s, people like Earl Robinson, who wrote the famous labor song "Joe Hill" in 1936 while directing the music program at another children's camp. Yiddish nursery songs, Irish jigs, Czech dances, and American slave ballads all made their way into the repertoire.

Jenny Wells Vincent was a classically trained musician who turned to folk music. She often performed at progressive gatherings (including one of the Mine-Mill conventions and a reception for the Asociación Nacional Mexicana Americana) and promoted the music and culture of northern New Mexico.[2] She had grown up in a privileged family in Winnetka, Illinois, and went to Vassar College, where she put to music the poetry of fellow students Muriel Rukeyser and Elizabeth Bishop. After graduation, she and her new husband, Dan Wells, moved to Europe, where they became alarmed at the rise of fascism and also developed a friendship with Frieda Lawrence, wife of D. H. Lawrence. It was because of the Lawrences' ties to Taos and its artists' colony that the couple moved to New Mexico later in the 1930s. They made friends with local families, most of them living and working on small farms, and soon found themselves helping to organize a school on their ranch. (The school closed during World War II.) In the late 1940s, Jenny Wells divorced her first husband and then married Craig Vincent, a former New Deal administrator. In 1949, the Vincents opened the San Cristóbal ranch as a vacation spot and summer camp for progressives from California to New York.[3] The Vincents advertised their ranch in progressive publications such as *PM*, a journal published in New York by independent radical Cedric Belfrage. It was, in one visitor's words, a "left-wing dude ranch."[4]

In San Cristóbal, the Jenckses met another family looking for some rest and relaxation. Paul and Sylvia Jarrico were from Hollywood, and Paul had just been blacklisted from the screenwriting profession. The two couples liked each other right away. Paul described the blacklist, how he and his friends "were really feeling a sense of freedom that now they could really make some films that they really wanted to make, and that they were looking for stories to tell." Clinton told them, "We've got a story to tell, let me tell you. You know, we're down on the Continental Divide in the southwestern corner of New Mexico and nobody knows we're on the planet. And we're engaged in what for us is a life and death struggle for ourselves and the existence of our union and nobody knows about it."[5] Excited by the story of the women's picket, the Jarricos later drove south to Hanover, where Sylvia and their son Bill joined the women on the picket. They returned to Los Angeles convinced that they had found the story for a movie.[6] Sylvia Jarrico recalled that she was attracted by "everything about it. . . . It was irresistible motion picture material."[7]

Progressive networks permitted the Jenckses and Jarricos to meet one another, and shared experiences of Cold War repression formed the basis for an immediate friendship and for their seeing their situations as two aspects of the same battle.[8] Clinton and Virginia Jencks, after all, worked for a left-wing union that had been expelled from the CIO in 1950 and would soon come under congressional scrutiny for "Communist domination."[9] Paul Jarrico had just been fired by RKO after his unfriendly appearance before the House Un-American Activities Committee (HUAC) in June, while Sylvia Jarrico had recently lost her job with the University of California because she refused to sign a state-mandated loyalty oath.[10] Mine-Mill thus had more in common with the Hollywood Ten and other blacklisted filmmakers than simply a narrowing of opportunities: its officials and representatives, like Clinton Jencks, would face prison for allegedly falsifying their Taft-Hartley affidavits, while the Hollywood Ten faced prison for contempt of Congress. Paul Jarrico commented that Mine-Mill was "kicked out of the CIO in 1949 for being a left-wing union. We were kicked out of Hollywood for the same reason. So if there was some similarity in the thinking, it was no accident."[11]

In Chapter 3 I described Mine-Mill's expulsion from the CIO. Here I move the story to Hollywood, explaining the growth and influence of the Communist Party (CP) in Hollywood, the studio system within which progressives in the industry were forced to work, the hearings conducted by HUAC, and the blacklist imposed by the movie industry.

THE COMMUNIST PARTY IN HOLLYWOOD

Progressives in Hollywood established the most flourishing CP presence outside of New York City and built organizations that attracted liberals and radicals alike. In 1936, the head of the CP's Cultural Commission, V. J. Jerome, organized the first clubs in Hollywood, which were composed of radicals—mostly screenwriters—who came out of Hollywood's union drives of the 1930s or from the New York literary scene.[12]

The party in Hollywood was independent of the Los Angeles chapter, its members enjoying an organizational leeway that reflected their importance in the eyes of party leadership. They faced looser discipline than did other Communists, and they were free of many party obligations, such as hawking the *Daily Worker* on street corners.[13] Every couple of weeks each "talent branch" held a meeting at a member's house.[14] One member would typically give a prepared talk about a subject, and then the dozen or so people who attended would discuss the topic. The meetings were "relatively informal," as Paul Jarrico recalled.[15] After the discussion, "there would be a checkup of activities, just going around the room asking people to report on what they'd been doing, usually on the basis of assignments that they'd undertaken at earlier meetings: 'How's that coming along? What's happening on that Guild committee? What's happening on that janitors' strike you were helping out with?'" The party pressured people to stay active, but, as Paul Jarrico explained,

> there was always a conflict, especially among writers, because writing is hard work, and a lot of people were reluctant to take the time off from their normal work of writing in order to engage in political activity. . . . "I haven't got time. I've got this assignment to do." "But, Christ, if you don't do this—if you don't talk to so-and-so in preparation for the next Guild meeting—it's not going to be done; you're the only one who knows him. You're the only guy who knows how to move him on this issue. You've got to do it." "All right, for Christ's sake, I'll do it!" More or less like that. It was not, "Comrade, you are expected to do this. Report next week that you have done it!" It wasn't quite as stiff and autocratic as some people might suppose.[16]

The achievements of the Hollywood talent branches matched their prestige. First, the Hollywood Communists raised more money than any other club in the country. Second, the 1930s and 1940s witnessed an overwhelming florescence of Hollywood progressive political organizations in which Communists participated. A leftist political culture, quite unlike post-McCarthy Hollywood liberalism, grew out of the labor struggles of the talent guilds and of industrial unions, often in jurisdictional conflict with the conservative and corrupt International Association of Theater and Stage Employees (IATSE).[17] This political culture reflected and deepened the commitment to radical causes among a broad spectrum of movie workers. And in a "world where networking meant everything, the Communist Party's Popular Front was, from the middle thirties until the late forties, *the* network for the cerebral progressive, the inveterate activist, and the determined labor unionist."[18] During the Popular Front period (1935–39), radical and liberal activists worked together on compelling issues such as support for Republican Spain. Indeed, the most successful Communist Party activity was probably in those groups with limited, immediate programs "directed toward democratic (and often highly patriotic) goals."[19] The Hollywood Anti-Nazi League, for instance, attracted liberals and even exiled European royalty to its banner. Sonja Dahl Biberman, Herbert Biberman's sister-in-law and later an assistant director of *Salt of the Earth*, observed that "the Communist Party was much in evidence in all anti-fascist activity, but then so were the Republican and Democratic Parties."[20] The Nazi-Soviet Pact of 1939–41 ended the Popular Front in Hollywood as elsewhere, convincing many liberals that Communists could not be trusted. American entry into World War II, though, pulled Communists back into the mainstream of American patriotism and therefore into American political life.[21]

Among the Hollywood Communists were several individuals, connected by family, as well as political, ties, who would later create *Salt of the Earth*. Sylvia and Paul Jarrico, the assistant producer and producer, respectively, of *Salt*, joined the party in the late 1930s. Both hailed from Russian Jewish immigrant families. Paul Jarrico was proud that his father, "a poet and a fighting man," had formed an armed self-defense group that prevented a pogrom in their native town of Kharkov.[22] He "simply grew up thinking that fathers go to political meetings every night."[23] He was a Young Communist in 1934 and 1935 while attending Berkeley and became a screenwriter almost immediately after graduating from the University of Southern California in 1936, an occupation he pursued "almost continuously" until his dismissal from RKO after receiving a subpoena in 1951 to appear before HUAC.[24] In the late 1930s, he wrote *No Time to Marry* (1938) and *Beauty for the Asking* (1939). His screenplay for *Tom, Dick and Harry* (RKO Radio) was nominated for an Academy Award in 1941, and during World War II he wrote *The Face Behind the Mask* (1941) and *Thousands Cheer* (1943) and cowrote *Song of Russia* (1944) for MGM.

Sylvia Jarrico, while not a screenwriter, immersed herself in the same left-wing milieu, joining the party toward the end of the Popular Front because she was attracted by the Marxist critique of economics and politics. Stunned by the news of the Nazi-Soviet Pact, she convinced herself that the party leaders had acted in good faith. Her faith was renewed by World War II: "We were heart and soul in the war effort. We felt ideologically well equipped for it. And we were glad to have so many others with us now."[25] After the war, she pursued graduate study of motion pictures and ideology, "how [motion pictures] reflect, how [they] influence reality."[26] From 1945 to 1951 she was the managing editor of the *Hollywood Quarterly*, a journal of film criticism published by the University of California Press. The *Hollywood Quarterly* grew out of the Hollywood Writers' Mobilization, a wartime collaboration between left-wing writers at the University of California at Los Angeles and in the motion picture industry.[27] She lost this job in 1951 after refusing to take the loyalty oath required by the State of California. "There was a panic . . . at UCLA that precisely mirrored the panic in the motion picture industry," she explained. "And the *Hollywood Quarterly* was the point of contact."[28]

Michael Wilson, who wrote the screenplay for *Salt*, came from a "zealously Catholic" family in Oklahoma that moved first to a Los Angeles suburb and then to the Bay Area.[29] Like his brother-in-law Paul Jarrico, Wilson became radicalized as a student at Berkeley in the mid-1930s.[30] He joined the "tiny, virtually inactive" CP branch on campus in the spring of 1937, and, after a year in Europe, "returned to Berkeley a dedicated Marxist-Leninist."[31] Rather than beginning graduate school, as he had planned, Wilson devoted his considerable energies to political organizing and teaching classes in Marxism, while still aiming to become a writer.[32] After trying to write short stories about minority workers, Wilson was persuaded by Paul Jarrico to try screenwriting. He moved to Hollywood in 1940 and earned five screen credits, including several Hopalong Cassidy movies, before serving in the Marines from 1941 to 1945.[33] Just before being blacklisted in 1951, Michael Wilson won the Academy Award for Best Screenplay for *A Place in the Sun*.

Herbert Biberman, *Salt*'s director, was a generation older than the Jarricos and Wilson and arrived in Hollywood after working in radical theater in the East. He had earned a master's degree in theater from Yale and had studied theater in the Soviet Union early in the 1930s. Shortly after moving to New York City, he joined the Theater Guild, where he met actress Gale Sondergaard, his future wife. At the Theater Guild, he directed a Soviet play called *Roar China*, in which workers from New York's Chinatown performed alongside professional actors.[34] His Hollywood career was apparently less successful than those of his comrades; at the time of the 1947 HUAC hearings, Biberman was under no contract with a major studio. His sister-in-law, Sonja Dahl Biberman, was also very active in Popular Front organizations, serving for several years as executive secretary of the Hollywood Anti-Nazi League and then of the Joint Anti-Fascist Refugee Committee. She would prove indispensable to the worker-artist alliance that produced *Salt of the Earth*.

THE HOLLYWOOD STUDIO SYSTEM

The Left flourished in Hollywood, but not in the sense of openly influencing the content of film. The Hollywood studio system successfully and consistently limited radical film content, if not radical political organizations, in order to appease outsiders clamoring for movie censorship. Motion pictures had long been a target for groups concerned with upholding morality, such as the Catholic Church, women's clubs, and the American Legion. Many people believed that the movies, like the theater, were inherently immoral and, if not controlled, would corrupt audiences. In key respects, as we will see in the next chapter, they shared with many left-wing cultural critics the view that audiences risked cultural degeneration in the face of offensive imagery.

In the 1910s, the industry frequently submitted its films to locally run boards of review, which used the volunteer labor of women's clubs to evaluate film content.[35] In the early 1920s, religious groups and other reformers threatened massive boycotts of Hollywood films. Unwilling to take a chance on reduced profits, Hollywood producers formed the Motion Picture Producers and Distributors of America (MPPDA) in 1922 and in 1930 adopted a production code by which the industry could regulate itself. All films had to pass through the Hays Office, which monitored voluntary adherence to the code.[36] Specifically banned were any depictions of "white slavery," miscegenation, sexual "perversion," and ridicule of the clergy; strongly discouraged were subjects like rape, drug use, murder techniques, and lustful kissing. Bowing to pressure from the Catholic Legion of Decency, as well as Protestant and Jewish groups, in 1934 the MPPDA strengthened the code with fines and more rules.[37] Unlike other kinds of writers, then, screenwriters labored under the censorship of an industry code. And unlike the press, motion pictures enjoyed no First Amendment protection before 1952.[38]

Hollywood executives bowed to the pressure of censors, and their ability to enforce the production code rested on their iron hold over the industry, itself partly a result of the Depression that drove many studios into bankruptcy and a few into efforts to make film production more efficient along industrial lines.[39] Five studios ran the show from 1930 to 1948: Warner Brothers, Loew's (which owned Metro-Goldwyn-Mayer), Paramount, RKO, and Twentieth Century Fox. Three others—Columbia, Universal, and United Artists—gradually edged their way into the market but wielded less power than the Big Five.[40] Vertical integration characterized this industry as it did the industries in the manufacturing sector; the same corporations owned production and distribution rights, and they used this power to control almost all of the films that made it into movie houses. The major studios may have appeared to compete with one another, but, in fact, they colluded to corner the market. Movie theater chains owned directly by the Big Five got the best deals; block booking and similar marketing strategies forced independent exhibitors to accept the entire programs that the major studios offered. Money came from New York corporate offices and dictated to Hollywood executives exactly how many films were to be made and at what cost.[41]

On their own turf, movie executives were autocrats. Screenwriters gathered in the writers' colonies of the studio lots to write assigned scripts or parts of scripts in return for a set salary. Creativity was cramped by studio bureaucracy: the story department, not the individual screenwriter, supplied the stories, and screenwriters adapted them to studio specifications. As one successful screenwriter put it, "[The producers] owned you; you were a commodity; they were paying you so much a week, and you belonged to them. And there was never any kidding about that."[42] A screenwriter's job security rested on accumulating screen credits, but before labor unions gained power in the late 1930s, no individual screenwriter could be certain of receiving them.[43] The nature of piece work, in which different parts of a script were farmed out to different writers, allowed less-than-scrupulous executives to attribute scripts incompletely.[44] Studio management monitored the comings and goings of all people associated with the studio and readily forced particular stories on its writers.

Adrian Scott, one of the Hollywood Ten who later helped form the company that produced *Salt*, developed ulcers and gastritis as he struggled to balance his own vision of *Crossfire* (1946), a film that dramatized the dangers of bigotry and anti-Semitism, against the prescriptions of studio executives. Speaking to a conference on thought control in 1947, shortly before the HUAC hearings began, Scott denounced the effects of movie censorship:

> Through all the long months before we started work, fear consumed us. . . . It is a fear produced with a Hollywood trademark. Throughout its comparatively short history, Hollywood has been the victim of an infinite variety of lobbyists who claim the right to dictate what pictures shall be made and what the content of those pictures shall be. As a result of these pressures, a complex and subtle system of thought control has grown up around the industry. At times it is not so complex and not so subtle. . . . The producer's first consideration of any property is: "Can I get this by the production Code?" Notice the wording: "Can I get it by?" It is not a deliberate thought process, it is a

reflex action—that automatic. . . . My colleagues and I are guilty. We imposed a censorship on ourselves, in first considering a picture on anti-Semitism and during its preparation. There is nothing in the code of the Producers' Association which prevents making this picture.[45]

Still, as historians Paul Buhle and Dave Wagner have argued, radical screenwriters managed to include humanist values and concern for the underdog in their movies, particularly those in less reputable genres like horror and science fiction, which attracted less scrutiny from the Production Code Administration than regular dramas.[46]

THE BLACKLIST

Radical politics—though never radical film content—had gained some legitimacy in Hollywood during the 1930s and 1940s, attracting conservatives to scrutinize the film industry as one especially vulnerable to communist infiltration. During World War II, Walt Disney had persuaded the Tenney Committee (California's state equivalent to HUAC) to investigate Hollywood's subversive films, but the hearings were widely ridiculed and their backers quickly gave up. After the war, Hollywood began to produce a few tentative offerings of a more sophisticated nature than its earlier fare. Films like *The Best Years of Our Lives*, *Crossfire*, and *Pinky* confronted social problems like veterans' adjustment to postwar America, anti-Semitism, and racism. But the Cold War, waged in HUAC hearings, froze any trend toward more films that dealt directly with social issues.

The Motion Picture Alliance for the Preservation of American Ideals (MPAPAI) invited HUAC to Hollywood in 1947. John Cogley, who wrote about the blacklist for the liberal Fund for the Republic, described the MPAPAI as a "militantly anti-Communist, pro–free enterprise group" that included such luminaries as Walt Disney, Ayn Rand, Gary Cooper, Robert Taylor, Adolphe Menjou, gossip columnist Hedda Hopper, and John Wayne.[47] HUAC quickly accepted this invitation, announcing that summer that it would investigate the CP infiltration of the motion picture industry. All of the MPAPAI members testified as "friendly witnesses" in the 1947 hearings. But nineteen of the other witnesses under subpoena declared that they would be "unfriendly." The committee had no right to question their political beliefs, they said, and none of them would cooperate with what they considered a serious threat to the Constitution.[48]

As the hearings opened in October 1947, with J. Parnell Thomas pre-
siding, the nineteen unfriendly witnesses enjoyed the support of a number of Hollywood liberals and leftists who criticized the congressional
investigation.[49] Representatives of the Committee for the First Amendment flew to Washington to register their opposition, and the studios'
producers testified that Communists did not influence film content or
other aspects of production. Paul McNutt, counsel for the producers,
denounced HUAC: "It does not require a law to cripple the right of free
speech. Intimidation and coercion will do it."[50] Eric Johnston, president
of the national Chamber of Commerce and representative of the studio
executives, sent word to the witnesses that the studios would not blacklist the unfriendlies.[51] During the hearings, Herbert Biberman returned
the favor by praising the editorials and the industry's spokespeople who
recognized that the hearings were only a "smokescreen under which [this
committee was] trying to prescribe a film diet for the American people"
and "to drive a wedge into the component parts of the industry."[52]

The unfriendly witnesses chose the First Amendment as their defense, and Biberman's comments typified their strategy and aggressive
rhetoric. HUAC was trying to replace the Bill of Rights with the "rule of
accusation," he said, to poison the public mind with scare tactics. "If I
were guilty of acts of force or violence," he continued, "I would never have
been called before this committee. I would be in the courts. And if I were
guilty of such acts . . . I *should* be in the courts, and convicted and
condemned. It is because I have been an active citizen that I am here.
No slothful, lazy, self-satisfied or cynical citizen is brought here—except
those who are in the service of, or in the same bed with, the members of
this committee."[53] For his part, Adrian Scott stressed that the Constitution guaranteed the rights of minorities.

Thomas stopped the hearings after only ten of the unfriendly witnesses had been called. Those witnesses, soon dubbed the Hollywood
Ten, were cited with contempt of Congress, a charge upheld by a House
vote of 346 to 17.[54] Some of them, like Adrian Scott, returned to their
jobs—but not for long. In December, the industry's executives issued the
"Waldorf Statement" (after meeting at the Waldorf-Astoria Hotel on
October 24), which explicitly blacklisted all of the unfriendly witnesses.
Dore Schary, widely perceived as one of the more liberal Hollywood
executives, testified in 1951 that he had tried to get Scott to sign a letter
denying CP membership so that RKO would not have to fire him. Scott,
according to Schary, agreed to sign an affidavit denying sympathy for a
party seeking to overthrow the government by force, but he would not

sign any letter denying he had ever been a Communist.[55] Scott's subsequent dismissal letter from the president of RKO declared that Scott and Edward Dmytryk, another of the Ten, had brought themselves and the studio into "disrepute" and had "otherwise violated the provisions of Article 16 of [their] employment agreement."[56] Article 16 was the "morals clause," a standard element of studio contracts that executives used to dismiss people for political beliefs.

As historian Ellen Schrecker has shown, anticommunism in the late 1940s and early 1950s employed complex set of mechanisms to expose supposed Communists.[57] The congressional committee, fueled by professional witnesses provided by the FBI, was one of the most important of these, setting the stage for government, private industry, and other organizations to prove their loyalty by expelling Communists and other progressives. In 1947, the industry claimed—as it had in the 1920s and again in the early 1940s—that it could regulate itself. This time, though, its leaders chose the blacklist as the means by which to do so. Industry executives would probably never have bothered to throw out radical screenwriters, but, faced with governmental hostility, they joined the campaign of national politicians to rid the industry of supposed Communist influence and, not coincidentally, to score political points. The government, moreover, might not have tried to force the issue directly had not the industry's big names sanctioned its political goals and methods.

Cast out from the industry, the Ten turned to fighting to stay out of prison. They produced a short documentary film, *The Hollywood Ten*, which their families and political allies distributed. A group of liberals signed an amicus curiae brief on their behalf, but their convictions were upheld in 1950. On the eve of sentencing, they issued a statement to the press. The Hollywood Ten, said Ring Lardner Jr., were the first victims of the Cold War. Although in 1947 the Truman administration did not explicitly condone the hearings, Lardner charged, events of the past three years had propelled the Democrats into the camp of the Republicans:

> In 1947 the administration was slowly and sometimes timidly launching the opening sallies of its Cold War. The Un-American Activities Committee had a standing something like the privateering captains of Queen Elizabeth [I]'s time, whose attacks on Spanish commerce were sometimes greeted with smiles and sometimes with frowns, but these contributions to the royal cause were always gratefully accepted. The queen had the eventual choice of repudiating them or making them an official part

of the national effort. In 1950 . . . the administration itself has a program that would have seemed prematurely anti-democratic to the [H]UAC of 1947.[58]

Alvah Bessie warned the country that while they were the first victims of the Cold War, they would not be the last: all Americans were "potential victims of the hot war that [was] being brewed in the Pentagon Building these days and nights."[59] Their comments came a matter of weeks before the start of the Korean War, in July 1950. They all went to prison, some for six months, some for a year. Sylvia Jarrico recalled that she was part of a diminishing group of supporters: "We were planning a large welcome home demonstration for the eight [who remained in prison]. We thought our fight to rehabilitate their reputations was going pretty well and that they would come home as heroes."[60] They came home, however, to a new round of HUAC hearings on Communist subversion.

In 1951, HUAC targeted the financial support that Hollywood furnished to the CP, rather than party influence—which it could never find—on film content. And this repression spread far beyond ten people. Hundreds were called before HUAC, each faced with the unpalatable choice of going to prison, being blacklisted, or informing on others.

The experience of the Hollywood Ten revealed the weakness of a defense based on freedom of speech and the First Amendment. Using that defense, the Hollywood Ten wound up in prison for contempt of Congress. The Fifth Amendment offered protection against self-incrimination, so it could protect witnesses from going to prison, but it could not protect them from the blacklist: central to the spectacle of the HUAC hearings was self-abnegation and the repudiation of any radical or even liberal past activities, and only by capitulating to the committee's agenda could one avoid the blacklist imposed by the studios. Hollywood interpreted "taking the Fifth" as an admission of guilt, and the studios were unwilling to run the risk of employing anyone so tainted. Nor could one simply admit one's own radical background; having once forfeited the Fifth Amendment's protection by answering *any* questions, one opened the door to further questioning and one could not withhold information about other people. According to this line of legal reasoning, answering questions about oneself but then refusing to answer about others constituted contempt of Congress. Many witnesses thus found themselves trapped between clearing their own names and drawing other people into HUAC's system of repression.[61]

Paul Jarrico appeared before HUAC on April 13, 1951, and, like most of the unfriendly witnesses in the second round of hearings, he invoked the Fifth Amendment, although he answered some questions. When Representative Doyle asked him if he would not want to help the committee uncover subversion, Jarrico replied, "One man's subversion is another man's patriotism. I consider the activities of this committee subversive of the American Constitution." Later, Jarrico filed a statement in which he declared: "It is not our loyalty to our country that is being judged, but our loyalty to the particular economic system that prevails here. And that is the biggest lie of all: that capitalism and democracy are somehow the same thing, that it's un-American to stand for social change."[62]

Sylvia Jarrico had already experienced political repression before McCarthy's rise: she had lost her job at the *Hollywood Quarterly* for refusing to sign a loyalty oath required by the state of California. Now her husband was blacklisted as well. Not only did Paul Jarrico lose his job with RKO, but Howard Hughes also denied him screen credit for *The Las Vegas Story*, which Jarrico had written before HUAC subpoenaed him. The Screen Writers' Guild took Hughes to court and lost. Thereafter, the union could not guarantee anyone's right to work or credit for work already done. Michael Wilson weathered similar storms. His Academy Award for *A Place in the Sun* guaranteed him no protection against the blacklist after he appeared before HUAC in September 1951. In 1953, Wilson and twenty-three other unfriendly witnesses filed a civil suit against Loew's, Inc., for conspiracy to blacklist, seeking $51 million in damages. Like Jarrico, they lost.[63] And like Jarrico, Wilson saw his name removed from a script—*Friendly Persuasion* (1956)—this time with the consent of the Screen Writers' Guild. During the blacklist, Wilson, along with Dalton Trumbo, operated a clearinghouse for others to take on scripts under pseudonyms; in this manner he wrote *The Bridge on the River Kwai* (1957) and *Lawrence of Arabia* (1962). His name appeared on no screen until 1965, and only in 1997 was his name restored to *The Bridge on the River Kwai*.[64]

The term "Cold War" aptly describes the events in Hollywood from 1947 to 1960. As HUAC hauled motion picture workers into hearings on Communist influence in Hollywood, and as producers agreed to an informal blacklist, a chill spread over film production in all its aspects. Who would propose a script dealing with racial justice or with the honest struggles of a trade union if it could elicit a subpoena? Who could afford, after the 1951 hearings began, to argue their First Amendment rights, the tactic that had landed the Hollywood Ten in jail, or to invoke their Fifth Amendment right to silence, which the studios treated as an admission of guilt and rewarded with a place on the blacklist? One major Hollywood film did take industrial unionism as its subject, but the union in question was portrayed as corrupt. Coming from a director who had recently protected his career by informing on his Hollywood colleagues, Elia Kazan's *On the Waterfront* raised the snitch to a heroic level.[65]

For the Hollywood Ten and others on the blacklist, the informer was no hero. They experienced abusive investigators, unsympathetic judges, and prison because they believed that to grant even a shred of legitimacy to HUAC by cooperating was to betray the Constitution, their beliefs, and their friends. Out of this experience, some radicals fought back by suing their former employers and by forming their own film company. Wilson's, Jarrico's, and Scott's visions of aligning their politics with their craft could now come to fruition, but only outside the system. As Paul Jarrico put it, "It wasn't until 1951, when we were good and dead professionally, that we could get involved in movies that packed a real social and political wallop."[66] Now they could finally commit "a crime to fit the punishment."[67]

According to Biberman, Paul Jarrico and Adrian Scott began to plan an independent film company just ten minutes after Jarrico's appearance before HUAC in April 1951.[68] When Biberman heard of their idea, he contacted an attorney for the Hollywood Ten to begin setting up a company. This lawyer told him that Simon Lazarus, a movie exhibitor who ten years before had suggested an independent company to Biberman, was again expressing interest in such an enterprise. With one share each, Lazarus, Herbert Biberman, Adrian Scott, Paul Jarrico, and an attorney formed the Independent Productions Corporation (IPC) in September 1951.[69] Lazarus, Scott, and Biberman took on the challenge of raising money, with Lazarus investing $5,000.[70]

Indeed, their efforts to finance the company show the paradoxical effect of anticommunism. They found investors in two groups of people, both responding—though in different ways—to the anticommunism that prevailed in American political culture. The first group consisted of opportunists who were simply not disturbed by the red tinge on the company and were eager to profit from the talents of blacklisted artists freed of the studios' control. "The blacklisted!" cried one businessman. "They're like gold laying [sic] in the streets!"[71] The second group of investors found ideological reasons to back IPC financially, although they were themselves not Communists, leftists, or necessarily even liberals. They supported IPC because they did not believe that politics should limit how they spent their money. When Lazarus or Biberman explained the possible consequences of supporting IPC—harassment from HUAC or other government agencies, from the American Legion, or from IATSE—these investors were positively insulted that anyone would presume to dictate the terms under which they could invest their own dollars.

After only a few months, the company had raised some $50,000, and by the summer of 1952, when IPC approached the Mine-Mill international to collaborate on a film, the company had raised about $95,000.[72] They planned to use it to produce the story of the women's picket in Hanover.

8

A Progressive Vision of Popular Culture

Henrietta Williams noticed him up on a hill. He was a stranger, dressed casually but not in workers' clothes, gray-haired but probably only in his late thirties. He was watching the women as they walked in their circle outside the Empire Zinc mine in Hanover early in the fall of 1951. Williams, a picket captain, suspected that "he was a company man, that he was writing down names to take us women to jail." She was certainly prepared to confront him: months on the picket line and a week in jail made her a force to be reckoned with. The picketing women were surprised to learn instead that he was a writer from Hollywood, interested in their stories. So "we let him come down and drink coffee with us, talk to us," she explained later.[1]

The man was Michael Wilson, and he had come to the women's picket because his brother-in-law, producer Paul Jarrico, and director Herbert Biberman wanted him to tell the women's story in a screenplay that would be produced by blacklisted artists in a new film company, Independent Productions Corporation. In fact, Wilson had been reluctant to visit Grant County. Blacklisted after invoking the Fifth Amendment before the House Un-American Activities Committee on September 21, 1951, Wilson had finally begun working on a novel. Only after Jarrico and Biberman agreed that the people of Local 890 would exercise final say over the script did he take on this new project instead. "If you think something's great and they think it's lousy," he warned, "they're going to win." They were "to be the censors of it and the real producers of it . . . in point of view of its content."[2]

There, by the picket line, Wilson interviewed the women, "what [they] thought, what [they] were doing, how hard [it was] walking in that sun, so hot." He wanted to know what the women thought would happen and whether they were going to win. "All those things he asked," Henrietta Williams recalled. "He asked a lot of questions, and we answered them. Everything that was true, we told what was going on there."[3] Wilson stayed in Grant County for a month, and he kept himself on the margins, not drawing attention to himself. "He sat by the picket line," Clinton Jencks remembered. "He sat in the union hall. He went to the dance. He sat in our homes. We talked, you know. But he didn't hardly say anything. You wouldn't know he was there. . . . He had this capacity to just become a part of the thing so that people weren't self-conscious and were just going ahead and doing what they were doing."[4]

Wilson may not have said much, but he was deeply affected by the solidarity that the union families demonstrated. Most men had first opposed the women taking over picket duties, fearing violence and a threat to their authority in the household. By the time Wilson visited, though, many had grudgingly taken on some of the women's work. The situation in Grant County also impressed him with its complexity: "There are battles for equality taking place there on so many levels I can hardly unskein them myself," he told Biberman when he returned to California.[5] Wilson did not rush to interpret those battles in a definitive way; indeed, it took him three months to figure them out and write an initial scenario. Wilson concluded that one form of equality was hollow in the absence of the others, and he anchored his screenplay in the idea of the "indivisibility of equality." The strike began as a struggle for ethnic equality. But once women took over the line, "the struggle for equality move[d] to a new level, which include[d] the old."[6] Only after men accepted women as equals, and Anglo and Mexican American workers allied with one another, could the mining families sustain and ultimately win the strike. Wilson's script did not focus on the history of Local 890's political and community activism of the 1940s. Instead, it centered on personal relationships, which may have been more suitable for the kind of drama he envisioned: something that would make viewers identify with the characters and appreciate the transformations they underwent. In this respect, *Salt of the Earth* was able to portray precisely the kind of conflict—one between a husband and a wife—that had been largely neglected by the union until the Empire Zinc strike brought it to center stage.

Wilson returned to Grant County in January 1952, just as the strike was coming to an end, to read the screenplay's outline to the union families.[7] Gathered in the union hall, at first "everybody just sat and

listened," Clinton Jencks recalled. But before long "they began to interrupt. It was not a self-conscious thing. They'd say, 'No, no, it wasn't like
that at all.' "[8] Virginia Chacón said that the script had "too much Hollywood stuff. We [told] him, 'It has to be the real thing.' "[9] Lorenzo Torrez
objected to a scene in which Esperanza used her dress to wipe up a beer
spill. He felt it reinforced "the stereotype that Chicanos are dirty, and that
they aren't smart enough to use a towel."[10] And one union member felt
that "the screenplay had the liberal white man—modeled on Clinton
Jencks—saving the Mexican masses."[11]

There was a clear gender division in the script's reception. The men
overruled an adultery subplot, an objection that the women derided. "Oh,
you're all so pure!" they jeered. "You don't do things like that?" The
women, for their part, rejected the depiction of too much drinking: "Our
husbands are not drunkards," they insisted.[12] Whether men or women
prevailed on a particular point depended on their relative strength in
articulating their positions, but women's recent history of organizing and
leading the strike gave them additional clout in the script discussions.
Had union men alone been consulted, for instance, it is doubtful that
men would have been portrayed as comically as they often were.

Michael Wilson understood his task to be honoring the people of
Grant County, and he believed that to do them justice meant to defer to
them—albeit after rigorous discussion—on critical matters. Whatever
beliefs about workers or ethnic minorities he brought with him, he did
not apply them indiscriminately to a passive and inarticulate people. He
listened carefully to the historical actors and tried to recast his own
thinking to match their situation. And whatever shyness Local 890 members may have initially felt upon meeting glamorous Hollywood people,
they clearly and forthrightly expressed their own opinions about the project and the way it should be done. After all, they had plenty of experience
seeing Mexican Americans portrayed stereotypically and disrespectfully
on film. This was true both of Hollywood's movies, as one might expect,
and of Mexican cinema, which stereotyped Mexican Americans as de-
racinated pachucos.[13] Perhaps the union families' predisposition to critique Wilson's script reflected the influence of the cultural activism of the
Asociación Nacional Mexicana Americana. In any case, they found a
ready listener in Michael Wilson. As Clinton Jencks put it, "Any communication is two-way. Since people were telling their own story, they
had a right to say it the way they wanted to say it. And that's one part. But
I think the other part of it is there was somebody that would . . . listen. So
it was worth saying. . . . We had to take some risks in criticizing these

Charles Coleman as Antonio Morales, ruefully hanging laundry to dry. Photo courtesy of the Wisconsin Center for Film and Theater Research, Lot #A108.

people that came from so far. . . . But similarly, it had to be important enough to [IPC] to be able to accept that criticism."[14]

Wilson accepted the criticisms. He did not, as Jencks put it, "have to defend [the script] as a child."[15] The excised scenes, Wilson explained to Biberman, were "perfectly legitimate dramatic scenes and illustrations. In a script in which you're after drama for its own sake, they'd be perfectly acceptable. But we're dealing with something else. Not just people. A people. And you don't necessarily express them in naturalistic detail. You have to really synthesize them, all of them; the weaknesses and the virtues, until the individual expresses a real element of the whole and not something untypical of the whole, even though a variant of it."[16] Some men were unfaithful to their wives, Wilson acknowledged, but to project that on screen might only reinforce stereotypes of "the sensuous, promiscuous, Latin male."[17] Even on purely dramatic grounds, he thought the adultery subplot was poorly resolved.

Another detail in the original outline that did not appear in the final script was the role of religion and the Catholic Church in Esperanza's life. In the outline, Esperanza's devotion to the Catholic Church serves as a barometer of her political consciousness: as she becomes more involved in the strike, the church exerts less influence on her. Perhaps this device rang untrue to the many Empire Zinc strikers who appreciated the support given by Father Smerke of Hanover's Holy Family Church; certainly these mining families had little trouble reconciling their religious beliefs with their union activism, and when they did encounter antiunion sentiment from priests they did not hesitate to criticize it.[18] In any case, Wilson's deference to criticism from the union was the key to synthesizing the disparate parts of the community. After six more months, Wilson came up with a script of which Local 890—men and women—approved.

The unique way in which Wilson crafted the script for *Salt of the Earth* was part of creating a new kind of popular culture, one in which working people themselves, allied with artists, would dramatize their own struggles. Independent Productions Corporation, incorporated in September 1951, was created in order to make this new kind of movie. Employing blacklisted artists, IPC would fight McCarthyism; even more importantly, it would contribute to a democratic culture, its entertainment presenting, as Biberman described it, "people to people in such a way as to give them their own experience clarified, organized, enriched—to such a degree that it gives confidence and faith and direction." And people would see more than their own individual stories. They would see the stories of other Americans and begin the hard process of talking to one another, of discarding "the distrusts and hatreds which have been foisted upon them—and [of finding] joy and hope and fulfillment in each other."[19]

The stakes were high in cultural politics, and Biberman knew precisely what he did *not* want: to follow the popular media's prescription for attracting a female audience. The "publication *True Experience*," he observed, "urges writers to submit 'hard-hitting, earthy love stories.' It continues: 'What does the everyday woman want? Give her marriage and seduction. Give her Cinderella and rape. Give her love and delinquency. Give her addiction, adoption and abandonment. Give her crime, abortion

and frigidity. Give her insanity and murder. Every man and woman having an affair must pull toward each other with so much gravity that the
earth stops spinning.' "[20] Without an alternative medium, Biberman believed, American cultural values would deteriorate. People would become inured to violence and brutality "until, little by little, the horrible
finality of official brutality, which yesterday they would have called fascism and resisted, tomorrow they accept only because they yielded little
by ever so little all along the way."[21] Perhaps Biberman, more than other
members of IPC, exaggerated the stakes in cultural politics, but all of
them shared a vision of popular culture in which filmmakers could venture onto socially critical or ambiguous terrain. They were convinced that
IPC could offer Americans something truer to life than anything *True
Experience* would publish.

This vision of cultural politics provided the foundation for *Salt of the
Earth*. It was influenced by, but not coextensive with, Hollywood Communists' theorizing on culture, which in turn influenced the way IPC
would address the themes of race and sex discrimination that Communists had long theorized about and organized around. Wilson's starting point was the Communist Party (CP) consideration of the "Woman
Question"—this was, in fact, the first title of his screenplay, and hardly
anyone besides Communists continued to use this nineteenth-century
term.[22] But Wilson parted company with CP thinking by placing the
Woman Question at the *center* of a feature film that addressed sexism,
first, as a serious and substantive problem and, second, as a problem
connected to but neither determinant of nor subordinate to ethnic and
class inequality. Wilson was probably predisposed to do so because left-
wing women in Hollywood had pushed the party to discuss women's
issues, including housework. When asked how he came to write a story
about miners that focused on miners' wives, Wilson replied, "I never
conceived of it any other way."[23] But even more important, the families in
Grant County wanted to portray their struggle in this way. If Wilson had
the lead female character, Esperanza, bravely confront her husband in
one of the turning points of the film, it was because the women in Grant
County told him to do so. The script reflected their recent history and the
leverage women had gained.

In this chapter I first analyze the efforts of Hollywood Communists
to determine their role in film production, efforts that took place in a
number of settings in the 1930s and 1940s. Next, I examine IPC's first
projects to show the lessons its filmmakers learned in trying to translate

In a climactic scene in Salt of the Earth, *Esperanza (Rosaura Revueltas) confronts her husband Ramón (Juan Chacón). Note the protective image of the Virgen de Guadalupe behind her. Photo courtesy of the Wisconsin Center for Film and Theater Research, Lot #A108.*

their political beliefs into art, lessons they brought to the production of *Salt of the Earth* in 1951–53. Finally, by analyzing the film's production, I take up the themes of authenticity and the meanings of representation in this most unusual worker-artist alliance.

COMMUNIST FILM THEORY

To work as a Communist in Hollywood was to work within severe constraints. No studio gave free rein to its writers' imaginations (as we saw in Chapter 7), and Communists, individually and as a group, struggled to define the relation of cultural production to political conviction. They never fully succeeded in developing a Marxist aesthetic that they could practice in Hollywood's film industry.[24]

Two positions regarding the place of Marxism in Hollywood film production emerged in the course of what Paul Jarrico later described as "knock-down/drag-out fights" on cultural politics.[25] The dominant view was reductionist and didactic: genuine communist art would explicitly advance the class struggle. Since the studio system was a purely capitalist institution, it would never brook radical film content; thus it was futile and fundamentally misguided for Communists to tamper with the ideological trappings of the superstructure, as opposed to the economic base —the real source of power and real site of political transformation. This analysis received some sanction from Earl Browder, who led the party from 1934 to 1945. According to Richard Collins, a former CP screenwriter who testified before HUAC (in the same hearings in which he named Paul Jarrico as a Communist), Browder instructed the Hollywood branches not to inject films with Communist ideology.[26]

While Browder may have subscribed to this reductive view of culture, he also represented the Popular Front and, during World War II, adopted an accommodationist policy toward American business, both positions helping to generate the alternative vision of culture discussed below. Thus, when the party repudiated "Browderism" in 1945 and predicted instead a period of unavoidable class conflict, it adopted an even more rigid cultural policy. An episode in 1946 reflected this change. Albert Maltz, soon to become one of the Hollywood Ten, raised the issue of creativity and radical politics in an article for the Communist publication *New Masses*. Thinking of art as no more than a weapon in the class struggle, Maltz argued, was a "straitjacket" that he had had to abandon in order to write anything at all.[27] Even though Maltz's opinion was widely— if tacitly—accepted among many CP members in the arts, his article provoked a storm of abuse from the centers of party power. Chastened, Maltz recanted his views within a month. V. J. Jerome, head of the party's Cultural Commission, also expressed the harder line when he reviewed postwar films about African Americans in 1950. Although films like *Pinky* and *Home of the Brave* portrayed African Americans in a sympathetic light, Jerome interpreted those slight improvements as diversionary tactics, which only bolstered the underlying strategy of monopoly capital.[28] Communists should not deceive themselves, either as audience or as creative artists, about the real nature of these cultural expressions.

The "Maltz Affair" was widely cited by anticommunists "as proof of a totalitarian Communist effect on popular culture."[29] But as historians Paul Buhle and Dave Wagner point out, the episode was more complex than that: when Maltz first submitted his article to *New Masses*, the editors approved it "virtually unanimous[ly]" and anticipated "vigorous and high[-]level discussion."[30] Moreover, when Maltz met with national leaders, he was joined by several other screenwriters who stoutly defended Maltz's position, and none of them was actually punished. Buhle and Wagner interpret the controversy "as a continuation of an old discussion" in a period when the national leadership was trying—and generally failing—to rein in the Popular Front aesthetic sensibilities of its Hollywood artists.[31]

Future IPC associates Herbert Biberman, Sylvia Jarrico, Paul Jarrico, and Michael Wilson shared those sensibilities, which placed them in the second camp of Hollywood Communists of the 1930s and 1940s. They believed that there was always room, and therefore always the obligation, to introduce progressive ideas into cinema. Films reached millions of people, and radicals should neither abandon commercial film production to the mercies of the politically reactionary nor forsake it for documentary production alone. Biberman related that Lazarus had approached him early in the 1940s to start an independent film company. At the time, however, Biberman believed that progressives needed to work within the mainstream of the industry—the good favor that Communists found during World War II was not to be passed up.[32] Sylvia Jarrico observed that radical writers "did not look to alternative film making. They believed that socially responsible writers belonged in the film industry because feature films were the most significant way in which the people of the world were being educated. The medium reached so far, that any victory was important."[33] Paul Jarrico insisted that "if you could change their attitude toward women, workers, Blacks, and minorities in general —*and you could*—then that was an important contribution. Sure they wouldn't let us make a really revolutionary picture, but if we were good writers and skillful at our craft we could subtly affect the content [toward progressive ends]. It was a battle we did not resolve at the time."[34] Michael Wilson believed that the humanist writer "did not meekly deliver what the philistine ordered, but struggled tenaciously to preserve human values in all his work; . . . Hollywood writers in particular, dealing like all their kind in the radioactive commodity of ideas, were accountable to the peoples of the world for the effects of their ideas."[35]

"Humanism" was not a term that most Communists employed, and perhaps Wilson's usage here, and elsewhere, points to his way of navigating the political waters of Communism in Hollywood and of fashioning a powerful feminist story in *Salt of the Earth*. Committed to Marxist class analysis, Wilson nonetheless asserted a standard of "human values" that would, first, supersede a reductionist Marxism and, second, open to artistic exploration a world of topics taking as their starting point a concern with the human condition. In speaking of "humanism," Wilson was asserting the legitimacy of artistic work that would otherwise have been dismissed by Marxists as "bourgeois." This position was considered the "right-wing opportunist" position, as opposed to the "left sectarian" position.[36]

In this manner, Wilson was carrying on the discussion that had developed in several Popular Front–style organizations for Hollywood artists. The League of American Writers (LAW) sponsored screenwriting classes beginning in 1939. Led by writers such as Paul Jarrico, these classes addressed technical and political questions alike and were conducted as workshops, rather than as formal lectures.[37] Jarrico recalled that these workshops fostered fruitful debates between "historians" and "humanists," the former trying to grasp characters' historical motivations and the latter "look[ing] to the story as story, probing . . . more for interpersonal conflicts."[38] The Hollywood Writers Mobilization (founded in 1943), in many ways a continuation of the Hollywood Anti-Nazi League, continued the Popular Front by bringing together leftists, liberals, some industry executives, and academics both to promote wartime unity and to set the stage for a transformed film industry after the war.[39] Finally, two film theory journals, *Hollywood Quarterly* (1945–51) and *Hollywood Review* (1953–56), pushed far beyond the film criticism of party organs like *New Masses* or the *Daily People's World*. *Hollywood Quarterly* grew out of the Hollywood Writers Mobilization and brought together leftists and liberals under the respectable aegis of UCLA, which in turn ensured institutional freedom from party control. Sylvia Jarrico was its managing editor; her graduate adviser, psychology professor Franklin Fearing, was its editor. Screenwriters, animators, composers—all sorts of film practitioners, as well as academics, wrote about the social and political implications of film technique and genre.[40] However, the journal did not survive the blacklist era with the same ecumenical theoretical approach or left-wing participation. *Hollywood Review* was an attempt by Helen Levitt and Sylvia Jarrico in 1953 to rekindle *Hollywood Quarterly's* critical edge. Jarrico herself wrote a piercing feminist critique of what she called the "Evil Heroines of 1953." "The complacent theme that submission is the natural state of women," she wrote, "has given way to the aggressive theme that submission is the *necessary* state of women. . . . Hollywood's sinister heroines [were] ruthless killers" who reflected the Cold War counterattack on women who had been mobilized for war.[41] Jarrico connected Hollywood images of women to the Cold War push to get women to leave paid employment. *Hollywood Review* also paid particular attention to race and racism in American film and film production.[42]

Conflicts over radical artists' role in creating popular culture—whether or not the media would permit progressive ideas, however defined, into the mainstream of cultural production—should not mask, however, one essential similarity between the two basic positions staked out by Hollywood Communists. Both were predicated on a left-wing critique of mass culture that assumed that the audience was only a passive receptacle for the media's productions.[43] In this formulation, the public simply ingested whatever the popular culture served, whether conservative or progressive on race and gender issues. Biberman's excoriation of *True Experience* was actually part of a long tradition of radical cultural criticism that labeled popular culture decadent and often pornographic, gratifying people's basest instincts without stimulating people to crave something nobler.[44]

EARLY IPC PROJECTS

The evolution and structure of IPC also tell us about its members' political beliefs, both implicit and explicit. While IPC members' ideas about representing working-class struggles, and the ethnic and gendered dimensions of those struggles, had their origins in CP theory, they transcended the confines of CP analysis. Even more importantly, IPC members developed their ideas in the course of implementing them in specific projects. By the end of 1951, IPC was considering several ideas for feature films, all of which concerned either the situation of ethnic minorities or the question of individual conscience and the state. A screenplay by Dalton Trumbo (exiled in Mexico) portrayed an African American nurse accused of being a Communist. Paul Jarrico wrote a script about an atomic scientist who came to accept the government's argument that the "bomb is our strength."[45] While she did not develop a screenplay herself, Sylvia Jarrico's ideas on women in cinema might also have influenced the development of IPC. The first project slated for production, though, was a feature about the Scottsboro Boys, nine African American men in Alabama who were convicted in the early 1930s of raping two white women.

One woman later admitted that she had fabricated the story, partly under coercion from local authorities. The CP's International Labor Defense had taken on the case and publicized it across the country at a time when the Birmingham African American elite and the National Association for the Advancement of Colored People (NAACP) backed away.[46]

IPC had trouble developing the Scottsboro story as a feature film, however, and never managed to write a successful screenplay. The company ran through "half a dozen approaches" before consulting African American artists in New York City.[47] Director Biberman reported that the IPC screenwriters were surprised and somewhat embarrassed not to have known more about the contemporary "Negro Liberation Movement." "Then we began to see some forest and some trees . . . that the Negro artists were not 'experts' on Negro subjects to be consulted when we white artists had come a cropper . . . but they were really leading the most vital and numerically significant cultural fight in our country today, and that it was a pretty late date for us to come to them . . . let us face it, a lily-white company . . . and ask for favors."[48] The shortcoming of the Scottsboro story, according to Biberman, was that it portrayed victims when it should have shown "the Negro people in action"; the reason IPC had failed in this respect was that "the stories had to be conceived by Negro artists and developed under their understanding [and] guidance."[49]

Underlying Biberman's explanation of the Scottsboro project's failure were complex ideas of political theory and practice. IPC sincerely desired to show African Americans in a favorable light, to restore dignity to their history through an artistic medium that had kept them subjected to white supremacy. This imperative came out of humanism and a CP analysis that kept the struggle of African Americans in the foreground; the party saw African Americans as an "oppressed nation," the struggles of which were in and of themselves revolutionary.[50] Yet, finally freed of studio censorship, and armed with the "correct" analysis and political sensibilities, IPC still had trouble creating a genuine and compelling reflection of African American life. None of its approaches rang true; the mere belief in racial equality, however sincere, was inadequate to the task.

Those same political convictions, challenged by what they first believed was no more than an aesthetic problem, nonetheless formed the basis of IPC's action on the Scottsboro project. For, to these Communists, the structure of their organizations had to embody their political convictions. Biberman and the others in IPC recognized that the "lily-white" composition of their company was more than a problem of image: it also compromised the very art that they sought to create. Frequently, the

party paid no more than lip service to full representation in leadership
and membership, just as the democratic centralism that characterized
the party's hierarchy was always more centralized than democratic. Still,
the CP was far ahead of other interracial organizations of its day in
searching for and promoting African American leadership. (The same
was not true of female leadership.) Indeed, Biberman's comments have
the timbre of the breast-beating confessions of white chauvinism that the
party occasionally demanded of its members.[51]

But any tendency toward histrionic self-abnegation was tempered by
Biberman's immediate action: not to purge the company of the people
who had been shortsighted but to solicit the active participation of two
notable African Americans in the arts. Carlton Moss and Frances Williams joined the company late in 1951 as vice presidents and producers.
Moss had written and produced plays for the Federal Theatre and had
written radio scripts for NBC. During World War II he produced a film
for the War Department, *The Negro Soldier*, which many white soldiers
and "almost every black [soldier] in the Army and Air Corps" saw between February 1944 and August 1945.[52] Williams was an actress who
had helped start an African American community theater in Cleveland
when she was a teenager. She served on the executive board of Actor's
Equity and on Los Angeles's Central Labor Council, and she had had
plenty of experience with Hollywood stereotyping, once "ma[king] a stir
by refusing seventeen different bandannas for her role in [a] remake of
Show Boat."[53] Never, according to Biberman, had black and white people
together formed a film company in the United States. He hoped that
IPC's example would inspire African Americans to prod Hollywood to
integrate its own studios. IPC scrapped the Scottsboro story and instead
adopted a project Moss had begun elsewhere, a biography of Frederick
Douglass in collaboration with the National Council of Negro Women.
John Howard Lawson agreed to write the screenplay. But once IPC got
the idea for *Salt of the Earth*, and a commitment from Mine-Mill to
support the movie, it moved forward with that project and placed the
others on the back burner.

FORGING A WORKER-ARTIST ALLIANCE

Michael Wilson reminded Biberman that the problem with earlier IPC
projects, like the Scottsboro script, was that they were trying to tell
people's story "from our point of view." *Salt of the Earth* would be some-

thing different. The goal was to convey the essence of this people, and the means to do so were to be found in a worker-artist alliance in which the workers provided more than raw material for artists to fashion into a movie. This alliance depended not only on workers' participation in creating the script, as we saw above, but also on careful decisions about casting and on a formal structure that ensured equal participation of union families and artists. These arrangements allowed the union families to reenact and recreate the drama of the strike and, in so doing, to process the changes wrought by the strike while making connections to blacklisted artists, blacklisted technicians, and sympathetic audiences.

Casting

Herbert Biberman came to *Salt* convinced that a nonprofessional cast consisting of the miners' families would prove vital to the film's success. Excited by Soviet theater in the early 1930s, as a young director in New York Biberman had united professional and nonprofessional Chinese American actors in the play *Roar China*. Biberman saw his role as one of drawing out the essence of "the people," and he discovered that "the Chinese developed a homogeneity, a group presence, that endowed each individual with stature that was a gift from the whole. It brought a power in relaxation to them that few *actors* achieve. If they brought less skill, they brought the authority and dedication of their own persons and that incomparable thing—the reality of a people."[54]

Biberman's correspondence with the leaders of Mine-Mill reflected his excitement at the thought of working with the mixture of "the skill per se" of professional actors and "the authenticity the real people have."[55] He showed a genuine commitment to utilizing the talents of Mexican Americans, not just to depicting them. (He preferred Mexican American over Mexican actors because with the former there would be "no accents.")[56] In casting the lead roles, Biberman had first turned to fellow blacklisted artists like his own wife, Academy Award–winning actress Gale Sondergaard. But shortly into the casting process the producers "were jolted by recognition of a primary obligation." As Biberman recounted it, "We had thought of ourselves as 'the blacklisted.' And we were the veriest newcomers. Culturally and socially, as well as politically and economically, vast numbers of our American people had been blacklisted for centuries. Had they not been, we might never have been. Were we, the new blacklisted, to blacklist the older ones?"[57] IPC decided that Sondergaard would not play Esperanza. In this instance we can see how political beliefs about

equality can be deepened—and made concrete, as in casting decisions—
by the flash of recognition of oneself in another's situation, or of another
in one's own situation. The blacklist had been a dramatic episode with a
clear beginning, the 1947 HUAC hearings. Realizing that blacklisting in a
wider sense, with no discrete event to mark its inception, happened to
"vast numbers" of Americans, and that this broader form of exclusion
was something they had all nominally opposed without connecting it to
themselves, pushed Jarrico, Wilson, and Biberman to change their approach. "The first humiliating recognition of our discriminatory inheritance," Biberman related in his memoirs, "was sufficient. We knew what
we had to do."[58]

And that was to engage Rosaura Revueltas, a respected Mexican
actress, to play Esperanza. Revueltas's mother came from a mining family
in northern Mexico, and in Mexico City, where Rosaura's father owned a
small shop, the family became prominent in the arts and in left-wing
politics. One brother had been a composer, another a painter, a third a
novelist and well-known Communist.[59] Revueltas herself had appeared in
only a few films, but she had won European and Mexican awards for
those performances. Biberman described her as "beautiful for this role,
sensitive, earthy and not Hollywoodesque in her beauty which is deeper
and richer."[60]

And until the last weeks before the shooting began, a Mexican actor
(never named in Biberman's letters or later memoir but identified by
Deborah Rosenfelt as Rodolfo Acosta) was to have played Ramón. Acosta
had "played some twenty-six pictures in Mexico, [was] a Mexican Academy Award winner, and [had] played some nine pictures for the studios in
Hollywood."[61] He had been waiting all his life, he told Biberman, to play
such a role. It would permit him "to express his national pride, his love of
a character such as Ramon, the heroic struggles of his own people."[62]
(This flowery language was Biberman's, not necessarily Acosta's.) In casting, then, IPC members were taking the lessons from the Scottsboro film
project to heart. People of Mexican descent needed to participate in the
production, not simply to provide the material for the story.

Biberman tried to work out the relationship between authenticity
and professionalism. It was important to him to have Mexican Americans perform in *Salt of the Earth*, and for some of them to be professional
actors. But the casting process elicited two challenges to his vision. The
first concerned working on a project that deliberately challenged the
dominant McCarthyism; the second inhered in the complicated process
of uniting workers and artists. Simply lining up professional actors and

actresses proved difficult, and finding them in the United States proved impossible. No Mexican American actors accepted the roles. Having only recently, and barely, made inroads into the studios, they understood that performing in *Salt of the Earth* would end their careers. Rodolfo Acosta changed his mind by the time Biberman was ready to move operations to the Silver City area.[63] "His agent," Biberman recalled, "had warned him against any association with us. It would sound the death-knell for his Hollywood career."[64] In the end, Biberman failed to find a satisfactory Mexican American professional actor to play Ramón.

Sonja Dahl and Rosaura Revueltas used this crisis, which erupted just days before shooting was to begin, as an opening for an actor whom Biberman had wholeheartedly dismissed: Kennecott employee Juan Chacón. Chacón was born and raised on a small ranch in the Mimbres Valley. During World War II, he worked as a welder in California and Hawaii shipyards, but after the war he decided to return to Grant County. Despite his training and experience, Kennecott hired him as a laborer. He quickly became active in the union and even ran for political office in 1948. By the time of the film production, Chacón was a Local 890 officer.[65] Chacón had been active in the Mine-Mill union since his return from defense industries in California and Hawaii after World War II. Dahl had met him in one of her early visits to Grant County to look for shooting sites and "felt that this man exuded a certain kind of posture in that cold union set-up, that . . . was very sympathetic." Chacón, she commented later, "commanded respect. . . . He [was] a very simple man. But there was a quality of dignity about him . . . that really impressed" her.[66] Revueltas, too, believed that Chacón could fill the role.

But Biberman deemed Chacón "much too shy, too small in stature, too sweet and retiring for Ramón."[67] He eventually agreed, however, to let the two women choose between Chacón and another auditioner. Dahl and Revueltas "were delighted when Herbert finally deigned to listen to [them], after [they] pushed and pushed him."[68] And despite what Biberman considered an "utterly pedestrian" reading, Chacón got the part.[69] Just as Michael Wilson responded both to Hollywood women and to local women in developing the story in *Salt*, so too did Herbert Biberman accept the interference by two women into what he had most emphatically deemed the director's prerogative. "I had been casting all my adult life," he commented. "There were certain attributes for a role!"[70]

Biberman worked closely with Chacón to make the best of what he thought was a dismal situation. He told Chacón to spend several hours on the top of a nearby mountain, remembering everything that has taken place in the valleys below you for three hundred years. . . . Not just remember it in your brain, but see it in your eyes. And everything you see I'd like you to feel yourself in the middle of. . . . And as you stand there, seeing yourself, seeing this country, seeing its history, seeing its struggles, seeing its strength and promise, I want you to talk back at it, and with *words*, spoken by your eyes. . . . If you do this you'll come back tomorrow no longer John Chacon. Not even Ramon. But the vital spark of the people of this valley out of which we will make Ramon.[71]

This kind of focus reflected Biberman's ideas—deeply romantic, to say the least—on how to draw out the essence of "the people."[72] Chacón had his own take on the process: "Herbert Biberman handed me the script, and he said, 'Here, take this. Go up to the hills and talk to those rocks up there, and learn it.' So I went up there, and I opened the script, and I started reading it. And I started looking at the rocks and reading the script. And I said, 'Well, I'll be darned. Here I am, an actor in *Salt of the Earth*. Trying to learn a script.' So, I went ahead, and I went up there several times. I looked at those rocks, and I kept on reading and reading the script. So finally, we started filming *Salt of the Earth*. And it didn't take me very long to learn the script."[73]

Romanticism inflected Wilson's and Biberman's ideas for *Salt*. Both men referred to "the people" without any direct or personal connection to them; in this respect, Biberman and Wilson resembled many writers on the Left who casually or effusively spoke of "the people" as a group that possessed singleness of purpose and for whom these writers claimed to speak. An outsider status, they thought, could help artists "enter into [the people's] lives [and] inspire them into resistance—into refusing to make the little day by day concessions of their decency."[74] Wilson was very attentive to the union families' own words and the texture of their lives: he did not apply preconceived ideas of how an oppressed minority feels or how it should act. But the very project of distilling an essence speaks of an illusory homogeneity, the imagination of which may have resulted, in part, from seeing Mexican Americans as exotic. Wilson essentialized Mexican Americans and workers, but on that basis he also deferred to them. In the context of producing a script, he attempted to integrate their understanding of their history with his ability to write a story.

Biberman went down the same path when he tried to capture the

Juan Chacón studying the script of Salt of the Earth. *Photo courtesy of the Wisconsin Center for Film and Theater Research, Lot #A108.*

essence of the people through art. He described his reaction to meeting the miners and their families: they were "such a beautiful group of people . . . that well photographed they will just knock people out of their seats with their strong and clean and incredibly attractive character."[75] Like Wilson, Biberman essentialized Mexican Americans and workers, but rather than deferring to them on this basis he confined them to his own vision of a worker-artist alliance in which nonprofessionals stayed in their place. Romanticism had a flip side in this case: condescension perceptible in some of Biberman's (and, to a lesser extent, Wilson's) comments about Mexican Americans. Biberman and Wilson respected the Mexican American community in Bayard; at the same time, they exalted or romanticized that community, finding in it an essence that obfuscated

Virginia and Clinton Jencks on the set of Salt of the Earth. *Photo courtesy of the Wisconsin Center for Film and Theater Research, Lot #A108.*

differences among its members. Mexican American working families in Grant County challenged Wilson and Biberman from a position of "authenticity." Wilson was already inclined to accept this, but Biberman could not, and did not, entirely do so.[76]

Casting the lead female character brought out this problem of authenticity. Union members in Grant County saw no reason why professional actors should play the lead roles. Intimidated, perhaps, by the "high society" that IPC seemed to represent, Local 890 families also wanted to protect their own story and feared that professional actors might compromise it. Virginia Chacón, for instance, said "We just didn't want a movie made and let somebody else come and take our places, you know."[77] Many a female picketer, in fact, probably thought the character Esperanza was modeled on herself.[78] This feeling grew even stronger

Angie Sánchez as Consuelo Ruiz, offering the ladies auxiliary's help to the striking Delaware Zinc miners. Sitting next to her are Clinton Jencks as Frank Barnes, Joe T. Morales as Sal Ruiz, and Ernesto Velásquez as Charley Vidal. Photo courtesy of the Wisconsin Center for Film and Theater Research, Lot #A108.

once Herbert Biberman cast Juan Chacón as Ramón. Union members—women particularly, but supported by the men and by union officials like Clinton Jencks—then saw even less reason to bring in an outsider to play the female lead. Angie Sánchez, who played Consuelo Ruiz, later stated that Biberman had originally slated her to play Esperanza.[79] Biberman had stopped in Bayard early in July 1952 to begin screening local people for roles. He wrote to Travis that he had "discovered a wonderful and natural-born actress in Bayard who has lifted my hopes considerably," but he neither identified her nor indicated that she might play Esperanza.[80]

The final cast featured nine 890 members—most having been in leadership positions in the union and auxiliary—in leading roles. Juan Chacón played Ramón. Clinton and Virginia Jencks played organizer

*Henrietta Williams as Teresa Vidal, proposing that women take over the picket
lines. Photo courtesy of the Wisconsin Center for Film and Theater Research,
Lot #A108.*

Frank Barnes and his wife, Ruth. Joe T. Morales, long a Kennecott employee and 890 leader, played Sal Ruiz, with Angie Sánchez playing his
wife, Consuelo. Henrietta Williams, who had been jailed during the Empire Zinc strike, played Teresa Vidal, and Ernesto Velásquez, the chairman of the Empire Zinc strike negotiating committee, played her husband, Charley. And rounding out the nonprofessional cast in prominent
roles were Clorinda Alderette and Charles Coleman as Luz and Antonio
Morales. Casting the scabs and deputies proved difficult; eventually two
brothers, E. A. and William Rockwell, agreed to take on the odious role of
the sheriff's deputies, but only after Biberman demonstrated that the violent scenes involved fake blows: neither wanted to hit a union brother.[81]
Some blacklisted professional actors played minor roles. Will Geer, who

E. A. and William Rockwell as the sheriff's deputies, delivering the court injunction to the union hall. Director Herbert Biberman had trouble casting the deputies, because no one wanted to hit a union brother. Only after showing the Rockwell brothers that the punches were fake did Biberman persuade them to accept the roles. Photo courtesy of the Wisconsin Center for Film and Theater Research, Lot #A108.

would later gain fame as Grandpa Walton on television, played the sheriff, and David Wolfe played the company's representative.

The Gender Politics of IPC

Interestingly, lessons from the Scottsboro project did not perceptibly shape the gender politics within IPC. Sylvia Jarrico and Sonja Dahl Biberman both worked on the production of *Salt*, but they were not afforded the same kind of formal recognition as women in a film on the Woman Question that Carlton Moss and Frances Williams received as African Americans in projects on the Negro Question. Rosaura Revueltas did not join IPC's production company but did join its distribution company.

Biberman referred to his sister-in-law as the "secretary of our company," instead of the assistant producer that she really was. Sonja Dahl Biberman first scouted out the county for possible locations and housing in December 1952.[82] She was trusted enough, and in sufficient contact with the set and crew, to be one of two signatories on the IPC bank account in Silver City.[83] She worked on the set as "script girl" and on whatever else needed to be done, alternating jobs with other crew members.[84] Later she was critical to the film's distribution. Historians Larry Ceplair and Steven Englund refer to Sylvia Jarrico as an associate producer; and, although the film credits do not list her, she certainly was on the set throughout shooting and, according to Biberman, very popular among the union families. She had walked the picket with union women when the Jarricos first visited the strike late in 1951. Clearly she had plenty to say and plenty to offer.

In IPC's film projects, as in CP thinking in general, there were obvious parallels between the treatment of African Americans and that of women. The first IPC project was a film about African Americans and racism, while the second addressed women and sexism. Furthermore, Communists and people in IPC used similar language to discuss the two issues: "the Negro Question" and "the Woman Question," "white chauvinism" and "male chauvinism." But these linguistic similarities did not carry over into concrete applications of theory on race and gender; the women's issues did not resonate in the same way with the leaders of IPC and did not, evidently, require the same formal attention to the place of women within the organization.

Here we witness a blindness regarding women's contributions that was characteristic of mixed-gender political and business organizations. This may have come from Sylvia Jarrico and Sonja Dahl Biberman having been family members of the principal players in IPC. To some degree, women were subsumed into the project as wives and sisters. This subsumption may be related to the romanticism regarding "the people" being represented: assumptions of a unity, a wholeness, obscured any divisions among its components. This is ironic given Wilson's own enthralled attention to the complex layers of struggle; still, it is not much of a surprise that in some instances there would be a neglect of that complexity in favor of a simpler whole, particularly when the complexity was in their own families and company.

This analysis is not meant to accuse IPC members of myopia or of acting at odds with the implications—implications that we perceive fifty years later—of their egalitarian beliefs. Instead of passing judgment, we should understand these issues as giving fuller shape to their political thought as they developed it in their personal lives and in collective endeavor, and seek to understand the reasons that their ideas and actions on gender and Mexican American ethnicity lagged behind their ideas on African Americans and racism. Even to discuss "lagging behind" is to apply standards that they may or may not have held. Still, Communists possessed enough theoretical commitment to women's equality and to Mexican American social advancement that those standards were indeed relevant.

The Production Committee

Once the project moved to Grant County in early January 1953, a production committee, consisting of six representatives each from IPC, Local 890, and Auxiliary 209, managed the daily work. The appointment of representatives from Local 890 and Auxiliary 209 in equal numbers hints at women's assertions of equal representation in putting their story on film; the structure affirmed that they could not be subsumed in the general category of "union members" but rather warranted their own standing. And with IPC in the minority on the production committee, the filmmakers were in no position to trump the decisions of the union families if the union representatives were united on a particular question. Although Mine-Mill's international executive board had agreed in the summer of 1952 to sponsor the picture (without contributing money), the international occupied no formal position on the production committee. Morris Wright, editor of Mine-Mill's national newspaper, served as public relations representative.[85]

Production involved many tasks: getting crew and cast to the film location, building sets, gathering props, coordinating the crowds for group scenes, feeding and housing everyone, scheduling the shooting to accommodate men and women who also had regular jobs. To assistant director Jules Schwerin, the ladies' auxiliary deserved most of the credit for these logistics.[86] He was also quite moved by "the relationship developing between the crew and the miners." It was "a wonderful thing to watch," he said, "a real spirit of brotherhood, each group learning from the other. . . . Every day more miners pitch in to help the crew, some of them after a grueling eight-hour day in the mines. Our construction team can take pride in the fact that the miners find our mine-head set authentic."[87]

Sonja Dahl Biberman made sure that the production committee also arranged adequate child care to allow women to participate, both behind

Meals on the set were provided by the production committee, composed equally of representatives from IPC, Local 890, and Auxiliary 209. Photo courtesy of the Wisconsin Center for Film and Theater Research, Lot #A108.

and in front of the camera. Some women had tried individual solutions to the problem of child care. Anita Torrez, for instance, persuaded her younger sister to come to Hanover to take care of the Torrezes' infant while Anita helped with production. But the problem posed by inadequate child care was of such great dimension that it required a collective solution. The mass scenes, in particular, were difficult to arrange and caused many changes in the production schedule. Herbert Biberman knew that the production would require "women, and child care," but he did nothing to arrange it; the men in Local 890 had overlooked the issue entirely.[88] It took Sonja Dahl Biberman's persistence to make men recognize babysitting as a legitimate concern of the filmmakers. "Most of the families have no phones and distances are fantastic," Schwerin noted. "Organizing a baby-sitting-and-jitney service for a hundred people is really something. . . . We are all impressed by the stamina and courage of the women and the relaxed nature of their children."[89]

The production committee was responsible for more than the day-to-day logistics. It was, as Juan Chacón explained, also "a policy-making body, with the responsibility of seeing that our picture ran true to life from start to finish. Occasionally there were meetings in which the union people pointed out to our Hollywood friends that a scene we had just shot was not true in certain details. When that happened we all pitched in to correct the mistake. Most of these mistakes were made because the movie craftsmen had not lived through all our struggles; but they had all the heart and the good will in the world."[90] Clinton Jencks corroborated Chacón's account but emphasized conflict within the committee: "This wasn't all easy. There were people who came in, making the film, [who] had very strong ideas about how the film should be made.... We'd have arguments.... We'd be working hard all day, ... and we'd have meetings until late at night, hammering out problems for the next day." Still, this conflict was productive because no one group could dominate. As Jencks put it, "It was a beautiful kind of process of interchange."[91]

The struggles within the production committee show how important it was to the mining families that the story be "true." This truth consisted not only of the fidelity of particular details to the events they portrayed but also of an ownership of both the strike and its representation. Making the strike into a movie was a transformative process. The movie was not, and could never be, the same thing as the strike, and the artistic distance between the two was necessary if the participants were either to process the events of the strike in an emotionally satisfying way or to share their story with audiences near and far. But the union families wanted to ensure that the transformation of their story would not also be an *expropriation* of their story.

Acting and Reenacting

Scenes before the camera felt real to the Grant Countians who performed them, and the casting process brought this out into the open: couples hesitated to play the spouses of other men and women; the Rockwell brothers did not want to play deputies because they were afraid of hurting a union brother. The experience of actually shooting the scenes, too, shortened the distance between acting and reenacting, while reliving the events provided some of the amateur actors with emotional release. For others, however, closeness to the real events made filming the scenes traumatic.

In one early scene, after an accident that precipitates the strike, Ramón assaults a foreman who calls him "Pancho" and a "liar, a no-good,

The lines between acting and reenacting were often blurred. Here, Ramón assaults the foreman, with Charley Vidal and Frank Barnes trying to restrain him. Chacón acted with such intensity—Jencks was kicked in the shin in the process— that Jencks was convinced this scene was a catharsis for pent-up anger toward managers. Photo courtesy of the Wisconsin Center for Film and Theater Research, Lot #A108.

dirty—." This was the first scene shot with dialogue, and, as assistant director Jules Schwerin noted in his diary, "Everyone was tense. One miner kept muffing his lines. He apologized, explaining that the actor-foreman reminded him of a real foreman he had known, and added: 'He gets me so damn mad I forget my lines.' If we can sustain this kind of reality, a few muffed lines won't matter."[92] For Juan Chacón, acting in this scene proved to be something of a catharsis for years of pent-up resentment at racist management. He tore into the actor playing the foreman with such force that Clinton Jencks and Ernesto Velásquez could barely restrain him; Jencks got a bruised shin in the deal. "He didn't pull all that anger out of the sky," Jencks commented.[93] Chacón later said, "One of the most surprising things to us was that we found we didn't have to 'act.' El Biberman, as we came to call him, was happiest when we were just ourselves. So after awhile, we stopped pretending and then, from the 'rushes' we saw, the movie began to look better."[94] Clinton Jencks felt that the movie was "so close to the time [of the strike]. It was a part of us. . . . I wouldn't even know the camera [was there]."[95]

The union families, like Biberman, were trying to distill an essence— not of "a people," necessarily, but of the meanings of the strike for them, their families, and their union community. By reenacting their experience they reordered it. Putting on the mask of a theatrical role allowed them to articulate what felt to them to be central truths and, they hoped, to reach and engage audiences everywhere. Watching the first "rushes" on January 29, 1953, the union people "howled and cheered and laughed . . . when they saw themselves on the screen. . . . It was a catharsis."[96]

Not everyone welcomed the chance to relive the strike experience, however. Willie Andazola, a child who had been jailed with his mother, Camerina Andazola, after the mass arrests of June 16, 1951, did not want to play any role in the picture and only did so unwillingly. The jail had scared him very deeply, and he had nightmares about the bars.[97] And Rachel Juárez, who had been struck by a car on the picket line, never saw the film: even fifty years later, the prospect of seeing fellow picketers like Consuelo Martínez wounded by strikebreakers and deputies on screen was too traumatic for her.[98]

What Making Salt of the Earth *Meant to the Participants*

The blacklist devastated progressives in Hollywood, but it also opened the space for trying a new kind of artistic project. Going into the project, the Jarricos, Biberman, and Wilson were excited at the prospects of crafting a worker-artist alliance; coming out of it, they were transformed. Biberman made the fight to distribute the movie into a lifelong battle, suing Hollywood studios for conspiring to block the movie's distribution and working strenuously to get the movie shown in countries around the globe. Sylvia Jarrico found that working on *Salt of the Earth* "refurbished [her] sense of political usefulness."[99] And for Michael Wilson, who would go on to write even more widely acclaimed screenplays, writing *Salt of the Earth* was the most important thing he had ever done.[100]

The worker-artist alliance appealed to technicians as much as to writers, directors, and actors. A veteran of the battles against racketeering in the International Association of Theater and Stage Employees, technician Paul Perlin was blacklisted after the big Hollywood studio strikes of 1945 and 1946. HUAC subpoenaed him in November 1951, but

Willie Andazola (left) as a striker's son. Photo courtesy of the Wisconsin Center for Film and Theater Research, Lot #A108.

Perlin was not intimidated—he "gave the committee a rough time." He was thrilled to work on *Salt of the Earth* because it was the first movie where he was encouraged to "cross the bridge between craft and talent crews"; gone was the "jungle-like competition" that compromised Hollywood productions.[101] Similarly, prop maker Irving Hentschel was proud to have been hired to work on *Salt*, seeing it as his reward for years of union activity. "Pictures in Hollywood had all the guts taken out of them," Hentschel observed, but the people in Grant County made an unabashedly pro-union movie.[102]

Making this movie was also a way to rekindle women's activism, which dwindled after the strike ended in January 1952. For example, the auxiliary had planned to start a nursery that would, as the union news-

Filming Salt of the Earth. *Paul Jarrico is on roof at far left, Herbert Biberman is seated on the roof beneath the camera, and Michael Wilson is seated on the ground at right. Photo courtesy of the Wisconsin Center for Film and Theater Research, Lot #A108.*

paper put it, "[benefit] our women who have been tied up and are having trouble in preparing care."[103] But the nursery plan fell through. While "the men are still fighting together, daily on the job," Virginia Jencks observed in March 1952, "the women who showed courage and determination seem almost like by-products of the strike now that it is over." *Salt of the Earth* would give picketers "recognition and a feeling of accomplishment and personal pride," she explained. "In socialist countries there are many ways of showing how a person is a public hero, but here we have let this historical strike and these historic people fade away."[104] Jencks understood that part of the trouble was women's isolation as housewives, but she was especially frustrated with the international leadership and its failure to take women's situation seriously. According to Jencks, a speaker sent to lead a workers' education class for women in February 1952 "said nothing to us as women, or for us, and although there were sixteen women there, they were not involved in the discussion in any way. I'm still sore about the way this progressive guy never spoke about women in his discussions. . . . I'm losing objectivity. Clint tells me I'm a man-hater. Lately, I'm damned sure he's right."[105] As historian James Lorence suggests, Wilson's script was able to affirm women's activism in a way that transformed the actual outcome of the strike into a longer-lasting and more positive lesson in solidarity than what the strikers could have achieved.[106]

Perhaps most importantly, and most simply, the union participants wanted to get their story out, and *Salt of the Earth* promised to help them do so. Henrietta Williams could hardly believe that so much ugliness could be unleashed during the Empire Zinc strike against working people just trying to improve their lives. Making the movie, she said, was a way to show people "one of the worst things that could happen here in the United States."[107] But this was not in order to discredit the United States in the eyes of a hostile world, as *Salt*'s anticommunist enemies would insist. Instead, it was to affirm the dignity and the humanity of the strikers. To Williams, the title, *Salt of the Earth*, meant "the sweat of the miner, and the ground of the mines"—powerful images of working-class strength and the force of nature.[108] Clinton Jencks saw in the movie a chance to affirm the heroism of ordinary people and to make connections with audiences. Making *Salt* was a high point in their lives precisely because, as he put it, "we were reaching out, and we were making ourselves naked in all our weaknesses, and our strengths. And we weren't trying to cover up the problems. But we also wanted to say we've learned how to overcome some of those problems. . . . And we found people that were willing to help us say it. And that was beautiful."[109] Juan Chacón believed that *Salt of the Earth* "help[ed] to expose the lie" that Mexicans were "naturally inferior," a lie told by the mining companies to prevent Anglo-Mexican unity.[110] For all of these participants, the essence of making the movie was making connections to others, just as Biberman had described. *Salt of the Earth* brought workers and artists together and had the potential to connect both groups to American audiences more broadly. It was this challenge to the isolation imposed by the blacklist and by anticommunism more broadly that most threatened the mining industry and the film industry. And it was the potential to bring people together that, ironically, allowed both the mining industry and the film industry to unite in order to stifle *Salt of the Earth*.

9

Anticommunist Assaults

"A WEAPON FOR RUSSIA"

On February 24, 1953, Donald Jackson, representative from California and a member of the House Un-American Activities Committee (HUAC), addressed his colleagues from the floor of the House of Representatives. Just next door to America's nuclear headquarters at Los Alamos, he declared, Communists were making a subversive film that would inflame race hatred by depicting the United States as the "enemy of all colored people." Jackson did not know the name of this film, but he was certain of its content. In one scene, he explained, "two deputy sheriffs arrest a meek American miner of Mexican descent and proceed to pistol-whip the miner's very young son."[1] (In fact, there was no such scene.) Jackson performed the anticommunist ritual that had become standard HUAC practice, reciting the names of people associated with the film and announcing that each had refused to answer HUAC's questions about the Communist Party (CP). This film, a "weapon for Russia," according to Jackson, warranted a full congressional investigation and legislation to ban the film's distribution. Jackson was ready to "do everything in his power to prevent the film from being shown in public theatres."[2]

Jackson had been warned about the movie by the American Federation of Labor's Hollywood Film Council president, Roy Brewer. "No motion picture made by Communists can be good for America," Brewer said on February 12. "Hollywood has gotten rid of these people, and we want the federal government to investigate carefully the picture being made at Silver City, New Mexico."[3] For his part, Brewer had become aware of the film both from the attempt by the Independent Productions Corporation (IPC) to line up a union crew and from Grant County residents. The events of February and March 1953, in fact, reveal how national and local anticommunism worked in tandem. Representative Jackson's speech reverberated far beyond the floor of the House of Representatives, and it marked a turning point in the film crew's experience in Grant County. For the next three weeks, the film crew was first intimidated, then threatened, and finally driven out of town by union antagonists set on freeing the county of communists. Nationally, the federal government chose this moment to charge Clinton Jencks with having falsified a Taft-Hartley affidavit with the National Labor Relations Board, and for the next several years he struggled to stay out of prison.

THE MOVIE CREW IN GRANT COUNTY

Things did not start out so badly. The relations between the film crew and the townspeople were friendly at first, not least because IPC had deposited tens of thousands of dollars in the American National Bank of Silver City and planned to spend it locally. Sonja Dahl Biberman and Paul Jarrico had persuaded the proprietor of the Bear Mountain Ranch, a few miles northwest of Silver City, to house the entire crew despite the presence of some African American technicians. No Jim Crow here, they were glad to find. An eccentric local rancher, Alford Roos, was pleased to offer his ranch as a shooting location. Will Geer shared his love of orchids with the ladies of the Green Thumb Garden Club, who were delighted to have a famous actor—even a blacklisted one—among them.[4] Most small businessmen appreciated the commerce that accompanied film production in the vicinity, and some of the local officials, like Central mayor Frank Romero, granted permits to shoot in public spaces.[5] Indeed, IPC had been quite careful in cultivating cordial relations with local officials.[6] One night Sheriff Owen Mathews invited prop man Irving Hentschel to his office and, "with the lights low, produced submachine guns and rifles to use as models in the prop man's workshop."[7] One of the local priests "urged area merchants to rent automobiles, furniture, and other goods [to the film crew] at low cost in exchange for God's blessings. 'Those sonsabitches,' the priest muttered to assistant director Jules Schwerin after leaving the shops. 'They hate the Mexican Americans. Let them make some sacrifices.' "[8]

But by the middle of February, local and national anticommunists had publicized the film in Grant County, forcing the filmmakers to respond to angry charges about the nature and purpose of *Salt of the Earth*. Late in January, a Hurley schoolteacher named June Kuhlman had written to columnist Victor Riesel (who joined the attack early in February), E. T. "Buck" Harris, public relations director for the Screen Actors Guild, and Eric Johnston of the Motion Picture Association of America, requesting advice on "how to do [her] American duty." She had nothing but love for "these people," she explained, and did not want to see them used by communists.[9] Buck Harris then asked for information on the movie from Grant County newspapermen and from Ward Ballmer, public relations director at Chino. According to historian James Lorence, "Harris described all his informants as 'most cooperative,' although Ballmer demanded confidentiality because Kennecott had publicly adopted a 'hands off policy' on the movie. Together, they provided extensive detail."[10] Harris "suggested that one 'positive step' . . . would be to have the Immigration and Naturalization Service 'check on' [actress] Rosaura Revueltas's citizenship status to see if she could be charged with violation of her visitor's visa."[11]

In the town of Central, the John R. Storz American Legion Post had set up its own "Un-American Activities Committee." On January 23, Leroy B. Bible, chairman of the American Legion committee, alerted Representative Harold Velde, HUAC chairman, of the movie being made in Grant County, and a few weeks later Bible asked Senator Dennis Chávez to help Velde "clean out this known group of 'Communists.'"[12] The two anticommunist committees must have continued to work with one another, for Bible knew ahead of time that Representative Jackson would deliver a speech on February 24. Bible asked Chávez to mail copies of Jackson's speech to radio station KSIL and to the American Legion "for local use."[13] Chávez's office mailed copies of the *Congressional Record* to KSIL on February 25 and to Bible a few days later.[14]

The day after Jackson spoke, February 25, two federal immigration officials arrested Rosaura Revueltas on an administrative warrant for having illegally entered the United States on January 4.[15] Her passport bore no stamp of legal entry. Revueltas explained that she had entered at El Paso in a station wagon operated by LAMSA Airlines and that the border official had simply waved them all through. But her account carried no weight with immigration officials, who took her to El Paso. "All the way," she recalled, "they kept interrogating me. Was I a Communist? Weren't the people I was working with Communists? Wasn't this a Communist picture? For the first time I began to feel frightened. Not for myself, but for the picture. Some powerful man or men were out to kill our picture."[16] District immigration director Joseph Minton said he had been investigating Revueltas's case for over a week and was "ready to move in on her" before Jackson's speech; he also intended to investigate other cast members to verify that they were legally in the country. Asked if the passport technicality prompted her arrest, Minton replied, "In view of what has been going on up there and the people involved, I think anyone has the right to assume there might be other angles to this case."[17] Revueltas's arrest might not have been sparked by Jackson's speech, but it was clearly motivated by similar political considerations.

Mine-Mill and its supporters acted quickly. Morris Wright, public relations representative for the film, denied Jackson's accusations. The film was not produced by the CP but rather by Mine-Mill. No one was "pistol-whipped," nor was violence directed against a Mexican boy. The picture promoted ethnic harmony and would "serve as a good ambassador for the United States" in Latin America.[18] Paul Jarrico spoke more bluntly. Jackson, he said, was an "unmitigated liar" who should "take off his cloak of congressional immunity and fight like a man" about the production of *Salt of the Earth*.[19] From Mexico, too, came criticism of Revueltas's detention. Mexico's foreign minister, Luis Padilla Nerva, instructed the consul in El Paso, Raúl Michel, to give "all possible protection" to Revueltas and to ask for a delay in deporting her.[20] The Mexican National Association of Actors angrily condemned her arrest; prominent actor Jorge Negrete, president of the association, stated that "unless Rosaura Revueltas is freed to continue her work on *Salt of the Earth* every Hollywood actor now in Mexico will be suspended and barred from continuing their productions." Productions that would be affected included *Growing Wild*, starring Gary Cooper and Barbara Stanwyck, and *Second Chance*, featuring Anthony Quinn, Ward Bond, Robert Mitchum, and Linda Darnell.[21] Revueltas's attorney, Ben Margolis, filed for a writ of habeas corpus from U.S. district judge R. E. Thomason, and Revueltas "regained [her] hope of an early release."[22]

Revueltas's optimism faded during the habeas corpus hearing, however, when she saw Margolis "win argument after argument and yet lose on the basic plea. . . . And [she] began to realize that the forces trying to stop the completion of [the] picture were more powerful than [she] had imagined."[23] Judge Thomason refused to release her on bond.[24] Her choice was simple: she could voluntarily return to Mexico and apply for readmittance—which no one in the film company believed she would receive—or she could undergo deportation hearings. Revueltas finally left the country "voluntarily" on March 6, crossing into Juárez and then flying to Mexico City.[25]

Thus the actions of a small number of political figures, administration officials, and journalists threatened the film's completion. IPC public relations director Morris Wright told the *Silver City Daily Press* that the film company could "go on for awhile shooting those scenes in which Miss Revueltas does not appear, . . . but we can't finish it without her."[26] For some scenes, Biberman simply used a double, Anita Torrez's sister, who had arrived in Hanover to babysit.[27] For other scenes, he continued filming without Revueltas and then, some weeks later, filmed her in Mexico. The Mexican shooting, predictably, drove up production costs.[28]

Extralegal violence also threatened the crew, IPC, and union families. People who had opposed the Empire Zinc strikers took Jackson's speech as license to exact their own vengeance on the union. And they did so through intimidation and violence, which they justified as the only way to fight communism. On March 2—after radio station KSIL rebroadcast all twenty minutes of Jackson's speech—a group of eight or ten men confronted the film crew in front of the Central post office. Larry Martin, of Martin's Grocery Store, later explained, "When the movie people said they had permission from the Mayor to take the pictures, they were told, 'The Mayor doesn't run this town.' After that we told the crew we would bust the cameras if they didn't leave."[29] Martin and his companions exchanged angry words with the crew members, who eventually left the area.

Central mayor Romero tried to remain neutral, supporting neither the members of the film crew nor the men who harassed them. Juan Chacón claimed that "Romero apologized to the film unit for the rude treatment."[30] But Romero quickly backed away from any association with the film company: "I didn't apologize to anyone," he said the next day. "I would like to refute that statement."[31] Romero admitted that he had granted a film permit to Jules Schwerin but that, because of the negative publicity, he had tried to discourage both Schwerin and Jencks from actually coming to Central. Romero's disavowal did not, however, directly sanction the assault on the film crew. Before the confrontation began, he had received a telephone call from Bayard. A "group of citizens [was] ready to help us out," Romero stated. They "wanted to know if I would back them up. I told them to stay in Bayard, because I didn't want any violence."[32]

The day after the incident in Central, Bayard citizens assaulted the crew, who had set up cameras just south of Bayard's business section, across the street from the 890 union hall. Mayor Bill Upton had not granted even nominal permission to film in that town, and he insisted that the land in question was private property and that the owner had placed it in Upton's care.[33] Joined by some twenty other "citizens," the mayor told the crew to "leave and not come back."[34] Pharmacist Earl Lett, who had proudly attacked Clinton Jencks during the Empire Zinc strike, assaulted him again and shared the story with the *Silver City Daily Press*. Lett "told the movie makers 'that we didn't want any communists taking pictures' [and] said he caught Jencks by the coat and hit him. About that time, . . . Juan Chacón . . . jumped on his back. A couple of others got into the fray."[35] Union members from the nearby Local 890 hall defended the crew; after fifteen minutes, Deputy Sheriff John Turney and City Marshal Leslie Goforth managed to break up the fistfight. No one was arrested. The crew returned to Alford Roos's ranch to resume shooting.[36]

Around 1:30 on the morning of March 4, vigilantes shot four bullets at Jencks's car. Later that day, Jencks filed assault charges against Lett and asked that Lett be put under a "peace bond" like those issued against Empire Zinc strikers the year before.[37] Recapitulations, and sometimes inversions, of events that had occurred during the Empire Zinc strike continued on both sides of the moviemaking conflict. Later in the afternoon of March 4, for instance, a parade of some 250 cars swept through Grant County, harking back to a similar car parade of Local 890's supporters in the summer of 1951. It formed in Central, drove past the Roos Ranch, and then passed through Santa Rita, Hanover, Bayard, and, finally, Silver City. "Citizens" organized this parade, one participant stated, "to show people we don't like communists or what they are doing." It was led by Charlie Smith, the former Asarco local officer who had invited the Steelworkers in during the Empire Zinc strike.

Events surrounding the film shooting may have occasionally looked like those surrounding the Empire Zinc strike, but vigilantes soon carried the tensions to an even higher pitch. About seventy small businessmen delivered an ultimatum to Jencks and the film crew on March 4: leave town in twelve hours, or leave in black boxes.[38] Fearing that the vigilantes would destroy the film itself, armed union men guarded the ranch throughout the following nights. Radio station KSIL suggested a less violent but no less virulent tactic: that Grant County citizens turn on their porch lights all day on March 5 as a "freedom demonstration" against communism. On March 6, businesses in the county closed and one movie theater screened an anticommunist film, *The Hoaxters*, all day long. Aircraft flew above the Roos ranch to disrupt filming with noise.

Anticommunism was the means by which some people expressed their citizenship. People who opposed the union and the film company consistently described themselves as "citizens," arrogating the mantle of legitimacy and patriotism and implying that the communist filmmakers had no place in Grant County or even the United States. Yet some of these citizens cheerfully broke the law to achieve their ends, resorting to physical assaults, gunfire, and death threats. To men like Bayard mayor Bill Upton and Earl Lett, it appears that the imagined nature of communism—underground, insidious, and aimed at undermining the very foundations of democratic government—warranted antisocial and lawless methods in order to defend democracy. Lett told journalist Elizabeth Kerby: "[I] asked [the film crew] as nicely as I could to leave town, but I have a son in Korea, and I'm against Communism."[39]

By taking the law into their own hands and running "undesirables" out of town, Grant County anticommunists were simultaneously waging a local battle in the international Cold War and drawing on the history and the mythology of vigilantism in the American West to justify their actions. They took Representative Jackson's call to action as license to exercise what they perceived as a local prerogative to act in self-defense, outside the law if necessary. For some, Jackson's words threw fuel on local fires still smoldering from the days of the Empire Zinc strike, renewing their determination to settle old scores. For others, the notion that a "weapon for Russia" was being built under their own noses was enough to mobilize them against the filmmakers, regardless of their feelings about the Empire Zinc strike. Coverage of the controversy in the *Silver City Daily Press* only fed the anticommunist fervor. One particularly pungent editorial on the subversive nature of the film stated,

> [At first,] Silver Citians looked on with naïve interest as the camera crew began to shoot sequences in the town's busy streets. If they had any premonition of future disagreeable sequences in the secret script they gave no voice to it. . . . It was soon evident the picture being produced by M-M [Mine-Mill] was no ordinary commercial film. The community became convinced that the picture was communist-inspired and was for no other purpose than to inflame class and race hatred here and to put the United States in a false light before the world, particularly Latin America. While there was no certainty what was being filmed, it seemed to local residents that the movie makers had an affinity for shacks and underprivileged characters.[40]

While the editorial appeared to be based on actual concerns of Grant County residents, in fact, the "community" expressed its fears of a "communist-inspired" film in exactly the same language in which Representative Jackson had denounced the film a week earlier; moreover, every *Daily Press* report on the film in the following months included Jackson's assertion, with no caveat or attribution, that the movie was a "weapon for Russia." Similarly, Central mayor Frank Romero, described in the *New York Times* as a "scholarly World War II veteran," affirmed that he was "as anti-Communist as anybody." "I hope the Government will find some way of preventing the export of this picture because it would be very bad for our Latin-American relations," he said. (Romero, unlike Lett and Upton, wanted the prevention to take place within the law.)[41] Media coverage on radio station KSIL and in the *New York Times* and the *El Paso Herald-Post* employed the same anticommunist rhetoric.

The rhetoric of anticommunism and citizenship was coupled with revealing comments on race, nationality, and class. The *Silver City Daily Press* took pains to contrast "Mexican Americans" with "Spanish Americans": "Most of Mine-Mill's devoted following are of Mexican background—as distinguished from New Mexico's own native people, who are Spanish-Americans and proud of it."[42] Bayard mayor Bill Upton, too, linked the working class with Mexicans and hinted that this combination was particularly conducive to the spread of communism: "We have Spanish-American families here who are just as fine a people as you ever saw. But on the other hand the laboring class is not the same class of people. . . . We're just sitting on dynamite here until something is done about these Communists."[43] For his part, Earl Lett asserted, "[I'm not] against Spanish Americans. Some of my best friends are Spanish Americans."[44] These commentators contrasted the "good" Hispanics (those who were Spanish Americans, whose families had resided in New Mexico for centuries and who, importantly, were not of the working class) with the "bad" Hispanics (presumed to be recent arrivals from Mexico) and blithely denied any racism in the distinction by claiming to like the good Hispanics. Making this distinction was a common way for New Mexicans to define social position, one that reflected "a statewide preoccupation with the supposed cultural uniqueness of New Mexico."[45] In fact, though, the ethnic and national mixture in Grant County did not lend itself to such a simple analysis. People who had recently come from Mexico joined those whose families had long lived in the Mimbres and Gila valleys to form the backbone of Mine-Mill in Grant County; small businesspeople not only came from the same mixture as did workers, but they often came from working-class families themselves.

Interestingly, the criticisms of *Salt* had nothing to say about women's activism. When critics talked about the film's content, it was to emphasize race hatred. This may be because the government was more concerned about international criticism of racism. The "weapon for Russia" was a weapon because of the influence of movies on foreign opinions of the United States and because the United States was sensitive to criticisms of racism and not, apparently, to criticisms of sexism (if there ever were such criticisms); the movie was a weapon for Russia because it was made by communists, who, by definition, owed allegiance to the Soviet Union. A simpler explanation for the absence of commentary on women's roles is that none of the film's opponents actually read the script. Thus, ironically, the very essence of the film project—that which attracted the Hollywood filmmakers in the first place, and which union families were most concerned with conveying—failed even to register in this anticommunist discourse.

Mine-Mill and its supporters did not suffer these affronts silently. Hundreds of men and women, meeting at the union hall on March 4, issued an indignant statement against the attacks. They connected the current uproar with the Empire Zinc strike, declaring that the attack on their movie was an attack on their union. And they drew attention to the people in Grant County—98 percent, they claimed, although there is no explanation for how they arrived at that figure—who did not "go along with gangsterism and Ku Klux Klan tactics."[46]

Some local clergy tried to defuse the crisis. They supported the filmmakers' right to dramatize the Empire Zinc strike on film, and four of them issued a statement requesting the public "to abstain from all physical violence in this time of tension and to leave all ultimate decisions to be made by properly constituted authorities." Even Bishop Sidney Metzger of El Paso, who had publicized what he considered to be a communist threat in El Paso's Mine-Mill Local 510 (and had encouraged a Steelworkers raid there), supported the Grant County priests' statement. One Catholic priest, probably Father Smerke of Hanover, criticized the "scandalously untrue news stories" about *Salt of the Earth*. He and Father Linnane of Silver City convened a group of law enforcement officials, local Mexican American business leaders, and the film crew to try to protect the crew from violence.[47]

The efforts of the clergy and state police prevented additional violence but did not create a climate in which the crew could continue to shoot the film. On March 7, with barely enough footage to make into a film, the crew left Grant County. But conflicts continued to rage in the region even after the filming ceased. The union hall in Bayard mysteriously caught on fire on March 8; the hall in distant Carlsbad was destroyed by arson; and union member and actor Floyd Bostick's house burnt to the ground the following week.

THE STRUGGLE WITH HOLLYWOOD

The problems in Grant county mirrored IPC's trouble in Hollywood, where the repressive political climate had made it hard to hire a film crew.[48] Earlier in 1952, Simon Lazarus tried to line up a union crew but got a definitive "no" from Roy Brewer, president of IATSE. Brewer had made a name for himself in the late 1940s as an uncompromising anticommunist. In 1945, a dramatic and violent strike by studio technicians belonging to the left-leaning but non-Communist Conference of Studio Unions became an opening for Brewer and his IATSE to secure jurisdiction over the entire Hollywood industry.[49] Brewer capitalized as well on his membership in the Motion Picture Alliance for the Preservation of American Ideals, an anticommunist organization, to wrangle for himself an unofficial position as arbiter of the blacklist. As someone whose own power rested precisely and firmly on the blacklist, Brewer was unlikely to smile upon an independent company consisting of blacklisted directors, producers, writers, and actors. Thus it was no surprise that he declared in 1952 that IPC's film would simply never be made. RKO mogul Howard Hughes echoed Brewer's comments shortly before IPC began shooting in early 1953.

The troubles with Hollywood craft unions had prompted IPC to seek a formal arrangement with Mine-Mill's international office in Denver in the summer of 1952, beyond the informal alliance that IPC and union families had created in Grant County. Biberman first toured southwestern mining towns with Mine-Mill executive board member Orville Larson in June, concluding that Bayard, or possibly San Cristóbal, would work best as a film site.[50] He requested Mine-Mill's collaboration later that month. Without the strength of the entire union behind this project, Biberman stressed, IPC might have to film the story in Mexico rather than among the very families whose story they were telling. Biberman seemed to think that Mine-Mill was in a better "bargaining position" than

IPC was with respect to IATSE, and he asked that Mine-Mill sign on as official producers.[51]

Biberman's hopes on that score were misplaced, to say the least. IATSE continued to block technical support for *Salt of the Earth*, even with a union's name on the production roster. From October to December, Biberman and Jarrico turned instead to the CIO's Association of Documentary Technicians and Film Cameramen (ADTFC) in New York. The ADTFC was interested in the project, but it hesitated to associate with IPC for fear of red-baiting: locked in a jurisdictional dispute with IATSE in New York, the ADTFC fretted that IATSE could lure technicians into the AFL union. Biberman had "two pretty tough weeks in New York" trying to persuade individual technicians that they could handle "association with [Biberman and Jarrico] and with" Mine-Mill.[52]

In October 1952, Mine-Mill and IPC agreed that the latter would place money in a bank account under the name "International Union of Mine, Mill and Smelter Workers Special Motion Picture Production Account," and that Mine-Mill would officially hire and pay all technicians and actors. This arrangement would both relieve Mine-Mill of financial obligations and reassure the ADTFC. The crew signed on in the middle of October, demonstrating, according to Biberman, "more than willingness, . . . actually real enthusiasm for the undertaking."[53] But Jarrico reported in December, just two weeks before shooting was to begin, that the ADTFC was still worried "about servicing this picture at all," not only because of red-baiting, but also because hostility toward the film could leave its members high and dry: there might not be money to pay them. Jarrico stressed that Mine-Mill's "formal responsibility for the hiring of the crew" was critical in "protect[ing] those within the AD[TF]C who have tried to overcome this trepidation." Mine-Mill, he stated, "must assure [them] that their own union regulations will be adhered to strictly, and that money is available to cover not only their travel expenses but their wages."[54] But even Mine-Mill's name behind the film could not get that crew to Grant County. It backed out at the very last minute, leaving Jarrico and Biberman to scrounge for a "rump" crew of blacklisted technicians just days before shooting was scheduled to begin in January 1953.

Once the film processing phase began, IPC found that negative publicity had scared all laboratories away from *Salt of the Earth*. The laboratory that had processed the sound refused to do any more work, and *Salt*'s editors had to work under cover of night, in a former bathroom, to process the film. IPC recorded the musical score with union musicians who had been told that they were working on a film called *Vaya con Dios*.

The company pinned its hopes, though, on winning audiences over once they did see the movie. Its strategy was to organize audiences, calling on trade unions to publicize the movie among their members; to this end, the company persuaded the Mine-Mill international to send an advance man, Bill Gately, to a number of cities to drum up support. Local promotion committees were to be formed in each community, and they were to include "representatives from trade unions, women's organizations, minority groups and prestige people (e.g., clergy, educators, artists, business men, etc.)."[55] The committee was supposed to arrange a preview of the movie, inviting about a hundred "leading citizens" who could then be counted on "to build the kind of audience for the film that will really represent a cross-section of the community."[56] Blacklisted actress Anne Revere toured the country, giving readings from the script that were very successful, according to Jarrico, Biberman, and Wilson. And to counter the negative publicity, IPC and Mine-Mill distributed copies of the screenplay for people to see for themselves. *California Quarterly*, the publication of the Hollywood Arts, Sciences and Professions Council of the Progressive Citizens of America, published the script along with photos and interviews with the cast and crew. "Today there is a battle going on," Juan Chacón wrote in an open letter printed in the *Silver City Daily Press*, "between the book-burners and Americans who recognize what these forces have in mind for the rights of all of us to read and write and speak and think. To us, our movie, 'Salt of the Earth,' is our part of this fight. First, our right to make it—and secondly, your right to see it and make your own judgments on its qualities."[57] On another front, Paul Jarrico sued Howard Hughes and Roy Brewer for conspiracy to suppress the movie's production and distribution. The suit failed.

"The simple fact," Biberman wrote to Maurice Travis late in March 1953, "is that the appearance of this picture, magnificently played by miners and their families, is going to pull the rug out from under the labor-baiters and red-baiting Congressional racketeers and put the real issue before millions and millions of Americans." *Salt of the Earth* would be a platform for labor unions to redefine, as he put it, "what Americanism really is and how you fight for a better America." And the union people's performances, Biberman anticipated, "will knock people into a new realization of the culture and beauty and artistic skill which resides in working people. How could this not be so. . . . Perhaps workers themselves had better begin to realise how talented they are in all ways."[58]

Biberman was far too optimistic in imagining *Salt*'s success. It is possible, of course, that *Salt of the Earth* could have had an effect similar to his vision. Certainly many of the people who did see the movie—particularly women—responded favorably to it. But *Salt of the Earth* did not reach many people. Movie houses that initially agreed to show the movie backed out, fearing that the American Legion would make good on threats to boycott the theaters and that Hollywood distributors would cut them off from other films. Labor unions like IATSE prohibited projectionists from working in theaters that contracted to show the film. In the end, the story that women had persuaded Michael Wilson to dramatize reached almost no one. After a rocky beginning in New York in April of 1954, the film reached commercial audiences in only a very few cities before fading away, only to be seen by small numbers of Americans. The only Grant County theater to show the film was the Silver Sky Vue drive-in.

As the film moved further and further away from Grant County, the alliance between the filmmakers and the union families encountered difficulties. Several people in the union could not understand why, month after month, the film was not released. And after the film finally opened, in April 1954, Mine-Mill and Local 890 could not understand why they saw absolutely no profits from the movie. Angie Sánchez, some twenty years later, believed that she was supposed to have received a salary for her role. In fact, only the people who had lost time from paid jobs drew a salary during the filmmaking, and IPC budgeted no salary for *Salt*'s director, writer, or producer.[59] But her suspicions point to the difficulty of sustaining the trust that had enabled the two groups to work together in Grant County in the face of violence and intimidation.

GOVERNMENT HARASSMENT OF MINE-MILL

The anticommunist assaults on *Salt of the Earth* were accompanied by similar attacks on Mine-Mill. In October 1952, a Senate subcommittee held hearings in Salt Lake City on the administration of the Internal Security Act of 1950. (That same month, Herbert Biberman was facing expulsion from the Screen Directors Guild for his Communist affiliation, despite the fact that he had helped found the guild in the 1930s.) Chaired by Nevada senator Pat McCarran, the Senate Internal Security Subcommittee (SISS) hearings were intended to publicize and thereby condemn the Communist "domination" of Mine-Mill.[60] McCarran had already denounced the union as "subversive" by the time the hearings began on October 6, 1952.[61] The hearings were similar to others held by the House

Un-American Activities Committee, the Senate Judiciary Committee, and the Subversive Activities Control Board, designed less to generate information than to cast Communists and progressives beyond the pale of civil society, often through the publicity that resulted in witnesses getting fired from their jobs.[62]

For four days the Senate subcommittee questioned past and present Mine-Mill members and officials, as well as paid informants like ex-Communist Harvey Matusow. The subcommittee established the parameters of debate by beginning with respectful questioning of a series of anticommunist witnesses, such as Homer Wilson, a former Mine-Mill vice president and CIO international representative from Alabama who had encouraged the Alabama locals to secede from Mine-Mill and join the Steelworkers in 1948.[63] R. B. Matthews of New York City, formerly the research director for HUAC in the 1930s, explained that Mine-Mill was "Communist-dominated" because its policies and published statements matched those of "the known line of the Communist Party."[64] The CIO's Stanley Ruttenberg shared details of the CIO's 1949–50 expulsion of Mine-Mill.[65]

The subcommittee's interactions with secretary-treasurer Maurice Travis, as with all of Mine-Mill's current leaders, immediately became hostile. Interrogators posed compound questions that included assumptions about Communist membership and about the nature of Communist activity and commitments. Chairman Pat McCarran asked attorney Nathan Witt where Witt had first met Whittaker Chambers. Witt, lawyer that he was, responded that McCarran's question was phrased much like the question, "Have you stopped beating your wife yet?"[66] Either way one answered would confirm the assumption contained in the question, that Witt had beaten his wife. Similarly, McCarran asked Graham Dolan, Mine-Mill's director of education and assistant editor of *The Union*, "Was your book number in the Communist Party No. 45712?"[67] And of executive board member Al Skinner, McCarran asked, "Were you living in Salt Lake City when you went to the Communist school?" When Skinner objected to the question, McCarran stated that the question "call[ed] for an answer of 'yes' or 'no.' "[68]

McCarran insisted that these hearings did not constitute a trial. The subcommittee, he claimed, sought only to uncover "facts" about the CP and its activities in defense industries, "so that the people may judge just how great is the danger to this country of ours from Communism."[69] Moreover, he portrayed himself as a stalwart friend of labor, one who had supported labor rights during almost twenty years in the U.S. Senate and, prior to that, as a Nevada legislator and judge.[70] McCarran's comments notwithstanding, witnesses opposed to the subcommittee's mission and methods believed that this was indeed a trial. The lines of questioning— along with McCarran's unabashed equation of love for labor with hatred of communism—signaled to these witnesses that "taking the Fifth" was the only protection against a citation for contempt of Congress.

Al Skinner, for example, criticized the subcommittee's attempt "to make the Fifth Amendment something sinister that you hide behind," but McCarran countered, "you are the one doing the hiding."[71] Jack Blackwell, a miner from Idaho, objected to the subcommittee putting "words in [his] mouth" whenever he invoked the Fifth Amendment.[72] And Clinton Jencks used the Fifth Amendment, despite the apparently innocuous nature of some of the questions, because he did not trust the subcommittee to interpret his comments fairly. It was "quite possible," he stated, "that any answers given before this committee might be" used to incriminate him.[73] Simple "facts" that the subcommittee was ostensibly seeking to uncover, Jencks felt, could be manipulated. The subcommittee equated invoking the Fifth Amendment with admitting guilt. "Do you not realize," McCarran asked him, "that by . . . [declining to answer on the grounds of the Fifth Amendment] you are inferentially declaring yourself to be a Communist? . . . If you were not a Communist, the word 'no' would be the answer, would it not?"[74]

Jencks knew perfectly well that "no" would not necessarily get him off the hook, because the House Un-American Activities Committee had already shown what would happen to people who answered any of its questions. A witness who admitted to being or once having been a Communist would be forced to name names and thus ultimately play into the subcommittee's agenda. The Salt Lake City hearings, like the HUAC hearings, were premised on a set of monolithic assumptions about what communism was and what CP membership meant. There was no room for nuance or explanation in answering questions designed only to elicit confessions and the naming of names.

CLINTON JENCKS UNDER FIRE

The 1952 Salt Lake City Mine-Mill hearings set the stage for many more years of government harassment of Mine-Mill. Reporting on the hearings, SISS recommended amending Taft-Hartley so as to forbid "a member of a 'Communist organization' to hold office or a job in a labor union and [to permit] employers to discharge 'persons who are members of organizations designated as subversive by the Attorney General.'" The subcommittee urged the Justice Department "to determine whether perjury prosecutions should be brought against union officers identified as Communist."[75] One of the first people targeted was Clinton Jencks, who was ultimately forced to resign from Mine-Mill in the late 1950s.

In March 1953, during the furor over making *Salt of the Earth*, New Jersey Zinc executive Richard Berresford spoke to the House Committee on Education and Labor, the committee considering SISS's recommendation. Berresford argued that the law should require international representatives, not just elected union officials, to sign noncommunist affidavits. Clinton Jencks was an example of why the existing law was inadequate. Jencks had signed Taft-Hartley affidavits twice while an officer of Local 890. At the time of the "disruptive, subtle, confusing, mean, tricky, and unfair" Empire Zinc strike, Jencks was no longer an officer of the local but remained an international representative.[76]

The timing of Berresford's testimony was more important than its content, for it built on the publicity surrounding *Salt of the Earth* and gave new impetus to the government strategy of prosecuting progressive unionists for falsifying their Taft-Hartley affidavits. Jencks could be convicted for having filed a false affidavit within the previous three years if the government could prove that Jencks was still a Communist at the time he filed it, but the government would have to indict him no later than April 1953, when the three-year window would close.[77] Jencks was "convinced that the government wouldn't have gone forward with the indictment if it hadn't been for all the publicity" surrounding the Empire Zinc strike and *Salt of the Earth*.[78]

For several years, the National Labor Relations Board had been pressuring the Justice Department to prosecute progressive unionists for perjury, but the Justice Department had hesitated for several reasons. First, the language of Taft-Hartley was ambiguous, and in the late 1940s it was unclear if the law would be modified or even overturned; second, the FBI was reluctant to identify its informants by putting them on the witness stand; and, third, the FBI seldom had evidence that these unionists belonged to the CP at the time they signed the affidavits.[79] This was certainly the case with Clinton Jencks: even FBI chief J. Edgar Hoover admitted that "the evidence [of perjury was] not substantial" against him.[80] But with the new Eisenhower administration in 1953 came a new attorney general, Herbert Brownell, who pursued Taft-Hartley cases more aggressively.[81]

And thus it was that on April 20, 1953, the FBI arrested Clinton Jencks. Jencks was playing with his son in front of his house when two agents "roared up and jumped out and told [him he] was under arrest." They showed him their badges. Jencks asked them if he could "just go inside and put on [his] shoes and socks," but they told him they could not let him out of their sight, "like [he] was an armed fugitive or something like that."[82] Jencks spent the night in the Grant County jail, and the next day he was released on $5,000 bail posted by the international. He told the press: "This is just another effort of the companies and their representatives to use the Taft-Hartley act to stop unions. I am guilty of nothing other than fighting for the rank and file of our local union, and I intend to keep right on doing that."[83] Unfortunately, the international decided that Jencks should *not* keep doing that, at least not in Grant County, and on June 1, 1953, it announced Jencks's transfer to the Denver office.[84]

Jencks's trial opened in El Paso in January 1954 before federal judge R. E. Thomason, the vocal anticommunist who had overseen Rosaura Revueltas's detention the previous year, and it followed the pattern of most anticommunist proceedings. There was a parade of experts on the nature of Communism and witnesses who offered circumstantial evidence for the Communist ties of the accused. Rev. J. W. Ford, who had been a member of the CP in Albuquerque and, beginning in 1948, worked as an FBI informant, testified that Clinton and Virginia Jencks were both Communists. He could not confirm Clinton's membership past 1949, though.[85] George Knott, who had helped organize Grant County locals in 1942, testified that he had been a Communist from 1937 to 1947 and returned to Grant County in 1946 to "lay the groundwork" for Jencks to be hired as business agent.[86] By naming Jencks a Communist, declaring himself a Communist, and emphasizing his own role in bringing Jencks to Grant County, Knott tried to establish Jencks's arrival as a Communist plan to establish a strong party presence in Silver City. Jesús Terrazas, a car dumper in Kennecott's mill, claimed that he had been expelled from Local 890 for "fighting communism on the job."[87] During his cross-examination, though, another explanation for his expulsion emerged: Terrazas was disappointed that a grievance had not been settled to his liking, and he took another union member to court over it. Union rules forbade individuals from taking grievances against other members to court.[88]

In understanding how anticommunism functioned in this period, it is also important to consider those people who did *not* testify against

Jencks. As he put it, "it was just fantastic" that Terrazas was the sole witness from Grant County's mining district, given the thousands of people there who had come into contact with Jencks and the union.[89] Among them was José Campos, a union man whom the FBI approached to testify against Jencks. Campos was imprisoned for attempted rape—a conviction of dubious legality for which he was serving at least ten years—and the FBI offered to free him if he testified that Jencks was a Communist. He refused. According to Jencks, who learned of this several years later, Campos told them, "I don't have any such information. And I won't go in and lie about it." Campos served his term and never got another mining job in Grant County.[90]

The single most important testimony in convicting Jencks was that of Harvey Matusow, the only government witness to link Jencks to the CP after Jencks signed the Taft-Hartley affidavit. Matusow had belonged to the CP in New York, working in a left-wing bookstore and gradually becoming frustrated that he was not becoming a more important figure in the party.[91] By 1950, he discovered that he could attain such importance—if he worked for the FBI. That summer, Matusow met Clinton Jencks at the Vincents' ranch in San Cristóbal. Jencks remembered "scrupulously, carefully avoiding him because everyone thought he was such a weirdo."[92] Jenny Vincent had the same opinion—he was "arrogant and unpleasant"—but she tolerated him because he was an outstanding square dance caller.[93] Matusow later reported to the FBI on his San Cristóbal visit: "I have never attended a meeting of the Communist Party in New Mexico, and have never been present at a Communist Party meeting where Jencks was in attendance. I have never been told by Jencks that he is a member of the Communist Party, and I have never seen any direct evidence to prove that he is a member of the Communist Party. However, there is no question in my mind but that Jencks is a member of the Communist Party."[94] Matusow soon found that life as a professional witness offered even more glory, and he joined the circuit of ex-Communist expert witnesses appearing before government committees and agencies. In the 1952 Mine-Mill hearings in Salt Lake City, Matusow told SISS that Jencks had confided to him that Mine-Mill was trying to sabotage the Korean War effort by striking against copper companies.[95] Matusow repeated these allegations at Jencks's trial.

Matusow's story was sufficient to convict Jencks of perjury and to sentence him to five years in federal prison. All along, Jencks had understood intellectually that this case was a political attack on his union; now, after the jury announced its verdict, Jencks understood the case on a deeper level: "I was standing there with the marshal holding one of my arms and [attorney] John McTernan holding the other, being pulled by both sides. That brought it really home that *they were talking about my body.*"[96] Jencks's attorneys filed an appeal, and Jencks was allowed to return to his family.

Matusow began to have doubts about his role in Jencks's trial, and later in 1954 he recanted but then denied recanting his story. By 1955, however, he was certain that he wanted to take back his testimony. He contacted a publisher, Cameron and Kahn, and soon holed up in New York to write a mea culpa and exposé of the government's system of paid witnesses. Armed with this information, Jencks's lawyers requested a new trial, which Judge Thomason denied. Thomason found that Matusow's new testimony was merely a ploy by Communists to besmirch the justice system. Matusow was later convicted of perjury, and he served three years in prison.

Jencks lost his appeal, and the U.S. Supreme Court agreed to hear the case. The Court accepted Jencks's argument that the defense should have been allowed to see the prosecution's evidence, including the interviews with paid informants, and it reversed his conviction. While Matusow's new testimony was less decisive in overturning Jencks's conviction than his false testimony had been in convicting him, his book played an important role in discrediting the FBI's use of paid witnesses, which in turn likely influenced the Supreme Court in restricting prosecutory conduct.[97] Jencks saw in Matusow's recanting a validation of his humanity. If Matusow "hadn't had a seed of human being that eventually gave him the courage to turn around and admit that he'd lied," Jencks later commented, "I would have served five to ten years in prison. I didn't win because of the overwhelming strength of the American people, but [because] one human being, after he had lied, finally couldn't live with it anymore. I wrote Harvey Matusow a letter. I said: congratulations for rejoining the human race."[98]

The international office in Denver, meanwhile, decided that Jencks was a lightning rod for union opponents and that the union simply could not afford to keep him on. In Jencks's opinion, members of the executive board had "lost the belief in their own capacity to survive, and [decided] that in the interests of the membership, they were going to have to sacrifice some of their principles, some people if necessary."[99] The board asked for Jencks's resignation, along with that of Maurice Travis, who had also been prosecuted for filing a false noncommunist affidavit. Jencks thought this was a strategic mistake; instead of easing the pressure on

Mine-Mill, such a move sent the message that the union was on the run. Mine-Mill kept Jencks on the payroll until the Supreme Court agreed to hear his case, but it would not send him back to New Mexico. Jencks believes that this was because he had stirred things up too much there. International officers joked that Jencks was "trying to build socialism in one county"—Grant County—and should ease up on the rank-and-file activism, referring in particular to Clinton and Virginia Jencks's emphasis on women's rights.[100] When members of Local 890 learned that the international would not allow Jencks to return to New Mexico, they were angry and wanted to hire Jencks themselves, but Jencks reminded them that they now had Mexican American leadership that made him redundant.[101] He regretfully took up organizing work in Arizona and Colorado until the Supreme Court took his case, and then he left Mine-Mill for good.

Freed from the threat of prison, Jencks was nonetheless trapped by the blacklist. He moved from job to job in the Southwest, impressing his employers with his skills as a machinist and millwright until they got wind of his politics and fired him. "We've got a new classification to cover you, Jencks," said one official in California's employment office. "You're politically unemployable."[102] In yet another paradox of McCarthyism, by making him unemployable in an industrial setting, the blacklist freed Jencks to consider a different career altogether, and he won a Woodrow Wilson fellowship to study economics at Berkeley. By this point, in the early 1960s, anticommunism had waned enough that the university and the Woodrow Wilson Foundation supported Jencks in the face of government intimidation. Jencks wrote his Ph.D. dissertation on miners in England—it was still too politically hot to write on Mine-Mill, which he had hoped to do—and joined the economics faculty at San Diego State University.[103]

Clinton Jencks's experience was one of hundreds of examples of individual lives damaged by the anticommunism of the 1950s. McCarthyism, as historian Ellen Schrecker has shown, rested on a complex network of government and private forces that relied most basically on denying people a livelihood. The blacklist paradoxically allowed Herbert Biberman, the Jarricos, and Michael Wilson to form an independent film company, but the repression generated by Grant County union opponents, Hollywood studio and union executives, and the federal government bankrupted IPC. The Hollywood blacklist did not completely prevent these artists from working, but it forced them into exile and closed off the alternative path they had tried to mark out for creating popular culture.

The blacklist also affected other Mine-Mill activists in New Mexico and other parts of the country. While many union men continued to work for the mine companies, some found that they could not get work easily if they ever left the jobs that had provided union security. Albert Millán, for example, worked for Kennecott for thirty-three years and was a union representative that whole time. In 1967, the Steelworkers (with whom Mine-Mill had recently merged) struck, and Millán went to California to look for a job. The first thing he heard, he recalled, was "You're a Communist," and he could not get a job.[104] Juan Chacón kept his job at Kennecott (although he had to fight to keep it in the 1970s), but his wife, Virginia, believes that their union activism prevented their sons from ever getting work in Grant County's mines.[105] The union could protect its members, but it was harder to protect people, like the children of union activists, trying to break into the industry.

Jenny and Craig Vincent were forced to close down their ranch in San Cristóbal in December 1953. The FBI was routinely shadowing ranch visitors and taking down their license plate numbers, and Craig Vincent was called before Senator McCarran's Senate Internal Security Subcommittee to answer charges that the ranch was a meeting place for Communists. "We decided," the couple said, "that we could no longer, in all fairness to our guests and ourselves, subject them to the overt danger of being framed in this way, to satisfy the evil political purposes of those who would subvert the constitution. . . . Our guest business is a casualty of war and McCarthyism—not of free enterprise."[106] Reflecting on these events fifty years later, Jenny Vincent said they "taught [her] what the FBI can do to somebody—they can practically kill your career."[107] Indeed, even without jeopardizing their jobs, government harassment took its toll on union activists and their supporters. Virginia Chacón recalled the FBI as a constant presence outside the Chacón home in the Mimbres Valley. She was especially angry that one of them was a Mexican American. "Do you know what you are?" she asked him in Spanish. "*Un vendido*, a sellout, that's what you are. That's all you are."[108]

10

Conclusion

In this book, I have examined a set of unusual events as a lens onto American gender, ethnic, and class relations in the changing political climate of the mid-twentieth century. Confined as they are to a small region and short span of time, the Empire Zinc strike and the production of *Salt of the Earth* allow us to see the interplay of historical contingency, individual action, and larger historical dynamics. Grant County's mining district was representative of the national mining economy in many ways; industrial mining, the masculine character of mine work, and the surge of labor activism in the 1930s and 1940s were national, as well as local, phenomena. But this mining district was not identical to other such places. Its patterns of settlement, demography, political economy, and the actions of individuals—John Sully and Daniel Jackling in the 1920s, Ysmael Moreno and Jack Kemp in the 1930s, Arturo Flores and the Jenckses in the 1940s, Elvira Molano and Tom Foy during the Empire Zinc strike, Michael Wilson and Sonja Dahl Biberman in the making of *Salt of the Earth*—all shaped events unique to Grant County. Micro-history allows a nuanced understanding of the texture of local society and of the relationship of local society to larger historical forces, but it also runs the risk of parochialism, that is, of remaining trapped by such a narrow scope as to leave us wondering if these events mattered for Grant County alone. If the history in this book is to affect how we think about other situations, it is important to generalize from the particularities and to follow some of the historical figures and institutions into later years.

OLD WAYS AND NEW

A turning point in *Salt of the Earth* takes place in the Quinteros' kitchen, with Ramón and Esperanza fighting over the "new way" that her strike activism seems to be charting for their family. For Esperanza, the new way is one of dignity; for Ramón, it is one of emasculation, her dignity apparently coming at his expense. Esperanza tries unsuccessfully to per- suade him that her status at home resembles his at work. "The Anglo bosses look down on you," she reminds him, "and you hate them for it. 'Stay in your place, you dirty Mexican'—that's what they tell you. But why must you say to me, 'Stay in *your* place'? Do you feel better having some- one lower than you? . . . Whose neck shall I stand on, to make me feel superior? And what will I get out of it? I don't want anything lower than I am." When she insists that he cannot win the strike—or anything— without her, Ramón raises his arm to hit her. But Esperanza stands up to him. "That would be the old way," she tells him. "Never try it on me again." It is an astonishing scene, for rarely did movies of this era address domestic violence so directly and in an effort to promote gender equality. Ramón is neither let off the hook nor portrayed as a monster; instead, he is allowed to change in a way that affirms the dignity of men and women alike. The movie ends on a triumphant note, with the mining community pouring in from all directions to protect the Quintero family from evic- tion and Ramón finally accepting that, together, men and women could "push everything up with us as we go." "Then I knew," Esperanza reflects in a voice-over, "we had won something they could never take away— something I could leave to our children—and they, the salt of the earth, would inherit it."[1]

The movie shows a fundamental transformation taking place in the relations of husbands to wives, a transformation made possible by a change of gender consciousness and by the success of the strike. The transformation is clear and unambiguous; the old way is distinguished from the new, and the new way is chosen. It is a transformation that will be sustained and enjoyed by the coming generations. The film's portrayal of transformation, though, was itself an effort to settle and make perma- nent in a cultural artifact that which was far more volatile in real life. For the conflicts taking place in Grant County were not fully resolved—for individuals or families, or in terms of gender relations more broadly.

The depth and permanency of changes in union families' gender relations varied from couple to couple. Some women found that the

strike and the process of making the film changed their husbands' behavior for the better or, if this were not the case, that they at least improved women's self-confidence enough for them to strike out on their
own. Henrietta Williams, for example, grew much closer to her husband,
Braulio, as a result of the strike and movie.[2] Mariana Ramírez and Anita
Torrez both "felt that their marriages became more egalitarian part-
nerships."[3] Dolores Jiménez felt that she "grew ten feet tall" as a result of
the strike, tall enough and strong enough to end her marriage to an
abusive husband. She got her GED, went to beauty school, and opened
her own salon—and she kept her ex-husband, Frank, from laying claim to
any of her earnings. She regretted, however, that her divorce lawyer persuaded her that changing her name "wouldn't be proper."[4]

But some women, like Virginia Chacón, believed that men slipped
too readily and too quickly back into the old ways. One wrenching story
comes from the late 1950s, after Chana Montoya finally pulled away from
an abusive marriage to Cipriano Montoya, a Kennecott employee and
union activist. She divorced him in 1954, but they continued to live
together off and on. In 1955, she moved to Los Angeles, where, with the
help of *Salt of the Earth* technician Paul Perlin, she got a job in a Los
Angeles hospital. When Cipriano went to Los Angeles to persuade her to
return to New Mexico, she got a restraining order against him.[5] The
restraining order did not work. One morning in July 1961, he waited for
her near a bus stop and then shot her four times with a rifle, killing her on
the spot. She was thirty-three years old, the mother of seven children.

Montoya launched an unusual defense: he claimed he shot his ex-wife
to protect his children from communism. "She was among the party's
cadre," he explained. "She was not only trying to poison the world with
filthy Communist propaganda, she was a threat to the future security of
our seven children."[6] He accused her of joining the Communist Party in
1948 and then of leading him into it. "From that hour on," he said, "we had
a very sorrowful marriage."[7] Her participation in the Empire Zinc strike,
which he attributed to a CP order, "made [him] angry." "That was no job
for a woman," he asserted. Moreover, he claimed that authorities at a CP
school at the San Cristóbal ranch in the mid-1950s accused him of "exercising undue 'masculine control' over his wife."[8] Montoya was convicted
and imprisoned for his wife's murder. Upon release he told Virginia and
Juan Chacón that he had been forced to testify in that manner. Shortly
after his release he committed suicide.

Obviously the Montoyas' story is not typical. But its very extremity
reveals some of what is at stake in attempting to change gender relations.

The movie, by ending on a positive note, makes us want the changes we see on screen to be permanent, but the variety of actual couples' experiences does not permit such a gratifying conclusion. Still, even though not all of the couples involved in the strike made permanent positive changes in gender relations, we can nonetheless appreciate the changes that some people made in gender consciousness.

Many of the picketing women had a profound change of consciousness, whether or not their marriages also changed. Several actively sought work outside the home, sometimes pursuing higher education to obtain it. In her late thirties, Aurora Chávez got her GED and then a teaching certificate and a master's degree. After her husband died in the early 1960s, she moved to Douglas, Arizona (another southwestern mining town), where she taught in a bilingual program.[9] Some men experienced a change in consciousness, too, "getting a lesson" from the women, as Local 890 official Angel Bustos reported to the Mine-Mill convention in 1953.[10] A more poignant story comes from the granddaughter of Joe T. Morales. Late in his life, suffering from Alzheimer's disease, Morales kept yelling at the hospital nurses to get back on the picket line: in his delusional state, he was back at the Empire Zinc picket.[11] In 1951, Morales had been uncomfortable with women's picketing, yet on some deep level the urgency and importance of their action impressed him. Finally, as the character Esperanza hoped, many children of union activists did inherit the dignity and compassion fostered by the union community, and they continued to work on behalf of social justice causes.

But while positive and powerful, the change of consciousness proved inadequate for sustaining activism in the ladies' auxiliary. In fact, Auxiliary 209 disbanded only a few years after *Salt of the Earth* was made. These observations suggest that gender consciousness and gender relations do not change at the same rate or in sync with one another; a dramatic change in the former, in this case, was accompanied by a less dramatic change in the latter. A permanent change in the division of labor, combined with a stronger feminist movement, might have helped women maintain the advances they had made and even, perhaps, move further.[12] Instead, we have the cultural artifact *Salt of the Earth*, which continues to resonate with audiences because it keeps us imagining a solidarity across gender, class, and ethnic lines.

The history of the Empire Zinc strike shows us how gender conflict can arise in the course of other conflicts—the unintended consequences of particular actions—while its origins lay in the larger social structure. Mine-Mill organizing in Grant County paid little heed to women or to gender issues, but its class- and ethnic-based mobilization was none-theless gendered from the beginning: men created a brotherhood that challenged management from a position of masculine honor and strength, and women joined efforts to redress class and ethnic inequities, inequities understood to affect families, not just male workers. Women did not aim to change their marriages, but in encountering their husbands' resistance in the charged atmosphere of the Empire Zinc strike, they demanded a reevaluation of the power relations between men and women.

The women's picket took place because of a confluence of factors, some long-standing and others more transitory, that made the Empire Zinc strike matter so much in the first place and then permitted women to propose the picket, men to go along with it, and the company and law enforcement to be taken enough by surprise so as to upset the balance of power in this labor-management battle. The strike mattered so much to union families in Grant County because they saw it as a showdown be-tween the collective power of management and the collective power of workers. It assumed the proportions that it did because over the previous three years mining companies had tried—and mostly failed—to defeat Local 890 by other means, often using anticommunism to try to persuade workers to abandon the red-tainted union. Workers were little disposed to do so, however, because the union they knew—and had built them-selves—was democratic and worked hard on their behalf. Because the stakes were so high, and because they had come to see their families' well-being tied up with that of the union, women stepped forward with their ambitious proposal to defend Local 890's picket.

In the story of the women's picket, we see how human agency takes the potential inherent in a given confluence of events and realizes that potential, in this case by women's dramatic and transformative confron-tations with husbands and law enforcement. The women picketers not only prevailed against their husbands and Empire Zinc but also attracted artists who were equipped to help union families make their story into a movie, and thereby to amplify the victory far beyond the boundaries of Grant County. As an explanatory model, a "showdown" like that between Local 890 and the Empire Zinc Company operates according to a clear narrative progression of crescendo, climax, and denouement. The de-nouement includes only those elements either explicitly or implicitly present in what preceded it; the showdown model is, in this respect, something of a closed system. By contrast, a "confluence of events" is inherently unstable and ambiguous, as new factors come into play and others recede. Both historical models are at work in the story of the women's picket and movie production, but only the former is at work in the cinematic rendition of the story. And it is the latter we must consider in gauging the long-term changes wrought by the strike and the movie production.

The Empire Zinc strike was important in confirming Mine-Mill as a powerful presence in Grant County. It held tremendous symbolic value throughout the mining Southwest, and both this symbolic value and the actual work Mine-Mill continued to do in this region challenged the dual-wage system and segregation more broadly. Mexican Americans continued to enter jobs from which they had been excluded, and they continued to use their union as a base from which to influence local politics. In turn, the strength of Mine-Mill locals in the Southwest (along with those in Montana, the original core of the Western Federation of Miners and then of Mine-Mill) helped the union withstand fifteen years of assault by the federal government, the U.S. Steelworkers, and others bent on stifling this left-wing union. Prosecutions for falsifying noncommunist affidavits and efforts to classify the union as an agent of a foreign government all foundered in the legal system because Mine-Mill was able, ultimately, to win on appeals. Mine-Mill's victories were hollow, however, for Mine-Mill's resources were drained by the endless legal battles until the union was forced to merge with the Steelworkers, its rival, in 1967.[13] Mine-Mill Local 890 became Steelworkers Local 890.

And other factors were at play in the local political economy. Corporate paternalism was on the wane, not just because of worker protest but also because of market forces and national trends. In 1955, Kennecott Copper Corporation sold off its company towns, including Santa Rita and Hurley. An Ohio real estate company bought the property and sold the lots to individuals, giving first choice to residents. Kennecott had lost a 1954 discrimination suit brought by Tommy Higgins, a Mexican American employee who had tried to rent a house in Anglo-dominated Hurley rather than in North Hurley, where most Mexican Americans lived. The suit may have played some role in the corporation's decision to get out of the business of providing housing and other services—and the business of maintaining segregation.[14]

Still other forces tempered the achievements of Grant County miners, most notably the collapse of the lead-zinc market in 1953. Absent government intervention, nothing—even an alliance with the mining companies that were usually the union's antagonists—could protect miners from the ravages of the international metals market.[15] So while the 1952 victory over Empire Zinc strengthened Local 890, the workers themselves had little opportunity to enjoy that victory. Empire Zinc and Asarco both shut down for a few years, and many union families had to move away.

Kennecott continued production until it sold its Santa Rita and Hurley operations to Phelps-Dodge (PD) in the mid-1980s. PD had just defeated the Steelworkers in Clifton-Morenci, Arizona, another Mine-Mill stronghold of Mexican American miners, in a strike that was another turning point in American labor relations: PD's victory effectively destroyed pattern bargaining in national industries.[16] (The only pattern bargaining that remained was in the form of union concessions to increasingly aggressive corporations.) Having succeeded in decertifying the Steelworkers in Clifton-Morenci, PD kept up the pressure on Local 890 but failed, ultimately, to decertify it.[17] But while the union has hung on, it has not been strong, and its members have enjoyed little job security in the face of plant closings and partial reopenings as the region undergoes the same deindustrialization that characterizes so much of contemporary America. From year to year, PD's Grant County workforce contracts or expands by hundreds of workers, fluctuating with the vagaries of the metals market and the operations at PD's other mines. Recently, Chino has been operating at full force, but the smelter at Hurley is unlikely to reopen.[18]

The blacklisted artists' story was similarly bittersweet. Rosaura Revueltas was blacklisted in her native Mexico and never made another film. The Jarricos and Wilsons moved to France in the mid-1950s and continued to work on film projects in exile. Herbert Biberman remained in the United States and in the 1960s directed *Slaves*, an ambitious but unsuccessful film. He wrote a memoir of making *Salt of the Earth* in 1965, just before the movie began to resurface and circulate on college campuses as part of the Chicano and feminist movements. Members of Independent Productions Corporation launched an antitrust suit against Hollywood studios and individuals like Roy Brewer for conspiracy to destroy *Salt of the Earth*, but their efforts finally failed in the mid-1960s. IPC was slightly more successful in distributing the movie abroad, where it won several prestigious awards, but only in the European and Asian countries that were not dominated by Hollywood. Even with these showings, IPC never recouped its costs. IPC went bankrupt and could make no more pictures, and that road to a more democratic popular culture was blocked.

COMMUNISM AND ANTICOMMUNISM

It is important to see how, in making *Salt of the Earth*, blacklisted artists managed to "hide in plain sight": they produced motion pictures and television shows that projected humanist values despite their opponents' strenuous efforts to enforce the blacklist.[19] But that perspective must encompass the overall picture of repression. The costs of anticommunism have been very high for individuals, who lost friendships, livelihoods, and reputations; for the film industry, which lost a vibrant alternative popular culture; for the labor movement, which lost a generation of committed organizers and a critical perspective on the American political economy; and for social justice causes of all sorts. Anticommunists operated, in part, by ferreting out people's membership, or alleged membership, in progressive organizations and forcing supposed communists to participate in public acts of renunciation. One defense against the witch hunt has been the principled refusal to answer the question, "Are you now or have you ever been a member of the Communist Party?" This understandable defensive posture has had the unfortunate consequence of keeping the history of the American Left in a shadow that is lifting only little by little.

The story of Mine-Mill in Grant County can tell us much about left-wing unionism and its importance to Mexican Americans. Mine-Mill offered Mexican American workers a powerful class analysis that took serious account of racism and its expression in class relations at the workplace and in claims to citizenship in local society. Labor rights and civil rights are intimately connected to one another, and, in the 1940s, left-wing unions like Mine-Mill recognized this connection and by doing so helped secure these rights for Mexican Americans. Mine-Mill matched its rhetoric with forceful, effective action and the fostering of local leadership, which inoculated most Mexican American workers against the anticommunism that surged around them in the late 1940s. The Left that those workers knew was a positive force in their lives, quite at odds with the terrible specter that anticommunists conjured up.

Progressive unionism like that in Grant County owed much to, but was not coterminous with, the Communist Party. This basic fact was lost on anticommunists, to whom communism meant one thing, and anything close to the CP was by definition defiled and perverted by it. But anticommunists in Grant County were correct in identifying a CP presence and sensing in it a threat to the social order. The thrust of CP-inspired activism was different from what anticommunists imagined—

Mine-Mill Local 890 threatened the class and racial order, not the functioning of democratic government—but it was no less a threat.

This disjuncture points us to another aspect of this story that may have broader significance: communism and anticommunism do not belong to the same analytical category. There is a relationship between them, one cemented by language (the prefix "anti" links the two), but it is not a simple relationship. Communism in the labor movement meant a Marxist class analysis and vision of the future, community with others who shared that analysis and vision, and organizations that were in some places rigidly hierarchical and in others, like Grant County, much more democratically run. Anticommunism was a defensive response to the perceived threat of communism, but it came to operate as a discourse in American society, a discourse manifest in powerful institutions like the House Un-American Activities Committee, the Hollywood blacklist, and the Congress of Industrial Organizations. It was a discourse that people employed to express other kinds of conflicts and thereby to take the higher moral ground accorded to anticommunism. Local class, racial, and, in the case of Chana and Cipriano Montoya, gender antagonisms all found expression in anticommunist rhetoric fueled by national efforts to suppress progressive unionism and cultural alternatives like *Salt of the Earth*. Anticommunism lent itself to opportunism, because it was sacrosanct: anything done in the name of anticommunism was unassailable. Cipriano Montoya took this view to its logical, if tragically absurd, conclusion when he tried to get away with the murder of his wife by saying he killed her to protect his children against communism.

THE EMPIRE ZINC STRIKE AND
SALT OF THE EARTH TODAY

The story of the strike and the movie illuminates a tumultuous period in the history of mid-twentieth century America. It fuses, in a clear and compelling fashion, the themes of class, ethnic, and gender conflict and struggles for solidarity. It embodies the connections between local and national historical trends: the workings of anticommunism, early efforts at Chicano civil rights, and the trajectory of the American labor movement. And it shows how important it was for workers to reenact their experiences in an artistic form. Unique among feature films of the 1950s, *Salt of the Earth* relied on a collaboration of workers and artists;

also unique among feature films, it was the subject of intense political and economic repression, but ultimately deemed by the U.S. Library of Congress one of a hundred films it is committed to preserving above all others.

Sensing these rich layers of historical meaning, artists, scholars, and activists have repeatedly returned to the Empire Zinc strike and *Salt of the Earth* as important tools in union campaigns, feminist consciousness-raising efforts, and the Chicano movement, as well as the subject of conferences, scholarship, documentary films, feature films, and even an opera.[20] All have been inspired by the combination of the story and the remarkable circumstances in which the story was then told, suppressed, and ultimately revived.

The legacy of the strike and movie production has been more ambiguous for Grant County's residents, however. As in many other labor conflicts, the people involved were forced to take sides and then to live, often for decades, with the ramifications of their choices. Powerful feelings of solidarity and betrayal alike have animated the people of Grant County ever since. The union's supporters, often the children of the 1950s activists, have also been saddened by the recent decline of the union, the sapping of its vitality at the very moment when the community is left with the environmental devastation of a century of mining and seventy-five years of smelting.

For this reason, some Grant County residents have recently worked on the remaking of *Salt of the Earth*. The way in which that iconic film might be remade, however, has not been determined, and the project may never be realized. True to the spirit of the original, this project relies on a close collaboration between filmmakers and Grant County residents. But, unlike the first, it must also take into account the existence of a complete script from fifty years ago. For some people involved in the project, this is the chance to film Michael Wilson's script with the resources it deserved but never received, in order to achieve higher production values and widespread distribution through a Hollywood studio. For others, the spirit of *Salt of the Earth* requires that the new movie not simply reshoot the same scenes with new actors but rather address current community issues—such as environmental reclamation or protecting the Kneeling Nun rock formation on the mountain behind Chino's open pit, a geological feature that has special meaning for Grant Countians. A new production committee has brought together the perspectives of Hollywood producer Moctezuma Esparza, writer-director David

Riker, Michael Wilson's heirs, and Grant County residents. Just as the union families struggled to represent their story as they understood it, so too are today's Grant County families struggling to honor the accomplishments of their parents and grandparents and to revive a community spirit that can meet the challenges of a new century.

NOTES

SHSWA   State Historical Society of Wisconsin Archives,
                 Madison, Wis.
WFMR   Western Federation of Miners/International Union
                 of Mine, Mill and Smelter Workers International,
                 District, and Local Records, University of Colorado
                 at Boulder Libraries, Boulder, Colo.

CHAPTER ONE

1. Collar-to-collar pay, also known as "portal-to-portal" pay, would compensate workers for the time spent traveling to the work site within the mine. The union's other demands were helpers for miners, preventing foremen from performing productive work, the deletion of a no-strike clause, and an end to a thirty-day trial period for new workers.

2. *SCDP*, October 17, 1950.

3. See Lorence, *Suppression of "Salt of the Earth,"* for a full account of this opposition.

4. For the script, see Michael Wilson, *Salt of the Earth.*

5. Prominent among them were the Cannery and Agricultural Workers Industrial Union (later the United Cannery, Agricultural, Packing, and Allied Workers of America) in California, Arizona, Colorado, and Texas; the International Longshoremen's and Warehousemen's Union in California; and the National Miners Union and the Liga Obrera de Habla Española, both active in New Mexico. This labor organizing took place in agriculture, manufacturing, warehousing, and many other industries. See Jamieson, *Labor Unionism in American Agriculture*, 80–114 and 164–99; Vargas, *Labor Rights Are Civil Rights*, 62–157; Ruiz, *Cannery Women, Cannery Lives*; Weber, *Dark Sweat, White Gold*; Daniel, *Bitter Harvest*; Mario T. García, *Memories of Chicano History*, 87–107; and Healey and Isserman, *California Red.*

6. For more on the southwestern organizing drive, see Dinwiddie, "Rise of the Mine-Mill Union." Vargas, *Labor Rights Are Civil Rights*, 159–74, and Mario T. García, *Mexican Americans*, 175–98, focus on organizing in El Paso's smelters.

7. Lichtenstein, *Labor's War at Home*, and Vargas, *Labor Rights Are Civil Rights*, make this argument.

8. For information on the Congreso, see García, *Mexican Americans*, 145–74; Vargas, *Labor Rights Are Civil Rights*; Gutiérrez, *Walls and Mirrors*, 110–16; Ruiz, "Una Mujer Sin Fronteras"; and Larralde and Griswold del Castillo, "Luisa Moreno." For LULAC, see Márquez, *LULAC*; Gutiérrez, *Walls and Mirrors*; Mario T. García, *Mexican Americans*; Orozco, "Regionalism, Politics, and Gender"; Orozco, "Origins of the League of United Latin American Citizens"; and Garza, "LULAC."

9. On the conservative end of the political spectrum, the American G.I. Forum was formed to secure rights for Mexican Americans while affirming a

patriotism that increasingly became anticommunist in the 1950s; further to the left was the American Veterans Committee, which was not limited to any one ethnic group but fought for veterans' benefits—in housing, health, education, and work—that would not be restricted to white people. For the American G.I. Forum, see Allsup, *American G.I. Forum*, and Ramos, *American G.I. Forum*. For the American Veterans Committee, see Bolte, *New Veteran*; Moore, "Search for Alternatives"; Saxe, "'Citizens First,'"; Severo and Milford, *Wages of War*; and Tyler, "American Veterans Committee."

10. Here I am drawing especially on the work of Horace Huntley and Robin Kelley, who have both studied Mine-Mill among African Americans in Alabama. Huntley uses a violent jurisdictional battle between Mine-Mill and the United Steelworkers in 1948 to evaluate Mine-Mill's record on race and racism. He finds that the union's formal commitment to racial equality distinguished Mine-Mill from many southern unions, and that the anticommunism unleashed in the late 1940s—which took the form of raids by the United Steelworkers, sanctioned by the CIO—set back the cause of interracial unionism. See Huntley's dissertation, "Iron Ore Miners and Mine-Mill"; for an abbreviated version, see his article, "Red Scare and Black Workers in Alabama." Kelley is more critical of the CP. He, too, finds a commitment to racial equality and, importantly, an active effort to mesh southern African American cultural practices with Communist ones. He shows that the CP was not monolithic in structure or ideology; local conditions and history mattered, and African Americans used the party more than the party used them. But Kelley finds that the shift from the ultra-left Third Period to the Popular Front—a shift that many historians have applauded as sanctioning indigenous radicalism—hurt the cause of African American self-determination. The Popular Front relaxed the party strictures against "white chauvinism," at least in Alabama, and Mine-Mill's interracialism had the effect of sanctioning white racism. See Kelley, *Hammer and Hoe*.

Huntley and Kelley belong to a revisionist school of historians examining the CP. By focusing on its workings in particular locales and around union organizing and racial equality, they diverge from the path marked out by Theodore Draper in the 1950s and since followed by historians such as Harvey Klehr and John Earl Haynes. In this interpretation, the American CP was little more than a puppet of the Soviet Union; riven by factionalism and dominated by immigrants, the CP lacked authentic connection to the United States and, instead, threatened American institutions. See Theodore Draper, *Roots of American Communism* and *American Communism and Soviet Russia*; Klehr, *Heyday of American Communism*; and Klehr, Haynes, and Anderson, *Soviet World of American Communism*. Vernon Jensen, who wrote important histories of Mine-Mill and its predecessor, the Western Federation of Miners, similarly dissects every policy shift in the 1930s to show the creeping influence of Communists and their sometimes violent clashes with moderates, who realized their peril only too late. See Jensen, *Nonferrous Metals Industry Unionism*.

11. Heidi Hartmann first developed this thesis in "Capitalism, Patriarchy, and Job Segregation by Sex."

12. The historical literature is rich in these themes. See Kaplan, "Female Consciousness and Collective Action"; Kessler-Harris, "Treating the Male as 'Other'"; Gordon, "What's New in Women's History"; essays in Baron, ed., *Work Engendered*; Jameson, *All That Glitters* and "Imperfect Unions"; Mercier, *Anaconda*; Faue, *Community of Suffering and Struggle*; Taillon, "'What We Want Is Good, Sober Men'"; Glickman, *Living Wage*; Lindsay, "Domesticity and Difference"; Yarrow, "Gender-Specific Consciousness"; Peck, *Reinventing Free Labor*; Penfold, "'Have You No Manhood in You?'"; and Finn, *Tracing the Veins*.

13. Tilly and Scott, *Women, Work, and Family*.

14. Boydston, *Home and Work*.

15. In *Cannery Women, Cannery Lives*, the first full-length book on Chicana labor history, Vicki L. Ruiz shows how cannery workers negotiated family responsibilities as they created a gender-specific work culture, a theme that anthropologist Patricia Zavella develops in her study of contemporary cannery workers, *Women's Work and Chicano Families*. Roslinda M. González offers a structural overview of Chicana family life and employment in "Chicanas and Mexican Immigrant Families." "Las Obreras: The Politics of Work and Family" was the theme of a special issue of *Aztlán* in 1991, featuring articles by sociologists, anthropologists, and historians. This collection of essays was republished in 2000 as a book, *Las Obreras*, edited by Vicki L. Ruiz. Sociologist Beatríz M. Pesquera finds that the contemporary division of household labor—and Chicanas' expectations of their husbands' household duties—varies noticeably by social class. See Pesquera, "'In the Beginning He Wouldn't Lift Even a Spoon.'" Margaret Rose organizes her study of women in the United Farm Workers around the figures of Dolores Huerta, who represented an independent woman activist—albeit one with many family commitments—and Helen Chávez, who represented what Rose considers a more traditional integration of family, union, and work. See articles by Rose, "Traditional and Nontraditional Patterns of Female Activism" and "From the Fields to the Picket Line," and her dissertation, "Women in the United Farm Workers."

16. Jameson, *All That Glitters*; Klubock, *Contested Communities*; Peck, *Reinventing Free Labor*; Finn, *Tracing the Veins*; Mercier, *Anaconda*; Yarrow, "Gender-Specific Consciousness"; Penfold, "'Have You No Manhood in You?'"; Guérin-Gonzales, "From Ludlow to Camp Solidarity."

17. See especially Jameson, *All That Glitters*; Finn, *Tracing the Veins*; Mercier, *Anaconda*; Faue, *Community of Suffering and Struggle*; Guérin-Gonzales, "From Ludlow to Camp Solidarity"; and Steedman, "Godless Communists and Faithless Wives."

18. See Jameson, *All That Glitters*; Mellinger, *Race and Labor in Western Copper*; Huginnie, "'Strikitos'"; Baker, "Women in the Ludlow Strike"; Peck, *Reinventing Free Labor*; O'Neill, "Domesticity Deployed"; Gordon, *Great Arizona*

Orphan Abduction; Byrkit, "Walter Douglas and Labor Struggles"; and Dubofsky, *We Shall Be All.*

19. I have chosen not to use the term "machismo," because it tends to flatten the range of masculinities into a stereotype of Mexican men.

20. As Cynthia E. Orozco has shown, feminists, especially women in subordinated ethnic groups, were not necessarily part of national women's organizations. An important example is Alice Dickerson Montemayor, a LULAC leader from Laredo, Texas, who criticized male leaders for their sexism. See Orozco, "Alice Dickerson Montemayor."

21. A very few historians have studied the CP from a feminist angle, investigating women's roles in the party and in left-wing organizations, how the party did and did not promote women's rights, and notions of gender implicit in party rhetoric and action. In general, these historians show the subordination of women's issues in an organization that saw class struggle as the principal force in history. Looking at the decade of the 1930s, Robert Schaffer argues that the party's structure permitted women's participation but that the absence of autonomous women's groups kept women's issues in the background. Buttressing this tendency were CP press images of women as militant strikers, beauty queens, and keepers of the family flame. Rosalyn Baxandall, surveying CP history over several decades, finds that the party's formal commitment to gender equality opened the way for women to criticize male authority. But, like Schaffer, she concludes that the party treated women's issues as subordinate matters that did not merit diversion of attention or resources from the class struggle. Women's liberation would follow class liberation, and to organize around women's oppression was not only a waste of time but, even more, a betrayal of working-class women in favor of "bourgeois" feminism. Clearly the party itself was only a limited vehicle for women's participation and for changes in gender relations, but Linn Shapiro and Kate Weigand have found a different situation in the "front" organizations of the late 1940s. At some distance from the party, but still influenced by its worldview, activism in organizations like the Congress of American Women began to take Communist women in new theoretical directions. Moreover, as Baxandall suggests, informal discussions of the Woman Question were important in changing the consciousness of some Communist women and men. This book takes off from the insights gained from this recent work. Instead of concentrating on the party itself, however, I am more interested in the ways that women who were associated with a left-wing union—although probably not Communists themselves—made use of left-wing feminism. See Schaffer, "Women and the Communist Party USA"; Baxandall, "Question Seldom Asked"; Shapiro, "Red Feminism"; Weigand, "Vanguards of Women's Liberation"; and Weigand, *Red Feminism.*

22. A useful starting point for this literature is Alma M. García, "Development of Chicana Feminist Discourse," and Alma M. García, ed., *Chicana Feminist Thought.*

23. See Rose, "Gender and Civic Activism," 179, and Ruiz, "Claiming Public

Space," 24. Irene Ledesma ("Texas Newspapers and Chicana Workers' Activism," 322–27) finds, by contrast, that maternalist representations of Chicana strikers limited strikers' power in that era. For the 1970s, Mary Pardo ("Creating Community" and *Mexican American Women Activists*) argues that a maternalism rooted in neighborhoods and ethnicity empowered the "Mothers of East L.A." These scholars are engaged in a larger debate about "political familism," or the theory, articulated most clearly by Maxine Baca Zinn in the 1970s, that Chicanas' political activism has been rooted in family ideology. Cynthia Orozco cautions against applying this theory uncritically to Chicana history. See Zinn, "Political Familism," and Orozco, "Beyond Machismo," 7–8.

24. For a fascinating study of a different cross-ethnic cultural collaboration— the "Mexican Players" and the San Gabriel Valley's Padua Hills Theater, which evolved from an Americanization program into an effort to combat Anglo prejudice—see Matt Garcia, *World of Its Own*, 121–54, and "'Just Put on That Padua Hills Smile.'"

25. On the complicated issue of labels, see Bean and Bradshaw, "Intermarriage Between Persons of Spanish and Non-Spanish Surname"; Hernández, Estrada, and Alvírez, "Census Data"; Gutiérrez, *Walls and Mirrors*; and Rodríguez, *Changing Race*.

26. Fields, "Ideology and Slavery."

27. See Gutiérrez, *Walls and Mirrors*; Griswold del Castillo, *Los Angeles Barrio*; and Kaminsky, "Gender, Race, *Raza*."

28. Cooper, "'Our Strike,'" 81.

CHAPTER TWO

1. Lasky, *Geology and Ore Deposits*, 69; Hernon and Jones, "Ore Deposits of the Central Mining District," 1222–23, 1228–33; Clemons, Christiansen, and James, *Southwestern New Mexico*, 68; Parsons, *Porphyry Coppers*, 340–43.

2. Clemons, Christiansen, and James, *Southwestern New Mexico*, 68. "Ore" is made up of both useful and useless mineral, the latter referred to as "gangue."

3. Hernon and Jones, "Ore Deposits of the Central Mining District," 1220–22; Clemons, Christiansen, and James, *Southwestern New Mexico*, 69.

4. Hernon and Jones, "Ore Deposits of the Central Mining District," 1216–20; Finlay, *Report of Appraisal*, 55.

5. Milbauer, "Historical Geography of the Silver City Mining Region," 28.

6. Ibid., 52.

7. Boyer and Gayton describe the lives of women in this part of the world in *Apache Mothers and Daughters*.

8. Parsons, *Porphyry Coppers*, 206; John P. Wilson, *Historical Profile of Southwestern New Mexico*, 9.

9. Mack Turner, "Mining Industry Writes 150 Years of History from Primitive Workings to Open Pit Projects," *SCDP*, December 13, 1954; Sinclair, "Town

That Vanished into Thin Air," 2−3. McWilliams, *North from Mexico*, 135, dates Carrasco's discovery as 1800.

10. John P. Wilson, *Historical Profile of Southwestern New Mexico*, 9.

11. McGaw, *Savage Scene*, 76; Albert H. Vigil, interview by author.

12. And unlike in other areas of the Southwest, including Grant County, Hispanics of northern New Mexico later became important in territorial and then in state politics. See Gómez-Quiñones, *Roots of Chicano Politics*, 257−62, for territorial politics, and 328−33 for the *Hijos del País* movement, which asserted Hispanic political power in the years following statehood in 1912.

13. Historical geographer D. W. Meinig succinctly describes these regional economic, demographic, and cultural patterns in *Southwest*. The eastern New Mexican highlands were also settled later than northern and central New Mexico, remaining under Comanche control until Mexicans and Texans started ranching there in the nineteenth century. Known as "Little Texas," this district resembled the Texas Panhandle geographically and culturally. Grant County differed from Little Texas in that its metal mines ensured that ranching never dominated the local economy.

14. John P. Wilson, *Historical Profile of Southwestern New Mexico*, 10; Humble, "Grant County, New Mexico."

15. John P. Wilson, *Historical Profile of Southwestern New Mexico*, 10.

16. Ibid.

17. Kirker's biographer casts Santa Rita's ownership in some doubt. At first Don Francisco's wife continued to run the mine and to lease it to other Mexicans and Americans. But the Mexican government restricted landownership by *gachupines*, or Spanish-born Mexicans such as Don Francisco. See McGaw, *Savage Scene*.

18. McGaw, *Savage Scene*.

19. Sinclair, "Town That Vanished into Thin Air," 3.

20. J. H. Lyman, cited in *Indian Affairs Report* (1871), cited in Twitchell, ed. and comp., *Leading Facts of New Mexican History*, 252 n. 104.

21. Sinclair, "Town That Vanished into Thin Air," 5.

22. Milbauer, "Historical Geography of the Silver City Mining Region," 64. Henkel's smelter used Mexican and German technology.

23. Sweeney, *Mangas Coloradas*. An abbreviated account can be found in Sweeney, "Mangas Coloradas and Mid-Nineteenth-Century Conflicts."

24. Debo, *History of the Indians of the United States*, 267−83. The Chiricahua who eventually surrendered, including Geronimo and other leaders, were shipped to Fort Marion, Florida, by train, and then to Mobile, Alabama, and Fort Sill, Oklahoma, before being finally settled back in New Mexico on the Mescalero Apache reservation near Tularosa.

25. See, for example, obituaries in *Silver City Daily Press* of Mrs. Patrocinio D. Acevedo, August 6, 1948; Pánfilo H. Becerra, September 10, 1943; Margarita Cordova, September 20, 1943; Mrs. Ysidora Y. Fletcher, July 10, 1954; Francisco

Grijalva, February 13, 1934; José Guerra, February 24, 1942; Trinidad Ponca Hernández, January 8, 1948; Domitila Morales, March 29, 1939; Annie Madrid Ogás, April 4, 1944; Urbana Lucero Ramírez, December 24, 1947; Luz Telles Tarín, December 24, 1944; Paulina Torres, August 13, 1949; and Josefa S. Trujillo, October 10, 1948. Many were from the Mimbres Valley, and a few were identified as miners or railroad workers. A number of equally longtime residents were not identified as pioneers, but I have not found differences in the two sets to account for the discrepancy. Into eastern New Mexico, too, came both Mexicans and Texans at this time, but their movements were always in the context of Texan imperial ambitions that treated Mexicans shabbily at best, violently at worst.

26. See Weinberg, *Manifest Destiny*. Juan Gómez-Quiñones explains further that partisan politics also delayed statehood, as Democrats who dominated what would become Arizona did not want to be subjected to the Republicans who dominated New Mexico. See Gómez-Quiñones, *Roots of Chicano Politics*, 325.

27. Joe T. Morales, interview by author.

28. On the San Pedro Valley, see Benton, "What About Women in the White Man's Camp?," for a superb analysis of racial formation in the context of distinct social and economic districts.

29. Darlis A. Miller, "Cross-Cultural Marriages," 100.

30. Deena J. González, *Refusing the Favor*, 72, 113–16. González finds that Spanish Mexican women who married Euro-Americans around the time of the U.S. conquest of Santa Fe ran into trouble as widows: unscrupulous Euro-Americans increasingly used the courts to defraud them of inheritance and, occasionally, to contest child custody. See ibid., 91–92. Looking at central Arizona mining towns in the 1860s, Johnson, in "Sharing Bed and Board," shows the very different cultural expectations brought by Mexicans and Anglos to cohabitation—whether among Mexicans, among Anglos, or between Mexicans and Anglos. Her emphasis on the flux of boomtowns makes for a good comparison with similarly booming Silver City but less so with the Mimbres Valley.

31. This is untrue of Asians. There were a few Japanese and Chinese in Grant County, and, as other historians have shown, the Chinese ranked below even Mexicans in the mining industry. See especially Johnson, *Roaring Camp*. By the 1940s, however, the few Chinese families were fairly well established as grocers.

32. Hyde, *Copper for America*, 82.

33. O. M. Bishop and R. L. Mentch, "Zinc," in U.S. Department of the Interior, Bureau of Mines, *Mineral Facts and Problems*, 979.

34. The New Jersey Zinc Company, *First Hundred Years*; Bishop and Mentch, "Zinc," 979. The United States imported most of its zinc until the 1890s.

35. Elliott et al., *International Control in the Non-Ferrous Metals*, 766. Finlay, *Report of Appraisal*, 59, classifies the other lead-zinc operations in Grant County as "Small Metal Mines of Doubtful Value." The lead-zinc industry spread from New Jersey and Pennsylvania into Wisconsin, Illinois, and what would become

known as the Tri-State region, the corner where Kansas, Missouri, and Oklahoma meet.

36. Bureau of the Census, *Fourteenth Census*, "New Mexico," table 3. The 1920 census did not break down data by county, but other sources confirm that most metal mines were located in Grant County. I take the state figures as a reasonable approximation of Grant County's figures.

37. Bureau of the Census, *Fifteenth Census, 1930, Mines and Quarries, 1929*, "Gold, Silver, Copper, Lead, and Zinc," table 7. A single enterprise could cover more than one mine.

38. Bureau of the Census, *Fourteenth Census*, table 3.

39. Coan, *History of New Mexico*, 2:365; Davis, ed., *Historical Encyclopedia of New Mexico*, 556.

40. See Spence, *Mining Engineers and the American West*, for the definitive history of this class of men.

41. The demand diminished in the 1910s, when the Mexican Revolution drove many engineers back to the United States and the mining schools turned out more graduates than the market could support. See ibid., 294–96.

42. Coan, *History of New Mexico*, 2:365.

43. Spence, *Mining Engineers and the American West*, 66.

44. *SCDP*, October 21, 1938, section C, Progress Edition, 10.

45. Ibid.

46. Sinclair, "Town That Vanished into Thin Air," 6.

47. Turner, "Mining Industry Writes 150 Years of History"; Himes, "General Managers at Chino," 1; John Murchison Sully obituary, n.p., July 18, 1933, in Silver City Public Library vertical file, "Santa Rita."

48. Parsons, *Porphyry Coppers*, 210.

49. Hyde, *Copper for America*, 129.

50. Rickard, *Interviews with Mining Engineers*, 194–96.

51. Jameson, *All That Glitters*, 24–25.

52. Twitchell, *Leading Facts of New Mexican History*, 270; Hyde, *Copper for America*, 140–41.

53. Hurley was named after J. E. Hurley, general manager of the Atchison, Topeka, and Santa Fe Railroad. See Pearce, ed., *New Mexico Place Names*, s.v.

54. This accounts, too, for how American and British companies were able to take over mining operations in copper-rich but capital-poor regions like Chile and Mexico. The Chilean owners of El Teniente mine in central Chile, for example, could not afford to invest in the transportation, housing, and processing that would make mining its inaccessible and low-grade ores profitable. They sold it to a company financed by the Guggenheims, who "merged their U.S. and Chilean mines [into] Kennecott Copper Company" in 1915. Kennecott would eventually purchase Chino, too. See Klubock, *Contested Communities*, 24–27.

55. National Labor Relations Board (NLRB), *Decisions and Orders*, 26:1188;

Peck, *Reinventing Free Labor*, 68–69. All of these companies employed Mexican immigrants. Seeking a stable fuel source during the boom years of war production, Chino had bought the Victor American Fuel Company in 1917 and renamed it the Gallup American Coal Company. See Huggard, "Environmental and Economic Change," 203.

56. By 1915, Chino's operations employed "853 men in the open pits and about 1,200 at the power plant and mill at Hurley." By the end of World War I, some 12,000 workers depended on Chino. See Huggard, "Environmental and Economic Change," 121, 128. Over the first half of the twentieth century, "with the exception of the Santa Fe Railroad, the [Santa Rita] copper mines were the state's largest employer" (Nash, "New Mexico in the Otero Era," 8).

57. Complicating the lexicon further is the fact that "miner" can also refer to the mine owner. I use the term "mine operator" to refer to the owners and managers (when I do not need to distinguish between the two).

58. Clearly a miner's work life depended as well on the work of others, principally women, to feed and clothe them. I discuss the family economy and the sexual division of labor in Chapter 6.

59. Cages, or man-cages, carried people; skips carried supplies down the shaft and ore and waste products back up. Occasionally, "skips" referred to the apparatus that carried both men and ore. See Wendel, "Mining in Butte Forty Years Ago," 60–61; Lewis, *Elements of Mining*; and Young, *Elements of Mining*.

60. Young, *Elements of Mining*, 209. Speeds increased for deeper shafts: a shallow shaft of 500 feet, for instance, could accommodate a hoisting speed of 1,200 feet per minute, while a shaft deeper than 3,000 feet permitted speeds up to 3,000 feet per minute.

61. National War Labor Board case 111-13879-D (22-D-185), WFMR, box 866, folder 1.

62. Geological features and the underground environment dictated the specific method of stoping. Shrinkage stoping depended on strong ore deposits. Miners worked from the floor level upward, blasting the rock face above them. They left broken ore in the stope to support the walls, which received further support from timbering and sometimes from pillars of unmined ore. Miners used cut-and-fill stoping when confronted with weak ore structures. In this process, miners removed the ore in parallel, vertical slices; as they removed each slice, they left waste in the stope as a support and also as a floor from which to continue mining. Even weaker ore required square-set stoping, a costly method in which miners immediately replaced the mined ore with timbers. Asarco's Groundhog mine used this method. See Lewis, *Elements of Mining*, and Young, *Elements of Mining*.

63. Ira Wright commented in 1944 that most of the district's mines used loader operators, not hand shovels. See *SCDP*, May 29, 1944.

64. The best account of Chino's technology and work processes is in Huggard, "Environmental and Economic Change," 90–218.

65. Clemons, Christiansen, and James, *Southwestern New Mexico*, 29. In March 1943, a carload of dynamite was used to move half a million tons of rock in a single blast. See "Big Blast at Chino," *New Mexico Miner and Prospector*, March–April 1943, 3.

66. Clemons, Christiansen, and James, *Southwestern New Mexico*, 29.

67. Ibid. *SCDP*, July 10, 1944, describes the short-lived New Mexico Ore Processing Company's zinc mill in Bayard. USSRMC later bought this mill.

68. NLRB, *Decisions and Orders*, 26:1225, 1227.

69. Memo from Carlos Castañeda, assistant to the chairman, to Bruce Hunt, hearing examiner, President's Committee on Fair Employment Practice, November 21, 1944, FEPCR, box 339. The manuscript censuses for 1920 and 1930 show the same job segregation but do not explain which jobs had lines of promotion.

70. Jeffrey Garcilazo ("*Traqueros*," 16) similarly argues that, by the 1880s, railroad "track labor became synonymous with racial subordination."

71. Six Mexican men, living in Central, were firemen for a stationary boiler in 1930. See 1930 manuscript census, Precinct 1, Central.

72. NLRB, *Decisions and Orders*, 26:1228; 1920 manuscript census, Precinct 13, Santa Rita.

73. NLRB, *Decisions and Orders*, 26:1226.

74. Moses's grandfather had been a St. Louis doctor, and his father, John, served in the Confederate army before selling shoes in St. Louis; Horace's mother also came from a moderately genteel southern family. John Moses set up as a merchant along the Mimbres River, where his three sons worked intermittently in commerce, on local Anglo ranches, and in the mines. See *New Mexico Miner and Prospector*, June 1944, 1, 8; Coan, *History of New Mexico*, 2:353; and Davis, ed., *Historical Encyclopedia of New Mexico*, 555.

75. *SCDP*, August 6, 1951; position roster, Santa Rita, July 13, 1944, WFMR, box 864, folder 4.

76. See Probert, "Discord at Real del Monte," 47; Woyski, "Women and Mining in the Old West," 40.

77. Murphy, *Gathering of Rivers*; Hurtado, *Indian Survival*; Woyski, "Women and Mining in the Old West," 40.

78. Guérin-Gonzales, "From Ludlow to Camp Solidarity," 303–9.

79. Rowse, *Cornish in America*, 344. Undoubtedly, some women worked underground; a sketch from 1870 shows one woman in a group of underground miners suffering from heat exhaustion in Nevada, and a few immigrant women in Pennsylvania may have worked underground as mine laborers in addition to helping their families by collecting coal from banks of anthracite waste. See Sloane and Sloane, *Pictorial History of American Mining*, 184, and Priscilla Long, *Where the Sun Never Shines*, 131.

80. "The Idol of Groom Creek Miners Union," *Miners' Magazine*, June 2, 1904, 7. Her husband presided over Arizona's State Federation of Labor in 1904.

81. *Miners' Magazine*, September 17, 1903, 3.

82. "The Idol of Groom Creek Miners Union," 7.

83. *Miners' Magazine*, September 17, 1903, 3. See Lawrence Glickman, *Living Wage*.

84. The approximation is necessary because the census statistics, which I used for the total female population, did not specify the sex breakdown of the age groups; to calculate adult females, I halved the number of persons under age fifteen, assuming that this sex ratio was more likely than not to be even, and subtracted that number from the total number of females.

85. 1930 manuscript census, Precincts 11, 13, and 16.

86. As Josiah McC. Heyman has argued, companies control towns openly, by threatening to take away jobs, housing, and tax payments, and discreetly, by controlling "real estate, zoning, and bank loans." Because all members of a family are connected to the company, "the social field of action—everyday give and take among people—is strongly coherent. The nature of social interaction in one domain, let us say segmented pay in the job market, is likely to be reproduced in another, say among children in school. Grievances accumulated at the company store overlap with grievances accumulated in the mine shafts by men. One's self-understanding, such as 'race,' is synonymous with other self-understandings, such as 'union.' . . . Residents take stances of loyalty or opposition to the ever-present company which persist for years, transmitted through family, union, and city politics" (Heyman, "In the Shadow of the Smokestacks," 158–59).

87. John Sully, commenting in 1910, cited in *SCDP*, March 31, 1951.

88. Ibid.

89. Milbauer, "Historical Geography of the Silver City Mining Region," 64.

90. Huginnie, " 'Strikitos,' " 183; Jameson, *All That Glitters*.

91. 1910 manuscript census; 1920 manuscript census. The 1920 census identifies them as zinc miners. I am assuming that these are Empire Zinc employees, since Peru had not begun operations and Blackhawk produced very little zinc: a yearly average of 712 tons of zinc in 1919 and 1920, compared to Empire Zinc's yearly average of 18,685 tons of zinc from 1911 to 1920. See Finlay, *Report of Appraisal*, 55, 59.

92. John Sully, commenting in 1910, cited in *SCDP*, March 31, 1951.

93. Bill Wood, interview by author. Wood's father was half Anglo and half Mexican, and Bill Wood attributes to his father's friendship with Chino foreman Harry Thorne his family's good fortune in getting a water pipe.

94. Arturo Flores, interview by author.

95. Mariana Ramírez, "The Road to Peace," *Union Worker*, January 1951, 2.

96. Southwest of Silver City, the Phelps-Dodge Company bought many mining claims in the Burro Mountain mining district and built a model company town, Tyrone, for its Anglo and Mexican workers. Urged by the wife of its president, the company designed buildings in the "Spanish mission" style that had been gaining currency in the Southwest. Appreciation of pre-Anglo culture went only so far, of course, and the company made sure that the actual Mexicans lived

in the cheapest houses with the fewest amenities. But the post–World War I depression forced Phelps-Dodge to shut down its Tyrone operations in 1921, and Chino was left alone to carry the torch of corporate paternalism. (Chino, too, closed down in 1921, but it reopened the following year.) See Magnusson, "Modern Copper Mining Town," and Willis, "Housing at Tyrone, New Mexico."

97. These claims are based on evidence from interviews, reminiscences, and a survey of news coverage, society pages, jury and electoral notices, graduations, and advertisements in the *Silver City Daily Press* from 1941 to 1955.

98. Aurora Chávez, interview by author; Alice Sandoval, interview by author. Hurley High School classrooms were integrated.

99. Except for two teachers in private Spanish-speaking classes, all teachers in the 1930 census for Hanover and Santa Rita were Anglo. (See Table 2.) Newspaper reports on school activities confirm this pattern for the 1940s in Santa Rita, Hurley, Bayard, Fierro, and Cliff. Two or three Spanish-named teachers taught at Central School in the 1940s, and both San Juan and San Lorenzo in the Mimbres Valley had Spanish-named teachers; Fortunata Valencia, for example, taught at the San Juan School from 1930 to 1947. Mrs. Cruz Galván Valenzuela taught at Hanover School in the mid-1940s. According to her nephew, Frank Ramirez, Valenzuela achieved her education against the wishes of her father, who opposed female education. She graduated from State Teachers College, taught school in Artesia, in eastern New Mexico, then returned to Grant County and later helped establish bilingual education. See Elizabeth Horcasitas, interview by Polly Evans, Rio Grande Historical Collections, New Mexico State University Library, RG-T253, Las Cruces, N.M.; Ramirez, *Remembering Fierro*, 64; and *SCDP*, July 1, 1943; September 20, 1943; September 11, 1945; February 12, 1948; February 27, 1948; March 19, 1948; March 26, 1948; May 7, 1948; September 2, 1948; January 29, 1949; August 31, 1949. On punishment for speaking Spanish in Grant County schools, see Elizabeth Horcasitas interview; Huggard, "Environmental and Economic Change," 259; Anita and Lorenzo Torrez, interview by author; Matías Rivera, interview by author; and Aurora Chávez, interview by author. Neither Arturo Flores nor Dora Madero recall being punished for speaking Spanish in school; Alice Sandoval said that such punishment depended on the individual teacher. See Flores, interview by author; Madero, interview by author; and Sandoval interview. In 1919, at the urging of Governor Octaviano Larrazolo, New Mexico's legislature passed an act supporting bilingual education, but the state board of education stressed English instruction and the act was repealed in 1923. See Erlinda Gonzales-Berry, "Which Language Will Our Children Learn?," 180–84.

100. Graduation rolls, *SCDP*, May 20, 1941; May 21, 1941; May 23, 1941; May 14, 1942; May 18, 1942; May 15, 1944; May 18, 1944; May 15, 1945; May 18, 1945; May 29, 1945; May 14, 1947; May 16, 1947; May 21, 1947; May 26, 1948; May 27, 1948; May 28, 1948; May 29, 1948; May 24, 1949; May 23, 1950; May 24, 1950; May 15, 1952; May 23, 1951; May 22, 1952.

101. Himes, "Unions and the Chino Mine," 6.

102. In this respect, they resemble the cross-class social organizations that historian Elizabeth Jameson found in Cripple Creek, before the violent and divisive strike of 1904. See Jameson, *All That Glitters*, 88–90.

103. For Boy Scouts, see *SCDP*, February 14, 1944; April 24, 1945; September 21, 1948. For Girl Scouts, see *SCDP*, February 17, 1944; February 14, 1945; January 2, 1948; April 6, 1948; February 27, 1950; March 11, 1950.

104. For movie theaters, see letter from J. P. Sepulveda to *SCDP*, January 26, 1942. Albert H. Vigil recalled an incident from his childhood when he and his mother went to the movies. A couple of Anglo women in the row ahead of them turned around and told them, "You have to go sit over there." Vigil's mother replied, "If you don't like it you can go back to Oklahoma," and that settled the issue. See Albert H. Vigil, interview by author. For dances, see *SCDP*, April 11, 1941; January 13, 1942; January 20, 1942; February 5, 1942; August 4, 1944; September 8, 1944; November 8, 1946; February 3, 1949; April 15, 1949; July 2, 1949; July 1, 1950; October 20, 1950; January 18, 1952; February 15, 1952.

105. Lists of precincts, *SCDP*, September 10, 1942; November 2, 1946; May 24, 1947; September 6, 1951; April 22, 1952.

106. New Mexico was exceptional in the enfranchisement of its Mexican American citizens. For contrasts with Texas, Arizona, and California, see Gómez-Quiñones, *Chicano Politics*.

107. Mariano Lucero and Cecilio Torres were Hanover's constables during this period, and Joe G. Arciero Jr. was Fierro's. See *SCDP*, November 10, 1942; January 3, 1947; April 5, 1950.

108. Lists of juries, *SCDP*, September 16, 1942; September 8, 1943; September 5, 1944; August 23, 1945; March 26, 1947; November 25, 1947; August 23, 1948; October 24, 1949; December 1, 1949; September 12, 1950; March 7, 1951; May 28, 1951. Voting rolls formed the basis for the first round of jury selection; since Mexican Americans did not vote significantly less than Anglos, it is puzzling that so few would serve on juries. Jury selection, though, was a mixture of random selection—names for the venire were drawn from the "wheel"—and the judgment of District Judge A. W. Marshall, who chose a smaller panel.

109. Dolores Jiménez, interview by author and Sam Sills. Jiménez is the daughter of Margarita and William Villines.

110. "Grant County Sheriffs for 100 Years"; James Blair obituary, *SCDP*, February 3, 1941; Jones, *Memories of Santa Rita*; Bill Wood, interview by author.

111. 1920 manuscript census; Santa Rita seniority list, 1947, WFMR, box 870, folder 15. Other Fletchers (possibly Frank's cousins or brothers) had Spanish first names and also worked menial jobs at Chino.

112. I am indebted to Bernard Himes for this and following descriptions of Jackling.

113. Back at home in San Francisco, Jackling liked to cruise the bay in his gigantic yacht, also named the *Cyprus*.

114. *SCDP*, October 21, 1935. In one scene in *Salt of the Earth*, the striking

miners come across a magazine article about the company president hunting big game in Africa. Their admiration prompts them to undertake a hunting expedition of their own, which jeopardizes the strike.

115. At least one Mexican American couple named their son "Sully"; Sully Armijo belonged to Hanover Lodge 54 of the Alianza Hispano Americana in 1951. See *SCDP*, January 30, 1951.

116. *Silver City Enterprise*, June 14, 1912.

117. See O'Neill, "Domesticity Deployed," for an excellent gender analysis of the Bisbee deportation.

118. Melzer, "Exiled in the Desert," 281. The Gallup residents were sent by railroad to Belen, "where they were held in custody just outside the town's railroad yards."

119. Peck, *Reinventing Free Labor*, 222.

CHAPTER THREE

1. See Chapter 4.

2. *SCDP*, November 14, 1950.

3. *SCDP*, June 8, 1951; June 9, 1951.

4. *SCDP*, June 9, 1951. Empire Zinc superintendent S. S. Huyett confirmed this when he testified before the NLRB. See *SCDP*, September 26, 1951.

5. *Bayard Journal*, June 3, 1950.

6. Grant County marriage records for Dorman Lee Capshaw, Lee Ross Capshaw, and Patricia Capshaw Ney identify their birthplaces as Cardin, Kiowa, and Picher, Oklahoma, respectively.

7. Local 890 activist José Carrillo identified these three men in a letter to Senator Dennis Chávez in July 1951. See José Carrillo to Dennis Chávez, July 12, 1951, Dennis Chávez Papers, box 208, folder 9, CSR.

8. *SCDP*, June 11, 1951.

9. NIRA was passed in 1933 during Roosevelt's "First Hundred Days." The Supreme Court struck it down in 1935, but the National Labor Relations Act, or Wagner Act (1935), codified similar prolabor principles and was upheld by the Supreme Court in 1937. The Wagner Act created the National Labor Relations Board (NLRB), which sponsored and oversaw elections for union representation and meditated some labor-management conflicts. NIRA also called on industries to set up codes that would regulate prices and curb overproduction, and in some industries, labor unions thrust themselves into the process. But as energetic as Mine-Mill was in organizing workers in the 1930s, it carried absolutely no weight in drafting the copper, lead, or zinc codes.

10. Himes, "General Managers at Chino," 10, 12.

11. 1930 manuscript census, Precinct 13, Santa Rita.

12. NLRB, *Decisions and Orders*, 26:1189. At the time, Local 63 represented workers at Santa Rita and Hurley.

13. Rubenstein, "Great Gallup Coal Strike of 1933," 175.

14. Ibid. For a fictional account of the labor conflict in Gallup, see Philip Stevenson's [Lars Lawrence's] series *The Seed*, consisting of *Morning, Noon and Night*, *Out of the Dust*, *Old Father Antic*, and *The Hoax*.

15. On agriculture, see Jamieson, *Labor Unionism in American Agriculture*; Daniel, *Bitter Harvest*; Weber, *Dark Sweat, White Gold*; Healey and Isserman, *California Red*. On canneries, see Ruiz, *Cannery Women, Cannery Lives*. On California organizing more broadly, see Mario T. García, *Memories of Chicano History*. For a synthesis of Mexican working-class history in the Southwest and Midwest, see Vargas, *Labor Rights Are Civil Rights*.

16. Santa Rita officers were C. M. Gumfory, president; Martin Gallegos, vice president; Jack Kemp, financial secretary and treasurer; Samuel Sáenz, recording secretary; Julián Horcasitas, warden; G. O. Biles, conductor; and Stone Mayes, T. B. Benjamin, and F. O. Smith, trustees. Hurley officers were Julio Grado, president; Ysmael Moreno, financial secretary and treasurer; and Marcelo Avalos, trustee. See *Nev. Consol. Copper Corp. v. NLRB*, 122 F.2d 587, 593 (10th Cir. 1941); and NLRB, *Decisions and Orders*, 26:1218, 1219, 1221.

17. See Arneson, " 'Like Banquo's Ghost,' " 1609.

18. Industrial unions organized all the workers in a workplace, regardless of occupation. Craft unions, by contrast, organized workers in a particular trade or occupation.

19. Huginnie, " 'Strikitos,' " 157. Huginnie comments that this 1902 effort failed and, in fact, "resulted in the entire Anglo work force being fired."

20. Jensen, *Nonferrous Metals Industry Unionism*, 4–5.

21. Resolution 25, in *Mine-Mill Conv. Proc.* (Salt Lake City, August 6–13, 1928), day 5, 3. The following year the convention cited Canadian and Mexican violations of U.S. immigration laws as reason for prohibiting any immigration for ten years; a resolution to this effect passed, but only after it was amended so that "in no way" would it refer to Canadians. See Resolution 32, in *Mine-Mill Conv. Proc.* (Salt Lake City, August 5–10, 1929), day 3, 1.

22. "Annual Report of the President, International Union of Mine, Mill and Smelter Workers, 1940," in *Mine-Mill Conv. Proc.* (Denver, August 5–10, 1940), 81–82.

23. The "communist take-over" of Mine-Mill is Jensen's primary concern in *Nonferrous Metals Industry Unionism*. I agree with Jensen that Mine-Mill became a union close to the CP, but I interpret this change more positively, in large part because of its effects on cross-ethnic organizing in the Southwest.

24. On Mine-Mill among African Americans, see Huntley, "Iron Ore Miners and Mine Mill" and "Red Scare and Black Workers," and Kelley, *Hammer and Hoe*.

25. See Vargas, *Labor Rights Are Civil Rights*, 90–113, and Rubenstein, "Great Gallup Coal Strike of 1933."

26. NLRB, *Decisions and Orders*, 26:1190–91.

27. Ibid., 1191.

28. Ibid.

29. Ibid., 1203. Cruz was born in Mexico, and his union work was especially courageous given the rash of deportations that took place during the Great Depression.

30. Ibid., 1191.

31. Benigno Montez, quoted in Deborah Rosenfelt, "Commentary," in Michael Wilson, *Salt of the Earth*, 114.

32. Mariana Ramírez, quoted in Rosenfelt, "Commentary," 115.

33. Nevada Consolidated alleged that union supporters made these threats, but the company's foremen, including Hap Thorne, admitted to the labor board that they never investigated these threats; by contrast, union men's testimony was either corroborated by management (indirectly) or simply never challenged.

34. NLRB, *Decisions and Orders*, 26:1204.

35. *Nev. Consol. Copper Corp. v. NLRB*, 122 F.2d 587, 594 (10th Cir. 1941).

36. Himes, "General Managers at Chino," 11.

37. Two years later, Mine-Mill workers at the American Metals Company in Terrero, N.M., were also defeated when the company shut down indefinitely. See *SCDP*, February 21, 1936.

38. *SCDP*, July 1, 1935; November 27, 1935; January 10, 1936. Chino insisted that its properties were worth only $7 million in 1935, while the state tax commission set the value at $12 million; the two parties eventually agreed on $9.5 million, which maintained Grant County's classification.

39. U.S. Department of the Interior, Bureau of Mines, *Minerals Yearbook 1935*, 275. Before closing in October 1934, the Chino Mines operated at only 20 percent of capacity. For Empire Zinc, see U.S. Department of the Interior, Bureau of Mines, *Minerals Yearbook 1937*, 470, and *SCDP*, March 11, 1937. Empire Zinc reopened with about 100 workers, many of whom were former employees.

40. Katherine Benton analyzes the corporate maternalism that accompanied corporate paternalism in Bisbee. See Benton, "What About Women in the White Man's Camp?,"; Finn, *Tracing the Veins*; O'Neill, "Domesticity Deployed"; Mercier, *Anaconda*; and Deutsch, *No Separate Refuge*.

41. *SCDP*, August 7, 1934; December 11, 1934.

42. Montoya, "Roots of Economic and Ethnic Divisions," 21. Although this was supposed to be a voluntary program, there is some evidence that families were pressured to send their sons to CCC in order to reduce the number of families on direct relief. Grant County's welfare administrator, Juanita Langer, was told by the assistant director of public welfare to "withdraw relief from families where eligible boys refuse to enlist in the CCC . . . in order that [Aid to Dependent Children] grants may be cut down" (ibid., 22).

43. New Mexican Hispanic youth encountered discrimination in the CCC,

but it was nothing compared to that faced by Tejanos. See Montoya, "Roots of Economic and Ethnic Divisions," 29–32, and Melzer, *Coming of Age in the Depression.*

44. This pattern fits analyses articulated by Gordon, *Pitied But Not Entitled,* and Kessler-Harris, *In Search of Equity,* on the gendered nature of the welfare state.

45. J. I. Kemp, Box 971, Santa Rita, to Gov. Clyde K. Tingley, April 1, 1935, Gov. Clyde K. Tingley Papers, box 10, folder 322, NMSRCA. The workers had protested their unsafe transportation to the work site, and the governor helped end the practice.

46. Ysmael Moreno to Gov. Clyde K. Tingley, July 12, 1935, Gov. Clyde K. Tingley Papers, box 10, folder 332, NMSRCA.

47. NLRB, *Decisions and Orders,* 26:1197.

48. Ibid., 1205–6. McCraney applied to general foreman Thorne the following spring, but Thorne turned him down.

49. Ibid., 1195.

50. Ibid., 1196, 1221.

51. This was the case for Rafael Kirker, Julián Horcasitas, Juan Vera, and Simon Sias. See ibid., 1208.

52. Himes, "General Managers at Chino," 7–8.

53. Sixty-one men filed the first complaint, another forty-two names were added after the first hearing, and thirteen more were added after the second hearing. See NLRB, *Decisions and Orders,* vol. 26, Appendix A, 1240–41.

54. *NLRB v. Nev. Consol. Copper Corp.,* 316 U.S. 105, 107 (1942).

55. Himes, "General Managers at Chino," 13.

56. Here I differ with Zaragosa Vargas, who argues in *Labor Rights Are Civil Rights* that Mine-Mill's commitment to the no-strike pledge fundamentally compromised its commitment to racial equality. I find instead that Mine-Mill both appealed to Mexican Americans and followed through with contracts and grievances that aimed to redress inequality.

57. Luis Leobardo Arroyo ("Chicano Participation in Organized Labor," 290–99) notes that while CIO labor unions were important to Mexican American workers in Los Angeles, the citywide CIO Council was also important as an organizational form that fought discrimination in the community beyond the workplace.

58. NLRB, *Decisions and Orders,* 19:596. The employment manager, Murray Bateman, probably regretted those words once they made their way into the 1939 NLRB hearings, because in almost every instance the board found that the company had wrongfully discriminated against union supporters.

59. Dinwiddie, "Rise of the Mine-Mill Union," 51.

60. *SCDP,* April 25, 1941; August 14, 1941.

61. *SCDP,* November 10, 1941. No one could take his vacation until November 1942. The union checkoff would have made collecting union dues more

efficient because the company's payroll office would have deducted the dues and given them directly to the union local.

62. Asarco leased the Hanover mill from Blackhawk Consolidated, and in 1950 it did not renew the lease, turning instead to its larger mill in Deming. Mine-Mill represented Asarco office workers but lost jurisdiction in 1944.

63. *CIO News—Mine-Mill Edition*, May 26, 1941, 2.

64. Staff Report, Silver City Area, District #2, March 21, 1942, WFMR, box 294, folder 3.

65. For Hurley membership, see Local 69 monthly reports, 1941–46, WFMR, box 865, folder 3. For Hurley officers, see *SCDP*, April 4, 1941. For Santa Rita officers, see *SCDP*, April 17, 1941. (There are no extant monthly reports for Santa Rita Local 63 for this period.)

66. Staff Report, Silver City Area, District #2, May 23, 1942, WFMR, box 294, folder 3; *SCDP*, May 27, 1942.

67. *SCDP*, July 20, 1942.

68. Ibid.

69. Ibid.

70. The Chino Metal Trades Council was founded in February 1941. It was composed of the International Association of Machinists, International Brotherhood of Electrical Workers, Steam and Operating Engineers International Union, United Brotherhood of Carpenters, International Boilermakers and Iron Ship Builders, United Association of Plumbers and Steamfitters, and International Union of Blacksmiths. See *SCDP*, February 7, 1941. A year later, the AFL created a Southwestern District Metal Trades Council, corresponding to Mine-Mill's Southwest Industrial Council. See *SCDP*, February 24, 1942.

71. Himes, "Unions and the Chino Mine," 9.

72. De la Torre's father had been a track laborer on the Santa Fe Railroad for twenty-five years. See *SCDP*, May 5, 1941; May 21, 1941.

73. Staff Report, Silver City Area, District #2, April 25, 1942, WFMR, box 294, folder 3; *SCDP*, February 1, 1943. The AHA was a *mutualista*, or fraternal organization, for Mexican Americans, founded in Tucson in 1894. It provided burial services for members and hosted U.S. and Mexican patriotic celebrations. Lodge No. 17 was formed in Silver City in 1904, and by the 1940s there were lodges in Hanover, Bayard, Santa Rita, and Hurley. See *SCDP*, February 1, 1943; August 2, 1944; June 17, 1947; March 30, 1951. Evidence that miners belonged to AHA comes from the lodges' locations—few people unaffiliated with the mines lived in those mining camps—and from obituaries. See, for example, *SCDP*, March 26, 1947. On the importance of *mutualistas*, see Gutiérrez, *Walls and Mirrors*.

74. *SCDP*, March 10, 1941.

75. *SCDP*, April 16, 1941.

76. Ernie De Baca, quoted in *SCDP*, October 10, 1941.

77. *SCDP*, October 6, 1942; October 30, 1948.

78. *SCDP*, May 22, 1942.

79. *SCDP*, May 25, 1942.

80. George Knott, Staff Report, Silver City Area, District #2, June 6, 1942, WFMR, box 294, folder 3.

81. Ibid.

82. *SCDP*, July 9, 1942.

83. "Agreement Covering Wages and Working Conditions between Nevada Consolidated Copper Corporation, Chino Mines Division, and International Union of Mine-Mill and Smelter Workers Locals Nos. 63 and 69, July 7, 1942," WFMR, box 864, folder 2; *SCDP*, January 26, 1942.

84. Staff Report, Silver City Area, District #2, July 25, 1942, WFMR, box 294, folder 3. At the Peru Mining Company, George Knott, Jess Nichols, Gussie Nard of the Copper Flats shaft, and Juan García of the Pewabic shaft negotiated workers' first contract in August 1942. (Workers at Peru's Kearney shaft had not yet finished a run-off election, so they were not immediately covered by the contract.) Their contract guaranteed job security and promotion according to seniority, rather than on the basis of "race, creed, color, and national origin," and granted vacations and time-and-a-half pay for overtime work. See *SCDP*, August 7, 1942.

85. Union's statement of position and brief, April 2, 1945, National War Labor Board case 111-13879-D (22-D-185), WFMR, box 866. The Fair Employment Practices Committee, discussed below, found that it was difficult to get Chino to upgrade Mexicans precisely because Chino's doing so would take them out of Mine-Mill's jurisdiction and place them in the AFL's jurisdiction—which lacked contract language forbidding discrimination on the basis of nationality. See Memo from Ernest G. Trimble to Lawrence W. Cramer re: Discrimination in the Southwest, [December 1944], FEPCR, box 339. It is interesting, however, that sometime between 1941 and 1945, Richard P. Erbacher, the corresponding secretary of Chino's Metal Trades Council, notified the committee that the "mining companies of the Southwest discriminated against Americans of Spanish descent, no matter [their] education, training, or ability." See "New Mexico Complaints," FEPCR, box 339.

86. Local 604 daybook, WFMR, box 866. The daybook, which covers 1942–46, lists initiations only in 1942.

87. Local 890 checkoff, New Mexico Consolidated Mining Co. and Peru Mining Co., January 1948, WFMR, box 882.

88. Asarco Local 530 daybook and petty cash record, WFMR, box 865, book 2.

89. Among the Anglo blacklisted workers who stayed in Mine-Mill were Earl Allen, locomotive engineer; Joseph Baxter, locomotive engineer; Asa T. Carr, railroad brakeman; Angus Gruwell, steam shoveler; John "Jack" Howe, locomotive engineer; James L. McCraney, steam shovel fireman; and Charles H. Williams, locomotive fireman.

90. The National War Labor Board (NWLB) upheld the union's position, but Kennecott general manager Horace Moses hesitated to fire so many workers. See *SCDP*, July 26, 1943.

91. Carlos Castañeda, assistant to the chairman, to Will Maslow, director of field operations, President's Committee on Fair Employment Practice, May 8, 1944, FEPCR, box 339. Its least objectionable stanza reads: "There is Mexicans, Indians, Wops, and Chinks. So damn many foreigners the damn place stinks. It's ajabber jabber here and jabber there. I am so disgusted I want to pull my hair" (Anonymous, "The C.I.O. and the A.F. of L.," April 9, 1944, FEPCR, box 339).

92. Based on Santa Rita position rosters from 1944, 1947, and 1949, the percentage of laborers with Spanish names increased from 85 percent in 1944 (196 of the 231 laborers) to 99 percent in 1949 (179 of the 181 laborers). See position roster, Santa Rita, July 13, 1944, WFMR, box 864, folder 4; seniority list, Santa Rita, July 1, 1947, WFMR, box 870, folder 15; and seniority list, Kennecott Copper Corporation, July 1, 1949, WFMR, box 870, folder 24. The departure of Navajo men from the wartime workforce partly accounts for the increased percentage of Mexican American laborers.

93. New Mexico Employment Security Commission, reported in SCDP, February 13, 1941; June 25, 1941; October 9, 1941. In May, the commission "placed 400 more workers than in April while the number of persons registered for employment dropped by 500." In 1941, the commission made 2,320 payments to Grant County recipients; that number dropped significantly over the following two years, to 1,054 in 1942 and 33 in 1943. The average monthly payment to Grant County recipients was quite small, although it increased over time: $9.84 in 1941, $10.11 in 1942, and $13.94 in 1943. See New Mexico Employment Security Commission, "Annual Report (1941)," 22; "Annual Report (1942)," 21; "Annual Report (1943)," 23.

94. Nevada Consolidated first raised wages in July and then again in November. See SCDP, July 21, 1941; November 14, 1941.

95. SCDP, April 1, 1942.

96. "Mine Managers Tell of Manpower Problems," New Mexico Miner and Prospector, November 1942, 8.

97. SCDP, July 17, 1944.

98. On women employees, see Chapter 6; on Navajo workers, see Huggard, "Environmental and Economic Change," 157–58.

99. Himes, "General Managers at Chino," 19; Franco, "Beyond Reservation Boundaries," 249.

100. Huggard, "Environmental and Economic Change," 275.

101. Clinton Jencks, interview by author. Bernard L. Himes disputes this characterization, reporting that "the cabins provided basic shelter, warmth, water, and, in the open yard, room to tether nanny goats. Mine-Mill protested the accommodations. . . . The company, unhappily, yielded to non-Navajo pressure, evicted the tenants, and did away with the mini-village" (Himes, "General Managers at Chino," 20).

102. Ibid. I have not been able to get employment records showing if Navajo women, as well as men, worked at Chino.

103. Morgan, Domestic Mining Industry, 213; New Mexico Miner and Pros-

pector, November 1942, 1. The New Mexico Miners and Prospectors Association, founded in 1939 by mine owners and engineers, approved of this government interference in the free market because by November 1942 this measure "had reduced labor loss in [logging and mining] by 80 percent or more" (*New Mexico Miner and Prospector*, November 1942, 2).

104. "5,306 soldiers were released by the Army [in this second round of furloughs], and of these 4,546 were hired—3,168 going to copper mines, 1,136 to zinc mines, and 242 to molybdenum mines" (Morgan, *Domestic Mining Industry*, 223).

105. Nelson Lichtenstein analyzes these problems most thoroughly in *Labor's War at Home*. See also Atleson, *Labor and the Wartime State*; Milkman, *Gender at Work*; Zieger, *CIO*; and Vargas, *Labor Rights Are Civil Rights*.

106. Daniel, *Chicano Workers*. President Roosevelt created the FEPC in 1941 to stave off the mass demonstration that A. Philip Randolph threatened to stage in Washington, D.C., against continued discrimination in defense industries. Vargas, *Labor Rights Are Civil Rights*, interprets the FEPC as especially weak.

107. Dinwiddie, "Rise of the Mine-Mill Union," 53.

108. Memo from Carlos Castañeda, assistant to the chairman, to Will Laslow, director of field operations, FEPC, June 23, 1944, and Report and Recommendations re Cases Involving Southwest Copper Mining Industry, May 18, 1945, FEPCR, box 339. In "Region X" as a whole (Texas, Louisiana, and New Mexico), 25 percent of the FEPC's cases from July 1943 to June 1944 were dismissed on the merits and 40 percent satisfactorily adjusted. See Committee on Fair Employment Practice, *First Report*, 115, table 1-B.

109. Memo from Carlos Castañeda, assistant to the chairman, to Will Laslow, director of field operations, FEPC, September 1, 1944, FEPCR, box 39.

110. Southwest Industrial Union of Mine-Mill meeting minutes, March 22, 1942, Miami, Arizona, WFMR, box 294, folder 3.

111. Local 530 represented office workers until 1944.

112. National War Labor Board case 111-613-D, FEPCR, box 339. Holguín had received a substantial wage increase in December 1942, and by the following summer he was earning the salary guaranteed by the union's new contract with Asarco. The case, then, concerned back pay between 1941 and December 1942, and the NMC took this into account in its decision.

113. 14 *War Labor Reports* 146, decision of the Nonferrous Metals Commission, upheld by the National War Labor Board in 18 *War Labor Reports* 591. The three Arizona companies were Miami Copper Company, International Smelting and Refining Company, and Inspiration Consolidated.

114. Dinwiddie, "Rise of the Mine-Mill Union," 54.

115. Ibid.

116. *New Mexico Miner and Prospector*, January 1943, 1. After the speeches, "the huge crowd rose and repeated the Oath of Allegiance, and then followed the spectacular demonstration of the Army in action, which thrilled everyone present" (ibid., September 1943, 5).

117. *SCDP*, September 28, 1942; *New Mexico Miner and Prospector*, November 1942, 1.

118. See Lichtenstein, *Labor's War at Home*, and Harris, *Right to Manage*. Similarly, the mining industry had stoutly resisted union influence on the industry codes mandated by the 1933 National Industrial Recovery Act.

119. *SCDP*, December 16, 1941.

120. *SCDP*, April 9, 1942; April 27, 1942. For more on Grant County's participation in the 200th, see Cave, *Beyond Courage*.

121. *SCDP*, December 11, 1941.

122. *SCDP*, December 22, 1941. There is no evidence that miners saw in Robinson's comments a concession of workers' rights or power.

123. At least one Bayard Anglo, L. A. Jesson, also saw in the war effort little room for discrimination. Shortly after Pearl Harbor, he wrote to the *Silver City Daily Press*: "Rather shocks me to see racial color mentioned in newspapers and even broadcasts [about the fighting. Our allies, the] Filipinos, Chinos, Sud-Americanos[,] ain't lilly-white [*sic*], amigo. Y ademas algunos de la fuerzas Americanos, incluyen tropas que no son blancos [And furthermore some of the American forces, include troops that aren't white]—but are damned good fighting men and real Americans." (*SCDP*, December 18, 1941; grammatical errors in Spanish are in the original).

124. Managers often "led" the meetings in which they explained the payroll-deduction system, but apparently most workers understood only when provided with a Spanish translation.

125. *SCDP*, February 11, 1942.

126. Staff Report, Silver City Area, District #2, [March 21, 1942], WFMR, box 294, folder 3. Other Mine-Mill defense bond promoters included Local 69 president Angus Gruwell and vice-president Julián Horcasitas, both of whom had been active in the 1930s disputes with Chino. Horcasitas was the brother-in-law of Juan Valencia, who was killed in action at Pearl Harbor and for whom New Mexico's first "Spanish American VFW Post" (Veterans of Foreign Wars Post 4150) would be named in May 1943. Horcasitas was also the junior vice-commander of this post. See *SCDP*, February 6, 1942, and May 22, 1942.

127. *SCDP*, January 27, 1943. Ninety-four percent of Hurley's workers, for instance, were signed up for payroll deduction, a figure that included all of the track gang, all of the boiler shop, and 97 percent of the labor department. See *SCDP*, January 13, 1943.

128. *SCDP*, September 29, 1944.

129. Southwest Industrial Union Council president Clyde Sparks, Miami, Arizona, and Secretary-Treasurer W. H. Solem, Carlsbad, New Mexico, to New Mexico governor John J. Dempsey, [1943], Governor John J. Dempsey Papers, box 2, 1943, NMSRCA.

130. Western Division, American Mining Congress, "Declaration of Policy," reprinted in *New Mexico Miner and Prospector*, March 1944, 3. Kennecott labor relations specialist James K. Richardson reaffirmed in 1946 "that collective bar-

gaining is here to stay" (James K. Richardson, Address to 1946 Meeting of New Mexico Miners and Prospectors Association, reprinted in *New Mexico Miner and Prospector*, June 1946, 4).

131. Zieger, *American Workers, American Unions*, 100. Over ten million belonged to the AFL. For the strike wave, see "Postwar Work Stoppages Caused by Labor-Management Disputes," *Monthly Labor Review* 63 (December 1946), 872. Most of these strikes concerned wages, and most involved members of the CIO.

132. Resolutions adopted by New Mexico Miners and Prospectors Association, published in *New Mexico Miner and Prospector*, May 1946, 7. Grant Countian Ira Wright chaired the resolutions committee. See also Harris, *Right to Manage*.

133. Even Taft-Hartley did not fully satisfy mine industry leaders, who wanted to prohibit industrywide bargaining, forbid "union proposals [in collective bargaining] incroaching [*sic*] on the employer's right to manage his business," and deny any representation rights or strike rights to unions that failed to get rid of Communist officers. See Western Division, American Mining Congress, "Declaration of Policy," reprinted in *New Mexico Miner and Prospector*, December 1947, 4. Both the AFL and the CIO opposed Taft-Hartley's movement through the legislature and persistently called for its repeal in the years after passage.

134. As Richard M. Freeland argues in *Truman Doctrine*, although President Truman opposed Taft-Hartley, and even vetoed it (the Senate overruled his veto), his foreign relations policy, first in Greece and then in the rest of Europe, emphasized the dangers of world communism. His domestic political opponents then used this very discourse to promote their own antilabor policies.

135. Clinton Jencks to Maurice Travis, June 26, 1948, WFMR, box 867, folder 1; *SCDP*, June 24, 1948; June 30, 1948; August 20, 1948.

136. Arthur Flores, B. G. Provencio, José T. Morales, and Clinton Jencks to W. H. Goodrich, July 10, 1948, WFMR, box 870, folder 7. This letter referred to Kennecott's letter of May 1. Flores was president of the Santa Rita unit, Provencio president of the Hurley unit, Morales the delegate to Mine-Mill's national Kennecott Council, and Jencks the president of Local 890.

137. Clinton Jencks to Senator Dennis Chávez, February 7, 1949, WFMR, box 294, folder 13. Local 890 also sent petitions signed by 500 members for the international office to circulate among congressmen. See Jencks to Elizabeth Sasuly, February 7, 1949, WFMR, box 294, folder 13.

138. Clinton Jencks, interview by author. Jencks recalled that both he and his wife, Virginia, worked to convince union members to give the new strategy a try.

139. Ibid. The June 11 date comes from the July 11, 1948, letter cited in note 136, above.

140. I analyze this political campaign in Chapter 4.

141. See Jensen, *Nonferrous Metals Industry Unionism*.

142. Local 890 financial secretary José S. Campos to John Clark, April 3, 1950, WFMR, box 294, folder 13. See also Paul B. Sáenz and Angel R. Bustos to

Reid Robinson, December 4, 1946, WFMR, box 865, folder 11. Sáenz and Bustos were officers of Asarco Local 530 in 1948.

143. Local 530 petty cash record and membership, WFMR, box 865, book 2. Rafael Lardizábal Sr. joined the NLRB suit against Nevada Consolidated, but the NLRB ruled that his failing eyesight, not the blacklist, accounted for his not being rehired.

144. C. J. "Bud" DeBraal [to Rafael Lardizábal], March 4, 1952, and Lardizábal to DeBraal, May 26, 1952, WFMR, box 872, folder 41.

145. Rafael Lardizábal, quoted in *SCDP*, June 3, 1952. He aired his criticisms over radio station KSIL on June 2, 1952.

146. Ibid. Local 890 did organize a gift drive and Christmas party for the Empire Zinc strikers' children.

147. *SCDP*, June 7, 1951.

148. Asarco Local 530 monthly reports, 1945–47, WFMR, box 865, folder 13.

149. Paul B. Sáenz and Angel R. Bustos to Reid Robinson, December 4, 1946, WFMR, box 865, folder 11.

150. Quoted in *SCDP*, November 10, 1951.

151. White's replacement, Paul Sáenz, thought little of White's accounting skills. Apparently White (and, to be fair, his predecessor) never deducted federal withholding or social security from salaries of union employees, and left "a veritable mess" for Sáenz to clean up. See Paul B. Sáenz to Reid Robinson, December 30, 1946, WFMR, box 865, folder 11.

152. Clinton Jencks, interview by author.

153. For one of many examples from Local 890 executive board minutes, see those for February 6, 1948, WFMR, box 868, book 10. This pattern of lively debate continued into the 1950s.

154. Interviews by author of Arturo Flores, Lorenzo Torrez, Virginia Chacón, and Clinton Jencks.

155. A spring 1948 membership drive at Kennecott by Local 890 yielded proportionately more Mexican new members. Of the 361 employees eligible for union membership in March and April 1948, 128 (35 percent) were Mexican and 233 (65 percent) were Anglo. At the end of May, 290 eligible workers still did not belong to the union, of whom 80 (28 percent) were Mexican and 210 (72 percent) were Anglo. See "Eligible workers not in union as of March 1948 at Kennecott, Hurley," "Eligible workers not in union as of April 1948 at Kennecott, Santa Rita," "Santa Rita workers eligible for Union not in Union May 25, 1948," and "Eligible workers not in Union as of May 25, 1948, Hurley," WFMR, box 870, folder 7. It is unclear if the change over time comes from individuals joining the union or ceasing to be eligible.

156. Asarco seniority list as of May 1, 1949, WFMR, box 870, folder 1; Local 890 petty cash record and membership book, WFMR, box 865, book 2; Asarco Unit meeting minutes, 1949, WFMR, box 868, book 7.

157. Statement of Floyd Bostick on behalf of Local 890, in U.S. Congress, House of Representatives, *Problems in the Metal Mining Industry*, 400. From the

beginning of the twentieth century, many people have moved to New Mexico for health reasons. Most of the literature on this phenomenon has shown the middle-class origins of the migrants; here we see examples of working-class people taking the same steps.

158. Local 890 became a civil rights and political organization as much as a labor union, a development I analyze in Chapter 4.

159. Arturo Flores, interview by author, and Clinton Jencks, interview by author. No one organized a ladies' auxiliary, which suggests little attempt to mobilize people beyond the workplace. Carlsbad, located some distance from Grant County, had New Mexico's only ladies' auxiliary before Grant County women formed Auxiliary 209 in 1948. See Chapter 4.

160. Santa Rita Local 63 minutes, January 30, 1947, WFMR, box 864, book 2. Reports from the 1941–42 organizing drive reinforce the sense that these organizers came from outside, and that the Grant County drive was considered part of a much larger project.

161. Virginia Chacón, interview by author. Arturo Flores echoed her comments. See Flores interview. (Palomino is a Spanish term for a white horse.)

162. The information for this section comes from Clinton Jencks, interview by author.

163. SLID was associated with the Socialist Party; years later it became the basis for Students for a Democratic Society.

164. *Los Angeles Times*, February 25, 1990, Sunday, home edition.

165. The Southern Tenant Farmers' Union began in the early 1930s as an interracial union affiliated with the Socialist Party. In the sit-down strike, hundreds of farm tenants lined the highway near Sikeston, Missouri, to protest their evictions. See Grubbs, *Cry from the Cotton*, and Mitchell, *Mean Things Happening in This Land*.

166. Curtis evidently had a misunderstanding with Orville Larson, Mine-Mill vice president for District 2, and Larson fired him from the Silver City position.

167. Clinton Jencks, interview by author.

168. These leadership and stewards' classes were no small commitment for any miner: one lasted from 9:30 A.M. to 4:30 P.M. on a Sunday, which meant a full day's work on top of a normal work week. See Local 890 executive board minutes, February 6, 1948, WFMR, box 868, book 10.

169. Flyer advertising leadership school, February 8, 1948, WFMR, box 870, folder 10.

170. Notes, shop stewards training class, WFMR, box 870, folder 10. This had been the preamble to the WFM's constitution. Mine-Mill initially dropped it when it reorganized in 1916 but readopted it in 1934. See Jensen, *Nonferrous Metals Industry Unionism*, 17.

171. Educational materials sent by Graham Dolan to Local 890 and letter from Graham Dolan to Howard Goddard, December 15, 1947, WFMR, box 870, folder 10.

172. Flyer advertising leadership school.

173. Clinton Jencks, interview by author. Yolanda Broyles-González makes a persuasive case that Chicano political theater of the 1960s came out of just this tradition, characterized by a "collective and *physical* manifestation" of cultural memory in storytelling, *dichos*, jokes, dance, and other forms of performance. See Broyles-González, *El Teatro Campesino*, 15.

174. Arturo Flores, interview by author.

175. Notes, shop stewards training class. Many grievance records in the WFMR contain these "five-cent notebook" sheets of paper.

176. Local 890 executive board minutes, February 6, 1948, WFMR, box 868, book 10.

177. Ibid., February 23, 1948.

178. Clinton Jencks to Taller de Gráfica Popular, September 29, 1948, WFMR, box 873, envelope 2. These "close ties" also found expression in efforts to ally with Mexican Asarco workers. In 1949, Angel Bustos and Ezekiel Santamaria, Local 890 representatives to the national Asarco Council, called on the council to "work closer with the Mexican workers in the AS&R in Mexico." See ASR Council minutes, January 30–31, 1949, Omaha, WFMR, box 870, folder 8.

179. C. E. Jencks to University of New Mexico Film Library and Extension Service, August 9, 1949, WFMR, box 873, envelope 2; Local 890 executive board minutes, February 6, 1948, and September 22, 1948, WFMR, box 868, book 10.

180. Cipriano Montoya to Graham Dolan, November 24, 1951, WFMR, box 867, folder 1.

181. Asarco Unit minutes, June 30, 1949, WFMR, box 868, book 7.

182. "Steward's Outline," n.d., WFMR, box 870, folder 10.

183. Clinton Jencks, interview by author.

184. "Steward's Outline."

185. Arturo Flores, interview by author.

186. Ibid.

187. Ibid.

188. Ibid.

189. Ramón A. Hurtado is listed as having begun work at Kennecott on August 19, 1945, and to have been classified as a pitman on May 1, 1947. See Kennecott seniority list, July 1947, WFMR, box 866, folder 4. Flores himself later had a chance for promotion out of the truck department. This opportunity arose precisely because of union-won seniority and antidiscrimination clauses in his contract, but Flores turned it down—also because of the union. As grievance committeeman for the Santa Rita unit, and as an 890 official, driving a truck was a surefire way to talk to workers in many different parts of the plant.

190. C. D. Smothermon to Clinton Jencks, July 20, 1950, WFMR, box 867, folder 1. Montoya resigned this position after about six weeks, citing his wife's health. He returned to Grant County and at the time of the Empire Zinc strike presided over Local 890.

191. Arturo Flores, interview by author.

192. Local 890 minutes, September 29, 1951, WFMR, box 868, book 9. This issue later came to a head in the early 1960s, when Al Skinner promised Mexican American supporters that a Mexican American would replace him as District 2 representative; the 1951 convention proceedings show Mexican Americans debating the issue some ten years before. See Maclovio Barraza, interview by Alice M. Hoffman, December 10, 1969, transcript, WFMR, box 950, folder 1.

193. M. E. Travis to C. D. Smothermon, July 30, 1951, WFMR, box 206, folder 10. Travis suggested that Smothermon call a conference of Mexican American unionists in the Southwest, but it is unclear what relation that conference (if it indeed took place) had to the Mexican American caucus at the September 1951 Mine-Mill convention in Nogales.

194. Anita Torrez, interview by author.

195. Virginia Chacón, interview by author.

196. Lorenzo Torrez, interview by author.

197. Anita Torrez, interview by author.

198. Lorenzo Torrez, interview by author.

199. Clinton Jencks, interview by author; *Jencks v. United States*, 226 F.2d 540 (5th Cir. 1955).

200. The secrecy surrounding CP membership set the stage for considerable trouble a few years later for Clinton Jencks, when he was convicted of having falsified a Taft-Hartley noncommunist affidavit in 1950. See Chapter 9 and Schrecker, *Many Are the Crimes*, 310–11, 336–55.

201. "Steward's Outline."

202. *SCDP*, April 5, 1951.

203. Cargill, "Empire and Opposition" (1983), 196–97.

204. Cipriano Montoya to Maurice Travis, February 3, 1951, WFMR, box 294, box 13.

205. Open letter from Clinton Jencks to Mine-Mill locals, March 20, 1951, WFMR, box 294, folder 13.

206. Receipts from the Southwestern Food and Sales Co., Inc., for January 8, January 9, and February 1, 1951, WFMR, box 294, folder 11.

207. Mine-Mill report, n.d., WFMR, box 294, folder 13; Anita and Lorenzo Torrez, interview by author.

208. Cargill, "Empire and Opposition" (1983), 199.

209. Anita and Lorenzo Torrez, interview by author.

210. Mine-Mill report, n.d., "Empire Zinc Strike," WFMR, box 294, folder 13.

211. Letters to the editor, *SCDP*, April 5, 1951.

CHAPTER FOUR

1. Cargill, "Empire and Opposition" (1979), 74. Cargill refers to union meeting minutes for June 12, 1951, in the WFMR, but I could not locate those minutes. My account of the meeting comes from his thesis and subsequent article, Mine-

Mill convention proceedings, and interviews I conducted with Aurora Chávez, Anita and Lorenzo Torrez, Virginia Chacón, and Clinton Jencks.

2. Aurora Chávez, interview by author.

3. Anita Torrez, interview by author.

4. Aurora Chávez, interview by author; Ernesto Velásquez, *Mine-Mill Conv. Proc.* (1951), 65; Virginia Chacón, interview by author.

5. Juan Chacón, OHALC interview.

6. Anita Torrez, interview by author.

7. Cargill, "Empire and Opposition" (1979), 74; Cargill, "Empire and Opposition" (1983), 203; Clinton Jencks, interview by author.

8. Aurora Chávez, interview by author.

9. *Mine-Mill Conv. Proc.* (1951), 64.

10. Ibid.

11. In this respect, the Empire Zinc strike was similar to many other such mining conflicts in which women's participation and the politics of gender proved pivotal, such as the Cripple Creek strikes of 1894 and 1904, the Ludlow strike of 1913–14, and the Bisbee strike of 1917. Women often acted to protect their family and class interests, a topic I pursue more fully below.

12. Penfold, " 'Have You No Manhood in You?,' " 275.

13. Yarrow, "Gender-Specific Consciousness."

14. Klubock, *Contested Communities*; Finn, *Tracing the Veins*.

15. James K. Richardson, Address to 1946 Meeting of New Mexico Miners and Prospectors Association, reprinted in *New Mexico Miner and Prospector*, June 1946, 4. Richardson was a labor relations specialist at Kennecott's Utah operations, and in the early 1950s he was transferred to New Mexico.

16. Ibid.

17. This account comes from the record of an inquest held March 30, 1947, New Mexico State Inspector of Mines Records, box 2, folder 125, NMSRCA.

18. To "bar down" was to loosen and remove the rock likely to separate from the wall; to "timber" was to provide wooden support.

19. Accident report, inquest, Findings on Hearing held by State Mine Inspector, May 8, 1947, New Mexico State Inspector of Mines Records, box 2, folder 127, NMSRCA.

20. Ibid.

21. The funerals of four men killed at U.S. Smelting, Refining, and Mining Company (USSRMC) on March 21, 1947, were conducted by the AHA. See *SCDP*, March 26, 1947.

22. *SCDP*, April 9, 1947.

23. See Kessler-Harris, "Providers," in *A Woman's Wage*, and Gordon, *Pitied But Not Entitled*. In her most recent work, *In Pursuit of Equity*, Kessler-Harris has shown that over the twentieth century, men and women have fought for something they understood as "equity" over and above something later feminists would consider "equality."

24. Empire Zinc negotiation notes, August 29, 1949, WFMR, box 868, book 8.

25. Ernest Rodríguez, handwritten summary of delegation to Santa Fe, [July 6, 1949], WFMR, box 870, "Unemployed" folder.

26. Handwritten lists of unemployed men and their dependents, n.d., WFMR, box 870, "Unemployed" folder.

27. Ibid. All but one of these eighteen veterans had Spanish names.

28. Chino reopened within a year, but Phelps-Dodge did not resume mining for thirty years; in the interim, it leased mine claims to individuals like H. E. McCray.

29. Ray Strickland was the local officer of the State Employment Security Commission, which administered federal and state unemployment benefits and placed unemployed workers in new jobs. In January, 1,866 people applied for nonagricultural work at Strickland's office in Silver City, but only 147 of them found jobs. By the middle of February, Strickland still had 221 active applications. See *SCDP*, February 17, 1949.

30. *SCDP*, June 16, 1949; *New Mexico Miner and Prospector*, July 1949, 11.

31. *SCDP*, June 28, 1949; June 29, 1949; *New Mexico Miner and Prospector*, July 1949, 11.

32. *SCDP*, June 30, 1949.

33. *SCDP*, July 13, 1949.

34. *SCDP*, August 9, 1949. The unemployment rate includes only those people looking for work.

35. John Steelman, Assistant to the President, List of labor market areas of very substantial unemployment, December 30, 1949, Dennis Chávez Papers, box 190, folder 13, CSR.

36. Open letter to New Mexico legislators from Gregorio Mesa, Angel Bustos, and Clinton Jencks, July 16, 1949, WFMR, box 870, "Unemployed" folder.

37. *SCDP*, June 29, 1949, 1. Two hundred applicants a day flooded the offices.

38. The Unemployed Councils were led by the Communist Party, and the Workers' Alliances were led by the Socialist Party; the latter organized workers on public relief projects. See Gosse, " 'To Organize in Every Neighborhood.' "

39. New Mexico Employment Security Commission, Thirteenth Annual Report, 1949, New Mexico Supreme Court Law Library State Agency Collection, box 16, folder "Employment Security Commission—Annual Reports, 1946–1950," 15, NMSRCA.

40. The six men were Gregorio Mesa, Henry Jaramillo, Ernest Trejo, Cipriano Montoya, Ernest Rodríguez, and Clinton Jencks.

41. Ernest Rodríguez, handwritten summary of delegation to Santa Fe, and Clinton Jencks, handwritten notes taken during trip, WFMR, box 870, "Unemployed" folder;

42. Open letter from Local 890's Unemployment Committee, July 16, 1949,

in WFMR, box 870, "Unemployed" folder. Mabry later denied that he had said he was willing to call a special session if three-fifths of the legislature requested it. See State Senator Guido Zecca to Clinton Jencks, July 30, 1949, WFMR, box 870, "Unemployed" folder. Zecca represented McKinley County and suggested that Grant County's unemployed miners apply for jobs at the Gallup American Coal Company, located in McKinley County.

43. Statement by Governor Thomas J. Mabry, n.d., Governor Thomas J. Mabry Papers, box 6, "Special issues—unemployment 1949–50, correspondence with Clinton Jencks" folder, NMSRCA.

44. Clinton Jencks to Morris Wright, editor of The [Mine-Mill] Union, August 18, 1949, WFMR, box 870, "Unemployed" folder.

45. Local 890 had several ideas for publicizing the union's view of the unemployment crisis, and the political economy more broadly, at the 1949 Labor Day parade. One parade float would show the union winning benefits, "which are then passed on to the Community," while the company sent its profits "away to Wall Street." A second idea connected consumers and workplace conditions—here, speedup and the resulting overproduction. With the mines shown shut down, as they were in 1949, consumers faced "a great need for bathtubs, plumbing, houses, cars, and even kitchen utensils," all of which were beyond their means. A third float would place a corporation above an Anglo worker and a Mexican worker, each holding a "list of their common needs for food, clothing, [and] housing." See Clinton Jencks to Research and Education Department, International Union of Mine, Mill and Smelter Workers, August 23, 1949, WFMR, box 870, folder 10.

46. Most newspaper discussion of veterans presumed that they were men; similarly, the state veterans' agency estimated a 1956 veteran population of 125,000 "service men and their dependents." See New Mexico Veterans' Service Commission, "Report of New Mexico Veterans' Service Commission." Interestingly, though, the first "mayor" of Western New Mexico University's Campus Village, which housed veterans, was a woman. See SCDP, September 22, 1947.

47. There is a growing historical literature that stresses the importance of World War II veterans on the civil rights movements of the 1950s and 1960s. The G.I. Forum, for example, began in 1948 to secure veterans' benefits for Mexican Americans. The G.I. Forum spread throughout the Southwest; New Mexico's 1954 convention anticipated 250 delegates and alternates (Forum News Bulletin, April 1954, 2, WFMR, box 118). But there does not seem to have been a chapter in Grant County—perhaps because Mine-Mill served similar purposes or perhaps because the G.I. Forum was vocally anticommunist and found little support among Mine-Mill members. For example, in 1954, Ed Idar Jr., executive secretary of the American G.I. Forum of Texas, angrily wrote to Mine-Mill's newspaper, the Union, demanding to be removed from the mailing list of "an organization whose record shows clearly that it is being used by elements whose loyalty is primarily to a foreign power and to a foreign ideology. . . . Our sympathy rests with the group of loyal Americans in the El Paso locals of your union that attempted to wrest

control . . . from the tainted leadership" (Ed Idar Jr. to editor, *The Union News-paper*, February 2, 1954, WFMR, box 118). For the American G.I. Forum nationally, see Allsup, *American G.I. Forum*, and Ramos, *American G.I. Forum*; for the G.I. Forum in Texas, see also Montejano, *Anglos and Mexicans*, 279–80. Clinton Jencks was a member of the left-wing American Veterans Committee, which experienced its own battle over communism in 1947. See *SCDP*, May 14, 1947; Bolte, *New Veteran*; Moore, "Search for Alternatives"; Saxe, " 'Citizens First, Veterans Second' "; Severo and Milford, *Wages of War*; and Tyler, "American Veterans Committee."

48. See Starobin, *American Communism in Crisis*, for a close analysis of national and international Communist policy in this period.

49. Report of communications and correspondence, Santa Rita Local 63 minutes, February 6, 1947, WFMR, box 864, book 2.

50. Chester R. Brooks, chairman of Mine-Mill's Kennecott Council, to Kennecott Council locals and delegates, May 8, 1947, WFMR, box 870, folder 2. Brooks specifically told Clinton Jencks, Felipe Huerta, and Brígido Provencio to pass this information on to the membership.

51. Santa Rita Local 63 minutes, July [17], 1947, WFMR, box 864, book 2.

52. Ibid.

53. Santa Rita Local 63 minutes, August [7], 1947, WFMR, box 864, book 2.

54. "The Zero Hour," *New Mexico Miner and Prospector*, April 1944, 1.

55. Here I am building on the arguments of Robert Korstad and Zaragosa Vargas, both of whom explicitly connect union organizing by African Americans and Mexican Americans to civil rights activism of the 1940s and 1950s. See Korstad, *Civil Rights Unionism*, and Vargas, *Labor Rights Are Civil Rights*.

56. *SCDP*, September 11, 1942.

57. *SCDP*, August 28, 1944. Anchondo belonged to Mexico's Federación Regional de Obreros y Campesinos and had worked in El Paso as part of the Mexican union's cross-border organizing in the early 1940s. See Arnold, "Humberto Silex," 9. The union drive angered Asarco Local 530 member E. A. Dowell, who resented "the dragooning of mine, mill and smelter workers into financing and supporting political candidates and parties that care little or nothing for the rank and file of union members." A union, in Dowell's view, should instead "secure better wages and working conditions for its members." Dowell's denunciation of Mine-Mill's political activity, though, seems to have been his tactic to draw attention to the real issue that he cared about: a delay in getting a pay raise that the Nonferrous Metals Commission had granted over the summer. See *SCDP*, October 16, 1944; for the union's response, see *SCDP*, November 3, 1944, and November 6, 1944.

58. The 1948 campaign became a showdown between liberals and leftists within the labor movement and in American political culture more broadly. The CIO insisted that unions support President Truman, while the CP and its supporters backed Progressive Party candidate Henry Wallace.

59. Local 890 executive board minutes, January 2, 1948, WFMR, box 868, book 10. Political platform quoted in *SCDP*, March 3, 1948. That September, the Grant County chapter of the New Party held its founding convention, which nominated a number of union leaders for political office; the statewide New Party convention then nominated them as well.

60. Henry Jaramillo dropped out before the election. See Local 890 executive board minutes, August 30 and October 5, 1948, WFMR, box 868, book 10; and *SCDP*, September 3, 1948; September, 20 1948.

61. Local 890 executive board minutes, September 22 and September 28, 1948, WFMR, box 868, book 10.

62. *SCDP*, May 11, 1948.

63. Ibid.

64. *SCDP*, June 9, 1948.

65. These figures are from *SCDP*, November 4, 1948, and presumably reflect local reportage. Strangely, an Associated Press report on congressional races (also published in this issue of *SCDP*) showed a much higher number of voters for Provencio (423) and Jencks (585), while the Associated Press report on state races (published in *SCDP*, November 5, 1948) did not even mention Chacón or Luján.

66. Wallace activists had also worked the year before through another organization with national aspirations, the Committee to Organize the Mexican People (COMP), whose executive secretary, Isabel Gonzales, organized the Wallace campaign among Mexican Americans and later worked with the Asociación Nacional Mexicana Americana, discussed below. COMP operated out of the same Denver building that housed Mine-Mill's international, and local COMP committees in July 1947 were clearly tied to Mine-Mill strongholds in Arizona, El Paso, and Grant County. Mine-Mill officers, in fact, constituted almost all of these committees; Albert Muñoz and Arturo López, Mine-Mill activists in Santa Rita, led New Mexico's only chapter. The strongest committees were in Denver, Pueblo, and Lafayette, Colorado; they drew on Mine-Mill support and ventured into agricultural areas, advocating labor legislation to improve the work and living conditions of sugar beet workers. See Committee for Organizing the Mexican People, Local Committees as of July 1, 1947, and Isabel Gonzales to Albert Muñoz, August 29, 1947, WFMR, box 870, folder 27. The overlapping of membership across organizations suggests both the continuing interest in ethnically based organizations and the difficulties in sustaining them over time. According to historian Mario T. García (*Mexican Americans*, 200), the Wallace campaign had brought together many leftist Mexican Americans in the Southwest; gathered in El Paso for a conference of "Amigos de Wallace" chapters in October 1948, they decided to reconvene later in order to create a permanent national organization. The story of COMP suggests an earlier set of connections.

67. This example of Mexican Americans running for political office may have encouraged Frank Romero, a small businessman in Central, to challenge incumbent mayor H. L. Barnett in 1952. Romero won that election but probably

regretted it the following year, when he was forced to mediate between the *Salt of the Earth* crew and local Anglos—Barnett included—who were seeking to drive the film crew away.

68. *SCDP*, May 26, 1944. Another sign of Morales's standing in Silver City came at the funeral of his sixteen-year-old daughter Dolores. Active pallbearers included Henry Jaramillo and Ray Leon, both Mine-Mill activists; "honorary pallbearers" included former mayor Frank Vesely, Carl Dunifon, and Sixth District Court judge A. W. Marshall. See *SCDP*, July 7, 1951.

69. The actual role of that bloc, though, was complicated. In 1947, Frank Druley secured the backing of Joe V. Morales, Tony Remigio, and Manuel Valdez, all prominent Democrats. Remigio and Valdez accused Druley's opponent, Melvin Porterfield, of having "dictated the election board . . . and [failing] to name a single Spanish American." Perhaps sensing that their support for Druley could backfire if perceived as part of a quid pro quo, Morales took pains to deny "that Spanish-speaking voters were promised a town clerk of their own race, a fire station on Chihuahua hill, manned by Spanish-Americans, and . . . that Mr. Druley had denied service to native people at his restaurant" (*SCDP*, March 28, 1947). Morales's disclaimer suggests, first, that Mexican Americans were quite interested in filling political posts from which they were apparently excluded and, second, that this kind of political horse trading might push some Anglo supporters away from Druley. In any case, Porterfield won the election. In 1951, Hal Hammack won the mayoral race in Silver City with the help of the "Spanish-speaking vote," although, again, the actual role of this vote is hard to assess. Some Mexican Americans may have been lured to Hammack's side by his advertisement in Spanish, featuring the endorsement of nineteen Mexican American men who declared Hammack "*un hombre justo y honrado [que] no tiene prejuicios*" ("a just and honorable man who has no prejudices").

70. Lorenzo Torrez, interview by author.

71. Mine-Mill activists and other progressives formed ANMA at a meeting in Phoenix in February 1949, timed to coincide with President Lincoln's birthday. It was most active in California, New Mexico, Colorado, Arizona, and El Paso, Texas.

72. For information on ANMA, see Urrutia, "Offspring of Discontent," and Mario T. García, *Memories of Chicano History*, 169–93, and *Mexican Americans*, 199–227.

73. *La Voz de ANMA* (Denver), October 1951, WFMR, box 206, folder 11; *The* [Mine-Mill] *Union*, February 25, 1952, 6, WFMR, box 324, folder 17; and C. D. Smothermon to Ernesto Velásquez, February 28, 1952, WFMR, box 867, folder 1. Mine-Mill's support for the boycott angered some auxiliary members in other parts of the country. Mrs. Charles Wadenklee of Avenel, New Jersey, wrote to the union's newspaper, "If the National Association of Mexican-Americans are so narrow minded that they can't take a little good natured kidding they shouldn't

tag the name Americans to the end of their name. Judy Canova also kids the hill-billy Americans and they aren't screaming for revenge. Don't the Mexican-Americans have any sense of humor at all?" Annie Petek of Helena, Montana, wrote a similar letter. See The [Mine-Mill] Union, February 25, 1952, 6.

74. See Garcilazo, "McCarthyism." Bert Corona remembers, by contrast, that the Left worked only on behalf of European Americans, not Latinos, in the deportation cases of the late 1940s and early 1950s. See Mario T. García, Memories of Chicano History, 119.

75. A Reuben [sic] Arzola was hired as a trackman at Kennecott on February 25, 1947; he does not appear on the 1949 employee list. A Felipe Arzola was later one of the Empire Zinc strikers.

76. ANMA, "Abusos e Injusticia Contra los de Origen Mexicano" (1949), 4, WFMR, box 294, folder 13.

77. SCDP, May 2, 1949. Interior quote is McDonald's. A Guadalupe Rodrí-guez was a machine miner at Empire Zinc in 1946.

78. SCDP, May 5, 1949.

79. Notes on Fierro Defense, n.d., WFMR, box 873, envelope 2.

80. SCDP, May 5, 1949.

81. Ibid.

82. ANMA, "Abusos e Injusticia," 6.

83. Arturo Flores, open letter, June 1, 1949, WFMR, box 873, envelope 3. It is interesting that Flores, who often went by "Art" or "Arthur," identified himself as "Arturo" in all ANMA business.

84. Lorenzo Torrez estimated ANMA membership by that point at about fifty, although they did not meet regularly. Art Flores, who at that time was working in El Paso, still got bundles of fifty copies each of El Progreso, ANMA's newspaper, for February through June 1953. See Alfonso Sena to Arturo Flores, August 12, 1953, WFMR, box 867, folder 5; and Lorenzo Torrez, interview by author.

85. Handwritten notes, [January 1953], WFMR, box 119, "Salt of the Earth" folder.

86. For more on ANMA in California, see Mario T. García, Memories of Chicano History.

87. Lorenzo Torrez, interview by author.

88. Ibid.

89. New Mexico's founding convention of ANMA welcomed the Grant County unemployed caravan to Albuquerque, and its delegates sent its new state executive secretary, Alfredo Montoya, "to consult with high state officials on the unemployed situation." The state association suggested that Grant County's miners look for work in Carlsbad, another Mine-Mill stronghold but one in which only 100 of the 2,000 potash miners were Mexican; ANMA planned to connect the issue of unemployment with that of discrimination against Mexicans.

See Alfredo C. Montoya, executive secretary of ANMA, to Governor Thomas J. Mabry, September 2, 1949, and minutes, Junta de la Mesa Directiva de ANMA, September 4, 1949, Albuquerque, WFMR, box 870, "Unemployed" folder.

90. Minutes, Junta de la Mesa Directiva de ANMA, September 4, 1949. Torrez also mentioned efforts to desegregate swimming pools and movie theaters, but it is unclear from the context if he was speaking of Grant County's chapter or of ANMA in general. See Lorenzo Torrez, interview by author.

91. See J. D., "On Chauvinism against the Mexican-American People"; and Burnhill, "Mexican-American Question"; "Mexican-Americans"; and "Plight and Struggles."

92. Burnhill, "Mexican-American Question," 53.

93. Tenayuca and Brooks, "Mexican American Question."

94. The United Farm Workers of America (UFW) is perhaps the best example of Chicano labor organizing around families; the UFW differed from Mine-Mill in that the industry employed families to perform agricultural work. As Margaret Rose shows, the UFW's family-based organizing benefited many farmworkers, but the divisions of labor were nonetheless gendered in ways that kept most women from direct leadership. See Rose, "From the Fields to the Picket Lines," 272, and "Women in the United Farm Workers."

95. Clinton Jencks, interview by author.

96. See critique of the Equal Rights Amendment in Cowl, "Struggle for Equal Rights for Women."

97. Cobble, *Other Women's Movement.*

98. Engels provided the theoretical base for other Communist considerations of women's status. One guide to discussing the Woman Question added to Engels some examples from the American experience, among them that "the oppression of Negro women is in many ways *qualitatively* different from that of white women, not merely quantitatively more intense" (Epstein and Wilkerson, *Questions and Answers on the Woman Question*, emphasis in the original).

99. Inman, *In Woman's Defense.*

100. See Dancis, "Socialist Women in the United States," 92; Baker, "Women Working for the Cooperative Commonwealth"; and Couturier, "'Women's Women.'"

101. Baxandall, "Question Seldom Asked," 156–57. Kate Weigand, studying Communist women after World War II, criticizes Baxandall for declaring that the party expelled Inman. Weigand found evidence that Inman herself spread the story that she was expelled in order to attack the party and to shore up her own credentials as an independent scholar. Weigand uses this episode, in fact, as part of her larger point that the CP was at least the source, if not the site, of a great deal of feminist discussion. See Weigand, *Red Feminism*, 28–45.

102. On the influence of such casual discussions, see Baxandall, "Question Seldom Asked," 159. The voices of some female midlevel leaders also come through in a 1950 *Daily People's World* article by Elizabeth Gurley Flynn, one of

the few high-ranking women in the CP. These women complained about the resistance they encountered from their husbands and about the assumption that their political lives were subordinate to their family lives. See Flynn, "What Do Communist Women Talk About?"

103. Millard, *Woman against Myth*, 21.

104. Swerdlow, "Congress of American Women," and Alonso, "Mayhem and Moderation." The attorney general listed the CAW as a "subversive organization" in 1948, and in 1950 the Justice Department demanded that CAW register with the state as a foreign agent. Rather than risk prison and fines, the CAW disbanded in 1950.

105. Historians Linn Shapiro and Kate Weigand have explored this area of Left and women's history most thoroughly. See Shapiro, "Red Feminism," and Weigand, "Vanguards of Women's Liberation" and *Red Feminism*.

106. Virginia Chacón, interview by author.

107. Local 890 executive board minutes, February 25, 1948, WFMR, box 868, book 10.

108. *Mine-Mill Conv. Proc.* (1936), 54–59, 182–83. The Chino locals did not attend this convention because Chino was still shut down.

109. Ora Valentine, chairman, "Report of the Continuations Committee of the Auxiliaries of the International Union of Mine, Mill and Smelter Workers," *Mine-Mill Conv. Proc.* (1941), 415. In 1940, Valentine attended a national CIO convention of auxiliaries where she discovered that women in auxiliaries of the United Mine Workers, the American Newspaper Guild, and the United Auto Workers "had been working years to accomplish this and as yet had not been successful" (ibid.).

110. Ibid., 413–16.

111. Garfield Ladies Auxiliary No. 59, Resolution No. 303, *Mine-Mill Conv. Proc.* (1941), 287. Mine-Mill had helped establish the Committee on Industrial Organization in 1935 within the American Federation of Labor, and the following year it and other founding organizations broke from the AFL to form the CIO.

112. *Mine-Mill Conv. Proc.* (1940), 372.

113. Mercier, *Anaconda*, 148–49.

114. Maurice Travis to Ladies Auxiliaries, December 9, 1947, WFMR, box 126.

115. Mercier, *Anaconda*, 148–49. Mercedes Steedman ("Godless Communists and Faithful Wives)" finds a similar crisis in the 1958 International Nickel Company strike in Sudbury, Ontario. Mine-Mill's uneven integration of women into the union community, the hardship caused by the strike, and, especially, a powerful anticommunist campaign by the Catholic Church divided strikers' wives and weakened the union.

116. Cargill, "Empire and Opposition" (1983), 203.

117. Vorse's observations are discussed in Yeghissian, "Emergence of the Red Berets," 1–2. In *Women, Community, and the Hormel Strike*, Neala Schleun-

ing shows a continuum of women's actions in the Hormel strike, ranging from the traditional to the militant, with an increase of the latter over time. Lynda Ann Ewen sees women's actions on their own behalf gradually spilling over into "larger goals"; in 1973–74, the Brookside Women's Club in Harlan County, Kentucky, started to help other pickets besides the coal miners' and "developed into a self-conscious women's organization committed to broader struggle for better living conditions" (Ewen, *Which Side Are You On?*, 54).

118. Aulette and Mills, "Something Old, Something New," 254–55.

119. In her otherwise excellent study, Schleuning (*Women, Community, and the Hormel Strike*) takes as a given a sharp, palpable divide between public and private spheres. Only against this backdrop does she perceive the significance of women's development into political activists. While it does make the changes over time stand out, this premise is faulty: many of the women in the support group had themselves worked at Hormel. Similarly, Yeghissian's analysis (in "Emergence of the Red Berets") of the Women's Emergency Brigade and Women's Auxiliary during the 1937 Flint sit-down strike rests on the premise of isolated, apolitical wives, sisters, and daughters who probably unwittingly helped General Motors through their ignorance of trade union principles. The strike, then, forged these women into new, militant, class-conscious viragoes. Yet her evidence erodes this model, as more and more of the women turn out to have been political activists prior to the strike.

120. Schofield, " 'Army of Amazons,' " 691.

121. Murray, "A la jonction du mouvement ouvrier et du mouvement des femmes," 15–16.

122. Temma Kaplan's 1982 article on Barcelona food rioters, "Female Consciousness and Collective Action," has been enormously influential. Traces of her basic argument can be found in most historical accounts of working-class women's activism.

123. Ewen, *Which Side Are You On?*, 48.

124. Cameron, *Radicals of the Worst Sort*, 5.

125. Baker, "Women in the Ludlow Strike." I disagree with Priscilla Long's interpretation of the Ludlow strike. Long suggests that wives developed class consciousness out of their relationships with their husbands; a woman's "consciousness was that of a miner's *wife*; her experience of class oppression was a particularly female one." She hints at but does not fully explore those aspects of company town life that affected women as workers. See Long, "Women of the Colorado Fuel and Iron Strike," 81, emphasis in the original.

126. Murray, "A la jonction du mouvement ouvrier et du mouvement des femmes."

127. *Union Worker*, January 1951.

128. Virginia Chacón, interview by author. Clinton Jencks confirmed that no one approached Cipriano Montoya about his abusiveness. See Clinton Jencks, interview by author.

CHAPTER FIVE

1. Dolores Jiménez, interview by author and Sam Sills.

2. Daría Chávez, interview by author, and Anita Torrez, interview by author.

3. Dolores Jiménez, interview by author and Sam Sills.

4. Virginia Chacón, interview by author.

5. Henrietta Williams, OHALC interview.

6. *SCDP*, June 13, 1951.

7. Ibid.

8. For an arrest warrant issued June 15, Anglos Blaine and Hartless could not name the three women charged with assault and battery; Jesús Avalos, by contrast, named three women: Daría Chávez, Anita Torrez, and Eva Becerra. See ibid.

9. Betty Jo [Hartless] Matthews, interview by author; *SCDP*, May 24, 1949.

10. Letter to the editor from Mrs. C. O. Hartless, *SCDP*, July 11, 1951.

11. For Franco, see obituary of his mother-in-law, Domitila Morales, *SCDP*, March 29, 1939. For Avalos, see Local 890 minutes, May 17, 1951, WFMR, box 868, book 9.

12. Local 890 minutes, June 14, 1951, WFMR, box 868, book 9. The picketers allowed salaried employees (management and office staff) and traffic to pass. The company said that "some employees managed to get thru [*sic*]," a claim that the women dismissed. See *SCDP*, June 13, 1951; June 14, 1951.

13. *SCDP*, June 15, 1951.

14. These ideas owe much to Kateri Carmola and Michael Rogin.

15. Virginia Chacón, quoted in *Mine-Mill Conv. Proc.* (1951), 63.

16. *El Paso Herald Post*, June 16, 1951.

17. *SCDP*, June 16, 1951.

18. Ibid.

19. *El Paso Herald Post*, June 16, 1951.

20. *New York Times*, June 17, 1951, 26.

21. *SCDP*, June 16, 1951.

22. Lucy Montoya, quoted in *The Union Worker*, June 1951, 3.

23. *New York Times*, June 17, 1951, 26; *SCDP*, June 16, 1951.

24. *New York Times*, June 17, 1951; Virginia Chacón, quoted in *Mine-Mill Conv. Proc.* (1951), 63.

25. *SCDP*, June 18, 1951.

26. Virginia Chacón, quoted in *Mine-Mill Conv. Proc.* (1951), 63.

27. *New York Times*, June 17, 1951.

28. Ibid.

29. *SCDP*, June 18, 1951.

30. *New York Times*, June 17, 1951.

31. Ibid., June 18, 1951.

32. Ibid., June 17, 1951.

33. *People's Daily World*, June 19, 1951.

34. Anita Torrez, "Class Matters," panel at "Salt of the Earth" conference.

35. Anita Torrez, interview by author.

36. *SCDP*, June 18, 1951.

37. Ibid.

38. Ibid. *SCDP*, May 23, 1953, reported that Haugland was elected president of the First Methodist Church's board of stewards. He had joined the Silver City congregation in 1929.

39. *SCDP*, June 21, 1951.

40. Filing record, Case No. 12812, *New Jersey Zinc Co. v. Local 890 of International Union of Mine, Mill and Smelter Workers*, Sixth New Mexico District Court Records, Grant County Courthouse, Silver City, N.M.

41. Lorenzo Torrez, interview by author.

42. *SCDP*, July 12, 1951.

43. Ibid.

44. Grant County marriage records for Patricia Capshaw, book 16, record 7513; and Ross Capshaw, book 16, record 7654, Grant County Courthouse, Silver City, N.M.

45. Bonnie May Capshaw Teckemeyer, interview by author.

46. *SCDP*, July 13, 1951.

47. *SCDP*, July 20, 1951.

48. Elvira Molano, quoted in *SCDP*, July 20, 1951.

49. Tomás Carrillo, comments on panel, "Bringing Salt of the Earth Home."

50. *SCDP*, August 21, 1951.

51. Local 890 press release, August 21, 1951, WFMR, box 873, envelope 1.

52. *SCDP*, August 18, 1951; September 5, 1951.

53. Tomás Carrillo, comments on panel, "Bringing Salt of the Earth Home."

54. *SCDP*, August 23, 1951.

55. Ibid.

56. Local 890 press release, August 23, 1951, WFMR, box 873, envelope 1.

57. Ibid. The *Silver City Daily Press* did not identify the shooter but described the same scene: "He shot about five shots, apparently wildly, during the peak of the fracas." See *SCDP*, August 23, 1951. Local 890 identified him as Denzil Hartless.

58. Local 890 press releases, August 23 and 25, 1951, WFMR, box 873, envelope 1; *SCDP*, August 23, 1951. *SCDP* reported that Agustín Martínez was first treated at the Santa Rita Hospital and then transferred to the Veterans' Administration hospital at Fort Bayard. Yguado was released that day from the hospital, and the other two remained overnight.

59. Local 890, Civil Rights Committee Report, September 20, 1951, WFMR, box 873, envelope 2. Mrs. Clanton was probably the wife of Deputy G. W. Clanton.

60. *SCDP*, August 23, 1951. The three companies were Kennecott (both Santa Rita and Hurley), Peru, and Asarco.

61. Within a few days, Mine-Mill reached a national agreement with Kennecott, but the other companies held out. Coming as it did in the middle of the Korean War, the national strike angered President Truman, who got a Taft-Hartley injunction against Mine-Mill and thirty-one companies on August 30, 1951, on the grounds that the labor dispute threatened national defense. The injunction prohibited both sides from strikes or lockouts. Yet, despite its apparent evenhandedness, the injunction affected the two sides unequally. Its net effect was to force Mine-Mill copper members back to work, because the injunction did not force the companies to negotiate. Thus the national copper strike ended in victory for the companies. Nevertheless, because the Taft-Hartley injunction concerned only the national copper strike, it had no effect on the Empire Zinc strike, which continued to drag on.

62. Anita Torrez, letter to editor, *SCDP*, June 16, 1951.

63. Local 890 press release, August 10, 1951, WFMR, box 873, envelope 1.

64. Local 890 press release, July 27, 1951, WFMR, box 873, envelope 1.

65. *SCDP*, July 21, 1951.

66. Ibid.

67. Ibid., parenthetical note in original.

68. *SCDP*, August 8, 1951.

69. Ibid.; Local 890 press release, August 9, 1951, WFMR, box 873, envelope 1. In a letter to New Mexico attorney general Joe L. Martínez, detailing all of the union's complaints about local law enforcement, Local 890 clarified that it was Assistant District Attorney Vincent Vesely who had charged the Juárezes with contributing to juvenile delinquency and that the case would be heard in juvenile court on September 18, 1951. I found no report of this proceeding in the local newspaper. See Cipriano Montoya and Ernesto Velásquez to Joe L. Martínez, September 15, 1951, WFMR, box 873, envelope 1.

70. No one recorded the hearings, but charges were published in the local newspaper.

71. The one woman justice I found was Mrs. J. J. Umscheid. She was appointed justice of the peace in Bayard to finish the term of her husband, who had died, and was later elected to the office in her own right.

72. Jack Miles, another Mine-Mill member, ran for the office and was endorsed by the Mine-Mill locals in 1944.

73. I have not determined exactly how Brewington was denied jurisdiction. In the case of charges against strikebreaker Grant Blaine, Brewington initially heard the complaint but when the ruling was recorded the following month it was in Andrew Haugland's court. A union letter to New Mexico attorney general Joe L. Martínez mentioned that "Mosely and Capshaw succeeded in disqualifying Brewington, a striker, and moving the case to Haugland's JP court." See Cipriano Montoya and Ernesto Velásquez to Joe L. Martínez, September 15, 1951, WFMR, box 873, envelope 1.

74. Ibid.

75. James Woolman eloquently makes this point in "Rough Draft for a New Cold War," which builds on C. Wright Mills's *Power Elite*.

76. *SCDP*, July 23, 1951.

77. Ibid.

78. *SCDP*, July 21, 1951.

79. Local 890 press release, July 24, 1951, WFMR, box 873, envelope 1; C. B. Ogás, interview by author.

80. *SCDP*, July 24, 1951.

81. *SCDP*, June 21, 1951.

82. *SCDP*, July 24, 1951.

83. Local 890 press release, July 24, 1951.

84. Local 890 telegram to Governor Mechem, July 25, 1951, Dennis Chávez Papers, box 208, folder 9, CSR.

85. Daría Chávez, letter to editor, *SCDP*, June 16, 1951.

86. Local 890 press release, August 22, 1951, WFMR, box 873, envelope 1.

87. Judge Charles D. Fowler, quoted in Local 890 press release, August 30, 1951, WFMR, box 873, envelope 1.

88. Local 890 minutes, August 22, 1951, WFMR, box 868, book 9.

89. Ibid.

90. Senator James Murray, Washington, to John Clark, Denver, June 25, 1951, WFMR, box 294, folder 1.

91. Stephenson, "Use of Troops in Labor Disputes in New Mexico," analyzes conflicts in 1919, 1922, 1927, and 1933 and concludes that in each instance troops were sent to break the strike rather than to restore order.

92. *SCDP*, August 11, 1951.

93. The *Silver City Daily Press* did not print the resolution when it was passed on June 25, 1951, but did so on July 20, 1951.

94. Gertrude Gibney, letter to the editor, *SCDP*, July 20, 1951.

95. Resolution of Central businesspeople, printed in *SCDP*, July 20, 1951.

96. Sullivan earned enough respect from Local 890 members that, five years later, the union declined to endorse for county sheriff one of its own officers, Gregorio Mesa, because Fred Sullivan was also in the race: "For sheriff our local has taken the position of not sponsoring a candidate, being that there are two candidates which our union approves of which will cause anamosity [*sic*] among our ranks" (Local 890 executive board minutes, February 12, 1956, WFMR, box 869).

97. Local 890 press release, September 21, 1951, WFMR, box 873, envelope 1.

98. 1930 manuscript census.

99. Local 890 press release, September 21, 1951.

100. Local 890 press release, October 12, 1951, WFMR, box 873, envelope 1. *SCDP* also reported that Father Smerke was holding a special mass, though the paper did not include the word "successful." Women apparently requested the mass of Father Smerke. See *SCDP*, October 13, 1951.

101. This section is based on my interview with Mr. Ogás.

102. Here Ogás could have been mixing up a couple of incidents, because I never found corroboration for this anecdote. He could have linked the widely publicized presence of Braulia Velásquez's six-week-old child in jail to Rachel Juárez's injury by Mosely's car.

103. *SCDP*, September 13, 1951.

104. Local 890 press release, September 29, 1951, WFMR, box 873, envelope 1.

105. *SCDP*, September 12, 1951.

106. Local 890 press release, September 29, 1951.

107. *SCDP*, September 12, 1951.

108. *SCDP*, September 27, 1951.

109. Virginia Chacón, interview by author; Local 890 press release, September 29, 1951; *SCDP*, September 27, 1951. Virginia Jencks was fined $40 and court costs. Justice of the Peace Andrew Haugland "said he would 'withhold judgment on a jail sentence for good behavior in the future.'" See *SCDP*, September 27, 1951.

110. Mrs. C. O. [Mary] Hartless, letter to the editor, *SCDP*, July 11, 1951. Her son, she said, had been drafted and was only trying to make some money before he got his final orders.

111. Betty Jo [Hartless] Matthews, interview by author.

· 112. Mrs. C. O. Hartless, letter to editor.

113. Betty Jo [Hartless] Matthews, interview by author.

114. Ibid.

115. Conversation with Juanita Escobedo, May 22, 2001, Silver City, N.M.

116. Cecilia Rodríguez Pino, "Children of Salt," panel at "Bringing Salt of the Earth Home."

117. *SCDP*, August 23, 1951.

118. Ibid.

119. *SCDP*, October 13, 1951; October 14, 1951; October 26, 1951; Ernesto Velásquez, open letter to business and professional people in Grant County, November 3, 1951, WFMR, box 873, envelope 1.

120. *SCDP*, September 20, 1951.

121. *SCDP*, September 25, 1951.

122. *Bayard Journal*, May 25, 1950.

123. *SCDP*, October 2, 1951; October 3, 1951.

124. Charles J. Smith, letter to the editor, *SCDP*, September 25, 1951.

125. Cargill, "Empire and Opposition" (1983), 235.

126. Ruiz, *Cannery Women, Cannery Lives*, 103–13.

127. Mercier, *Anaconda*, 149–64.

128. The Steelworkers were more successful in the 1960s, after years of government and CIO harassment had so weakened Mine-Mill that it could no longer work effectively on behalf of its members and the Steelworkers could argue

that it offered better economic benefits to workers. See Jensen, *Nonferrous Metals Industry Unionism*, and Keitel, "Merger."

129. Local 890 press release, October 5, 1951, WFMR, box 873, envelope 1. The reference to Mine-Mill organizing the area must have referred more specifically to amalgamation in 1947, since Mine-Mill was the only union to have organized Asarco.

130. Ibid.

131. Virginia Chacón, interview by author.

132. *SCDP*, July 18, 1951. In this respect, union opponents behaved as had white Cuban nationalists upon hearing Afro-Cuban complaints of discrimination early in the twentieth century. Armed with a color-blind ideology, white Cubans accused Afro-Cubans of racism when the latter tried to draw attention to patterns of political discrimination. See Rebecca J. Scott, "Fault Lines, Color Lines," 101–3.

133. Lupe Elizado, letter to the editor, *SCDP*, July 16, 1951.

134. Mrs. Tex Williams, letter to the editor, *SCDP*, June 29, 1951.

135. Lupe Elizado, letter to the editor.

136. As historian Nancie L. González observed in the 1960s, "Not only are persons in [the working] class more tolerant of recent immigrants from Mexico, but they object less to the term 'Mexican-American' when applied to themselves. They recognize the obvious cultural similarities between themselves and those south of the border, and they respect the modern Mexican nation. They are also becoming aware that they share a minority-group status with Mexican-American populations elsewhere—particularly in California and Texas" (González, *Spanish Americans of New Mexico*, 82).

137. Cargill, "Empire and Opposition" (1983), 237.

138. Bob Hollowwa to Local 890, March 3, 1952; Hollowwa to Cipriano Montoya, April 23, 1952, WFMR, box 867, folder 1.

139. Cargill, "Empire and Opposition" (1983), 263 n.

140. Local 890 minutes, September 19, 1951, WFMR, box 868, book 9. The minutes say "July 19," but the content concerns later events.

141. Telegram from Auxiliary 209 to John Clark, September 29, 1951, WFMR, box 294, folder 13.

142. The women's challenge took place at the same time that Mexican American unionists were demanding a place on the international executive board. See Chapter 3.

143. Frank, "Housewives, Socialists," 256.

144. Local 890 minutes, January 24, 1952, WFMR, box 868, book 9.

145. *SCDP*, September 12, 1951.

146. Clinton Jencks, interview by Sam Sills. In the contract discussion on January 24, Fred Barreras described an upcoming "trip to San Lorenzo on a pilgrimage[,] where all the Empire Zinc strikers will feel [part of an] honorable union with a clean heart and conscience" (Local 890 minutes, January 24, 1952).

147. Ernesto Velásquez raised $20,280, and the international posted $27,600 in its own behalf. $27,600 came from friends in northern New Mexico: Craig and Jenny Vincent, who owned the ranch where Clinton and Virginia Jencks met up with blacklisted Hollywood filmmakers and discussed producing a feature film about the Empire Zinc strike. (See Chapter 7.) See Local 890 press release, March 19, 1952, WFMR, box 873, envelope 1.

148. Ibid.

149. Local 890 press release, September 9, 1952, WFMR, box 873, envelope 1.

150. Torres had been a temporary constable in Hanover, but Sheriff Goforth fired him in August 1951 for "failing to do his duty" (*SCDP*, May 7, 1952).

CHAPTER SIX

1. Aurora Chávez, interview by author.

2. *Union Worker*, January 1951.

3. Aurora Chávez, interview by author.

4. Conversation with Rachel Juárez Valencia, May 7, 2004, Bayard, N.M.

5. Angel Bustos, quoted in *Mine-Mill Conv. Proc.* (1953), 30.

6. Guillermo "Willie" Andazola, interview by author.

7. Local 890 minutes, June 14, 1951, WFMR, box 868, book 9.

8. Local 890 minutes, October 17, 1951, WFMR, box 868, book 9.

9. See Ulrich, *Good Wives.*

10. See Gordon, *Heroes of Their Own Lives*, v–vi, and Boydston, *Home and Work*, 135.

11. As Patricia Zavella has shown for contemporary Chicana cannery workers, "The decision for a woman to seek work was critical and subject to negotiation between husband and wife" (Zavella, *Women's Work and Chicano Families*, 98).

12. Dolores Jiménez, interview by author and Sam Sills.

13. Daría Chávez, interview by author.

14. Josephine and Arturo Flores, interview by author.

15. Census statistics inform us of sex segregation but not ethnic segregation. I relied on qualitative sources, such as oral history interviews and references to women's work in the local newspapers, to get a sense of ethnic differences in occupations. For information on census classifications, see Bureau of the Census, *Two Hundred Years of Census Taking.*

16. Dora Gutiérrez Madero, interview by author; Alice Sandoval, interview by author.

17. Virginia Chacón, interview by author.

18. Grant County had an unusually large number of automobiles beginning after World War II—3,284 in 1947, in a population of roughly 20,000—but this does not mean that they were available for women to take to work. See Bureau of

the Census, *Statistical Abstract Supplement,* Items 32–33. Parrish Stage Lines ran buses from Silver City to the distant towns of Deming, Lordsburg, and Hot Springs. But these buses could hardly have served commuters from the nearby mining towns to Silver City, because even though they stopped in these towns, they would get a passenger to Silver City no earlier than 11:30 A.M. See ad for Parrish Stage Lines, *SCDP,* June 12, 1948.

19. Bureau of the Census, *Sixteenth Census, 1940,* table 23, 990; Bureau of the Census, *Seventeenth Census, 1950,* table 43. These figures describe the labor force before and after World War II and cannot, therefore, delineate wartime trends, but they do suggest that even the postwar adjustments did not return women's labor force participation rates to their prewar levels. Nor can we attribute the increase in women's labor force participation over that decade simply to the higher unemployment levels of 1940, a depression year, because the census category of "labor force" includes unemployed workers seeking work. The census definition of unemployment poses some interpretive difficulties for women's labor force participation rates: those people discouraged from looking for work do not appear in these statistics, and it is easy to imagine that women might fall into the category of discouraged potential employees. See Blau and Ferber, *Economics of Women, Men, and Work,* 281–82.

20. Bureau of the Census, *Sixteenth Census,* table 23, 990; Bureau of the Census, *Seventeenth Census,* table 43.

21. Bureau of the Census, *Sixteenth Census,* table 23, 990; Bureau of the Census, *Seventeenth Census,* table 43.

22. Bureau of the Census, *Fifteenth Census, 1930. Population,* did not break down county employment figures by sex, so I counted (in the manuscript census) those women employed in three towns: Santa Rita, Hanover, and Central. That year the Census Bureau added "Mexican" to the category of "race or color." Across the three towns, Mexican women were much more likely to work in service jobs and Anglos were much more likely to work in professions; paid manual labor outside the service sector was uncommon for both groups.

23. Position roster, Santa Rita, July 13, 1944, WFMR, box 864, folder 4. Ten additional women worked at Santa Rita that year, seven as laborers in other departments, and three as janitresses. Women entered mines, mills, and smelters elsewhere in the country during World War II but never to the same extent as in other defense industries. Laurie Mercier argues that "a sixty-year tradition of an exclusively male industry" in Anaconda, Montana, kept down the numbers of women smelter workers there, as did the fears of postwar unemployment in the copper industry, "which had been declining except during the war boom" (Mercier, *Anaconda,* 72–73). Anaconda Copper and Mine-Mill Local 117 agreed that women smelter employees "had to be Anaconda residents, wives of former smelter workers . . . , and with children or parents to support. Both company and union believed that local women, steeped in the culture that favored male breadwinners, would obligingly return to a prewar economic and social order after the [war]." The women workers were laid off early in 1946. See ibid., 67–68, 73.

24. Huggard, "Environmental and Economic Change," 157.

25. Dora Gutiérrez Madero, interview by author.

26. Ibid.

27. Santa Rita seniority list, Kennecott Corporation, June 1944, WFMR, box 866, folder 4.

28. Lacking seniority lists or other documentation, I cannot determine the jobs that the other women held.

29. Kirker was identified incorrectly as "Corinne Kirker" in the *Silver City Daily Press* article that lauded her mine work. See *SCDP*, December 4, 1942; and Local 604 membership day book, WFMR, box 866.

30. Huggard, "Environmental and Economic Change," 157.

31. Bureau of the Census, *Seventeenth Census*, table 23.

32. 64 percent of all adult women kept house in Grant County in 1940; 61 percent did so in 1950. The percentage of adult women keeping house is even higher when we exclude employed women: 78 percent of all adult women who did not belong to the labor force kept house in 1940 and in 1950. See Bureau of the Census, *Sixteenth Census*, table 23, and Bureau of the Census, *Seventeenth Census*, table 43.

33. *SCDP*, February 15, 1950.

34. Only nineteen men kept house in 1940, a number representing less than 1 percent of all adult men and just over 1 percent of those men who did not belong to the labor force. In other words, almost 99 percent of the men who were not in the labor force—perhaps because they were unemployed, or because they were unemployable due to disability or age—did not take up housework in place of paid work. This number more than doubled by 1950, but it still represented a tiny proportion of adult men. See Bureau of the Census, *Sixteenth Census*, table 23, and Bureau of the Census, *Seventeenth Census*, table 43.

35. See Jameson, "Imperfect Unions," and Kaplan, "Female Consciousness and Collective Action," for analyses of women's potentially contradictory experiences in this kind of moral economy.

36. See Boydston, *Home and Work*, 130–35, for calculations of the cash value of women's unpaid work in the antebellum Northeast.

37. U.S. Department of Labor, Women's Bureau, *Home Environment*, 16–17.

38. Alice Sandoval, interview by author.

39. Bill Wood, interview by author.

40. See advertisement in the *Bayard Journal*, December 21, 1950, and notice in Local 890's *Union Worker*, January 1952, for reference to Ynostroza's business. The 1950 ad announced that the factory would "be open all day December 23 and 24 to grind masa at any time," suggesting that women took the masa home and made the tortillas themselves.

41. Cowan, *More Work for Mother*, 86.

42. Virginia Chacón, interview by author. Some individuals delivered water for a fee, as Juan L. Vera did in Central. See *SCDP*, May 22, 1951; May 23, 1951.

43. Cowan, *More Work for Mother*, 87.

44. Ibid.

45. Bill Wood, interview by author.

46. C. B. Ogás, interview by author. This was true of Alice Sandoval's Santa Rita neighborhood. See Alice Sandoval, interview by author.

47. Matías Rivera, interview by author.

48. Bureau of the Census, *County and City Data Book 1952*, table 3.

49. Michael Wilson, *Salt of the Earth*, 17.

50. *Bayard Journal*, February 8, 1951; February 12, 1951.

51. Ibid., November 9, 1951.

52. Ibid., August 24, 1950.

53. Cowan, *More Work for Mother*, 93; Matías Rivera, interview by author; Aurora Chávez, interview by author. The percentage of residences wired for electricity grew from 8 in 1907 to almost 35 in 1920.

54. Cowan, *More Work for Mother*, 94.

55. Anita and Lorenzo Torrez, interview by author.

56. Albert H. Vigil, interview by author.

57. "Prices, Costs and Standards of Living," *Monthly Labor Review* 61 (December 1945): 1220–21.

58. Matías Rivera, interview by author; Bill Wood, interview by author; Ramirez, *Remembering Fierro*, 26. Note the importance here of children's labor, which merits considerably more discussion than is possible here.

59. Mining affected housecleaning, too. As Josephine Flores recalled, every blast at Chino made bits of sand and cement trickle down the walls of their home in Santa Rita. See Josephine Flores, interview by author.

60. Matías Rivera, interview by author.

61. Bill Wood, interview by author.

62. Elvira Acuña Ogás, interview by author; Arturo Flores, interview by author. Ogás grew up in Tyrone and appreciated the houses that Phelps-Dodge built there. Flores stated that Santa Rita's company housing was segregated in terms of quality, as well as in location: the Anglos had all the plumbing.

63. Clark, "Architecture and Town Development," 51.

64. Ibid., 120–21.

65. *SCDP*, April 14, 1944; December 11, 1946.

66. *SCDP*, July 17, 1948.

67. De Luna, "The Mexican American," 3.

68. Virginia Chacón, interview by author.

69. Anita and Lorenzo Torrez, interview by author; Elena and Raymundo Tafoya, interview by author; Clinton Jencks, interview by author.

70. *SCDP*, April 5, 1951.

71. Michael Wilson, *Salt of the Earth*, 17.

72. Envelopes of canceled checks, Locals 63, 69, 530, and 890, WFMR, boxes 864, 865, 866, and 884. The *SCDP*, reporting on a "record pay day" at Nevada Consolidated during the war, commented that most employees "immediately cash their checks either at the [mining] camps or at mercantile establishments

there and elsewhere in the course of shopping or payment of personal accounts. The enormous payrolls at the mines are largely spent right here in Silver City and other communities of Grant County" (*SCDP*, June 25, 1942).

73. *SCDP*, October 11, 1943.

74. Ernesto Velásquez, quoted in *Mine-Mill Conv. Proc.* (1951), 68.

75. The Santa Rita Store Company, Kennecott's company store, was used 230 times to cash checks drawn on the union's account between 1945 and 1948, more than any other single store in the period. Other local retail stores were used 268 times, and grocery stores and banks 96 times each. See envelopes of canceled checks, Locals 63, 69, 530, and 890, WFMR, boxes 864, 865, 866, and 884.

76. Elena Tafoya, interview by author; Matías Rivera, interview by author. See also Martín, *Songs My Mother Sang to Me*; Ruiz, *From Out of the Shadows*; Goldman, *Gold Diggers and Silver Miners*; and Jameson, *All That Glitters*.

77. *SCDP*, September 14, 1943; December 20, 1944; September 3, 1946; December 18, 1946; August 12, 1948; August 11, 1949.

78. *SCDP*, November 7, 1946; December 4, 1946.

79. *SCDP*, November 7, 1946; November 15, 1946; November 29, 1946. This estimate is based on impressionistic evidence.

80. Dolores Jiménez, interview by author and Sam Sills.

81. *SCDP*, April 19, 1947; September 11, 1947; May 20, 1948; August 6, 1948; August 10, 1948; September 9, 1948.

82. Dolores Jiménez, interview by author and Sam Sills.

83. *SCDP*, May 14, 1948; August 30, 1948. Posting bail for Homer McNutt was Lem Watson, the deputy sheriff later involved in the Fierro case.

84. Comment in "Picket Line Chatter," *The Union Worker*, June 1951, 3.

85. Hollowwa, Jencks, and Montoya to Travis, Clark, Larson, Wilson, Smothermon, and Dolan re: Empire Zinc strike, etc., August 19, 1951, WFMR, box 294, folder 11.

86. Biberman, *Salt of the Earth*, 64.

87. Dolores Jiménez, comments on panel, "Bringing Salt of the Earth Home."

88. Ernesto Velásquez, quoted in Local 890 minutes, October 17, 1951, WFMR, box 868, book 9.

89. Ernesto Velásquez, quoted in *Mine-Mill Conv. Proc.* (1951), 63.

CHAPTER SEVEN

1. Clinton Jencks, interview by Sam Sills.

2. She is still performing, and recently her trio released a CD of New Mexican songs that had been collected by the Works Progress Administration during the Depression.

3. Vincent's biographical information comes from a conversation with her biographer, Craig Smith, October 22, 2004, and from Nott, "Song of Jenny Vincent."

4. Sylvia Jarrico, OHALC interview. The ranch also attracted the attention of

the Federal Bureau of Investigation, and FBI harassment of ranch visitors forced the Vincents to sell the property in 1954.

5. Clinton Jencks, interview by Sam Sills.

6. Deborah Rosenfelt, "Commentary," in Michael Wilson, *Salt of the Earth*, 108; Sylvia Jarrico, OHALC interview.

7. Sylvia Jarrico, OHALC interview.

8. Many of Mine-Mill's national officers already knew the members of Jarrico's film company, Independent Productions Corporation, and the attorneys representing Mine-Mill and IPC—Nathan Witt in New York and Charles Katz in Los Angeles, respectively—were colleagues on a first-name basis.

9. I take this up in Chapter 9.

10. Sylvia Jarrico, OHALC interview.

11. Paul Jarrico, quoted in Rosenfelt, "Commentary," 96.

12. Communist Party organizations on the local level were generally called "clubs" or "cells"; I use "clubs" because "cells" has a tinge of conspiracy to it, and these groups in Hollywood were hardly conspiratorial.

13. Cogley, *Report on Blacklisting*.

14. The term "talent branch" refers to the organizations of people in the arts.

15. Paul Jarrico, interview in McGilligan and Buhle, *Tender Comrades*, 332.

16. Ibid.

17. See Horne, *Class Struggle in Hollywood*, for details on Hollywood unionism.

18. Buhle and Wagner, *Radical Hollywood*, 56.

19. Cogley, *Report on Blacklisting*, 34–35.

20. Sonja Dahl Biberman, quoted in Ceplair and Englund, *Inquisition in Hollywood*, 81.

21. On the Communist Party in the 1930s and 1940s, see Isserman, *Which Side Were You On?*; Brown et al., eds., *New Studies*; Cochran, *Labor and Communism*; Keeran, *Communist Party*; Levenstein, *Communism, Anticommunism, and the CIO*; and Klehr, *Heyday of American Communism*.

22. Transcript of Paul Jarrico's testimony before the House Un-American Activities Committee, April 13, 1951, Washington, D.C., Biberman-Sondergaard Papers, box 53, folder 6, SHSWA.

23. Quoted in Ceplair and Englund, *Inquisition in Hollywood*, 301.

24. Ibid.; transcript of Paul Jarrico's testimony before HUAC. Buhle and Wagner (*Radical Hollywood*, 179) state that Jarrico joined the Young Communist League at UCLA in 1930.

25. Quoted in Ceplair and Englund, *Inquisition in Hollywood*, 179.

26. Sylvia Jarrico, OHALC interview.

27. Ibid. I analyze this periodical in the context of Communist cultural politics in Chapter 8.

28. Ibid.

29. Quoted in Ceplair, "Michael Wilson," 481. His paternal grandfather had

been president of the Southern Baptist Convention. See Buhle and Wagner, *Radical Hollywood*, 226.

30. Michael Wilson's wife, Zelma, was Sylvia Jarrico's sister. She was an architect at a time when that profession included almost no women.

31. Quoted in Ceplair, "Michael Wilson," 481.

32. Ceplair, "Michael Wilson," 481; Buhle and Wagner, *Radical Hollywood*, 227.

33. Ceplair, "Michael Wilson," 481; Buhle and Wagner, *Radical Hollywood*, 227. His wife spent the war years working in a defense plant.

34. Sondergaard, "Artist and Man," 18.

35. On the board of review and its contradictory position as a "censorship organization that opposed censorship," see Budd, "Film Censorship and Public Cultures."

36. Named for its director, Will Hays, who was hired by the MPPDA.

37. Robert Sklar, *Movie-Made America*, 173–74.

38. Randall, "Censorship," 432. In a case involving exhibition of Roberto Rossellini's film *The Miracle*, the Supreme Court held that films were "a significant medium for the communication of ideas" and thus entitled to First Amendment protection. See *Joseph Burstyn, Inc. v. Wilson*, 343 U.S. 495, 501 (1952).

39. Buhle and Wagner, *Radical Hollywood*, 10.

40. Huettig, *Economic Control of the Motion Picture Industry*, 63, 84. United Artists, formed in 1919 by Hollywood stars Mary Pickford, Charlie Chaplin, Douglas Fairbanks, and producer D. W. Griffith, was a distribution company for the films produced by its members.

41. Ibid., 2–6. The studios were forced to divest themselves of movie chains on antitrust grounds following a 1948 Supreme Court decision. See *United States v. Paramount Pictures, Inc.*, 334 U.S. 131 (1948).

42. Donald Ogden Stewart, quoted in Ceplair and Englund, *Inquisition in Hollywood*, 16.

43. Screenwriters tried to organize a labor union in the early 1930s but were effectively stalled by company unions backed by the Academy of Motion Picture Arts and Sciences. The Academy included producers, actors, directors, writers, and technicians, and it projected the image of a unified Hollywood that masked the substantial divisions among groups. But by the end of the decade, talent guilds protected screenwriters, directors, and actors from the most outrageous violations of workers' rights.

44. Michael Wilson earned a credit for a "script contribution" to *It's A Wonderful Life* (1946), although he did a great deal of the work polishing the script; Dalton Trumbo, who became one of the Hollywood Ten, received no credit for his work on the script.

45. Adrian Scott, "You Can't Do That," 327–28.

46. Buhle and Wagner, *Radical Hollywood*, 111–53.

47. Cogley, *Report on Blacklisting*, 11. The Fund for the Republic was a liberal

organization founded by former Yale Law School dean Robert Maynard Hutchins to protect civil liberties.

48. The nineteen were Alvah Bessie, Herbert Biberman, Bertolt Brecht, Lester Cole, Richard Collins, Edward Dmytryk, Gordon Kahn, Howard Koch, Ring Lardner Jr., John Howard Lawson, Albert Maltz, Lewis Milestone, Samuel Ornitz, Larry Parks, Irving Pichel, Robert Rossen, Adrian Scott, Waldo Scott, and Dalton Trumbo. The majority were screenwriters. Parks was an actor, Adrian Scott was a producer, and Biberman, Dmytryk, Milestone, Pichel, and Rossen were directors.

49. Thomas would later be convicted of embezzlement and sentenced to the same prison that housed two of the Hollywood Ten.

50. Quoted in Cogley, *Report on Blacklisting*, 10.

51. Ibid., 11.

52. Herbert Biberman, statement during the second week of HUAC hearings, October 1947, Biberman-Sondergaard Papers, "Speeches—HUAC and Hollywood Ten," box 25, folder 2, SHSWA.

53. Herbert Biberman, prepared statement before the House Un-American Activities Committee, October 1947, Biberman-Sondergaard Papers, "Speeches —HUAC and Hollywood Ten," box 25, folder 2, SHSWA.

54. The Hollywood Ten were Bessie, Biberman, Cole, Dmytryk, Lardner, Lawson, Maltz, Ornitz, Adrian Scott, and Trumbo.

55. *Los Angeles Times*, February 13, 1952, 5.

56. Quoted in Ceplair and Englund, *Inquisition in Hollywood*, 331.

57. Schrecker, *Many Are the Crimes*, xiv–xv.

58. Press release, June 19, 1950, Biberman-Sondergaard Papers, "Speeches— HUAC and Hollywood Ten," box 25, folder 2, SHSWA.

59. Ibid.

60. Quoted in Ceplair and Englund, *Inquisition in Hollywood*, 367.

61. In 1952, Mine-Mill would experience this kind of repression as well, and the following year Clinton Jencks would be convicted of perjuring himself when he signed a Taft-Hartley affidavit in 1950. See Chapter 9.

62. Transcript of Paul Jarrico's testimony before HUAC, April 13, 1951.

63. *Daily People's World*, March 11, 1953, 3.

64. *The Bridge on the River Kwai* won the 1957 Academy Award for best screenplay. The award, however, went to Pierre Boulle, who had written a first version in French. Although Michael Wilson and Carl Foreman, who wrote the English screenplay, received posthumous Oscars in 1984, it took another thirteen years for their names to be restored to the actual screen credits. Wilson also received a posthumous Oscar nomination in 1995 for *Lawrence of Arabia*.

65. Peter Biskind analyzes *On the Waterfront* and other films from the 1950s in *Seeing Is Believing*. See also Victor Navasky's *Naming Names* on Kazan's decision to inform on Communists.

66. Paul Jarrico, quoted in Ceplair and Englund, *Inquisition in Hollywood*, 416–17.

67. Paul Jarrico, commenting in the documentary film *A Crime to Fit the Punishment*.

68. Biberman, *Salt of the Earth*, 31.

69. Independent Productions Corporation, Certificate of Incorporation, September 4, 1951, Biberman-Sondergaard Papers, box 51, folder 11, SHSWA. The board of directors included Lazarus and attorney Katherine Sims.

70. *New York Times*, March 27, 1953.

71. Biberman, *Salt of the Earth*, 32.

72. Maurice Travis informed the Mine-Mill executive board that IPC had $100,000. See memo from Travis to Mine-Mill international executive board, June 23, 1952, Biberman-Sondergaard Papers, box 52, folder 7. When Lazarus appeared before HUAC on March 26, 1953, he stated that IPC had $5,000 in capital stock, which he owned, and another $90,000 in promissory notes from "a lot of people" (*New York Times*, March 27, 1953).

CHAPTER EIGHT

1. Henrietta Williams, OHALC interview.

2. Michael Wilson, quoted in Biberman, *Salt of the Earth*, 38.

3. Henrietta Williams, OHALC interview.

4. Clinton Jencks, OHALC interview.

5. Biberman, *Salt of the Earth*, 39.

6. Ibid.

7. Michael Wilson, "Outline for *The Woman Question*," [December 1951], Biberman-Sondergaard Papers, box 17, folder 5, SHSWA. The lead female character in the draft is named China, possibly referring to the Chino copper mine.

8. Clinton Jencks, OHALC interview.

9. Virginia Chacón, interview by author.

10. Lorenzo Torrez, quoted in Tom Miller, "*Salt of the Earth* Revisited," 32.

11. Tom Miller, "*Salt of the Earth* Revisited," 32.

12. Michael Wilson, quoted in Biberman, *Salt of the Earth*, 40.

13. Maciel, "Los desarraigados," 165–66. According to the movie listings in the *Silver City Daily Press*, movie theaters in Silver City and Santa Rita regularly showed Mexican movies in the 1940s and 1950s, usually one or two a week.

14. Clinton Jencks, OHALC interview.

15. Ibid.

16. Michael Wilson, quoted in Biberman, *Salt of the Earth*, 40–41.

17. Ibid., 40.

18. Virginia Chacón, interview by author; Anita and Lorenzo Torrez, interview by author.

19. Herbert Biberman, report to IPC, [1951], 2, Biberman-Sondergaard Papers, box 17, folder 2, SHSWA.

20. Ibid., 1.

21. Ibid., 2.

22. See Chapter 4 for analysis of the Woman Question in Communist theory and practice.

23. Deborah Rosenfelt, "Commentary," in Michael Wilson, *Salt of the Earth*, 102, 107. Rosenfelt suggests that the Hollywood clubs were more likely than others to discuss the Woman Question and its personal and political dimensions.

24. Ceplair and Englund, *Inquisition in Hollywood*; Wagner and Buhle, *Radical Hollywood* and *Hide in Plain Sight*. The dozens of interviews by Patrick McGilligan and Paul Buhle for *Tender Comrades* confirm this assessment.

25. Quoted in Ceplair and Englund, *Inquisition in Hollywood*, 302.

26. Cogley, *Blacklisting in Hollywood*, 43.

27. Maltz, "What Shall We Ask of the Writers?"

28. Jerome, "Negro in Hollywood Films."

29. Buhle and Wagner, *Radical Hollywood*, 264.

30. Isidor Schneider to Albert Maltz, February 6, 1946, cited in ibid.

31. Buhle and Wagner, *Radical Hollywood*, 265.

32. Biberman, *Salt of the Earth*, 31–32.

33. Quoted in Ceplair and Englund, *Inquisition in Hollywood*, 320.

34. Quoted in ibid., 301.

35. Michael Wilson, speech delivered at "A Salute to John Howard Lawson," November 12, 1955, quoted in ibid., 299.

36. Buhle and Wagner dismiss "democratic humanism" as a politically necessary "smokescreen or evasion" to fend off anticommunist attacks, but I think it was also a means of maneuvering within CP cultural theory.

37. Buhle and Wagner, *Radical Hollywood*, 275–76.

38. Ibid., 282–83.

39. Ibid., 284–86. By contrast, Lary May interprets the wartime collaboration of radicals with the Office of War Information as a sign of capitulation to patriotic imperatives, which ultimately undermined any democratic promise in Hollywood films. See May, *Big Tomorrow*, 141–48.

40. Buhle and Wagner, *Radical Hollywood*, 292–300.

41. Jarrico, "Evil Heroines of 1953."

42. Buhle and Wagner, *Hide in Plain Sight*, 130.

43. Gorman, *Left Intellectuals and Popular Culture*.

44. Ibid., 115–16.

45. Herbert Biberman, Report to IPC, [1951], 2–4.

46. Robin D. G. Kelley discusses this case at length in *Hammer and Hoe*, 78–91. The Supreme Court twice reversed convictions, but only in 1937 did the State of Alabama release five of the men. In the 1940s, three more were freed and the ninth escaped to Michigan.

47. Herbert Biberman, Report to meeting of Independent Productions Corporation, March 22, 1952, 5, Biberman-Sondergaard Papers, box 17, folder 2, SHSWA.

48. Ibid., ellipses his.

49. Ibid.

50. On the Negro Question in the CP, see Naison, *Communists in Harlem*; Gerald Horne, "The Red and the Black: The Communist Party and African-Americans in Historical Perspective," in Brown et al., eds., *New Studies in the Politics and Culture of U.S. Communism*, 199–238; and Kelley, *Hammer and Hoe*.

51. See comments on the party's drive to eliminate white chauvinism in Healey and Isserman, *Dorothy Healey Remembers*; Dennis, *Autobiography of an American Communist*; and Kelley, *Hammer and Hoe*.

52. Cripps and Culbert, "*Negro Soldier*," 123.

53. Charles Champlin, "Life After 'Frank's Place,'" *Los Angeles Times*, October 18, 1988, calendar section, part 6.

54. Biberman, *Salt of the Earth*, 46.

55. Biberman to Maurice Travis, August 7, 1952, WFMR, box 119, "Salt of the Earth" folder.

56. Biberman, notes, [June 1952], WFMR, box 129, folder 8, "Salt." Biberman's comments also appear in the memorandum Maurice Travis sent to the Mine-Mill executive board, outlining Biberman's proposal. See Memorandum from Maurice Travis to executive board re: Film Entitled "Salt of the Earth," June 23, 1952, WFMR, box 119, "Salt of the Earth" folder.

57. Biberman, *Salt of the Earth*, 43–44.

58. Ibid., 44.

59. Ibid., 54; Sandoval T., *Mexikos Esperanza*, 16–25.

60. Biberman to Maurice Travis, September 14, 1952, WFMR, box 119, "Salt of the Earth" folder.

61. Ibid.; Rosenfelt, "Commentary," in Wilson, *Salt of the Earth*, 129.

62. Biberman, *Salt of the Earth*, 47.

63. Herbert Biberman to Maurice Travis, December 7, 1952, WFMR, box 119, "Salt of the Earth" Folder.

64. Biberman, *Salt of the Earth*, 47. Acosta went on to perform in B-grade movies and television.

65. Virginia Chacón, interview by author; *SCDP*, November 4, 1948.

66. Sonja Dahl Biberman, OHALC interview.

67. Biberman, *Salt of the Earth*, 71.

68. Sonja Dahl Biberman, OHALC interview.

69. Biberman, *Salt of the Earth*, 72.

70. Ibid., 71.

71. Ibid., 73.

72. Eventually Biberman came to admire Chacón's performance. While editing the film, he wrote to Maurice Travis: "That man Chacon is just incredible—the color, the variety, the authority!" See Biberman to Maurice Travis, April 20, 1953, WFMR, box 119, "Salt of the Earth" folder.

73. Juan Chacón, OHALC interview.

74. Biberman, Report to IPC [1951], 2.

75. Biberman to Maurice Travis, June 16, 1952, WFMR, box 119, "Salt of the Earth" folder.

76. Clinton Jencks later commented that Biberman "over-romanticized some things. . . . [S]ometimes I winced as I read" Biberman's memoir. See Clinton Jencks, OHALC interview.

77. Angie Sánchez and Virginia Chacón, OHALC interview.

78. Two women I interviewed believed that the story was based on them. Sonja Dahl Biberman thought that the character was a composite: "I don't think there was any one woman, and yet, each one had so much of her particular point of view, or her particular level of understanding. Her particular background would bring her own contribution" (Sonja Dahl Biberman, OHALC interview).

79. Angie Sánchez and Virginia Chacón, OHALC interview.

80. Biberman to Maurice Travis, July 23, 1952, WFMR, box 119, "Salt of the Earth" folder.

81. Biberman, Salt of the Earth, 65–66; Jencks, interview by Sam Sills. The Rockwell brothers were itinerant miners who hired on to sink shafts—very dangerous, skilled work. They were pro-union but did not belong to Local 890 because they worked outside its bargaining unit.

82. Sonja Dahl Biberman and Edward Biberman, OHALC interview.

83. Paul Jarrico to Nathan Witt, December 20, 1952, Clinton Jencks Papers, box 24, University of Colorado at Boulder Libraries, Boulder, Colo. The original signatories were to be Herbert Biberman and Paul Jarrico, but Sonja Dahl Biberman replaced her brother-in-law even though he was still in the area.

84. Sonja Dahl Biberman and Edward Biberman, OHALC interview.

85. IPC felt its primary connection and obligation was to the people of Grant County, and this led to some difficulty with the international union. Formal contract negotiations snagged on the distribution of profits. IPC and Mine-Mill agreed that 5 percent of the profits would go to the union, but it became clear in September 1952 that the "union" meant different things to IPC and Mine-Mill. IPC intended that Local 890 should receive the profits, but the Mine-Mill office in Denver assumed that the profits would benefit the union as a whole, since the contract would be signed by the international. Ultimately they compromised, with the 5 percent designated for an Empire Zinc Defense Fund. See Biberman to Maurice Travis, October 14, 1952; Charles Katz to Nathan Witt, September 17, 1952; and Witt to Katz, September 19 and October 15, 1952, WFMR, box 119, "Salt of the Earth" folder.

86. Jules Schwerin, "On Location," in Wilson, Salt of the Earth, 178.

87. Ibid., 177.

88. Biberman, notes, [June 1952].

89. Jules Schwerin, "On Location," 178.

90. Juan Chacón, "Union Made," in Wilson, Salt of the Earth, 181–82.

91. Clinton Jencks, OHALC interview.

92. Schwerin, "On Location," 177.

93. Clinton Jencks, interview by Sam Sills.

94. Chacón, "Union Made," 182.

95. Clinton Jencks, OHALC interview.

96. Schwerin, "On Location," 177.

97. Willie Andazola, interview by author.

98. Rachel Juárez Valencia, comments on panel, "Bringing Salt of the Earth Home."

99. Sylvia Jarrico, quoted in Ceplair and Englund, *Inquisition in Hollywood*, 418.

100. Becca Wilson and Rosanna Wilson Farrow, comments on panel, "Bringing Salt of the Earth Back Home."

101. "Paul Perlin," handwritten notes, WFMR, box 129, folder 6.

102. "Irving Hentschel," handwritten notes, WFMR, box 129, folder 6.

103. *The Union Worker*, January 1952, 2. The nursery would initially be for union members but would eventually "extend to cover the needs of all the mining area." Mariana Ramírez and Carrie Gonzales were designated the leaders of this project.

104. Virginia Jencks to Michael and Zelma Wilson, March 6, 1952, quoted in Lorence, *Suppression of "Salt of the Earth,"* 43.

105. Virginia Jencks to Mike Wilson, Zelma Wilson, and Sylvia Jarrico, February 24, 1952, quoted in ibid., 41.

106. Lorence, *Suppression of "Salt of the Earth,"* 41.

107. Henrietta Williams, OHALC interview.

108. Ibid.

109. Clinton Jencks, OHALC interview.

110. Chacón, "Union Made," 180.

CHAPTER NINE

1. *SCDP*, February 24, 1953.

2. *New York Times*, February 25, 1953, 22.

3. Ibid., February 13, 1953, 8.

4. Biberman, *Salt of the Earth*, 82. Members of the garden club included the wife of Carl Elayer, onetime superintendent of Asarco's Groundhog Mine, Republican leader, and owner of his own company by 1953. See *SCDP*, February 6, 1950.

5. Elizabeth Kerby, "Violence in Silver City," 8.

6. Biberman asked for Mine-Mill's opinions on how best to "address the local authorities in Bayard concerning the use of public thoroughfares and streets." This was, he said, "a pretty crucial question and I would not like to make any initial blunders" (Biberman to Maurice Travis, September 14, 1952, WFMR, box 119, "Salt of the Earth" folder).

7. Tom Miller, "*Salt of the Earth* Revisited," 33. Matthews defeated Leslie Goforth in the 1952 sheriff's election.

8. Ibid.

9. June Kuhlman to E. T. "Buck" Harris, January 28, 1953, and Kuhlman to "Dear Sir," January 22, 1953, in Screen Actors Guild Archives, Los Angeles, cited in Lorence, *Suppression of "Salt of the Earth,"* 78.

10. Lorence, *Suppression of "Salt of the Earth,"* 79.

11. Ibid.

12. Leroy B. Bible to Senator Dennis Chávez, February 17, 1953, Dennis Chávez Papers, box 208, folder 9, CSR. Bible wrote Chávez at the request of their "mutual friend, Commander J. F. Foy." This was probably Jack Franey Foy, District Attorney Tom Foy's brother.

13. Leroy B. Bible, telegram to Senator Dennis Chávez, February 23, 1953, Dennis Chávez Papers, box 208, folder 9, CSR.

14. Senator Dennis Chávez to Manager, Radio Station KSIL, Silver City, February 25, 1953, and handwritten note on copy of letter from Senator Dennis Chávez, Washington, to Leroy Bible, Fort Bayard, February 24, 1953, Dennis Chávez Papers, box 208, folder 9, CSR.

15. *New York Times*, February 27, 1953, 6.

16. Rosaura Revueltas, "Reflections on a Journey," in Michael Wilson, *Salt of the Earth*, 175.

17. *SCDP*, February 26, 1953.

18. *SCDP*, February 24, 1953.

19. *SCDP*, February 25, 1953.

20. *SCDP*, February 27, 1953; *New York Times*, March 1, 1953, 14.

21. *New York Times*, March 1, 1953, 14. Protest in Mexico drew on recent criticisms of Hollywood's domination over the Mexican film industry. For an insightful analysis of the relationships among Hollywood, the Mexican film industry, and the Mexican government, see Fein, "From Collaboration to Containment." In the end, the Hollywood actors were permitted to continue their work in Mexico.

22. Revueltas, "Reflections on a Journey," 176.

23. Ibid.

24. *New York Times*, March 1, 1953, 14. Thomason ruled at a habeas corpus hearing on March 3 that the district immigration director "was within his rights in denying her bond" (*New York Times*, March 4, 1953, 23).

25. *New York Times*, March 8, 1953, 86.

26. *SCDP*, February 27, 1953.

27. There is one scene, for instance, when Esperanza knocks a gun out of the hand of a deputy, and this Esperanza was played by Torrez's sister.

28. Close-ups of Revueltas at the end of the film were shot in Mexico.

29. Larry Martin, quoted in Kerby, "Violence in Silver City," 8. Among the group of men who confronted the crew in front of the Central post office were Franey Foy and H. L. Barnett. Barnett had recently lost the mayoralty to Romero.

30. *SCDP*, March 3, 1953.

31. Ibid.

32. Ibid.

33. Ibid.; *El Paso Herald Post*, March 4, 1953, 1.

34. *SCDP*, March 3, 1953.

35. Ibid.

36. *El Paso Herald Post*, March 4, 1953, 1.

37. *SCDP*, March 4, 1953.

38. Ibid.; *New York Times*, March 5, 1953, 20.

39. Kerby, "Violence in Silver City," 10.

40. *SCDP*, March 4, 1953.

41. *New York Times*, March 8, 1953, 86.

42. *SCDP*, March 4, 1953. For a different take on ethnic labels, see the comments by teenager Lupe Elizado during the Empire Zinc strike in Chapter 5.

43. Kerby, "Violence in Silver City," 10.

44. Ibid.

45. Nancie L. González, *Spanish Americans of New Mexico*, 78.

46. *The Union* (Bayard, N.M.), n.d., Clinton Jencks Papers, University of Colorado at Boulder Libraries, Boulder, Colo.

47. Statement of Revs. John P. Linnane, Francis Smerke, Pedro Ruiz, and Henry Saxon, quoted in *SCDP*, March 4, 1953.

48. Lorence, *Suppression of "Salt of the Earth,"* explains this process in more detail, using many of the same sources that I have consulted.

49. See Horne, *Class Struggle in Hollywood*.

50. Herbert Biberman to Maurice Travis, June 16, 1952, WFMR, box 119, "Salt of the Earth" folder.

51. Biberman, notes, [June 1951], WFMR, box 129.

52. Biberman to Travis, October 14, 1952, WFMR, box 119, "Salt of the Earth" folder.

53. Ibid., ellipsis his.

54. Paul Jarrico to Nathan Witt, December 20, 1952, Clinton Jencks Papers, box 24, University of Colorado at Boulder Libraries, Boulder, Colo.

55. IPC Distributors, Inc., "Organizational Steps to Be Taken with Regard to Showing 'Salt of the Earth,'" Biberman-Sondergaard Papers, box 17, folder 2, SHSWA.

56. Ibid.

57. Juan Chacón, open letter published in *SCDP*, August 3, 1953.

58. Herbert Biberman to Travis, March 26, 1953, WFMR, box 119, "Salt of the Earth" folder.

59. "Summary Production Costs" and "Detailed Production Costs," memos accompanying letter from Kevin Smith to Nat Witt, February 9, 1953, Clinton Jencks Papers, box 24, University of Colorado at Boulder Libraries, Boulder, Colo.

60. U.S. Congress, Senate, *Hearing on Communist Domination*.

61. At its 1952 convention, the Mine-Mill delegates passed a resolution

condemning McCarran's efforts to "bust the union" by calling it Communist-dominated. See *New York Times*, September 12, 1952, 45.

62. Victor Navasky analyzes this ritual in *Naming Names*, as does Ellen Schrecker in *Many Are the Crimes*.

63. Jensen, *Nonferrous Metals Industry Unionism*, 234–35. Wilson opposed Mine-Mill leadership but recognized the critical need for Alabama secessionists to include black people. Local leaders evidently disliked his racial policies, for they dismissed Wilson and hired Van Jones "with the understanding that the Steelworkers would be a *white* union" (ibid., 235, italics his).

64. U.S. Congress, Senate, *Hearing on Communist Domination*, 6.

65. Ibid., 26–30.

66. Ibid., 114.

67. Ibid., 225.

68. Ibid., 252.

69. Ibid., 2.

70. Ibid., 158.

71. Ibid., 261.

72. Ibid., 291.

73. Ibid., 170.

74. Ibid.

75. *New York Times*, December 30, 1952, 5.

76. Richard Berresford testimony, House Committee on Education and Labor, March 16, 1953, quoted in Schrecker, *Many Are the Crimes*, 343.

77. Jencks first filed a noncommunist affidavit in 1949, and by the time of Berresford's testimony the statute of limitations had expired for prosecuting him for perjury in connection with that affidavit. The Justice Department charged him instead with falsifying a second affidavit signed in April 1950.

78. Clinton Jencks, interview by Sam Sills.

79. Schrecker, "McCarthyism and the Labor Movement," 151–52.

80. Schrecker, *Many Are the Crimes*, 342.

81. Ibid., 342–43.

82. Clinton Jencks, interview by Sam Sills.

83. *New York Times*, April 22, 1953, 21.

84. *SCDP*, June 1, 1953.

85. *SCDP*, January 13, 1954.

86. *SCDP*, January 14, 1954.

87. *SCDP*, January 19, 1954.

88. Clinton Jencks, interview by Sam Sills. In Jencks's opinion, this rule and the procedure for upholding it were evidence of the union's democratic structure: union men settled disagreements internally and could not be "railroaded" (ibid.).

89. Ibid. Bill Upton, who had been mayor of Bayard during the strike, appeared at the trial as president of Bayard's Grant County Savings Bank. Upton admitted disliking Jencks, but his testimony was limited to confirming Jencks's

signature on the Taft-Hartley affidavit; he was not asked to confirm or deny Jencks's Communist ties. See *SCDP*, January 12, 1954.

90. Clinton Jencks, interview by Sam Sills.

91. See Matusow, *False Witness*, for a full account of his transformation from Communist to informer to professional witness.

92. Clinton Jencks, interview by Sam Sills.

93. Jenny Vincent, quoted in Nott, "Song of Jenny Vincent," 38, and Schrecker, *Many Are the Crimes*, 312.

94. Schrecker, *Many Are the Crimes*, 342.

95. *New York Times*, December 30, 1952, 5.

96. Clinton Jencks, quoted in Schrecker, *Many Are the Crimes*, 348, emphasis in the original.

97. *Jencks v. United States*, 353 U.S. 657 (1957), was a landmark decision granting defense attorneys access to FBI reports. It later played a minor role in the Watergate prosecutions. See *New York Times*, July 28, 1973, 10.

98. Clinton Jencks, interview by Sam Sills.

99. Ibid.

100. Clinton Jencks, interview by author. The phrase was a play on the Communist term "socialism in one country."

101. Clinton Jencks, interview by Sam Sills.

102. Clinton Jencks, quoted in Schrecker, *Many Are the Crimes*, 354.

103. Clinton Jencks, interview by author. See also Jencks, *Men Underground*.

104. Albert Millán, comments on panel, "Bringing Salt of the Earth Home."

105. Virginia Chacón, interview by author.

106. Jenny and Craig Vincent, quoted in *SCDP*, December 11, 1953. Predictably, the *Silver City Daily Press* mentioned the fact that the San Cristóbal ranch "lies just 90 miles from Los Alamos, top-secret atomic research center." Craig Vincent also faced contempt of court charges for refusing to give pretrial evidence in Clinton Jencks's case; those charges were dropped on March 8, 1954. See *SCDP*, March 10, 1954.

107. Jenny Vincent, quoted in Nott, "Song of Jenny Vincent."

108. Virginia Chacón, interview by author.

CHAPTER TEN

1. Michael Wilson, *Salt of the Earth*, 80–82, 90.

2. Henrietta Williams, OHALC interview.

3. Deborah Rosenfelt, "Commentary," in Wilson, *Salt of the Earth*, 143.

4. Dolores Jiménez, interview by Sam Sills and author.

5. *SCDP*, July 26, 1961.

6. *Los Angeles Times*, July 28, 1961.

7. *SCDP*, August 25, 1961.

8. Ibid. Two of the Montoyas' children—María, fourteen, and José, thirteen

—took the stand to refute their father. According to the *Los Angeles Examiner* (August 26, 1961), they "said their mother encouraged them to attend church and sometimes took them there herself." Feliciana Montoya's mother, Dolores Doñez, moved to Los Angeles to take care of the couple's children, who were living with Feliciana's brother, Max Doñez. (He had been an Empire Zinc striker and was now a Los Angeles postal clerk.) See *SCDP*, July 26, 1961.

9. Aurora Chávez, interview by author.

10. Angel Bustos, quoted in *Mine-Mill Conv. Proc.* (1953), 30.

11. Guadalupe Cano, panel, "Bringing Salt of the Earth Home."

12. In her study of the United Farm Workers, Margaret Rose similarly finds that women's union participation did not fundamentally change gender relations in families, in the UFW, or in the fields. See Rose, "Women in the United Farm Workers."

13. Only in Sudbury, Ontario, did the local reject the merger and remain a Mine-Mill local.

14. Higgins brought his complaint to the New Mexico Fair Employment Practices Commission, which ordered Kennecott to stop its segregation of housing, payroll numbers, and washrooms. Kennecott complied and told its employees that future housing assignments would be made "regardless of the applicant's racial extraction" (New Mexico Fair Employment Practices Commission, "Seventh Annual Report," 4–8).

15. Mine-Mill members, including Asarco employee and *Salt of the Earth* costar Floyd Bostick, and companies spoke at congressional hearings on the 1953–54 lead-zinc crisis. See *Problems in the Metal Mining Industry*.

16. Pattern bargaining was a practice established by industrial unions in the 1940s whereby a contract won at one major company would set the pattern for contracts in other companies within the same industry. It was the norm for the period 1950–80, and its destruction was part of the antilabor offensive of the Reagan era. See Rosenblum, *Copper Crucible*.

17. In the 1990s, PD managed to decertify Chino's Machinists, Pipefitters and Carpenters, Boilermakers, and Office Workers, but the Steelworkers and Electrical Workers have survived.

18. The Santa Rita mine and Hurley smelter closed down in 2002, when the price of copper dropped to 72 cents a pound. Chino then discovered that some of the tailings (waste) at Hurley, dating from the 1910s and 1920s, had enough copper left in it to process, and in 2003 the company began hauling it to Santa Rita for leaching. When copper prices rose to $1.23 a pound in early 2004, the Santa Rita mine and concentrator were reopened, but the Hurley smelter remained closed.

19. The phrase is the title of Paul Buhle and Dave Wagner's study of the effect of blacklisted artists on the movies and television, *Hide in Plain Sight*.

20. Movies include *A Crime to Fit the Punishment*, *One of the Hollywood Ten*, and *Memorias de Sal*; the opera is *Esperanza!*, which premiered in Madison, Wis., in 2001.

BIBLIOGRAPHY

PRIMARY SOURCES

Manuscript Collections

Albuquerque, N.M.
  Center for Southwest Research, University of New Mexico
    Dennis Chávez Papers
Boulder, Colo.
  University of Colorado at Boulder Libraries
    Clinton Jencks Papers
    Western Federation of Miners/International Union of Mine, Mill and
      Smelter Workers International, District, and Local Records
Las Cruces, N.M.
  New Mexico State University Library
    Rio Grande Historical Collections
Madison, Wis.
  Archives, State Historical Society of Wisconsin
    Herbert Biberman and Gale Sondergaard Papers
New York, N.Y.
  Tamiment Library, New York University
    Oral History of the American Left Collection, Series IV "A Crime to Fit
      the Punishment"
Santa Fe, N.M.
  New Mexico State Records Center and Archives
    Governor John J. Dempsey Papers
    Governor Thomas J. Mabry Papers
    New Mexico State Inspector of Mines Records
    New Mexico Supreme Court Law Library State Agency Collection
    Governor Clyde K. Tingley Papers

Silver City, N.M.
    Grant County Courthouse
        Grant County Record of Marriages
        Sixth New Mexico District Court Records
    Silver City Public Library
        Treasure Room
Washington, D.C.
    National Archives
        Records of the Committee on Fair Employment Practices, RG 228
        Manuscript Census, Grant County, N.M., Twelfth Census of the
        United States, 1900, in Microfilm Collection T-623-1000
        Manuscript Census, Grant County, N.M., Thirteenth Census of the
        United States, 1910, in Microfilm Collection T-624-915
        Manuscript Census, Grant County, N.M., Fourteenth Census of the
        United States, 1920, in Microfilm Collection T-625-107
        Manuscript Census, Grant County, N.M., Fifteenth Census of the
        United States, 1930, in Microfilm Collection T-626-1395
        Records of the National Labor Relations Board, RG 225

Interviews Conducted by Author

Andazola, Guillermo (Willie). March 4, 2003. Santa Clara, N.M.
Chacón, Virginia. September 29 and 30, 1995. Faywood, N.M. Tape recording.
Chávez, Aurora. May 8, 1997. Telephone interview.
Chávez, Daría. March 14, 1996. Hanover, N.M.
Flores, Arturo and Josephine. March 17, 1996. Rio Rancho, N.M. Tape recording.
Jencks, Clinton E. May 10, 1997. Telephone interview.
Jiménez, Dolores. Interview by Sam Sills and author. March 2, 2003. Santa Fe,
    N.M. Video and tape recording.
Madero, Dora Gutiérrez. May 31, 2001. Telephone interview.
Matthews, Betty Jo [Hartless] and John. March 5, 2003. Silver City, N.M.
Morales, Joe T. March 14, 1996. Silver City, N.M. Tape recording.
Ogás, C. B. and Elvira Acuña. March 13, 1996. Silver City, N.M. Tape recording.
Rivera, Matías. March 11, 1996. Silver City, N.M.
Sandoval, Alice. [Pseudonym.] June 1, 2001. Silver City, N.M. Telephone
    interview.
Tafoya, Elena and Raymundo. March 14, 1996. Hanover, N.M. Tape recording.
Teckemeyer, Bonnie May Capshaw. March 6, 2003. Silver City, N.M.
Torrez, Anita and Lorenzo. October 4, 1995. Tucson, Ariz.
Vigil, Albert H. March 13, 1996. Silver City, N.M. Tape recording.
Wood, Bill (Sonny). June 1, 2001. Silver City, N.M. Tape recording.

Other Interview

Jencks, Clinton. By Sam Sills. May 2, 1999. San Diego. Video and tape recording.

Government Reports

Clemons, Russell E., Paige W. Christiansen, and H. L. James. *Southwestern New Mexico*. Scenic Trips to the Geologic Past, no. 10, revised. Socorro, N.M.: New Mexico Bureau of Mines and Mineral Resources, 1980.

Committee on Fair Employment Practice. *First Report: Fair Employment Practice Committee: July 1943 – December 1944*. Washington, D.C.: U.S. Government Printing Office, 1945.

——. *Final Report: Fair Employment Practice Committee: June 28, 1946*. Washington, D.C.: U.S. Government Printing Office, 1947.

File, Lucien A. "Labor Unions in New Mexico's Nonferrous-Metals Mining Industry." Bureau of Business Research, University of New Mexico, *New Mexico Business Reprint* (October 1964).

Finlay, J. R. *Report of Appraisal of Mining Properties of New Mexico*. N.p.: 1921–22. New Mexico State Tax Commission Files, New Mexico Supreme Court Law Library State Agency Collection, New Mexico State Records Center and Archives, Santa Fe.

Jamieson, Stuart. *Labor Unionism in American Agriculture*. United States Department of Labor Bulletin no. 836. Washington, D.C.: U.S. Government Printing Office, 1945. Reprint, New York: Arno Press, 1976.

Lasky, Samuel G. *Geology and Ore Deposits of the Bayard Area, Central Mining District, New Mexico*. United States Geological Survey Bulletin no. 870. Washington, D.C.: U.S. Government Printing Office, 1936.

Morgan, John Davis, Jr. *The Domestic Mining Industry of the United States in World War II: A Critical Study of the Economic Mobilization of the Mineral Base of National Power*. Washington, D.C.: U.S. Government Printing Office, 1949.

New Mexico Employment Security Commission. Annual Reports, 1939–45. New Mexico Supreme Court Law Library State Agency Collection, New Mexico State Records Center and Archives, Santa Fe.

New Mexico Fair Employment Practices Commission. "Seventh Annual Report of the New Mexico Fair Employment Practices Commission, Fiscal Year ending June 30, 1955." Fair Employment Practices Commission, Annual Reports, 1949, 1954–66. New Mexico Supreme Court Law Library State Agency Collection, New Mexico State Records Center and Archives, Santa Fe.

New Mexico Veterans' Service Commission. "Report of New Mexico Veterans' Service Commission, 1955–1956." New Mexico Supreme Court Law Library State Agency Collection, New Mexico State Records Center and Archives, Santa Fe.

U.S. Congress. House of Representatives. *Problems in the Metal Mining Industry (Lead, Zinc, and Other Metals)*. Hearings before the Select Committee on Small Business, House of Representatives, 83rd Cong., 1st Sess., pursuant to

H. Res. 22, April 30, 1953, Phoenix. Washington, D.C.: U.S. Government Printing Office, 1953.

U.S. Congress. Senate. *Hearing on Communist Domination of Union Officials in Vital Defense Industry—International Union of Mine, Mill and Smelter Workers.* Subcommittee to Investigate the Administration of the Internal Security Act and Other Internal Security Laws of the Committee on the Judiciary, 82nd Cong., 2d Sess., October 6–9, 1952, Salt Lake City. Washington, D.C.: U.S. Government Printing Office, 1953.

U.S. Department of Commerce. Bureau of the Census. *County and City Data Book 1952.* Washington, D.C.: U.S. Government Printing Office, 1953.

———. *Fourteenth Census of the United States, 1920.* Vol. 11, *Mines and Quarries, 1919.* Washington, D.C.: U.S. Government Printing Office, 1922.

———. *Fifteenth Census of the United States, 1930. Mines and Quarries, 1929.* Washington, D.C.: U.S. Government Printing Office, 1933.

———. *Fifteenth Census of the United States, 1930. Population.* Vol. 3, Reports by States. Part 2, *Montana-Wyoming.* Washington, D.C.: U.S. Government Printing Office, 1932.

———. *Sixteenth Census of the United States: 1940. Population.* Vol. 2, *Characteristics of the Population.* Part 4, *Minnesota–New Mexico.* Washington, D.C.: U.S. Government Printing Office, 1943.

———. *Seventeenth Census of the United States: 1950.* Vol. 2, *Characteristics of the Population.* Part 31, *New Mexico.* Washington, D.C.: U.S. Government Printing Office, 1952.

———. *A Statistical Abstract Supplement: County and City Data Book 1949.* Washington, D.C.: U.S. Government Printing Office, 1952.

———. *Two Hundred Years of Census Taking: Populations and Housing Questions, 1790–1990.* Washington, D.C.: U.S. Government Printing Office, 1989.

U.S. Department of the Interior. Bureau of Mines. *Mineral Facts and Problems.* Washington, D.C.: U.S. Government Printing Office, 1956.

———. *Minerals Yearbook.* Washington, D.C.: U.S. Government Printing Office, 1932–57.

U.S. Department of Labor. *Monthly Labor Review* (Washington, D.C.), 1940–51.

U.S. Department of Labor. Women's Bureau. *Home Environment and Employment Opportunities of Women in Coal-Mine Workers' Families.* Washington, D.C.: U.S. Government Printing Office, 1925.

United States. National Labor Relations Board. *Decisions and Orders of the National Labor Relations Board.* Vol. 19. Washington, D.C.: U.S. Government Printing Office, 1940.

———. *Decisions and Orders of the National Labor Relations Board.* Vol. 26. August 1–26, 1940. Washington, D.C.: U.S. Government Printing Office, 1942.

United States. National War Labor Board. *War Labor Reports.* Washington, D.C.: Bureau of National Affairs, 1942–46.

321

Wilson, John P. *Historical Profile of Southwestern New Mexico.* Report no. 21.
    Las Cruces, N.M.: Cultural Resources Management Division, Department
    of Sociology and Anthropology, New Mexico State University, for the U.S.
    Department of the Interior, Bureau of Land Management, 1975.

Newspapers and Periodicals

Bayard Journal (Bayard, N.M.), 1950–52
CIO News: Mine, Mill and Smelter Workers Edition (Chicago), 1938–40
Daily Worker (San Francisco), 1950–53
El Paso Herald Post (El Paso, Tex.), 1951–54
Engineering and Mining Journal, 1941–55
Los Angeles Times, 1950–54, 1961
[Mine-Mill] Union (Denver), 1940–55
Miners' Magazine (Denver), 1900–1905
New Mexico Miner and Prospector (Silver City and Carlsbad, N.M.), 1942–55
New York Times, 1950–57
Political Affairs (New York), 1940–53
Silver City Daily Press (Silver City, N.M.), 1939–55
Union Worker (Bayard, N.M.), 1950–54

Published Proceedings

*Official Proceedings of the Convention of the International Union of Mine, Mill
    and Smelter Workers.* Salt Lake City: The Union, 1928–54.
*Thought Control in U.S.A.: The Collected Proceedings on the Subject of Thought
    Control in the U.S.* Los Angeles: Progressive Citizens of America, Southern
    California Chapter, 1947.

Unpublished Proceedings

"Bringing Salt of the Earth Home: A Fiftieth Anniversary Symposium." Western
    New Mexico University and Silver City Museum, Bayard and Silver City,
    N.M., May 5–8, 2004.
"Salt of the Earth." College of Santa Fe, Santa Fe, N.M., February 27–March 1,
    2003.

Books and Articles

Biberman, Herbert. *Salt of the Earth: The Story of a Film.* Boston: Beacon Press,
    1965.
Burnhill, James. "The Mexican People in the Southwest." *Political Affairs* (Sep-
    tember 1953): 43–53.
Cowl, Margaret. "The Struggle for Equal Rights for Women." *The Communist* 19
    (September 1940): 860–61.
Dennis, Peggy. *Autobiography of an American Communist: A Personal View of a
    Political Life, 1925–1975.* Westport, Conn.: L. Hill, 1977.

Engels, Friedrich. *Origin of the Family, Private Property, and the State, in the
     Light of the Researches of Lewis H. Morgan.* Introduction and notes by Elea-
     nor Burke Leacock. New York: International Publishers, 1972.
Epstein, Irene, and Doxey Wilkerson. *Questions and Answers on the Woman
     Question.* New York: Jefferson School of Social Science, 1953.
Flynn, Elizabeth Gurley. "What Do Communist Women Talk About?" *Daily Peo-
     ple's World,* October 24, 1950, 8.
"The Idol of Groom Creek Miners Union." *Miners' Magazine,* June 2, 1904, 7.
Inman, Mary. *In Woman's Defense.* New York: International Publishers, 1939.
Jarrico, Sylvia. "Evil Heroines of 1953." *Hollywood Review,* June–July 1953.
J. D. "On Chauvinism against the Mexican-American People." *Political Affairs*
     (February 1952): 51–56.
Jerome, V. J. "The Negro in Hollywood Films." *Political Affairs* (June 1950):
     58–92.
Maltz, Albert. "What Shall We Ask of the Writers?" *New Masses,* February 12,
     1946.
Matusow, Harvey. *False Witness.* New York: Cameron and Kahn, 1955.
"The Mexican-Americans—Their Plight and Struggle." *Political Affairs* (May
     1949): 71–80.
Millard, Betty. *Woman against Myth.* New York: International Publishers, 1948.
The New Jersey Zinc Company. *The First Hundred Years of the New Jersey Zinc
     Company: A History of the Founding and Development of a Company and
     an Industry.* New York: New Jersey Zinc Company, 1948.
"The Plight and Struggles of the Mexican-Americans." *Political Affairs* (July
     1949): 75–84.
Scott, Adrian. "You Can't Do That." Speech to the Conference on Thought Con-
     trol in the U.S.A., called by the Hollywood Arts, Sciences and Professions
     Council, PCA, July 9–13, 1947. Printed in *Thought Control in U.S.A.: The
     Collected Proceedings on the Subject of Thought Control in the U.S.* Los
     Angeles: Progressive Citizens of America, Southern California Chapter,
     1947.
Tenayuca, Emma, and Homer D. Brooks. "The Mexican Question in the South-
     west." *The Communist* 18 (March 1939): 257–68.

Films

A Crime to Fit the Punishment. Directed and produced by Barbara Moss and
     Steve Mack. Mass Productions, 1976.
The Hollywood Ten. Directed by John Berry. Produced by Paul Jarrico. Southern
     California Chapter of the National Council of the Arts, Sciences, and Pro-
     fessions, 1950.
Memorias de Sal. Directed by Ricardo Trujillo. KRWG-TV (Las Cruces, N.M.),
     1994.
One of the Hollywood Ten. Directed and produced by Karl Francis. Morena
     Films, 2002.

Salt of the Earth. Directed by Herbert Biberman. Produced by Paul Jarrico. Independent Film Corporation, 1954.

SECONDARY SOURCES

Books and Articles

Allsup, Carl. *American G.I. Forum: Origins and Evolution*. Austin: Center for Mexican American Studies, University of Texas at Austin, 1982.

Alonso, Harriet Hyman. "Mayhem and Moderation: Women Peace Activists during the McCarthy Era." In *Not June Cleaver: Women and Gender in Postwar America, 1945–1960*, edited by Joanne Meyerowitz, 128–50. Critical Perspectives on the Past. Philadelphia: Temple University Press, 1994.

Arneson, Eric. "'Like Banquo's Ghost, It Will Not Down': The Race Question and the American Railroad Brotherhoods, 1880–1920." *American Historical Review* 99 (December 1994): 1601–33.

Arnold, Frank. "Humberto Silex: CIO Organizer from Nicaragua." *Southwest Economy and Society* 4 (Fall 1978).

Arrieta, Olivia. "The Alianza Hispano Americana in Arizona and New Mexico: The Development and Maintenance of a Multifunctional Ethnic Organization." *Renato Rosaldo Lecture Series* 7 (1989–90).

Arroyo, Luis Leobardo. "Chicano Participation in Organized Labor: The CIO in Los Angeles, 1938–1950." *Aztlán* 6, no. 2 (Summer 1975): 277–303.

Atleson, James B. *Labor and the Wartime State: Labor Relations and Law during World War II*. Urbana: University of Illinois Press, 1998.

Aulette, Judy, and Trudy Mills. "Something Old, Something New: Auxiliary Work in the 1983–1986 Copper Strike." *Feminist Studies* 14 (Summer 1988): 251–68.

Baron, Ava, ed. *Work Engendered: Toward a New History of American Labor*. Ithaca, N.Y.: Cornell University Press, 1991.

Baxandall, Rosalyn. "The Question Seldom Asked: Women and the CPUSA." In *New Studies in the Politics and Culture of U.S. Communism*, edited by Michael E. Brown et al., 141–61. New York: Monthly Review Press, 1993.

Bean, Frank D., and Benjamin S. Bradshaw. "Intermarriage Between Persons of Spanish and Non-Spanish Surname: Changes from the Mid-Nineteenth to the Mid-Twentieth Century." *Social Science Quarterly* 51 (September 1970): 389–95.

Biskind, Peter. *Seeing Is Believing: How Hollywood Taught Us to Stop Worrying and Love the Fifties*. New York: Pantheon Books, 1983.

Blau, Francine D., and Marianne A. Ferber. *The Economics of Women, Men, and Work*. Englewood Cliffs, N.J.: Prentice-Hall, 1986.

Bolte, Charles. *The New Veteran*. New York: Reynal and Hitchcock, 1945.

Boydston, Jeanne. *Home and Work: Housework, Wages, and the Ideology of Labor in the Early Republic*. New York: Oxford University Press, 1990.

Boyer, Ruth McDonald, and Narcissus Duffy Gayton. *Apache Mothers and*

Daughters: Four Generations of a Family. Norman: University of Oklahoma
    Press, 1992.
Brown, Michael, et al., eds. *New Studies in the Politics and Culture of American
    Communism.* New York: Monthly Review Press, 1993.
Broyles-González, Yolanda. *El Teatro Campesino: Theater in the Chicano Move-
    ment.* Austin: University of Texas Press, 1994.
Buhle, Paul, and Dave Wagner. *Hide in Plain Sight: The Hollywood Blacklistees
    in Film and Television, 1950–2002.* New York: Palgrave Macmillan, 2003.
——. *Radical Hollywood: The Untold Story Behind America's Favorite Movies.*
    New York: The New Press, 2002.
Byrkit, James W. "Walter Douglas and Labor Struggles in Early Twentieth-
    Century Arizona." *Southwest Economy and Society* 1 (1976): 14–27.
Cameron, Ardis. *Radicals of the Worst Sort: Laboring Women of Lawrence, Mas-
    sachusetts, 1860–1912.* Women in American History. Urbana: University of
    Illinois Press, 1990.
Cargill, Jack. "Empire and Opposition: The 'Salt of the Earth' Strike." In *Labor in
    New Mexico: Unions, Strikes, and Social History since 1881*, edited by
    Robert Kern, 183–267. Albuquerque: University of New Mexico Press,
    1983.
Cave, Dorothy. *Beyond Courage: One Regiment against Japan, 1941–1945.* Rev.
    ed. Las Cruces, N.M.: Yucca Tree Press, 1996.
Ceplair, Larry. "Michael Wilson." In *The Political Companion to American Film*,
    edited by Gary Crowdus. N.p.: Lakeview Press, 1994.
Ceplair, Larry, and Steven Englund. *The Inquisition in Hollywood: Politics in the
    Film Community, 1930–1960.* Berkeley: University of California Press, 1984.
Coan, Charles F. *A History of New Mexico.* Vol. 2. New York: American Histori-
    cal Society, 1925.
Cobble, Dorothy Sue. *The Other Women's Movement: Workplace Justice and
    Social Rights in Modern America.* Politics and Society in Twentieth-
    Century America. Princeton, N.J.: Princeton University Press, 2004.
——. "Rethinking the Troubled Relations between Women and Unions: Craft
    Unionism and Female Activism." *Feminist Studies* 16 (Fall 1990): 519–48.
Cochran, Bert. *Labor and Communism: The Conflict That Shaped American
    Unions.* Princeton, N.J.: Princeton University Press, 1977.
Cogley, John. *Report on Blacklisting. I. Movies.* N.p.: Fund for the Republic, 1955.
Cooper, Frederick. "'Our Strike': Equality, Anticolonial Politics and the 1947–48
    Railway Strike in French West Africa." *Journal of African History* 37 (1996):
    81–118.
Cowan, Ruth Schwartz. *More Work for Mother: The Ironies of Household Tech-
    nology from the Open Hearth to the Microwave.* New York: Basic Books,
    1983.
Cripps, Thomas, and David Culbert. "*The Negro Soldier* (1944): Film Propaganda
    in Black and White." In *Hollywood as Historian: American Film in a Cul-*

tural Context, edited by Peter Rollins, 109–33. Lexington: University Press of Kentucky, 1983.

Dancis, Bruce. "Socialist Women in the United States, 1900–1917." *Socialist Revolution* 6, no. 1 (January–March 1976): 81–144.

Daniel, Cletus E. *Bitter Harvest: A History of California Farmworkers, 1870–1941*. Ithaca, N.Y.: Cornell University Press, 1981.

———. *Chicano Workers and the Politics of Fairness: The FEPC in the Southwest, 1941–1945*. Austin: University of Texas Press, 1991.

Davis, Ellis Arthur, ed. *Historical Encyclopedia of New Mexico*. Albuquerque: New Mexico Historical Association, 1945.

Debo, Angie. *A History of the Indians of the United States*. The Civilization of the American Indian Series, vol. 106. Norman: University of Oklahoma Press, 1970.

Denning, Michael. *The Cultural Front: The Laboring of American Culture in the Twentieth Century*. New York: Verso, 1996.

Deutsch, Sarah A. *No Separate Refuge: Culture, Class, and Gender on an Anglo-Hispanic Frontier in the American Southwest, 1880–1940*. New York: Oxford University Press, 1987.

Dinwiddie, D. H. "The Rise of the Mine-Mill Union in Southwestern Copper." In *American Labor in the Southwest: The First Hundred Years*, edited by James C. Foster, 46–56. Tucson: University of Arizona Press, 1982.

Draper, Theodore. *American Communism and Soviet Russia*. New York: Viking Press, 1960.

———. *The Roots of American Communism*. New York: Viking Press, 1957.

Dubofsky, Melvyn. *We Shall Be All: A History of the Industrial Workers of the World*. Chicago: Quadrangle Books, 1969. Reprint, Urbana: University of Illinois Press, 1988.

Elliott, William Yandell, et al. *International Control in the Non-Ferrous Metals*. New York: Macmillan Co., 1937.

Ewen, Lynda Ann. *Which Side Are You On? The Brookside Mine Strike in Harlan County, Kentucky, 1973–74*. Chicago: Vanguard Books, 1979.

Faue, Elizabeth. *Community of Suffering and Struggle: Women, Men, and the Labor Movement in Minneapolis, 1915–1945*. Gender and American Culture. Chapel Hill: University of North Carolina Press, 1991.

Fein, Seth. "From Collaboration to Containment: Hollywood and the International Political Economy of Mexican Cinema after the Second World War." In *Mexico's Cinema: A Century of Film and Filmmakers*, edited by Joanne Hershfield and David R. Maciel, 123–63. Wilmington, Del.: Scholarly Resources, 1999.

Fields, Barbara J. "Ideology and Slavery in American History." In *Region, Race, and Reconstruction: Essays in Honor of C. Vann Woodward*, edited by J. Morgan Kousser and James M. McPherson, 143–77. New York: Oxford University Press, 1982.

Finn, Janet. *Tracing the Veins of Copper, Culture, and Community from Butte to Chuquicamata*. Berkeley: University of California Press, 1998.

Franco, Jeré. "Beyond Reservation Boundaries: Native American Laborers in World War II." *Journal of the Southwest* 36 (Autumn 1994): 242–54.

Frank, Dana. "Housewives, Socialists, and the Politics of Food: The 1917 New York Cost-of-Living Protests." *Feminist Studies* 11 (Summer 1985): 255–85.

Freeland, Richard M. *The Truman Doctrine and the Origins of McCarthyism: Foreign Policy, Domestic Politics, and Internal Security, 1946–1948*. New York: New York University Press, 1970. Reprint, 1985.

García, Alma M. "The Development of Chicana Feminist Discourse, 1970–1980." *Gender and Society* 3 (1989): 217–38.

———, ed. *Chicana Feminist Thought: The Basic Historical Writings*. New York: Routledge, 1997.

García, Mario T. "The Chicana in American History: The Mexican American Women of El Paso, 1880–1920—A Case Study." *Pacific Historical Review* 49 (May 1979): 315–37.

———. *Memories of Chicano History: The Life and Narrative of Bert Corona*. Berkeley: University of California Press, 1994.

———. *Mexican Americans: Leadership, Ideology, Identity, 1930–1960*. Yale Western Americana Series, 36. New Haven: Yale University Press, 1989.

Garcia, Matt. "'Just Put on That Padua Hills Smile': The Mexican Players and the Padua Hills Theater, 1931–1974." *California History* 74, no. 3 (1995): 244–61.

———. *A World of Its Own: Race, Labor, and Citrus in the Making of Greater Los Angeles, 1900–1970*. Studies in Rural Culture. Chapel Hill: University of North Carolina Press, 2001.

Garcilazo, Jeffrey M. "McCarthyism, Mexican Americans, and the Los Angeles Committee for the Protection of the Foreign-Born, 1950–1954." *Western Historical Quarterly* 32 (Autumn 2001): 273–95.

Glickman, Lawrence B. *A Living Wage: American Workers and the Making of Consumer Society*. Ithaca, N.Y.: Cornell University Press, 1999.

Goldman, Marion S. *Gold Diggers and Silver Miners: Prostitution and Social Life on the Comstock Lode*. Women and Culture Series. Ann Arbor: University of Michigan Press, 1981.

Gómez-Quiñones, Juan. *Chicano Politics: Reality and Promise, 1940–1990*. Albuquerque: University of New Mexico Press, 1990.

———. *Roots of Chicano Politics, 1600–1940*. Albuquerque: University of New Mexico Press, 1994.

Gonzales-Berry, Erlinda. "Which Language Will Our Children Learn? The Spanish Language and Public Education Policy in New Mexico, 1890–1930." In *The Contested Homeland: A Chicano History of New Mexico*, edited by Erlinda Gonzales-Berry and David R. Maciel, 169–89. Albuquerque: University of New Mexico Press, 2000.

González, Deena J. *Refusing the Favor: The Spanish-Mexican Women of Santa Fe, 1820–1880*. 2nd ed. New York: Oxford University Press, 2001.

González, Nancie L. *The Spanish Americans of New Mexico: A Heritage of Pride*. Albuquerque: University of New Mexico Press, 1967. Revised and enlarged, 1969.

González, Rosalinda M. "Chicanas and Mexican Immigrant Families, 1920–1940: Women's Subordination and Economic Exploitation." In *Decades of Discontent: The Women's Movement, 1920–1940*, edited by Lois Scharf and Joan M. Jensen, 59–84. Boston: Northeastern University Press, 1983.

Gordon, Linda. *The Great Arizona Orphan Abduction*. Cambridge, Mass.: Harvard University Press, 1999.

———. *Heroes of Their Own Lives: The Politics and History of Family Violence*. New York: Penguin, 1988.

———. *Pitied But Not Entitled: Single Mothers and the History of Welfare, 1890–1935*. New York: Free Press, 1994.

———. "What's New in Women's History." In *Feminist Studies/Critical Studies*, edited by Teresa de Lauretis. Theories of Contemporary Culture, vol. 8. Bloomington: Indiana University Press, 1986.

Gorman, Paul. *Left Intellectuals and Popular Culture in Twentieth-Century America*. Chapel Hill: University of North Carolina Press, 1996.

Gosse, Van. " 'To Organize in Every Neighborhood': The Gender Politics of American Communists between the Wars." *Radical History Review* 50 (Spring 1991): 109–41.

"Grant County Sheriffs for 100 Years." *La Ventura Magazine*, July 27, 1968, sec. 2, p. 4.

Griswold del Castillo, Richard. *The Los Angeles Barrio, 1850–1890: A Social History*. Berkeley: University of California Press, 1979.

Grubbs, Donald H. *Cry from the Cotton: The Southern Tenant Farmers' Union and the New Deal*. Chapel Hill: University of North Carolina Press, 1971.

Guérin-Gonzales, Camille. "From Ludlow to Camp Solidarity: Women, Men, and Cultures of Solidarity in U.S. Coal Communities, 1912–1990." In *Mining Women: Gender in the Development of a Global Industry, 1670 to 2000*, edited by Jaclyn J. Gier and Laurie Mercier, 296–324. New York: Palgrave Macmillan, 2006.

Gutiérrez, David G. *Walls and Mirrors: Mexican Americans, Mexican Immigrants, and the Politics of Ethnicity*. Berkeley: University of California Press, 1995.

Harris, Howell John. *The Right to Manage: Industrial Relations Policies of American Business in the 1940s*. Madison: University of Wisconsin Press, 1982.

Hartmann, Heidi. "Capitalism, Patriarchy, and Job Segregation by Sex." *Signs: Journal of Women in Society* 3 (Spring 1976): 137–69.

Healey, Dorothy, and Maurice Isserman. *Dorothy Healey Remembers: A Life in the Communist Party*. New York: Oxford University Press, 1990. Republished as *California Red: A Life in the Communist Party*. Urbana: University of Illinois Press, 1993.

Henderson, Jean W. *The History of the Church of the Good Shepherd and the Life of Christ of Copper*. Silver City, N.M.: n.p., 1983.

Hernández, José, Leo Estrada, and David Alvírez. "Census Data and the Problem of Conceptually Defining the Mexican American Population." *Social Science Quarterly* 53 (March 1973): 671–87.

Hernon, Robert M., and William R. Jones. "Ore Deposits of the Central Mining District, Grant County, New Mexico." In *Ore Deposits of the United States*. Vol. 2, edited by John D. Ridge. New York: American Institute of Mining, Metallurgical, and Petroleum Engineers, Inc., 1968.

Heyman, Josiah McC. "In the Shadows of the Smokestacks: Labor and Environmental Conflict in a Company-dominated Town." In *Articulating Hidden Histories: Exploring the Influence of Eric R. Wolf*, edited by Jane Schneider and Rayna Rapp, 156–74. Berkeley: University of California Press, 1995.

Horne, Gerald. *Class Struggle in Hollywood, 1930–1950: Moguls, Mobsters, Stars, Reds, and Trade Unionists*. Austin: University Press of Texas, 2001.

Huettig, Mae D. *Economic Control of the Motion Picture Industry: A Study in Industrial Organization*. Philadelphia: University of Pennsylvania Press, 1944; and London: Oxford University Press, 1944.

Huginnie, A. Yvette. "A New Hero Comes to Town: The Anglo Mining Engineer and 'Mexican Labor' as Contested Terrain in Southeastern Arizona, 1880–1920." *New Mexico Historical Review* 69 (October 1994): 323–44.

Huntley, Horace. "The Red Scare and Black Workers in Alabama: The International Union of Mine, Mill and Smelter Workers, 1945–1953." In *Labor Divided: Race and Ethnicity in United States Labor Struggles, 1835–1960*, edited by Robert Asher and Charles Stephenson, 129–45. Albany: State University of New York Press, 1990.

Hurtado, Albert L. *Indian Survival on the California Frontier*. Yale Western Americana Series, 35. New Haven: Yale University Press, 1988.

Hyde, Charles K. *Copper for America: The United States Copper Industry from Colonial Times to the 1990s*. Tucson: University of Arizona Press, 1998.

Isserman, Maurice. *Which Side Were You On? The American Communist Party during the Second World War*. Middletown, Conn.: Wesleyan Press, 1982. Reprint, Urbana: University of Illinois Press, 1993.

Jameson, Elizabeth. *All That Glitters: Class, Conflict, and Community in Cripple Creek*. The Working Class in American History. Urbana: University of Illinois Press, 1998.

———. "Imperfect Unions: Class and Gender in Cripple Creek, 1894–1904." *Frontiers* 1 (Spring 1976): 89–117.

Jencks, Clinton E. *Men Underground: Working Conditions of British Coal Miners Since Nationalization*. Social Science Monograph Series, vol. 1, no. 4. San Diego: San Diego State College Press, 1969.

Jensen, Vernon H. *Nonferrous Metals Industry Unionism, 1932–1954: A Story of*

Leadership Controversy. Cornell Studies in Industrial and Labor Relations, vol. 5. Ithaca, N.Y.: Cornell University Press, 1954.

Johnson, Susan L. *Roaring Camp: The Social World of the California Gold Rush*. New York: W. W. Norton, 2000.

———. "Sharing Bed and Board: Cohabitation and Cultural Difference in Central Arizona Mining Towns, 1863–1873." In *The Women's West*, edited by Susan Armitage and Elizabeth Jameson, 36–42. Norman: University of Oklahoma Press, 1987.

Jones, Paul M. *Memories of Santa Rita*. N.p.: Author, 1985.

Kaminsky, Amy. "Gender, Race, *Raza*." *Feminist Studies* 20 (Spring 1994): 7–31.

Kaplan, Temma. "Female Consciousness and Collective Action: The Case of Barcelona, 1910–1918." *Signs: Journal of Women in Culture and Society* 7 (Spring 1982): 545–66.

Keeran, Roger. *The Communist Party and the Auto Workers Unions*. Bloomington: Indiana University Press, 1980.

Keitel, Robert S. "The Merger of the International Union of Mine, Mill and Smelter Workers into the United Steelworkers of America." *Labor History* 15 (Winter 1974): 36–43.

Kelley, Robin D. G. *Hammer and Hoe: Alabama Communists during the Great Depression*. Fred W. Morrison Series in Southern Studies. Chapel Hill: University of North Carolina Press, 1990.

Kerby, Elizabeth. "Violence in Silver City—Who Caused the Trouble?" *Frontier: The New Voice of the West* (May 1953): 5–10.

Kessler-Harris, Alice. *In Pursuit of Equity: Women, Men, and the Quest for Economic Citizenship in Twentieth-Century America*. New York: Oxford University Press, 2001.

———. *A Woman's Wage: Historical Meanings and Social Consequences*. Lexington: University Press of Kentucky, 1990.

Kirstein, Peter N. "American Railroads and the Bracero Program, 1943–1946." *Journal of Mexican American History* 5 (1975): 57–90.

Klehr, Harvey. *The Heyday of American Communism: The Depression Decade*. New York: Basic Books, 1984.

Klehr, Harvey, John Earl Haynes, and Kyrill M. Anderson. *The Soviet World of American Communism*. Annals of Communism. New Haven: Yale University Press, 1998.

Kleinberg, Susan J. "Technology and Women's Work: The Lives of Working-Class Women in Pittsburgh, 1870–1900." *Labor History* 17 (1976): 58–72.

Klubock, Thomas Miller. *Contested Communities: Class, Gender, and Politics in Chile's El Teniente Copper Mine, 1904–1951*. Comparative and International Working-Class History. Durham, N.C.: Duke University Press, 1998.

Korstad, Robert Rodgers. *Civil Rights Unionism: Tobacco Workers and the Struggle for Democracy in the Twentieth-Century South*. Chapel Hill: University of North Carolina Press, 2003.

Larralde, Carlos C., and Richard Griswold del Castillo. "Luisa Moreno: A His-
    panic Civil Rights Leader in San Diego." *Journal of San Diego History* 41
    (Fall 1995): 284–311.
Ledesma, Irene. "Texas Newspapers and Chicana Workers' Activism, 1919–
    1970." *Western Historical Quarterly* 26 (Autumn 1995): 309–31.
Levenstein, Harvey. *Communism, Anticommunism, and the CIO.* Contributions
    in American History, no. 91. Westport, Conn.: Greenwood Press, 1981.
Lewis, Robert S. *Elements of Mining.* 3rd rev. ed. New York: John Wiley and
    Sons, 1964.
Lichtenstein, Nelson. *Labor's War at Home: The CIO in World War II.* Cam-
    bridge: Cambridge University Press, 1982.
Lindsay, Lisa A. "Domesticity and Difference: Male Breadwinners, Working
    Women, and Colonial Citizenship in the 1945 Nigerian General Strike."
    American Historical Review 104 (June 1999): 783–812.
Long, Priscilla. *Where the Sun Never Shines: A History of America's Bloody Coal
    Industry.* New York: Paragon House, 1989.
——. "The Women of the Colorado Fuel and Iron Strike, 1913–1914." In
    Women, Work and Protest: A Century of U.S. Women's Labor History,
    edited by Ruth Milkman, 62–85. New York: Routledge, 1985.
Lorence, James J. *The Suppression of "Salt of the Earth": How Hollywood, Big
    Labor, and Politicians Blacklisted a Movie in Cold War America.* Albu-
    querque: University of New Mexico Press, 1999.
Maciel, David R. "Los desarraigados: los chicanos vistos por el cine mexicano."
    In *México Estados Unidos: Encuentros y desencuentros en el cine,* edited by
    Ignacio Durán, Iván Trujillo, and Mónica Verea, 165–88. México D.F.: Uni-
    versidad Nacional Autónoma de México.
Magnusson, Leifur. "A Modern Copper Mining Town." *Monthly Labor Review* 3
    (September 1918): 276–84.
Márquez, Benjamin. *LULAC: The Evolution of a Mexican American Political
    Organization.* Austin: University of Texas Press, 1993.
Martín, Patricia Preciado. *Songs My Mother Sang to Me: An Oral History of Mex-
    ican American Women.* Tucson: University of Arizona Press, 1992.
May, Lary. *The Big Tomorrow: Hollywood and the Politics of the American Way.*
    Chicago: University of Chicago Press, 2000.
McGaw, William Cochran. *Savage Scene: The Life and Times of James Kirker,
    Frontier King.* New York: Hastings House Publishers, 1972.
McGilligan, Patrick, and Paul Buhle. *Tender Comrades: A Backstory of the Black-
    list.* New York: St. Martin's, 1999.
McWilliams, Carey. *North from Mexico: The Spanish-Speaking People of the
    United States.* New ed., updated by Matt S. Meier. New York: Praeger Pub-
    lishers, 1990.
Meinig, D. W. *Southwest: Three Peoples in Geographical Change, 1600–1970.*
    New York: Oxford University Press, 1971.

Mellinger, Philip J. *Race and Labor in Western Copper: The Fight for Equality, 1896–1918.* Tucson: University of Arizona Press, 1995.

Melzer, Richard. *Coming of Age in the Depression: The Civilian Conservation Corps Experience in New Mexico, 1933–1942.* Las Cruces, N.M.: Yucca Tree Press, 2000.

———. "Exiled in the Desert: The Bisbee Deportees' Reception in New Mexico, 1917." *New Mexico Historical Review* 67 (July 1992): 269–84.

Mercier, Laurie. *Anaconda: Labor, Community, and Culture in Montana's Smelter City.* The Working Class in American History. Urbana: University of Illinois Press, 2001.

Meyer, Doris L. "Early Mexican-American Responses to Negative Stereotyping." *New Mexico Historical Review* 53 (January 1978): 75–91.

Milkman, Ruth. *Gender at Work: The Dynamics of Job Segregation by Sex during World War II.* The Working Class in American History. Urbana: University of Illinois Press, 1987.

Miller, Darlis A. "Cross-Cultural Marriages in the Southwest: The New Mexico Experience, 1846–1900." In *New Mexico Women: Intercultural Perspectives,* edited by Joan M. Jensen and Darlis A. Miller, 95–119. Albuquerque: University of New Mexico Press, 1986.

Miller, Tom. "*Salt of the Earth* Revisited." *Cineaste* 13, no. 4 (1984): 30–36.

Mills, C. Wright. *The Power Elite.* New York: Oxford University Press, 1956.

Mitchell, H. L. *Mean Things Happening in This Land: The Life and Times of H. L. Mitchell, Co-Founder of the Southern Tenant Farmers Union.* Montclair, N.J.: Allanheld, Osmun, 1979.

Montejano, David. *Anglos and Mexicans in the Making of Texas, 1836–1986.* Austin: University of Texas Press, 1987.

Montoya, María E. "The Roots of Ethnic and Economic Divisions in Northern New Mexico: The Case of the Civilian Conservation Corps." *Western Historical Quarterly* 26 (Spring 1995): 14–34.

Murphy, Lucy Eldersveld. *A Gathering of Rivers: Indians, Métis, and Mining in the Western Great Lakes, 1737–1832.* Lincoln: University of Nebraska Press, 2000.

Naison, Mark. *Communists in Harlem during the Depression.* Urbana: University of Illinois Press, 1983.

Nash, Gerald D. "New Mexico in the Otero Era: Some Historical Perspectives." *New Mexico Historical Review* 67 (January 1992): 1–12.

Navasky, Victor. *Naming Names.* New York: Viking Press, 1980. Reprint, New York: Penguin Books, 1981.

Nott, Robert. "The Song of Jenny Vincent." *The New Mexican* (Santa Fe), February 21–27, 2003, 38–39.

O'Neill, Colleen. "Domesticity Deployed: Gender, Race, and the Construction of Class Struggle in the Bisbee Deportation." *Labor History* 34 (1993): 256–73.

Orozco, Cynthia E. "Alice Dickerson Montemayor: Feminism and Mexican

American Politics in the 1930s." In *Writing the Range: Race, Class, and Culture in the Women's West,* edited by Elizabeth Jameson and Susan Armitage, 435–56. Norman: University of Oklahoma Press, 1997.

———. "Beyond Machismo, La Familia, and Ladies Auxiliaries: A Historiography of Mexican-Origin Women's Participation in Voluntary Associations and Politics in the United States, 1870–1990." *Perspectives in Mexican American Studies* 5 (1995): 1–34.

———. "Regionalism, Politics, and Gender in Southwest History: The League of United Latin American Citizens's Expansion into New Mexico from Texas, 1929–1945." *Western Historical Quarterly* 29 (Winter 1998): 459–83.

Pardo, Mary. "Creating Community: Mexican American Women in Eastside Los Angeles." *Aztlán* 20, nos. 1 and 2, Las Obreras: The Politics of Work and Family (1991): 39–72.

———. *Mexican American Women Activists: Identity and Resistance in Two Los Angeles Communities.* Philadelphia: Temple University Press, 1998.

Parsons, A. B. *The Porphyry Coppers.* Rocky Mountain Fund Series. New York: American Institute of Mining and Metallurgical Engineers, 1933.

Pearce, T. M., ed. *New Mexico Place Names: A Geographical Dictionary.* Albuquerque: University of New Mexico Press, 1965.

Peck, Gunther. *Reinventing Free Labor: Padrones and Immigrant Workers in the North American West, 1880–1930.* Cambridge: Cambridge University Press, 2000.

Penfold, Steven. " 'Have You No Manhood in You?' Gender and Class in the Cape Breton Coal Towns, 1920–1926." In *Gender and History in Canada,* edited by Joy Parr and Mark Rosenfeld, 270–93. Toronto: Copp Clark, Ltd., 1996.

Pesquera, Beatríz M. " 'In the Beginning He Wouldn't Lift Even a Spoon': The Division of Household Labor." In *Building with Our Hands: New Directions in Chicana Studies,* edited by Adela de la Torre and Beatríz M. Pesquera, 181–95. Berkeley: University of California Press, 1993.

Probert, Alan. "Discord at Real del Monte." *Journal of the West* 14 (April 1975).

Ramos, Henry A. J. *American G.I. Forum: In Pursuit of the Dream, 1948–1983.* Houston: Arte Público Press, 1998.

Ramirez, Frank. *Remembering Fierro.* Silver City, N.M.: Mother Bird Books, 1998.

Randall, Richard S. "Censorship: From 'The Miracle' to 'Deep Throat.' " In *American Film Industry,* edited by Tino Balio, 432–57. Madison: University of Wisconsin Press, 1985.

Rickard, T. A. *A History of American Mining.* New York: McGraw-Hill, 1932.

———. *Interviews with Mining Engineers.* San Francisco: Mining and Scientific Press, 1922.

Rodríguez, Clara E. *Changing Race: Latinos, the Census, and the History of Eth-*

nicity in the United States. Critical America Series. New York: New York University Press, 2000.

Rose, Margaret. "From the Fields to the Picket Line: Huelga Women and the Boycott, 1965–1975." *Labor History* 31 (Summer 1990): 271–93.

——. "Gender and Civic Activism in Mexican American Barrios in California: The Community Service Organization, 1947–1962." In *Not June Cleaver: Women and Gender in Postwar America, 1945–1960*, edited by Joanne Meyerowitz, 177–200. Critical Perspectives on the Past. Philadelphia: Temple University Press, 1994.

——. "Traditional and Nontraditional Patterns of Female Activism in the United Farm Workers of America, 1962 to 1980." *Frontiers* 11, no. 1 (1990): 26–32.

Rosenblum, Jonathan D. *Copper Crucible: How the Arizona Miners' Strike of 1983 Recast Labor-Management Relations in America*. Ithaca, N.Y.: ILR Press, 1995.

Rowse, A. J. *The Cornish in America*. New York: Macmillan Company, 1969.

Rubenstein, Harry R. "The Great Gallup Coal Strike of 1933." *New Mexico Historical Review* 52 (July 1977): 173–92.

Ruiz, Vicki L. *Cannery Women, Cannery Lives: Mexican Women, Unionization, and the California Food Processing Industry, 1930–1950*. Albuquerque: University of New Mexico Press, 1987.

——. "Claiming Public Space at Work, Church, and Neighborhood." In *Las Obreras: Chicana Politics of Work and Family*, edited by Vicki L. Ruiz, 13–39. Aztlán Anthology Series, vol. 1. Los Angeles: UCLA Chicano Studies Research Center Publications, 2000.

——. *From Out of the Shadows: Mexican Women in Twentieth-Century America*. New York: Oxford University Press, 1998.

——. "Una Mujer Sin Fronteras: Luisa Moreno and Latina Labor Activism." *Pacific Historical Review* 73 (February 2004): 1–20.

——, ed. *Las Obreras: Chicana Politics of Work and Family*. Aztlán Anthology Series, vol. 1. Los Angeles: UCLA Chicano Studies Research Center Publications, 2000.

Sánchez, George J. *Becoming Mexican American: Ethnicity, Culture, and Identity in Chicano Los Angeles, 1900–1945*. New York: Oxford University Press, 1993.

Sandoval T., Ivett. *Mexikos Esperanza: Un acercamiento a Rosaura Revueltas*. Durango, Dgo., México: Instituto de Cultura del Estado de Durango, 2002.

Saxe, Robert Francis. "'Citizens First, Veterans Second': The American Veterans Committee and the Challenge of Postwar 'Independent Progressives.'" *War and Society* [Australia] 22 (October 2004): 75–94.

Schaffer, Robert. "Women and the Communist Party USA, 1930–1940." *Socialist Review* 45 (May–June 1979): 73–118.

Schleuning, Neala. *Women, Community, and the Hormel Strike of 1985–86*.

Contributions in Women's Studies, no. 137. Westport, Conn.: Greenwood Press, 1994.

Schofield, Ann. "An 'Army of Amazons': The Language of Protest in a Kansas Mining Community, 1921–1922." *American Quarterly* 37 (Winter 1985): 686–701.

Schrecker, Ellen. *Many Are the Crimes: McCarthyism in America*. Boston: Little, Brown and Company, 1998.

——. "McCarthyism and the Labor Movement: The Role of the State." In *The CIO's Left-Led Unions*, edited by Steve Rosswurm, 139–57. Class and Culture Series. New Brunswick, N.J.: Rutgers University Press, 1992.

Scott, Rebecca J. "Fault Lines, Color Lines, and Party Lines: Race, Labor, and Collective Action in Louisiana and Cuba, 1862–1912." In *Beyond Slavery: Explorations of Race, Labor, and Citizenship in Postemancipation Societies*, edited by Frederick Cooper, Thomas C. Holt, and Rebecca J. Scott, 61–106. Chapel Hill: University of North Carolina Press, 2000.

Severo, Richard, and Lewis Milford. *The Wages of War: When American Soldiers Came Home—Valley Forge to Vietnam*. New York: Simon and Schuster, 1989.

Sinclair, John L. "The Town That Vanished into Thin Air." *New Mexico Magazine*, March 1997, <http://www.southernnewmexico.com/Articles/Southwest/Grant/SantaRita-Thetownthatvani.html> (accessed March 17, 2003).

Sklar, Robert. *Movie-Made America: A Cultural History of American Movies*. New York: Random House, 1975.

Sloane, Howard N., and Lucille L. Sloane. *A Pictorial History of American Mining*. New York: Crown Publishers, 1970.

Sondergaard, Gale. "Artist and Man." *American Dialogue* (Winter 1972): 18–23.

Spence, Clark D. *Mining Engineers and the American West, 1849–1933: The Lace-Boot Brigade*. Yale Western Americana Series, 22. New Haven: Yale University Press, 1970.

Starobin, Joseph. *American Communism in Crisis, 1943–1957*. Cambridge, Mass.: Harvard University Press, 1972.

Steedman, Mercedes. "Godless Communists and Faithful Wives, Gender Relations and the Cold War: Mine Mill and the 1958 Strike against the International Nickel Company." In *Mining Women: Gender in the Development of a Global Industry, 1670 to 2000*, edited by Jaclyn J. Gier and Laurie Mercier, 233–53. New York: Palgrave Macmillan, 2006.

Stevenson, Philip [Lars Lawrence]. *The Hoax*. The Seed, part 2, vol. 2. New York: International Publishers, 1961.

——. *Morning, Noon and Night*. The Seed, part 1., vol. 1. New York: G. P. Putnam's Sons, 1954.

——. *Old Father Antic*. The Seed, part 2, vol. 1. New York: International Publishers, 1961.

——. *Out of the Dust*. The Seed, part 1, vol. 2. New York: G. Putnam's Sons, 1956.

Sweeney, Edwin R. *Mangas Coloradas: Chief of the Chiricahua Apaches*. The Civilization of the American Indian Series, vol. 231. Norman: University of Oklahoma Press, 1998.

——. "Mangas Coloradas and Mid-Nineteenth-Century Conflicts." In *New Mexican Lives: Profiles and Historical Stories*, edited by Richard W. Etulain, 131–62. Albuquerque: University of New Mexico Press, 2002.

Swerdlow, Amy. "The Congress of American Women: Left-Feminist Peace Politics in the Cold War." In *U.S. History as Women's History: New Feminist Essays*, edited by Linda Kerber et al., 296–312. Gender and American Culture. Chapel Hill: University of North Carolina Press, 1995.

Taillon, Paul Michel. "'What We Want Is Good, Sober Men': Masculinity, Respectability, and Temperance in the Railroad Brotherhoods, c. 1870–1910." *Journal of Social History* 36 (2002): 319–38.

Tilly, Louise A., and Joan W. Scott. *Women, Work, and Family*. New York: Holt, Rinehart and Winston, 1978. Reprint, New York: Routledge, 1989.

Twitchell, Ralph Emerson, ed. and comp. *The Leading Facts of New Mexican History*. Vol. 3. Cedar Rapids, Iowa: Torch Press, 1917.

Tyler, Robert. "The American Veterans Committee: Out of a Hot War and into the Cold." *American Quarterly* 18 (Fall 1966): 419–36.

Ulrich, Laurel Thatcher. *Good Wives: Image and Reality in the Lives of Women in Northern New England, 1650–1750*. New York: Vintage Books, 1980.

Urrutia, Liliana. "An Offspring of Discontent: The Asociación Nacional México-Americana, 1949–1954." *Aztlán* 15 (Spring 1984): 177–84.

Vargas, Zaragosa. *Labor Rights Are Civil Rights: Mexican American Workers in Twentieth-Century America*. Politics and Society in Twentieth-Century America. Princeton, N.J.: Princeton University Press, 2004.

Weber, Devra. *Dark Sweat, White Gold: California Farm Workers, Cotton, and the New Deal*. Berkeley: University of California Press, 1994.

Weigand, Kate. *Red Feminism: American Communism and the Making of Women's Liberation*. Reconfiguring American Political History. Baltimore: Johns Hopkins University Press, 2001.

Weinberg, Albert Katz. *Manifest Destiny: A Study of Nationalist Expansion in American History*. Baltimore: Johns Hopkins University Press, 1935.

Wendel, Clarence Adami. "Mining in Butte Forty Years Ago." *Montana: The Magazine of Western History* 31 (July 1981): 60–66.

Willis, Charles F. "Housing at Tyrone, New Mexico." *Chemical and Metallurgical Engineering* 19 (October 1918): 627–29.

Wilson, Michael. *Salt of the Earth*. New York: Feminist Press, 1978.

Woyski, Margaret S. "Women and Mining in the Old West." *Journal of the West* 20 (April 1981): 38–47.

Yarrow, Michael. "The Gender-Specific Consciousness of Appalachian Coal

Miners: Structure and Change." In *Bringing Class Back In: Contemporary and Historical Perspectives*, edited by Scott G. McNall, Rhonda Levine, and Rick Fantasia, 285–310. Boulder, Colo.: Westview Press, 1991.

Yeghissian, Patricia. "Emergence of the Red Berets." *Michigan Occasional Papers in Women's Studies* 10 (Winter 1980).

Young, George J. *Elements of Mining*. 4th ed. New York: McGraw-Hill, 1946.

Zavella, Patricia. *Women's Work and Chicano Families: Cannery Workers of the Santa Clara Valley*. Anthropology of Contemporary Issues, 8. Ithaca, N.Y.: Cornell University Press, 1987.

Zieger, Robert H. *American Workers, American Unions*. 2nd ed. The American Moment. Baltimore: Johns Hopkins University Press, 1994.

———. *The CIO, 1935–1955*. Chapel Hill: University of North Carolina Press, 1995.

Zinn, Maxine Baca. "Political Familism: Toward Sex-Role Equality in Chicano Families." *Aztlán* 6 (Spring 1975): 13–37.

Unpublished Secondary Sources

Baker, Ellen R. "*Salt of the Earth*: Women, the Mine, Mill and Smelter Workers' Union, and the Hollywood Blacklist in Grant County, New Mexico, 1941–1953." Ph.D. diss., University of Wisconsin–Madison, 1999.

———. "Women in the Ludlow Strike." Unpublished paper, University of Wisconsin–Madison, 1991.

———. "Women Working for the Cooperative Commonwealth: Populists and Socialists Address the Woman Question, 1890–1914." M.A. thesis, University of Wisconsin–Madison, 1992.

Benton, Katherine A. "What About Women in the White Man's Camp? Gender, Nation, and the Redefinition of Race in Cochise County, Arizona, 1853–1941." Ph.D. diss., University of Wisconsin–Madison, 2002.

Budd, Mike. "Film Censorship and Public Cultures: The National Board of Review and Women's Voluntary Associations, 1909–1950." Paper presented to the American Studies Association, Washington, D.C., October 30, 1997.

Cargill, Jack. "Empire and Opposition: Class, Ethnicity and Ideology in the Mine-Mill Union of Grant County, New Mexico." M.A. thesis, University of New Mexico, 1979.

Clark, Carol L. "Architecture and Town Development in the Mining Camps of Southwestern New Mexico." M.A. thesis, University of New Mexico, 1982.

Couturier, Michelle. "'Women's Women': Socialist Party Activists and Writers for the *Progressive Woman*, 1907–1915." M.A. thesis, University of Wisconsin–Madison, 1985.

De Luna, George. "The Mexican American: Two Generations in Santa Rita and Kennecott." Typescript, December 1, 1972. Silver City Public Library Treasure Room, Silver City, N.M.

Garcilazo, Jeffrey. "*Traqueros*: Mexican Railroad Workers in the United States, 1870–1930." Ph.D. diss., University of California–Santa Barbara, 1995.

Garza, Edward D. "LULAC: League of United Latin American Citizens." M.A. thesis, Southwest Texas State Teachers College, 1951.

Himes, B. L. "The General Managers at Chino." Typescript, 1987. Silver City Public Library Treasure Room, Silver City, N.M.

——. "The Unions and the Chino Mines." Typescript, 1987. Silver City Public Library Treasure Room, Silver City, N.M.

Huggard, Christopher J. "Environmental and Economic Change in the Twentieth-Century West: The History of the Copper Industry in New Mexico." Ph.D. diss., University of New Mexico, 1994.

Huginnie, A. Yvette. "'Strikitos': Race, Class, and Work in the Arizona Copper Industry." Ph.D. diss., Yale University, 1991.

Humble, Terence M. "Grant County, New Mexico—Santa Rita history." USGen-Web Archives (ftp://ftp.rootsweb.com/pub/usgenweb/nm/grant/ceme teries/srhist.txt, 1998). Accessed November 1, 2002.

Huntley, Horace. "Iron Ore Miners and Mine-Mill in Alabama, 1933–1952." Ph.D. diss., University of Pittsburgh, 1977.

Milbauer, John Albert. "The Historical Geography of the Silver City Mining Region of New Mexico." Ph.D. diss., University of California–Riverside, 1983.

Moore, Thomas. "The Search for Alternatives: Veterans, Unions, and Veterans' Organizations, 1944–1950." Paper presented to the North American Labor History Conference, Detroit, October 19–21, 1995.

Murray, Sylvie. "A la jonction du mouvement ouvrier et du mouvement des femmes: la ligue auxiliaire de l'Association Internationale des Machinistes, Canada, 1903–1980." M.A. thesis, University of Québec at Montréal, 1988.

Orozco, Cynthia E. "The Origins of the League of United Latin American Citizens (LULAC) and the Mexican American Civil Rights Movement in Texas with an Analysis of Women's Political Participation in a Gendered Context, 1910–1929." Ph.D. diss., University of California, Los Angeles, 1992.

Rose, Margaret Eleanor. "Women in the United Farm Workers: A Study of Chicana and Mexicana Participation in a Labor Union, 1950–1980." Ph.D. diss., University of California, Los Angeles, 1988.

Shapiro, Linn. "Red Feminism: American Communism and the Women's Rights Tradition, 1919–1956." Ph.D. diss., American University, 1996.

Stephenson, Richard B. "The Use of Troops in Labor Disputes in New Mexico." M.A. thesis, University of New Mexico, 1952.

Weigand, Kathleen Anne. "Vanguards of Women's Liberation: The Old Left and the Continuity of the Women's Movement of the United States, 1945–1970s." Ph.D. diss., Ohio State University, 1995.

Woolman, James. "Rough Draft for a New Cold War: U.S. Foreign Aid, the Aswan Dam, and the Rise of Economic Development, 1951–1958." B.A. thesis, Columbia University, 2002.

INDEX

Page numbers in italics refer to illustrations.

Accidents, mining, 91–92, 93, 99
Acosta, Rodolfo, 206, 207
African Americans, 166, 202–4, 224
Alderette, Clorinda (Kirker), 113, 119, 157, 160, 212
Alderette, Frank, 160
Alianza Hispano Americana (AHA), 59, 92–93, 273 (n. 73)
Alvarado, Luis, 91
American Federation of Labor (AFL), 48, 51, 61, 131; limited success of, in Grant County, 50, 57–58, 59–60, 62
American Legion, 183, 225, 235
American Mining Congress, 68
American Smelting and Refining Company (Asarco), 28, 31, 69, 131, 160, 250, 273 (n. 62); Mine-Mill organizing in, 56, 57, 82, 161 (*see also* Local 530); and 1949–50 unemployment crisis, 95, 99
Anchondo, Seferino, 100, 286 (n. 57)
Andazola, Camerina, 219
Andazola, Willie, 219, *220*
"Anglo" (term), 12, 23
Anglo workers, 60–62; in Mine-Mill locals, 47, 48, 50, 61–62, 72, 73
Anticommunism, 70–72, 187, 239–40, 242, 251–52; limited appeal of, to Grant County mine workers, 2, 49, 82, 248, 251; use of, against *Salt of the Earth*, 2, 223–35; use of, by mining employers,

7–8, 48, 68, 69, 82, 113, 243, 248; and conflicts within Mine-Mill, 48, 70–71, 110; in motion picture industry, 185–91, 223–24, 232–35, 242; violent, 227–29
Apaches, 19–21, 22
Aragón, Fidel, 95
Arzola, Rubén, 103–4
Asarco. *See* American Smelting and Refining Company
Asian Americans, 262 (n. 31)
Asociación Nacional Mexicana Americana (ANMA), 102–7, 194, 288 (n. 71)
Association of Documentary Technicians and Film Cameramen (ADTFC), 233
Attorney general's list, 106, 291 (n. 146)
Auxiliaries. *See* Ladies' auxiliaries
Avalos, Jesús, 84, 122, 123, 144, 149
Avalos, Marcelo, 53

Ballmer, Ward, 225
Banks, 169
Barnett, H. L., 287–88 (n. 67), 312 (n. 29)
Barreras, Fred, 137, *138*, 298 (n. 146)
Bars, 90, 168
Baseball, 40
Bayard, N.M., 31, 54, 104, 165; not a company town, 37, 55; businesses in, 55, 141, 142–43, 163, 166, 168; and Empire Zinc strike, 85, 141, 142–43; union hall in, 85, 231, 232; and *Salt of the Earth*, 227–28, 311 (n. 6)
Bear Mountain Ranch, 224

Becerra, Eva, 149

Becerra, Vicente, 144, 148, 150

Bell, James, 26

Bencomo, Felipe, 90–91

Berresford, Richard, 238

Bessie, Alvah, 188

Biberman, Herbert, 186, 200, 235; background of, 182; and Independent Productions Corporation, 190–91, 200, 203, 204; views of, on cultural politics, 196–97, 202; as director of *Salt of the Earth*, 205–11, 212, 216, 218–19, 221, 227, 232–35; romanticizing by, 209–10

Biberman, Sonja Dahl, 180–81, 182; and *Salt of the Earth*, 207, 213–14, 215–16, 224

Bible, Leroy B., 225

Bisbee, Ariz., 41

Blackhawk Mining Company, 26, 37–38, 58, 160

Blacklisting: in mining industry, 55, 56–57, 242. *See also* Motion picture industry

Blackwell, Jack, 237

Blaine, Grant, 121, 123, 128

Blair, Jim, 40–41

Bostick, Floyd, 73, 232, 316 (n. 15)

Boyd, W. S., 55

Breadwinner ethic, 93–94, 156

Brewer, Roy, 223–24, 232, 234, 250

Brewington, Bob, 134, 295 (n. 73)

Brooks, Homer D., 106–7

Brotherhood: model of unionism based on, 88–94, 97–98

Browder, Earl, 199

Brown, Lewis, 125

Brownell, Herbert, 238

Buhle, Paul, 185, 200

Burro Chief mine (Tyrone, N.M.), 92

Bustamante, Jesús, 84

Bustos, Angel, 104, 153, 247

California Quarterly, 234

Campbell, Stanley, 64–65

Capshaw, Robert "Bobby," 46, 128–29, 131, *132*, 133

Carlsbad, N.M., 232, 289 (n. 89)

Carrasco, José Manuel, 20

Carrillo, José, 105, 269 (n. 7)

Carrillo, Tomás, 129

Catholic Church, 39, 140, 196; priests in, 140, 224, 231. *See also* Smerke, Father Francis

Central, N.M., 37, 225, 227; and Empire Zinc strike, 139, 140

Ceplair, Larry, 214

Chacón, Juan, 80, 101, 163, 166–67, 243

—in *Salt of the Earth*: as actor in, 207–8, 209, 211, 217, *218*–19, 309 (n. 72); and anticommunist attacks, 227, 228, 234

Chacón, Virginia, 74, 80, 108, 146, 157, 163, 243, 246; and Empire Zinc strike, 86, 113, 125–26; and *Salt of the Earth*, 194, 210

Chapin, Rudy, *124*, 139–40

Chávez, Agustín, 151–52

Chávez, Aurora, 39, 86, 123, 151–52, 165, 247

Chávez, Daría (Escobar), 119–20, 123, *124*, 131, 136, 156

Chávez, Senator Dennis, 69, 225

Child care, 220–21; during Empire Zinc strike, 86, 119–20, 152, 172; in *Salt of the Earth* filming, 215–16

Chino Copper Company, 28, 31, 37, 78, 166, 250, 264 (n. 56), 274 (n. 85), 316 (n. 18); as subsidiary, 28; unionization in, 47–48, 50, 52–53, 55–56, 57–58, 61; in Great Depression, 49, 50, 52–54, 55–56, 271 (nn. 38, 39); in World War II, 57–58, 61–63; women's employment by, 62–63, 158–61; and job discrimination, 79. *See also* Kennecott Copper Corporation; Nevada Consolidated

Chino Metal Trades Council (AFL), 57–58, 59, 61, 273 (n. 70), 274 (n. 85)

Churches, 39, 140. *See also* Catholic Church

CIO. *See* Congress of Industrial Organizations

Civilian Conservation Corps (CCC), 54, 78, 271 (n. 42)

Clanton, G. W., 150

Clanton, Mrs., 130, 294 (n. 59)

Clark, John, 71, 148

Class consciousness: men's, 3, 51, 52, 88–90; women's, 10–11, 111–12, 157, 171, 292 (nn. 119, 125)

Clifton-Morenci mining district (Arizona), 61–62, 250

Cobble, Dorothy Sue, 107

Coleman, Charles, *195*, 212

Committee to Organize the Mexican People (COMP), 287 (n. 66)

Communist Party (CP), 80–82, 145, 246, 251–52; Mine-Mill national leaders

and, 2, 8, 48, 71; and Local 890, 2, 8,
  80–82, 251–52; in motion picture
  industry, 2, 179–82, 197, 198–202; and
  gender issues, 11, 107–8, 114, 126, 197,
  214, 259 (n. 21), 290 (n. 101); Mexican
  American workers and, 50, 80–82,
  106–7. *See also* Anticommunism
Compa, Juan José, 21
Company towns, 37–38, 266 (n. 86). *See also*
  Hurley, N.M.; Santa Rita, N.M.
Congreso National del Pueblo de Habla
  Española (National Congress of
  Spanish-Speaking People), 8
Congress of American Women (CAW), 108,
  291 (n. 104)
Congress of Industrial Organizations (CIO),
  52, 71, 100–101, 131; and Mine-Mill,
  7–8, 48, 52, 71, 100–101, 179; purge of
  left-wing unions from, 7–8, 48, 71, 179;
  and Taft-Hartley Act, 69, 70. *See also*
  United Steelworkers
Cooking, 163, 164–65
Costales, Francisco, 32
Cowan, Ruth Schwartz, 164
Craft workers, 29, 32, 33, 57–58, 59, 60–61
Crittenden, Victor H., 33, 53
Cruz, Antonio, 53, 271 (n. 29)
Curtis, Verne, 52, 56–57, 60, 67, 74, 75, 100,
  280 (n. 166)

Dahl, Sonja. *See* Biberman, Sonja Dahl
Dances, 39–40, 152
Dannelly, Claude, 53
Day, Roberto, 134, 145
De Baca, Ernie, 59
DeBraal, Cornelius "Bud," 71, 146
De la Torre, Reymundo, 59
De Luna, George, 166
Democracy in Local 890, 8, 47, 49, 73–74, 75,
  77, 81–83
Dempsey, Gov. John J., 67
Deportation, 52, 57, 103, 289 (n. 74)
Deputies. *See* Sheriff's deputies
"Deputy husband" role, 154
Derr, Virginia. *See* Jencks, Virginia (Derr)
Dimas, Joe, 91
Divorce, 170, 246
Dmytryk, Edward, 187
Dolan, Graham, 236
Domestic violence, 153, 170–71, 245
Domínguez, Anita, 165

Domínguez, Manuel, 165
Doñez, Max, 46, 316 (n. 8)
Dual-wage system, 1, 17, 23, 63, 168; Mine-
  Mill's challenge to, 1, 7, 62, 98
Dunbar, Carl, 142
Duncan, James, 142

Education, 38–39, 106, 246, 247, 267 (n. 99)
Eisenhower administration, 238
Elections, 40, 45, 100–102, 105–6, 150
Elguea, Francisco, 20
Elizado, Lupe, 147
El Paso, Tex., 56, 105–6
El Paso Herald-Post, 230
El Paso Times, 67
Empire Zinc Company, 24, 31, 58; as subsidiary of New Jersey Zinc Company, 24,
  138–39; impact of, on Hanover, 37–38,
  167; plant shutdowns by, 54, 95, 250,
  271 (n. 39). *See also* Empire Zinc strike
Empire Zinc strike, 1–2, 3–4, 45–47, 82–84,
  113–14, 115, 249; demands of, 1, 256
  (n. 1); gender relations in, 2, 4, 10, 86–
  87, 115, 152–54, 171–74; success of, 3,
  4, 149, 173, 249; injunctions in, 3, 46–
  47, 84, 85–88, 120–21, 123, 127–28;
  company's attempt to resume production during, 46, 84; arrests in, 46, 125–
  26, 135, 137; community attitudes
  toward, 103, 124, 139–47, 168; strikebreakers in, 121–23, 125, 128–29, 143,
  149; violence in, 128–31, 142–44, 145,
  149; and nationwide copper strike, 131,
  295 (n. 61); women's picket in (*see*
  Women's picket)
Englund, Steven, 214
Escobar, Daría. *See* Chávez, Daría (Escobar)
Escobar, Elena. *See* Tafoya, Elena (Escobar)
Escobedo, Juanita, 144
Esparza, Moctezuma, 253
Ethnic division of labor, 32, 155. *See also*
  Dual-wage system; Grant County min-
  ing industry: ethnic discrimination in
"Ethnicity" (term), 13

Fair Employment Practices Committee
  (FEPC), 61, 63–64, 274 (n. 85), 276
  (n. 106)
"Family wage," 93, 167–69; and sexual division of labor, 9, 93; and household budgets, 168. *See also* Breadwinner ethic

Fearing, Franklin, 201
Federal Bureau of Investigation (FBI), 187,
    238–39, 240, 241, 243
Female-headed households, 36–37
Feminism, 11, 107–8, 161–62, 259 (nn. 20–
    21)
Fierro, N.M., 40, 102–3, 164
Fifth Amendment, 188–90, 192, 237
First Amendment, 186, 188, 189
Fletcher, Abigail, 41
Fletcher, Frank, 41
Fletcher, Guadalupe, 158, 160
Fletcher, William, 41
Flexner, Eleanor, 108
Flint sit-down strike (1937), 111
Flores, Arturo, 38, 76, 77, 78–79, 156, 281
    (n. 189); as Mine-Mill activist, 79, 80,
    145; and Asociación Nacional Mexi-
    cana Americana, 104, 105, 106
Flores, Josephine "Josie," 156, 302 (n. 59)
Ford, Rev. J. W., 239
Foremen, 34
Forsythe, Harvey, 55
Fowler, Charles, 137
Foy, Thomas P., 46, 124–25, 127, 129, 136,
    150
Franco, Francisco, 122, 125, 129
Frank, Dana, 149
Fraternal organizations, 39

Gallup, N.M., 49–50, 52, 63, 97
García, David, 46
García, Delfino, 91
García, Wallace, 46
Gately, Bill, 234
Geer, Will, 212–13, 224
Gibney, Gertrude, 139–40
G.I. Forum, 285–86 (n. 47)
Gillespie, Glenn, 56, 67
Goforth, Leslie, 45–46, 144, 228; election of,
    as sheriff, 45, 102; and sheriff's depu-
    ties, 45–46, 83, 128, 131–33; and
    women's picket in Empire Zinc strike,
    120–21, 124–25, 126, 128; defeat of, for
    reelection, 150
Gómez, Tomás, 46
Gonzales, Carrie, 311 (n. 103)
González, Deena J., 23
Grant County, N.M.: ethnic mixture in, 19–
    23, 37–41, 230–31, 262 (n. 31); poverty
    and relief in, during Great Depression,

54–55, 271 (n. 42); soldiers from, in
    World War II, 66; elections in, 101–2,
    150, 288 (n. 69); attitudes in, toward
    Empire Zinc strike, 124, 139–48, 168;
    response in, to Salt of the Earth film-
    ing, 224–32, 235; housing in (see Hous-
    ing); mining towns in (see Mining
    towns). See also Grant County mining
    industry
Grant County Miners Association, 82
Grant County mining industry, 17, 244;
    geological setting of, 17–19; in nine-
    teenth century, 19–23; corporate struc-
    ture in, 23–28; work processes in, 26,
    29–32, 264 (n. 62); craft workers in, 29,
    32, 33; ethnic discrimination in, 32–34,
    63–65, 274 (n. 85) (see also Dual-wage
    system); women workers in, 34–36, 63,
    158–61, 300 (n. 23); antiunionism in,
    41–42, 47–48, 54, 55–56, 68, 69; in
    1930s, 47, 49–56; shutdowns in, 53–54,
    94–96, 250; in World War II, 56–67; in
    late 1940s, 67–70, 94–96; safety con-
    cerns in, 90–93. See also specific firms
Grant County Organization for the Defeat of
    Communism, 145, 146
Grant County Welfare Association, 54
Graves, Charles, 84
Gray, David, 142–43
Great Depression, 47, 49–56, 93; New Deal
    programs in, 47, 51–52, 54–55; Mine-
    Mill organizing campaigns during, 47–
    50, 51–56
Grissom, Roy, 52–53
Grocery stores, 142–43, 168–69
Ground Hog mine (Vanadium, N.M.), 57, 72
Gruwell, Angus, 55, 277 (n. 126)

Hafner, Harry, 56
Hales, Jack, 92
Hanett, A. T., 150
Hanover, N.M., 33, 34, 36, 54, 59, 95, 150;
    founding of, 22; and Empire Zinc strike,
    24, 37–38, 54; Mexican Americans in,
    33, 34, 38, 59, 72, 152, 164; as "semi-
    independent" town, 37–38; housing in,
    38, 93–94, 152, 164, 167, 173; Asarco
    mill in, 57, 72, 273 (n. 62)
Harris, E. T. "Buck," 225
Hartless, Betty Jo, 143–44
Hartless, Carl, 122

Hartless, Denzil, 121–22, 123, 130, 294 (n. 57)
Hartless, Mary, 143, 297 (n. 110)
Hartless, Odell, 143
Haugland, Andrew, 104, 294 (n. 38); and Empire Zinc strike, 46, 127, 129, 133, 137, 139–40, 143, 297 (n. 109)
Hentschel, Irving, 220, 224
Herrera, Valdemar, 103
Heymann, Josiah McC., 266 (n. 86)
Higgins, Tommy, 249, 316 (n. 14)
Hiler, Jim, 126
Himes, Bernard, 39, 58
Hinojosa, Luis, 130
Hitler-Stalin pact, 66
Holguín, Arnulfo, 64–65
Hollowwa, Bob, 86, 147–48, 171–72
Hollywood. See Motion picture industry
Hollywood Quarterly, 181–82, 189, 201–2
Hollywood Review, 201–2
"Hollywood Ten," 186–88
Hollywood Writers Mobilization, 201
Holy Family Church (Hanover), 39, 140. See also Smerke, Father Francis
Hoover, J. Edgar, 238–39
Horcasitas, Julián, 32, 57, 82, 277 (n. 126)
Household budgets, 162–63, 167–69
House Un-American Activities Committee (HUAC), 179, 185–91, 192, 223, 237
Housework, 9, 108, 161–67, 197, 301 (n. 34); and Empire Zinc strike, 2, 4, 171–72; invisibility of, 9; theories about, 108, 161–62; and women's paid work, 169
Housing, 163–64; poorer, for Mexican Americans, 37, 38, 143, 163, 166–67; company-owned, 37, 38, 173, 249, 316 (n. 14); in Hanover, 38, 93–94, 143, 152, 164, 167, 173
Howard, Asbury, 72
Huerta, Felipe, 34, 52
Hughes, Howard, 189, 232, 234
Hughey, J. D., 91
Huginnie, Yvette, 38
Humphrey, Senator Hubert, 137
Huntley, Horace, 257 (n. 10)
Hurley, N.M., 28, 50, 58, 250; Chino mill in, 28, 31; Chino smelter in, 31, 250; segregation in, 37, 38–39, 40, 167, 249. See also Local 69
Hurtado, Ramón, 79
Huyett, S. S., 84

Immigration officials, 225–26
Independent Productions Corporation (IPC): formation of, 190–91; goals of, 196, 197; relation of, to Communist Party ideas, 202, 203–4; early projects of, 202–4; gender politics of, 213–15; and Salt of the Earth, 215, 224, 232–33, 250; repression of, 232–33, 242, 250. See also Biberman, Herbert
Independent Progressive Party. See New Party
Industrial Workers of the World (IWW), 41–42, 51
Injunctions, 68–69; in Empire Zinc strike, 3, 46–47, 84, 85–88, 120–21, 123, 127–28
Inman, Mary, 107–8
Intermarriage, 21, 23, 40–41, 50, 262 (n. 30)
International Association of Machinists, 69
International Association of Theater and Stage Employees (IATSE), 180, 232–33, 235
International Union of Mine, Mill and Smelter Workers (Mine-Mill):
—at national level: and Communist Party, 2, 8, 48–49, 52, 71, 80–82; and CIO, 7–8, 48, 52, 71–72, 100–101, 179; historical roots of, 34–35, 50–51; internal controversies in, 48, 70–71, 110, 241–42; Mexican Americans and, 51, 52, 56, 249; on immigration policy, 51, 52, 270 (n. 21); raiding against, 71–72, 145, 146, 148, 297–98 (n. 128); and gender issues, 87, 109–11, 146, 173, 221–22; political action of, 100–102, 286 (n. 57); and Salt of the Earth, 215, 226, 232–33, 234, 235, 310 (n. 85); government harassment of, 235–37, 249; merger of, with United Steelworkers, 243, 249
—in Grant County: fight of, against ethnic discrimination, 7–8, 48, 58, 59–62, 63–65, 78–79, 100, 104, 251; Anglo workers and, 47, 48, 50, 61–62, 72, 73; Mexican American workers' centrality to, 56, 57, 58, 62, 242; in World War II, 47–48, 56, 62, 63–64, 66–67, 98; in late 1940s, 67–70, 96; veterans in, 68, 73, 94, 97–98, 101; amalgamation of locals by (into Local 890), 72–73. See also Empire Zinc strike; Local 63; Local 69; Local 530; Local 604; Local 890
Ironing, 166

Jackling, Daniel Cowan, 27–28, 37, 41
Jackson, Rep. Donald, 223, 225, 226, 227,
   229, 230
Jameson, Elizabeth, 38
Jaramillo, Henry, 101, 105
Jarrico, Paul, 178, 179, 181, 182, 188–89; and
   Hollywood blacklist, 178, 179, 181; and
   Communist Party, 180, 181, 199, 200;
   and initial IPC projects, 190, 202; and
   Salt of the Earth, 221, 224, 226, 233,
   234; in later years, 250
Jarrico, Sylvia, 178, 179, 181–82, 200, 201–2;
   and Hollywood repression, 179, 181–
   82, 188, 189; and Salt of the Earth, 213,
   214, 219; in later years, 250
Jencks, Clinton, 70, 96, 101, 105, 178–79;
   noncommunist affidavits by, 69, 81, 314
   (n. 77); and amalgamation of Grant
   County locals, 72–73; background of,
   74–75; organizing style of, 74, 75–78,
   99, 108–9; encouragement of women's
   activism by, 86, 107, 108–9, 114, 171–
   72; violence against, 104, 145, 228; persecution of, 224, 237–42, 314 (n. 77);
   and Mine-Mill national office, 239,
   241–42; later career of, 242
—in Empire Zinc strike, 46, 136, 141, 145,
   149, 150, 177; and women's picket, 86,
   171–72
—and Salt of the Earth, 193–95, 210, 217,
   219, 222, 228; as actor in, 211–12, 218
Jencks, Virginia (Derr), 74, 75, 86, 108, 178–
   79, 221–22; background of, 75; and
   Salt of the Earth, 210, 211–12, 221, 297
   (n. 109)
—and Empire Zinc strike, 113, 142–43, 177,
   221; and women's picket, 86, 120, 126
Jerome, V. J., 179, 199
Jiménez, Dolores (Villines), 119, 120, 156,
   170, 171, 172, 246
Jiménez, Frank, 119, 156, 170, 171, 246
Jiménez, Rita S., 160–61
Johnson, James, 21
Johnston, Eric, 186, 225
Jones, LeRoy, 92
Jones, Oscar "Red," 91
Juárez, Domitilio, 152
Juárez, Rachel, 129, 131, 152, 219

Kazan, Elia, 190
Keays, Mrs. H. H., 35

Kelley, Robin, 257 (n. 10)
Kemp, Joseph I., 49, 52, 55
Kennecott Copper Corporation, 37, 69, 70,
   131, 225, 249, 250, 316 (n. 14); as owner
   of Chino Copper company, 28; in Gal-
   lup, N.M., 49–50, 52; and postwar labor
   relations, 69, 70, 95, 98. See also Chino
   Copper Company
Kerby, Elizabeth, 229
Kirker, Clorinda. See Alderette, Clorinda
   (Kirker)
Knott, George, 56, 59, 60, 239
Korean War, 113, 188
KSIL (radio station), 77; and Empire Zinc
   strike, 131, 136, 142; and Salt of the
   Earth filming, 225, 227, 228, 230
Kuhlman, June, 225

Labor-Management Relations Act of 1947.
   See Taft-Hartley Act
Ladies' auxiliaries, 87, 109–14, 280 (n. 159).
   See also Ladies' Auxiliary 209
Ladies' Auxiliary 209 (part of Local 890), 110,
   112–14, 215, 220–21, 247
Lardizábal, Rafael, 71–72
Lardner, Ring, Jr., 187–88
Larson, Orville, 148, 232, 280 (n. 166)
Laundries, 166
"Law and Order Committee," 145, 148
Lawrence, Mass., 112
Lawson, John Howard, 204
Lazarus, Simon, 190, 200, 232
League of American Writers (LAW), 201
League of United Latin American Citizens
   (LULAC), 8
Lerner, Gerda, 108
Lett, Earl, 145, 228, 229, 230
Levitt, Helen, 201
Linnane, Father John, 140, 231
Local 63 (Chino local at Santa Rita), 74, 99;
   in 1930s, 49, 53, 56; cross-ethnic orga-
   nizing in, 50, 57, 58, 61; in World War
   II, 57, 58, 59, 67
Local 69 (Chino local at Hurley), 50, 53, 56,
   57, 58, 60, 61
Local 530 (Asarco local), 57, 64–65, 73; eth-
   nic composition of, 57, 58, 61, 73; con-
   troversy in, 71, 72, 145
Local 604 (Peru, Blackhawk, and Empire
   Zinc local), 58, 61
Local 890 (amalgamated local as of 1947), 99,

239, 242; and Communist Party, 2, 8, 48–
49, 80–82; use of anticommunism
against, 7–8, 69, 239, 248; democracy in,
8, 47, 49, 73–74, 77, 81–83, 314 (n. 88); in
electoral politics, 45, 100–102, 105–6,
296 (n. 96); after the 1950s, 48, 249, 250;
and Mine-Mill national union, 71, 83,
147–49, 242; formation of, 71, 145; leadership training in, 75–78, 280 (n. 168);
union hall of, 85, 231, 232; workers'
strong loyalty to, 87–88; diverse issues
addressed by, 93–94, 96, 104; civil rights
activism of, 100, 104; and vision of union
family, 107–15; and *Salt of the Earth*,
215, 216, 235. *See also* Empire Zinc strike
—women's participation in, 10, 85–87, 108–
11, 112–15, 136, 137, 153–54. *See also*
Ladies' Auxiliary 209; Women's picket
Locomotive engineers, 32, 50
Lorence, James, 222, 225
Loya, Pete, 130
Lucero, Mona, 136
Ludlow, Colo., 112
Luján, Magdaleno, 101

Mabry, Gov. Thomas J., 96
Macías, Antonio, 84
Madero, Dora, 157, 158–59
Madrid, Jack, 46
Maltz, Albert, 199–200
Mangas Coloradas, 21, 22
Margolis, Ben, 226
Márquez, Lopi, 103–4
Marriage, 156–57, 169–71; power relations
in, 2, 4, 10, 115, 153–54, 173–74 (*see
also* Domestic violence); common-law,
170. *See also* Divorce; "Family wage";
Intermarriage
Marrufo, Ray, 46
Marshall, Judge A. W., 134–35, 150, 170, 268
(n. 108), 288 (n. 68); injunctions issued
by, 46–47, 127–28, 134
Martin, Larry, 227
Martínez, Augustín, 130, 294 (n. 58)
Martínez, Consuelo, 130, 219
Martínez, José, 139
Martínez, José M., 32
Martínez, Lola, 149
Martínez Sanchez, Adelaida, 164
Marxist economic theory, 76
Masculinity, 10, 99–100; challenge posed to,

by women's picket, 4, 10, 154, 248; and
mining, 9, 88–89, 90; and breadwinner
ethic, 9–10; and rejection of paternal-
ism, 90, 97–98
Mata, Arturo, 57, 58, 60
Mathews, Owen, 224
Matthews, R. B., 236
Matusow, Harvey, 236, 240, 241
McCarran, Senator Pat, 235–37
McCraney, James L., 55
McCray, H. E., 92
McDonald, Bartley, 45, 102, 103–4
McGrath, Herbert, 42
McNutt, Homer, 144, 171
McNutt, Oleta, 144, 171
McNutt, Paul, 186
Mechem, Gov. Edwin, 136, 137–38
Metzger, Bishop Sidney, 231
"Mexican Americans" (term), 12, 147, 230
"Mexican" jobs, 23, 32
Mexican National Association of Actors, 226
"Mexican wage," 168. *See also* Dual-wage
system
Millán, Albert, 243
Millard, Betty, 108
Mine-Mill. *See* International Union of Mine,
Mill and Smelter Workers
"Miner" (term), 29, 264 (n. 57)
Mining: technology of, 24, 26–27; as men's
work, 88–89; dangers in, 90–92. *See
also* Grant County mining industry
Mining engineers, 25
Mining technology, 24, 26–27
Mining towns, 37–41, 267 (n. 99); female-
headed households in, 36–37; ethnic
segregation in, 38–39, 106, 166; small
businesses in, 168–69, 224, 228, 230–
31, 262 (n. 31); housing in (*see* Hous-
ing). *See also specific towns*
Minton, Joseph, 226
Models of unionism, 87; of union as brotherhood, 88–94, 97–98; of union as family, 107–15
Molano, Elvira, 46; in Empire Zinc strike, 46,
120, 123, 129, 131–33, 137, *138*, 149
Montes, Manuel, 46
Montez, Benigno, 53
Montoya, Cipriano, 77, 80, 83, 105, 291
(n. 190); in Empire Zinc strike, 86, 136,
150, 171–72; as husband, 114, 153–54,
170–71, 246, 252

Montoya, Feliciana "Chana," 114, 153, 170–
    71, 246, 252
Montoya, Joseph, 96
Montoya, Lucy, 125
Montoya, Pablo, 150
Morales, Joe T., 23, 102, 144–45, *211*, 212,
    247
Morales, Joe V., 102
Moreno, Pat, 91
Morrell, Charles, 77, 95
Mosely, Marvin, 46, 129, 131, 133, 150, 152
Moses, Horace, 33–34, 50, 52, 62, 63, 97, 99,
    265 (n. 74)
Moss, Carlton, 204
Motion Picture Alliance for the Preservation
    of American Ideals (MPAPAI), 185, 232
Motion picture industry: Communists in, 2,
    179–82, 197, 198–202; blacklist in, 178,
    185–91, 219, 232, 242–43; censorship
    in, 182–83, 184–85; studio system in,
    182–85, 198, 199
Motion Picture Producers and Distributors
    of America (MPPDA), 183
Movie theaters, 39–40, 234–35; in Grant
    County, 39–40, 235, 307 (n. 13); and
    Salt of the Earth, 234–35
Mracek, Albert, 99–100
Muñoz, Alberto, 77, 101, 105
Murray, Senator James, 137

National Industrial Recovery Act (NIRA), 49,
    54, 269 (n. 9)
National Labor Relations Act (Wagner Act),
    68, 269 (n. 9)
National Labor Relations Board (NLRB), 51;
    and Mine-Mill's winning of union rec-
    ognition, 51–52, 53, 55–56, 57; and
    noncommunist affidavits, 69, 238
National Miners Union, 50
National War Labor Board (NWLB), 64
Native Americans, 19–21, 34, 63
Navajos, 63, 275 (nn. 92, 101)
Nazi-Soviet Pact, 181
Negrete, Jorge, 226
Nevada Consolidated, 28, 34, 57–58; as
    owner of Chino Copper Company, 28,
    34; as subsidiary of Kennecott Copper
    Corporation, 28; NLRB ruling against,
    55–56, 61
New Deal, 49–52, 54
New Jersey Zinc Company, 24; NLRB ruling

against, in Empire Zinc strike, 138–39,
    150. *See also* Empire Zinc Company
New Masses, 199–200
New Mexico Consolidated Mining Com-
    pany, 160
New Mexico Miner and Prospector, 99–100
New Mexico Miners and Prospectors Asso-
    ciation, 26, 89–90, 99–100
New Party (later called Independent Progres-
    sive Party), 100–101
New York Times, 126, 230
Noncommunist affadavits, 69, 70–71, 238;
    by Maurice Travis, 48, 71, 81, 241; by
    Clinton Jencks, 81, 224, 238, 314 (n. 77)
Nonferrous Metals Commission (NMC), 64,
    286 (n. 57)
North Hurley, 37, 40, 59, 167, 249
No-strike pledge, 66–67, 98

Ogás, C. B., 140–41, 142, 164
Ogás, Elvira, 302 (n. 62)
Open-pit mining, 31
Operating Engineers union, 58
Orlich, Mary, 110
Ortiz, Leo, 98

Padilla, Claudio, 46
Padilla Nerva, Luis, 226
Parra, Albert, 103
Paternalism, 37, 41, 90, 249; and antiunion-
    ism, 41–42; challenge to, 42, 90, 97–98;
    ethnic dimension to, 90, 97; waning of,
    249
Patton, L. H., 143
Patton, Vivian, 143
"Peace bonds," 137
Penfold, Steven, 88–89
Perea, Julián, 46
Pérez, Mary, 137, 149
Perlin, Paul, 219–20, 246
Peru Mining Company, 31, 95, 160; in Han-
    over, 31, 37–38; Mine-Mill in, 58, 274
    (n. 84); accidents in, 91, 93
Phelps-Dodge Company, 92, 166, 266–67
    (n. 96), 284 (n. 28); 1983 strike against,
    111
Pino, Cecilia, 144
Plumbing, indoor, 163–64, 173
Polanco, Anselma, 129
Polanco, Henry, 129
Pool halls, 59, 90

Popular Front, 180–81, 201
Porter, Harry, 91
Portos, José, 53
Provencio, Brígido, 77, 101

Queveda, Tony, 95
Quintana, Pete, 144

"Race" (term), 13
Radio. *See* KSIL
Railway brotherhoods, 32–33, 50, 58
Ramírez, Joe, 148
Ramírez, Mariana, 38, 172, 246, 311 (n. 103)
"Raza" (term), 13
Recreation, segregated, 39–40
Refrigerators, 165
Religion, 39, 196
"Reproductive labor" (term), 161–62
Revere, Ann, 234
Revueltas, Rosaura, 206; and *Salt of the Earth*, 198, 206, 207, 213; repression suffered by, 225–27, 250
Richardson, James K., 89–90
Riesel, Victor, 225
Riker, David, 253–54
Ríos, Jesús, 82
Rivera, Antonio, 137
Rivera, Matías, 164, 165, 169
Rivera, Mrs. Antonio, 84, 128
Roach, Joe, 138
Robinson, James, 56, 66
Rockwell, E. A., 212, *213*, 310 (n. 81)
Rockwell, William, 212, *213*, 310 (n. 81)
Rodríguez, Ernest, 94, 95, 96
Romanticism, 11, 208–10
Romero, Frank, 224, 227, 230, 287–88 (n. 67)
Roos, Alford, 224, 228
Roosevelt, Franklin D., 49, 63, 100, 276 (n. 106)
Royall, C. C., Jr., 104
Royall, C. C., Sr., 101, 136
Ruttenberg, Stanley, 236

Safety, 90–93, 99, 151; as spur to collective action, 93
Salas, Daniel, 46
Salazar, Sabina, 137, *138*
Salt of the Earth (1954), 4–7, 125, 250, 252–54; as collaborative project, 2–3, 12, 192–96, 197, 204–5, 215–17, 252; anti-communist attacks on, 4–5, 223–35;

depiction of gender conflict in, 5–6, 113, 164, 197, 245; high hopes for, 196–97, 204–5, 219, 220–21, 222; casting process for, 205–13; and townspeople, during filming, 224–32; filming of, 232–33; showings of, prevented, 234–35; latter-day high reputation of, 247, 253
Sánchez, Angie, 211, 212, 235
Sanders, Roy, 144
Sandoval, Alice (pseud.), 39, 157, 162
Santa Rita, N.M., 95, 140, 166, 316 (n. 18); as center of Grant County mining, 26–27; as company town, 28, 31, 37, 41, 249; shrinking of, by open-pit mine, 31; employment patterns in, 33, 36; segregation in, 38–39, 166. *See also* Local 63
Santa Rita Mining Company, 27
Savanna Copper Company, 25–26
Schary, Dore, 186
Schools, 38–39, 106, 267 (n. 99)
Schrecker, Ellen, 187, 242
Schwerin, Jules, 215, 216, 218, 224, 227
Scott, Adrian, 184–85, 186–87, 190
Scottsboro Boys, 202–3
Segregation, ethnic, 38–39, 106, 166
Sena, Tony, 168
Senate Internal Security Subcommittee (SISS), 235–38, 240, 243
Serna, David, 126
Sexual division of labor, 9; in labor market, 9, 34–36, 88–89, 93 (*see also* Women's employment); in families, 9 (*see also* Housework); as especially pronounced in mining districts, 34–36, 88–89
Sheriff's deputies, 150; selection of, 45–56; paid by Empire Zinc, 46, 131; and women's picket, 120, 125, 128, 131–33, 152; strikers' complaints about, 131–33
Silver City, N.M., 23, 102, 140, 158, 166; segregation in, 38–39, 106, 166
Silver City Daily Press, 60, 93, 103, 160, 170; and Empire Zinc strike, 12, 130, 147, 148; and *Salt of the Earth*, 227, 228, 229–30
Skinner, Al, 236, 237
Slover, E. A., 60
Small business owners, 168–69, 224, 228, 230–31, 262 (n. 31)
Smerke, Father Francis, 150, 196, 231
Smith, Charles J., 72, 145

Smith, Ida, 109
Smothermon, Chester, 80
Snedden, T. H., 77
Sondergaard, Gale, 205
Southwestern Food and Sales (Bayard), 142–43, 168
"Spanish American" (term), 147, 230
Sports, 40
State police, 138, 231
Stewards, 75–78, 82
Stewart, Dutch, 53
Strickland, Ray, 94–96
Strikebreakers (in Empire Zinc strike), 121–22, 128–29, 143; and women's picket, 122–23, 125, 128, 129–30, 149
Strikes, 68, 82, 107, 111, 112, 168, 283 (n. 11). See also Empire Zinc strike
Strike wave of 1945–46, 68
Sullivan, Fred, 139, 296 (n. 96)
Sully, John, 26–27, 28, 37, 41, 49
Sussex Zinc and Copper Mining Company, 24

Tafoya, Elena (Escobar), 120, 156, 164, 169
Tafoya, Julio, 92
Tafoya, Raymundo, 164
Taft-Hartley Act (Labor-Management Relations Act of 1947), 68–69, 238; noncommunist affidavits required by, 69, 70–71, 81, 224, 238
Tempest, Rone B., 49, 53, 55, 56
Tenayuca, Emma, 106–7
Terrazas, Jesús, 239
Terrazas, Mike, 46
Thomas, Rep. J. Parnell, 186, 306 (n. 49)
Thomason, Judge R. E., 226, 239, 241, 312 (n. 24)
Thorne, Harry "Hap," 53
Torres, Cecilio, 150, 299 (n. 150)
Torrez, Anita, 80, 81, 165, 167, 246; and Empire Zinc strike, 83, 86, 119, 126–27, 131; and Salt of the Earth, 216
Torrez, Cruz, 91
Torrez, Lorenzo, 80–81, 83, 84, 102, 105, 194
Towns. See Mining towns
Travis, Maurice, 80, 110, 148, 236, 241; and Communist Party, 48, 71; and noncommunist affidavit, 48, 71, 81, 241; and Empire Zinc strike, 83, 136
Truman, Harry S., 70, 101
Trumbo, Dalton, 189, 202

Turney, John, 228
Tyrone, N.M., 92, 166, 266–67 (n. 96)

Udero, Utimio, 99
Ulrich, Laurel Thatcher, 154
Unemployment, 94–96, 99, 168; and housework, 161
Union family, vision of, 107–15
United Mine Workers, 42
United Steelworkers, 48, 243; raids on Mine-Mill by, 71–72, 145, 146, 148, 297–98 (n. 128); merger of Mine-Mill with, in 1960s, 243, 249
Upton, Bill, 228, 229, 230, 314–15 (n. 89)
U.S. Library of Congress, 253
U.S. Office of Price Administration (OPA), 168
U.S. Smelting, Refining, and Mining Company (USSRMC), 31, 69, 82, 95, 99
U.S. Supreme Court, 55–56, 57–58, 61, 241
Utah Copper Company, 28

Valentine, Ora, 109–10
Vanadium, N.M., 37, 57, 72
Vásquez, Sal, 46
Velásquez, Braulia, 87, 113–14, 125, 126, 148, 172, 173
Velásquez, Ernesto, 72, 136, 149, 150, 153, 172–73; and Salt of the Earth, 211, 212, 218
Velde, Rep. Harold, 225
Vesely, Vincent, 129, 149
Veterans: social activism of many, 8, 73, 97; in Mine-Mill, 68, 73, 94, 97–98, 101; in New Mexico, 285 (n. 46)
Vigil, Albert, 105, 165
Vigilantes, 227–29, 232
Villines, Dolores. See Jiménez, Dolores (Villines)
Villines, Margarita, 40
Villines, William, 41
Vincent, Craig, 177, 178, 243
Vincent, Jenny Wells, 177–78, 240, 243, 315 (n. 106)
Violence: against Salt of the Earth filming, 5, 227–28; and women's picket, 122–23, 125, 126–27, 128–31
Vorse, Mary Heaton, 111

Wages: in Mine-Mill contracts, 57, 60, 63; during World War II, 62, 63. See also Dual-wage system

Wagner, Dave, 185, 200
Wagner Act. *See* National Labor Relations
    Act
Wallace, Henry A., 70, 101
War Manpower Commission (WPC), 63, 65
War Production Board (WPB), 64, 65
Washing machines, 165–66
Watson, Lem, 103–5, 303 (n. 83)
Western Federation of Miners (WFM), 34–
    35, 50–51. *See also* International Union
    of Mine, Mill and Smelter Workers
White, Leslie T., 72, 279 (n. 51)
Whitney, J. Parker, 26
Williams, Braulio, 246
Williams, Frances, 204
Williams, Henrietta, 157, 246; in Empire
    Zinc strike, 120, 137, 149, 192, 193; and
    Salt of the Earth, 192, 193, 212, 222
Williams, Lester, 46
Williams, Mrs. Tex, 147
Williams, T. L., 109
Wilson, Homer, 236, 314 (n. 63)
Wilson, Michael, 182, 189, 200–201, 208;
    and *Salt of the Earth*, 192–96, 204–
    5, 219, 221; in later years, 250, 306
    (n. 64)
Wolfe, David, 213
"Woman Question," the, 107–8, 197
Women's Bureau (of U.S. Department of
    Labor), 162
Women's employment, 36, 156–57, 169, 300
    (n. 22); in mining industry, 34–36, 63,
    158–61, 300 (n. 23)
Women's picket (in Empire Zinc strike), 2,

119–24, 148, 149–50, 171–74, 247–48;
    and power relations within families, 2,
    4, 10, 115, 153–54, 173–74; and house-
    hold responsibilities, 2, 4, 119–20, 151,
    153–54, 171–73; approval of, at Local
    890 meeting, 86–87; and competing
    models of unionism, 87–88; and strike-
    breakers, 121–23, 125, 128, 129–30;
    seven-month duration of, 123; jailing of
    participants in, 125–28; extension of
    injunction to, 127–28; and clashes with
    sheriff's deputies, 128, 129, 131–33
Wood, Bill, 38, 165, 166
Woodbury, J. F., 77
Works Progress Administration (later Work
    Projects Administration), 54, 62
World War II, 8, 56, 65–66, 78–79, 170, 181;
    and challenges to ethnic discrimina-
    tion, 8, 48, 56, 62, 63–65, 98; boost
    given to Mine-Mill organizing by, 47–
    48, 56, 62, 63–64, 66–67, 98; women's
    employment during, 63, 158–60; no-
    strike pledge during, 66–67, 98. *See
    also* Veterans
Worthington, Jesse, 91
Wright, Ira L., 25–26, 278 (n. 132)
Wright, Morris, 215, 226, 227

Yeghissian, Patricia, 111
Yguado, Bersabé, 130, 294 (n. 58)
Ynostroza, Eligio, 163

Zamora, Mariano, 46
Zelitti, John, 92